Alcohol and Drug Abuse

Nicotinism and the Emerging Role of E-Cigarettes (With Special Reference to Adolescents)

Volume 2

Concepts, Mechanisms, and Clinical Management

ALCOHOL AND DRUG ABUSE

Additional books and e-books in this series can be found on Nova's website under the Series tab.

Alcohol and Drug Abuse

Nicotinism and the Emerging Role of E-Cigarettes (With Special Reference to Adolescents)

Volume 2

Concepts, Mechanisms, and Clinical Management

Sushil Sharma

Copyright © 2018 by Nova Science Publishers, Inc.

All rights reserved. No part of this book may be reproduced, stored in a retrieval system or transmitted in any form or by any means: electronic, electrostatic, magnetic, tape, mechanical photocopying, recording or otherwise without the written permission of the Publisher.

We have partnered with Copyright Clearance Center to make it easy for you to obtain permissions to reuse content from this publication. Simply navigate to this publication's page on Nova's website and locate the "Get Permission" button below the title description. This button is linked directly to the title's permission page on copyright.com. Alternatively, you can visit copyright.com and search by title, ISBN, or ISSN.

For further questions about using the service on copyright.com, please contact:
Copyright Clearance Center
Phone: +1-(978) 750-8400   Fax: +1-(978) 750-4470   E-mail: info@copyright.com.

NOTICE TO THE READER

The Publisher has taken reasonable care in the preparation of this book, but makes no expressed or implied warranty of any kind and assumes no responsibility for any errors or omissions. No liability is assumed for incidental or consequential damages in connection with or arising out of information contained in this book. The Publisher shall not be liable for any special, consequential, or exemplary damages resulting, in whole or in part, from the readers' use of, or reliance upon, this material. Any parts of this book based on government reports are so indicated and copyright is claimed for those parts to the extent applicable to compilations of such works.

Independent verification should be sought for any data, advice or recommendations contained in this book. In addition, no responsibility is assumed by the publisher for any injury and/or damage to persons or property arising from any methods, products, instructions, ideas or otherwise contained in this publication.

This publication is designed to provide accurate and authoritative information with regard to the subject matter covered herein. It is sold with the clear understanding that the Publisher is not engaged in rendering legal or any other professional services. If legal or any other expert assistance is required, the services of a competent person should be sought. FROM A DECLARATION OF PARTICIPANTS JOINTLY ADOPTED BY A COMMITTEE OF THE AMERICAN BAR ASSOCIATION AND A COMMITTEE OF PUBLISHERS.

Additional color graphics may be available in the e-book version of this book.

Library of Congress Cataloging-in-Publication Data

ISBN: 978-1-53613-679-1

Published by Nova Science Publishers, Inc. † New York

This book is dedicated particularly to the most vulnerable young adolescents who become victims of nicotinism and suffer from its deleterious consequences in their entire life. The book is also dedicated to the author's close friends, relatives, and colleagues who died early on in their lives in miserable pain and agony from smoking tobacco due to ignorance, poverty, early childhood physical and psychological abuse, uncontrolled family planning, child neglect, corporal punishments, peer pressure, physical and mental stress, bad company, illiteracy, hostile environment, unemployment, and poor socioeconomic status.

Contents

Preface		ix
Introduction		xi
Acknowledgments		xxxi
Abbreviations		xxxv
Section 1:	**Concepts and Mechanism**	1
Chapter 1	Basic Molecular Mechanisms of Nicotinism	3
Chapter 2	Nicotinism in Chronic Diseases and Its Clinical Management (Emerging Concepts and Mechanisms)	45
Chapter 3	Nicotinisms: Emerging Concepts and Mechanisms	67
Chapter 4	Nicotinism: Its Prevention and Treatment	85
Chapter 5	Pharmacogenomics of Nicotinism	93
Chapter 6	Molecular Biomarkers of Nicotinism (Prevention and Treatment)	107
Chapter 7	Harmful Effects of Nicotine and Personalized Theranostics of Nicotinism	125
Section 2:	**Clinical Management of Nicotinism**	147
Chapter 8	Harmful and Beneficial Effects of Tobacco and Clinical Management of Nicotinism	149
Chapter 9	Recent Update on Nicotine Research	205

Conclusion and Recommendations 225

Appendix 229

Glossary 235

About the Author 239

Index 247

Preface

Nova Science Publishers now introduce an interesting book on 'Nicotinism and the Emerging Role of Electronic Cigarettes" to reduce global tobacco-related diseases in four volumes. Volume 1 describes general topics on nicotinism and the emerging role of electronic cigarettes; Volume 2 describes basic molecular biology of nicotinism; Volume 3 describes emerging biotechnology in nicotinism; and Volume 4 describes chronic diseases associated with nicotinism and disease-specific-spatiotemporal (DSST) charnolosomics and charnolopharmacotherapeutics for the targeted, safe and effective personalized theranostics of nicotinism. The book is written primarily for readers interested in learning more about the basic molecular biology, recent biotechnology, and molecular genetics, diseases linked to nicotinism and their possible prevention and cure. A novel disease-specific spatiotemporal charnolosomics along with conventional omics (genomics, proteomics, metabolomics, lipidomics, and metallomics) with correlative and combinatorial bioinformatic analysis is proposed for the first time to accomplish targeted, safe, and effective personalized theranostics of nicotinism for a better quality of life.

The book is written primarily for the health and well-being of highly vulnerable adolescents, who engage in drug seeking behavior (particularly tobacco and alcohol), become victims of chronic addiction, and suffer from poor quality of life, early morbidity, and mortality. Moreover, nicotine exposure during intrauterine life can induce diversified embryopathies (such as abortion, still birth, sudden infant death syndrome, microcephaly, craniofacial abnormalities, growth retardation, ADHD, and autism) in the developing infants; and asthma, COPD, cancer, and infertility in adults. The primary goal is to minimize nicotine-induced early morbidity and mortality due to asthma, emphysema, cancer, heart attack, diabetes, obesity, infertility, major depressive disorders, schizophrenia, Alzheimer's disease, and several other neurological and neuropsychiatric disorders, as described elegantly in this book.

Volume-2 describes basic molecular biology of nicotinism in two sections. Section-1 Concepts & Mechanism consists of seven chapters including: Chapter 1 Basic Molecular

Mechanisms of Nicotinism; Chapter 2 Nicotinism in Chronic Diseases and its Clinical Management (Emerging Concepts and Mechanisms); Chapter 3 Nicotinisms: Emerging Concepts and Mechanisms; Chapter 4 Nicotinism: Its Prevention and Treatment, Chapter 5 Pharmacogenomics of Nicotinism Chapter 6 Molecular Biomarkers of Nicotinism (Prevention and Treatment), Chapter-7 Harmful Effects of Nicotine and Personalized Theranostics of Nicotinism. Section-2 Clinical Management of Nicotinism consists of 2 chapters: Chapter 8 Harmful and Beneficial Effects of Tobacco and Clinical Management of Nicotinism; Chapter 9 Recent Update on Nicotine Research, and Conclusions and Recommendations

While each volume will serve as a text book for biomedical students and reference book for researchers, scientists, doctors, and professors; going through all the four volumes systematically will certainly enhance the existing knowledge and wisdom regarding nicotinism and drug addiction in general.

It is envisaged that readers (researchers, doctors, nurses, teachers, students (particularly high school and college going) and public will enjoy learning the most recent and novel personalized theranostic approaches currently being implemented in this clinically-significant discipline by carefully going through the most interesting and thought-provoking contents of this book.

Respectfully submitted,

Sushil Sharma, PhD, DMRIT

Introduction

This book is an extension of the knowledge regarding tobacco-induced compromised mitochondrial bioenergetics-based charnoly body (CB) formation, charnolophagy, charnolosome (CS) destabilization, and inhibition of argyrophilic nucleolar organizer (AgNOR) involved in the synthesis of ribosomes for protein synthesis in a cell. Protein synthesis is significantly compromised in the most vulnerable cells of a smoker. In the developing embryo, the most vulnerable neural progenitor cells and cardiac progenitor cells, derived from induced pluripotent cells are selectively destroyed by free-radical-induced CB formation to cause microcephaly and other craniofacial and developmental disorders in the progeny of cigarette-smoking pregnant woman. A habitual cigarette smoker experiences significant depression, anxiety, and other withdrawal symptoms.

Recently, the author published (a) two volumes of Beyond Diet and Depression; (b) Monoamine Oxidase Inhibitors: Clinical Applications, Health Benefits and Risks; (c) Alleviating Stress of the Soldier and Civilian; (d) Progress in PET Radiopharmaceuticals; (e) Personalized Medicine (Beyond PET Biomarkers); (f) Zika Virus Disease (Prevention and Cure); and (g) Fetal Alcohol Spectrum Disorder (FASD) [Concepts, Mechanism, and Cure], through NOVA Science Publishers, New York, U.S.A. The author described the induction of hippocampal CB formation in major depressive disorders (MDDs) in his book "Beyond Diet Depression" Volume-2. An increased prevalence of depression among cigarette smokers during abstinence can occur due to nicotine-induced hippocampal CB formation and charnolosome (CS) destabilization during degenerative apoptosis.

This book on "Nicotinism and Emerging Role of e-Cigarettes (Concepts, Mechanisms, and Clinical Management) confers a novel basic molecular mechanism of nicotinism involving diversified charnolopathies (particularly in the lungs and other vulnerable internal organs) involving COPDs, cardiovascular diseases, malignancies, neurodegenerative diseases, nephrotoxicities, and impotencies and their possible prevention and treatment as >70 diseases have been directly or indirectly linked to smoking.

The author was motivated to write this book because he has closely and carefully watched the unique life style and peculiar behavior of chars, sulfa, ganja, cigarette, marijuana, alcohol, and morphine addicts in India, Canada, U.S.A, and China. China is the world's biggest consumer of cigarettes. One in three cigarettes smoked globally and the world's biggest tobacco producer is China. More than 300 million people - about a quarter of the population - smoke, with an average smoker consuming 22 cigarettes a day. According to WHO report, there are ~120 million smokers in India. India is the home to 12% of the world's smokers. More than 1 million die each year due to tobacco smoking in India. According to a 2002 estimate, 30% of adult males in India smoke. Majority of them are so called sadhus and monks. They pretend to be recognized as religious saints and remain renunciated from this world. These drug addicts in reality are escapists who forget about themselves, their family responsibilities, and claim that they are very near to God. Although some of them could be real saints with tremendous knowledge and wisdom, majority of them may not have even high school diploma, yet they claim to possess extraordinary knowledge, power, and wisdom regarding religion and philosophy. They believe more in smoking and drinking than working hard to earn their livelihood and are indeed persistent burden to society. Some of them remove all hair whereas others keep long beard and mustaches and wear no or minimum clothes. Some of them apply ash on their body and even distribute ash to innocent people for their health and happiness. Some of them are even quacks and engage public in superstitions, supernatural powers, witch-crafts, and false claims of treating almost any intractable, multidrug resistant disease currently incurable by modern medicine. In every walk of their life, they take pride and shelter of religion to earn their livelihood and win the favor of general public. While remaining in religious places they collect considerable revenue in the name of God. The government has limited control on their activities and movements as they have their own unions all over the country.

Usually, people smoke tobacco for recreation and during pain, depression, and agony with a false belief to alleviate social, physical, mental, economical, psychological, and environmental stress. It has been estimated that ~1 billion people are currently smokers in this world. Although smoking is becoming less popular in many parts of the world, the total number of smokers is growing. A numerical data from 187 countries revealed that in 2012, 967 million people smoked every day compared with 721 million in 1980. An estimated 36.5 million adults in the USA currently smoke cigarettes and >16 million are suffering from smoking-related diseases. In 2005, the smoking rate among military personnel in the USA was 32.2% compared to the civilian rate of 21%. The risk of suicide rate among military men increased with the number of cigarettes smoked daily. Although Federal Bureau of Prisons is officially banning smoking, 80% of prison and jail inmates are smokers. Smoking rates currently are highest among Native Americans regions and territories where the poor and less-educated live. For instance, 29% of people in these regions are living below poverty line. Some racial, ethnic groups continue smoking cigarettes at higher rates. Native Americans are smoking at 38.9%. According to National reports of 2015, men (16.7%) were more likely to be current cigarette smokers than women (13.6%) [CDC, 2016]. Current cigarette smoking was higher among persons aged 18–24 years, 25–44 years, and 45–64 years than among those aged 65 years and older. Current cigarette smoking was highest among non-Hispanic American Indians/Alaska Natives and people of multiple races and lowest among Asians. *Non-Hispanic Asians does not include Native Hawaiians or Other Pacific Islanders. Current cigarette smoking was highest among persons with a graduate education degree certificate (GED) and lowest among those with a graduate degree. The current cigarette smoking was higher among persons living below the poverty level than those living at or above this level. Poverty thresholds are based on U.S. Census Bureau data. About 26 of every 100 adults who live below the poverty level (26.1%), ~14 of every 100 adults live at or above the poverty level (13.9%). By U.S. Census Region, current cigarette smoking was highest in the Midwest and lowest in the West. Current cigarette smoking was higher among persons with a disability/limitation than among those with no disability/limitation. According to sexual orientation, lesbian/gay/bisexual adults were more likely to be current smokers than straight adults. In 2015, current smoking ranged from ~9 of every 100 adults in Utah (9.1%) to ~26 of every 100 adults in Kentucky (25.9%). In China, ~280 million smoked as of 2012 in a population of 1.35 billion. Just over half of Russian men smoke every day, or 52%, the sixth highest proportion in the world in a list topped by Timor-Leste with 61%. However, only about 15% of Russian women smoke. Current cigarette smoking among U.S. adults aged 18 years and older. Tobacco use remains the single largest preventable cause of death and disease in the U.S.A. Cigarette smoking kills >480,000 Americans each year, with >41,000 of these deaths from exposure to secondhand smoke.

Cigarette Smoking among Specific Populations in USA

Cigarette smoking is very common among specific population in the USA. For example, a high prevalence of cigarette smoking has been noticed among American Indians/Alaska Natives, Asians, Blacks, Hispanics, Lesbian, Gay, Bisexual, and Transgender (LGBT), Military, Pregnant or Planning for a Baby, People Living With HIV, Mental Health Conditions, Adults with Disabilities.

American Indians/Alaska Natives (Non-Hispanic)

American Indians/Alaska Natives (AI/ANs) have a higher prevalence of current smoking than other racial/ethnic groups in the US (CDC, 2016). Factors that may affect smoking prevalence include sacred tobacco's ceremonial, religious, and medicinal roles in Native culture, which may affect attitude, belief, and behavior toward commercial tobacco use (CDC, 1998). Also, tobacco sold on tribal lands is not subject to state and national taxes, which reduces costs. Lower price is linked to increased smoking rates. In 2015:

a) 21.9% of AI/AN adults in the US smoked cigarettes, compared with 15.1% of U.S. adults overall.
b) The prevalence of cigarette smoking was about 1 in 5 (or 19.0%) among AI/A men and about 1 in 4 (or 24.0%) among AI/A women.
c) From 2005 to 2015, current cigarette smoking prevalence has decreased significantly among AI/AN adults.

Asians (Non-Hispanic)

Asian Americans represent a wide variety of languages, dialects, and cultures. While non-Hispanic Asian adults have the lowest current cigarette smoking prevalence of any racial/ethnic group in the US, there are significant differences in smoking prevalence among subgroups in this population. Many Asian Americans emigrate from countries where smoking rates are high and smoking among men is the social norm. However, an association between cigarette smoking and acculturation has been noticed among Asian Americans, with those having higher English-language proficiency and those living in the US longer being less likely to smoke (CDC, 2013, CDC, 2016). In 2015:

a) 7.0% of non-Hispanic Asian adults in the US smoked cigarettes, compared with 15.1% of U.S. adults overall.
b) Cigarette smoking prevalence was significantly higher among non-Hispanic Asian men (12.0%) than among non-Hispanic Asian women (2.6%).

From 2005 to 2015, a decline in smoking prevalence among non-Hispanic Asian adults occurred (from 13.3% in 2005 to 7.0% in 2015). Surveys conducted during 2010-2013 by the National Survey on Drug Use and Health reflect a more comprehensive representation of current smoking among Asian subpopulations (CDC, 2013). The percentage of respondents who reported smoking within the past 30 days by subpopulations surveyed were:

a) Chinese – 7.6%
b) Asian Indian – 7.6%
c) Japanese – 10.2%
d) Filipino – 12.6%
e) Vietnamese – 16.3%
f) Korean – 20.0%

Among women, cigarette smoking prevalence ranged from 2.9% among Chinese women to 20.4% among Koreans. Among men, cigarette smoking prevalence ranged from 11.6% among Asian Indians to 24.4% among Vietnamese individuals.

Blacks (Non-Hispanic)

Although cigarette smoking rates are lower among Black high school students than among U.S. high school students overall (5.7% compared with 9.3% in 2015), this difference is not sustained in adulthood (CDC, 2016). In 2015:

a) 16.7% of non-Hispanic Black adults in the US smoked cigarettes, compared with 15.1% of adults overall.
b) Smoking prevalence was significantly higher among non-Hispanic Black men (20.9%) than among non-Hispanic Black women (13.3%).
c) From 2005 to 2015, current cigarette smoking prevalence decreased among non-Hispanic Blacks (from 21.5% in 2005 to 16.7% in 2015).

Hispanics

The prevalence of cigarette smoking among Hispanics is generally lower than the prevalence among other racial/ethnic groups in the US, except non-Hispanic Asians. However, smoking prevalence among Hispanic men is higher than among Hispanic women, and there are significant differences in smoking prevalence among subgroups in this population. It has been shown that acculturation plays a significant role and that smoking prevalence is higher among Hispanics who were born in the US. In 2015:

a) 10.1% of Hispanic adults in the US smoked cigarettes, compared with 15.1% among U.S. adults overall.
b) Cigarette smoking prevalence was higher among Hispanic men (13.1%) than among Hispanic women (7.1%).

c) From 2005 to 2015, a decline in current smoking prevalence among Hispanics was noted (from 16.2% in 2005 to 10.1% in 2015).

Surveys conducted during 2010-2013 by the National Survey on Drug Use and Health also reflect a more comprehensive representation of current smoking among Hispanic subpopulations.

The percentage of respondents who reported smoking within the past 30 days by subpopulations surveyed were:

a) Central or South American – 15.6%
b) Mexican – 19.1%
c) Cuban – 19.8%
d) Puerto Rican – 28.5%

Among women, smoking prevalence ranged from 11.4% among central or South Americans to 25.1% among Puerto Ricans. Among men, smoking prevalence ranged from 19.8% among central or South Americans to 32.1% among Puerto Ricans.

Lesbian, Gay, Bisexual, and Transgender (LGBT)

Smoking prevalence among lesbian, gay, bisexual, and transgender (LGBT) individuals in the US is higher than among the total population. This may be due to the aggressive marketing of tobacco products to this community. LGBT individuals are also likely to have risk factors for smoking that include daily stress related to prejudice and stigma that they may face (CDC, 2014).

a) In 2015, the prevalence of current cigarette smoking among LGBs was 20.6%, compared with 14.9% among heterosexual/straight individuals.
b) In 2013, the prevalence of current cigarette smoking among transgender adults was 35.5% compared with 20.7% among adults whose gender identity corresponds with their birth sex (cisgender) (Buchting et al., 2017).

Military Service Members and Veterans

In the US, cigarette smoking prevalence is higher among people currently serving in the military than among the civilian population (Institute of Medicine, 2009; CDC, 2012). Cigarette smoking prevalence is even higher among military personnel who have been deployed. In 2011, 24.0% of all active-duty military personnel reported currently smoking cigarettes, compared with 19.0% of civilians (Barlas et al., 2011). During 2007–2010, male veterans aged 25–64 years were more likely to be current smokers than nonveterans (29.0% versus 24.0%).

Women who are Pregnant or Plan to Become Pregnant

In the US, modest decreases in cigarette smoking during pregnancy and after delivery occurred between 2000 and 2010, according to a study of 39 states and New York City (CDC, 2013). In 2010, data from 27 sites, representing 52% of live births, showed that among women with recent live births:~23% reported smoking in the 3 months prior to pregnancy.

a) More than half of these smokers (54.3%) reported that they quit smoking by the last 3 months of pregnancy.
b) 11% reported smoking during the last 3 months of pregnancy.
c) 16% reported smoking after delivery.

Among racial and ethnic groups, smoking during pregnancy was highest among American Indians/Alaska Natives (26.0%) and lowest among Asians/Pacific Islanders (2.1%). The highest prevalence of smoking after delivery was reported in women aged 20–24 years (25.5%), American Indians/Alaska Natives (40.1%), those who had less than 12 years of education (24.5%), and those who had Medicaid coverage during pregnancy or delivery (24.3%).

Smoking Status—Women With Recent Live Births, 2010	Prevalence*
Smoked before pregnancy	23.2%†
Smoked during pregnancy	10.7%
Smoked after delivery	15.9%

* Pregnancy Risk Assessment Monitoring System 2010, 27 sites.
† Among those who smoked before pregnancy, 54.3% quit smoking during pregnancy.

People Living with HIV

Cigarette smoking prevalence is at least two times higher among adults living with HIV than in the general population. HIV is now a chronic, manageable disease. Many people with HIV lead healthy, happy lives. However, smoking has deleterious health effects on people with HIV, including higher risks for cancer; COPD; heart disease; stroke; and HIV-related infections, including bacterial pneumonia (U.S. Department of Health and Human Services, 2014; U.S. Department of Health and Human Services,

2014; Mdodo et al., 2015). In 2009, among adults with HIV, 42.4% were current cigarette smokers (Mdodo et al., 2015). Factors associated with higher smoking prevalence among adults with HIV included:

a) Age: Persons aged 40–49 years are more likely to smoke than those aged 18–29 years.
b) Race/ethnicity: Non-Hispanic Whites and Blacks are more likely to smoke than Hispanics and Latinos.
c) Education: Persons who only achieved a high school education or less are more likely to smoke than those with more than a high school education.
d) Poverty level: Persons living below the poverty level are more likely to smoke than those living at or above the poverty level.

People with Mental Health Conditions

Nationally, nearly 1 in 5 adults (or 45.7 million adults) have some form of mental health condition, and 36% of these people smoke cigarettes. In comparison, 21% of adults without mental health conditions smoke cigarettes. (Mental health condition is defined as diagnosable mental, behavioral, or emotional conditions and does not include developmental and substance use disorders (CDC, 2013). Following are other important facts:

a) 31% of all cigarettes are smoked by adults with a mental health condition.
b) 40% of men and 34% of women with a mental health condition smoke.
c) 48% of people with a mental health condition who live below the poverty level smoke, compared with 33% of those with a mental health condition who live above the poverty level.

Adults with Disabilities

Adults with disabilities are more likely to be cigarette smokers than those without disabilities, because a smoker's disability is the result of smoking or because of possible higher stress associated with disabilities (CDC, 2016). In 2015, the prevalence of current cigarette smoking among adults with disabilities was 21.5% compared with 13.8% among adults with no disability.

Extensive studies have demonstrated a pivotal role of the meso-cortico-limbic system and its connections in several behavioral and affective responses to drugs of abuse, such as nicotine. Decreases in DA in the nucleus accumbens is also associated with withdrawal from other drugs of abuse, such as ethanol, morphine, cocaine, and amphetamine (Rossetti et al., 1992). In contrast, the increases in dialysate DA in the frontal cortex (Hildebrand et al., 1998; Carboni et al., 2000) were similar to those observed during withdrawal from other drugs of abuse (Imperato et al., 1986), indicating that common substrates are involved in the mediation of the withdrawal symptoms associated with different drugs of abuse that involve alterations in DAergic neurotransmission in the nucleus accumbens and the frontal cortex.

Like depression not induced by drugs, the depression-like aspects of nicotine withdrawal may be mediated by a decrease in monoaminergic neurotransmission. Data from the 1999 National Survey on Drug Use & Health suggest that the average age at first use of cigarettes is 15.4 years and initiation of daily smoking is 18 years (Kopstein 2001). The progression of cigarette smoking is associated with pre-contemplation, contemplation or preparation, initial trying, experimental or irregular smoking, and established daily smoking (Mayhew et al., 2000). It has been suggested that movement across these stages is determined by different factors (Flay et al., 1983). For instance, social factors such as peer modeling and opportunities to experiment may have a significant influence on initial experimentation with smoking, whereas factors such as genetic risk, negative affect, and propensity to develop tolerance to nicotine play a significant role in determining movement across later stages of smoking (Flay et al., 1983).

Dierker et al., (2001) demonstrated an association of nicotine dependence with anxiety disorder, affective disorder, conduct disorder, oppositional defiant disorder, substance abuse dependence, and parental substance dependence. They reported that affective disorders and drug abuse remained predictors of nicotine dependence after adjustment for confounding comorbidities. The lifetime prevalence of DSM-III-R diagnosis of nicotine dependence in the U.S. ranged from 20-24%, and past-year prevalence of DSM-IV diagnosis of nicotine dependence was 9-13%. It was recognized that the prevalence of lifetime nicotine dependence was higher for cigarette smoking than for any other substance abuse (Anthony et al., 1994; Giovino et al., 1995). Almost one-third of persons who had ever tried smoking cigarettes became dependent on nicotine. It was recognized that the more a person smokes, the greater is the likelihood of nicotine dependence (CDC 1995b). Thereafter, the increase in the percentage of smokers with a dependence tends to rise minimally; however, at higher than one and one-half packs of cigarettes per day. Females demonstrated a higher prevalence of dependence than did males. The duration of cigarette smoking was related to the prevalence of nicotine dependence (Kandel and Chen 2000). The prevalence of dependence was higher among Whites than among Blacks, and this difference was particularly evident at the lower rates of cigarette smoking. It was estimated that nearly one-half of all cigarettes sold in the US (44%) are consumed by people with mental illnesses or substance abuse disorders. In addition, the prevalence of tobacco abuse among those with either addictions and/or mental illness was between 38-98%, as opposed to 19.8% for the general population (Schroeder 2009).

An earlier study in Michigan noticed that young adults with nicotine dependence reported higher prevalence of alcohol and drug dependence and major depression and anxiety disorders than those who had never experienced nicotine dependence (Breslau et al., 2004a, b). The antidepressant treatment for both depression and smoking cessation, regardless of a history of depression supported the concept of shared substrates that mediate nicotine dependence and depression. The strong relationship between nicotine dependence and some psychiatric disorders may be a function of nicotine dependence. For example, in a study conducted by Breslau and Johnson (2000), nicotine dependence, as defined by the FTND score, was not related to major depression. These researchers attributed the strong relationship between the DSM-III-R definition of nicotine dependence and major depression to the behavioral symptoms associated with nicotine dependence. Therefore, the effects of dose, age, race, and gender may be related to the prevalence of nicotine dependence. The number of cigarettes smoked per day and the duration of smoking were related to the diagnosis of nicotine dependence.

The prevalence of nicotine dependence among adolescent smokers may be higher than that among adult smokers, particularly for those who smoke fewer cigarettes per day. The prevalence of nicotine dependence, as defined by DSM criteria, is higher among Whites than among Blacks but is lower in Whites when time to the first cigarette of the day is the criterion for dependence. It remains uncertain whether the prevalence of nicotine dependence differs by gender, suggesting the need to further explore reasons for the inconsistent findings across subgroups of smokers. A significant association exists between psychiatric disorders and smoking, but the nature of this association remains uncertain. Depending on the disorder, the relationship may be causal; for example, smoking may increase the odds of panic disorder and MDD and may lead to self-medication with tobacco abuse. On the other hand, this association may result from factors that involve psychological or physiological processes, such as intolerance to states of negative affect or neurotransmitter dysfunction in a common pathway, which lead to nicotine dependence, substance abuse, and depression. To date, understanding the causal relationships has relied on cross-sectional data sets. Prospective studies are limited and have examined only a few psychiatric disorders, but this type of study is necessary to lend solid evidence for any bidirectional causality or for common underlying causes of cigarette smoking and nicotine dependence with specific psychiatric disorders. A better understanding of these relationships will result in a deeper knowledge and wisdom regarding the basic pathophysiology of nicotinism.

In studies of adolescents, externalizing disorders may play a greater role than do internalizing disorders in the development of nicotine addiction. Therefore, studies encompassing a broader range of diagnoses are needed. Studying recovery from smoking can provide valuable information on the nature of tobacco addiction and the factors affecting it. Every year about 45% of daily smokers in the US stop smoking for 24 hrs. But only 5% or less achieve long-lasting abstinence (CDC, 2004). Thus, relapse is the limiting factor in the transition from smoking to nonsmoking status. This finding highlights the need to understand the exact basic molecular mechanism of relapse and the factors affecting it.

According to CDC report, current cigarette smoking among US adult aged 18 years and older can be categorized by race, ethnicity, sex, age, education, and economical status. Tobacco use remains the single largest preventable cause of death and disease in the US. Cigarette smoking kills >480,000 Americans each year, with >41,000 of these deaths from exposure to secondhand smoke. In addition, smoking-related illness costs >$300 billion a year, including ~$170 billion in direct medical care for adults and $156 billion in lost productivity (U.S. Department of Health and Human Services, 2014; Xu et al., 2015). In 2015, an estimated 15.1% (36.5 million) U.S. adults were current* cigarette smokers. Of these, 75.7% (27.6 million) smoked every day, and 24.3% (8.9 million) smoked some days (CDC, 2016). The percentage of U.S. adults who smoke cigarettes declined from 20.9% in 2005 to 16.8 % in 2014. Cigarette smoking reduced from 17.8% in 2013 to 16.8% in 2014. The prevalence of cigarette smoking in men is 16.7% and among women is 13.6%.

Nicotine is the tobacco plant's natural protection from being eaten by insects. The use of synthetic nicotine as a farm crop insecticide is being blamed for killing honey bees. A toxin, nicotine has proven to be as lethal as strychnine and 3 times deadlier than Arsenic in animal studies. Yet, this natural insecticide's chemical signature is so similar to the neurotransmitter ACh in size and polarity, that in the human brain, it fits a host of chemical locks permitting it direct and indirect control over the flow of several neurotransmitters, mostly, DA. The brain's DAergic pathways serve as a built-in guide. It uses a desire, yearning or wanting sensation to get our attention when time to pound home a survival lesson necessary to keep us alive and thriving. Any drug addiction, including nicotinism, has four major phases "craving, desire, rush, and crash". DAergic pathway stimulation is the common mechanism in addictions (including cocaine, heroin, meth, nicotine and alcoholism). Aside from enhancing DA release, nicotine is a CNS stimulant and activates the body's fight or flight response through enhanced release of NE from the adrenal gland. This allows nicotine addicts to feel different or even superior to illegal drug addicts who fill the world's prisons. While nicotine stimulates the CNS, alcohol has the opposite effect in depressing it and slowing normal brain function. DAergic stimulation of heroin is accompanied by an endorphin release, resulting in a short yet intense numbing or analgesic effect. Cocaine's high is a stimulated euphoria associated with delaying normal re-uptake of multiple neurotransmitters (DA, 5-HT, and NE) and METH is the maximum speed stimulant. Nicotine dependency, like alcoholism, is a real mental illness and disease. While able to completely arrest addiction, there is no cure. It has been reported that 86.8% of students who smoke nicotine at least once daily are chemically-dependent under DSM IV mental health standards (Journal of Pediatric Psychology June, 2005 30(4): pages, 319-332). Diminished autonomy and control over smoking is seen in 25% of students after smoking nicotine only once and in 35% after smoking it 3 to 4 times. (Addictive Behaviors, May 2008, Volume 33(5), pages 689-698).

Most of the nicotine addicts became trapped while children or teens. ~26% start losing control over continued smoking after just 3 to 4 cigarettes, rising to 44% after smoking 5 to 9. Within 7 seconds of first puff, ~50% of our brain's DAergic pathway ACh receptors become occupied by nicotine, or prior to finishing the first cigarette that nicotine would saturate almost all of them. Once saturated, continued smoking causes the receptors to become de-sensitized, which cause the brain to grow or activate millions of extra receptors, a process known as receptor up-regulation. Every 2 hrs. the amount of nicotine remaining in our bloodstream declines by half (known as nicotine's elimination half-life). Continued stimulation, de-sensitization and up-regulation of nAChR keeps the brain desire for more nicotine. An addiction is born as the brain regional neurocircuitry gradually increases the amount of nicotine. The longer we smoke nicotine, the more receptors that became saturated and desensitized, the more grown, and the more nicotine needed to satisfy resulting "want" for replenishment.

According to Dr. Nora Volkov from NIDA, drug addiction is a disease where brain changes translate into an inability to control drug intake similar to when we are starving and need food and that the drug becomes necessary for survival modulated by DAergic pathways to sustain long-lasting memory of salient events. The nicotine addiction may also be called as nicotine-induced brain high jacking and becomes as important as food for survival. As knowledge is power, that is why we have now more ex-smokers in the U.S. than smokers. Although our brain has tremendous capability for recovery, the addicted persons must take responsibility that they have a disease. Consciously, ~70% of daily smokers want to quit smoking. A specific time, place, person, situation or emotion train the mind to expect a new supply of nicotine. The catalyst and foundation for both conscious rationalizations and subconscious conditioning is the underlying chemical dependency.

There are primarily five recovery hurdles:

(1) appreciation for where they now find themselves,
(2) reclaiming their hijacked DAergic pathways,
(3) breaking and extinguishing smoking cues,
(4) abandoning smoking rationalizations, and
(5) relapse prevention.

It takes multiple failed quitting attempts before the user self-discovers the key to success. What they fail to tell is the lesson eventually learned, or that it can be learned and mastered during the first try. Successful recovery isn't about strength or weakness.

It's about a mental disorder where by chance the DAergic pathway receptors have 8 times greater attraction to a nicotine molecule than to the receptor's own neurotransmitter (ACh). It is named as the "Law of Addiction" as: "Administration of a drug to an addict will cause re-establishment of chemical dependence upon the addictive substance." ~50% of relapsing quitters report thinking that they thought they could get away with using just once. The benefit of fully accepting that we have a true chemical dependency and permanent priorities, disorder can't be over-emphasized. It simplifies the rules of recovery while helping protect against relapse. Nicotine activates the body's fight or flight response, feeding the addict instant energy by pumping stored fats and sugars into the bloodstream. It allows to skip breakfast and/or lunch without experiencing low blood sugar symptoms such as feeling nervous or jittery, trembling, irritability, anxiousness, anger, confusion, difficulty thinking or an inability to concentrate. Hence it is advised to minimize or avoid those symptoms, eat little, healthy and often. If diet and health permit, drink some form of natural fruit (cranberry) juice for the first three days. It will aid in stabilizing blood sugar while accelerating removal of nicotine from the bloodstream. Also, heavy caffeine users need to know that, nicotine doubles the rate by which the liver eliminates caffeine from the bloodstream. One cup of coffee, tea or one cola may now feel like two. While most caffeine users can handle a doubling of intake, consider a modest reduction of up to one-half if feeling anxious, irritable or unable to sleep following caffeine use. Use extreme caution with early alcohol use as it is associated with ~50% of all relapses. The average quitter experiences a maximum of 6 crave episodes per day on the third day of recovery, declining to about 1.4 per day by day ten. If each crave is less than 3 minutes and the average quitter experiences a maximum of 6 on their most challenging day. Contrary to convenience store tobacco marketing, and as the vaping e-Cigarettes addict will attest, we did not smoke for the flavor or taste of fine tobacco. In fact, there are no taste-buds inside human lungs. Contrary to hundreds of "pleasure" signs, drug addiction isn't about seeking pleasure but about satisfying a brain "wanting" disorder. Most of us convince ourselves that we smoke to relieve stress, when in reality, addiction intensifies it.

While nicotine is an alkaloid, stress, alcohol and vitamin C are each acid generating events that accelerate renal (kidney) elimination of nicotine from the bloodstream. Stressful situations cause release of several hormones which turn urine more acidic. A urine acid increase from a pH of 5.6 to 4.5 would increase the rate of nicotine elimination by 208%. The onset of early withdrawal due to accelerated elimination would force immediate nicotine replenishment. Within ten seconds of replenishment the crisis was over, at least the dependency induced portion. The silencing of stress-related wanting was recorded in long-term high definition memory, guaranteeing a deep-rooted belief that nicotine is a stress-buster, when all it had done was service the addiction. Will power cannot stop smoking, vaping, chewing or stopping nicotine from arriving in the brain. Dr. Volkow pointed out that by instructing users that they have a chemical addiction that is both a mental illness and disease, that some will use it as an excuse for avoiding responsibility in arresting it. But, does a person who is informed that he/she has cancer or heart disease pretend helplessness, or does he/she instead fight to save and extend their life? Combining the "Law of Addiction" with a "one day at a time" recovery philosophy is needed to remain free and keep mind's priorities disorder arrested for life. "Nearly all smokers who lapse experience a full-blown relapse." The e-cigarettes industry want us to remain slave to buying and vaping its nicotine. Although we stand < 72 hrs. from moving beyond peak withdrawal, it hides this truth to play, prey and feed upon our wanting for that next fix. The nicotine replacement therapy (NRT) industry wants smokers to believe that a natural poison is medicine, it is a therapy, and that it is somehow different from the tobacco plant's nicotine molecule.

Symptoms of Tobacco Addiction

Nicotine use can have many different effects on the body. It can: Decrease the appetite; fear of weight gain makes some people unwilling to stop smoking; boost mood, confer a sense of well-being, and possibly even relieve minor depression; increase activity in the intestine, create more saliva and phlegm; increase the heart rate by around 10 to 20 beats per minute; increase blood pressure by 5 to 10 mm Hg; possibly cause sweating, nausea, and diarrhea; stimulate memory and alertness. To smokers, tobacco helps them accomplish certain tasks and perform well. Symptoms of nicotine withdrawal appear within 2 to 3 hrs. after last use of tobacco. People who smoked the longest or smoked a greater number of cigarettes each day are more likely to have withdrawal symptoms. For those who are quitting, symptoms peak about 2 to 3 days later. Common symptoms include: Intense craving for nicotine; anxiety; depression; drowsiness or trouble sleeping; bad dreams and nightmares; feeling tense, restless, or frustrated; headaches; increased appetite, weight gain; and problems concentrating. Some, or all of these symptoms may be noticed when switching from regular to low-nicotine cigarettes or reducing the number of cigarettes.

Treatment of Nicotinism

There are many ways to quit smoking. There are also resources to help quit. Family members, friends, and co-workers may be supportive. Quitting tobacco is hard if we are trying to do it alone. To be successful, we must really want to quit. Most people who have quit smoking were unsuccessful at least once in the past. We should not view past attempts as failures. Instead, we should see them as learning experiences. Most smokers find it hard to break all the habits they have created around smoking. A smoking cessation program may improve the chance for success. These programs are offered by hospitals, health departments, community centers, work sites, and national organizations. Nicotine replacement therapy may also be helpful. It involves the use of products that provide low doses of nicotine, but none of the toxins found in smoke. Nicotine replacements are sold in the form of: Gums; inhalers, throat lozenges, nasal spray, skin patches one can buy many types of nicotine replacement without a prescription. The goal is to relieve cravings for nicotine and ease withdrawal symptoms. Health experts warn that e-cigarettes are not a replacement therapy for cigarette smoking. It is not known exactly how much nicotine is in e-cigarettes cartridges, because information on labels is often wrong. The health care provider can also prescribe other types of medicines to help quit and prevent from starting again. He/she can refer to stop smoking programs. These are offered by hospitals, health departments, community centers, work sites, and national organizations. People who are trying to quit smoking, often become discouraged, when they do not succeed in the beginning. Research shows that the more times we try, the more likely we are to succeed. If we start smoking again after we have tried to quit, we should not give up. We should look at what worked or did not work, think of new ways to quit smoking, and try again. There are many reasons to quit using tobacco. Knowing the deleterious health risks from tobacco may help motivate to quit as tobacco and related chemicals can increase risk of serious health problems such as cancer, lung disease, and heart attack. Nicotine addiction may occur due to cigarette smoking, cigar smoking, pipe smoking, smokeless snuff, tobacco use, and chewing tobacco.

Quitting Smoking or Switching

If a smoker wants to quit using nicotine entirely, and believes that he/she can quit soon, he/she should go ahead and quit. There are plenty of sites on the web that offer advice for quitting, or better yet, consult with the doctor. Tobacco harm reduction is focused on people who choose to continue using nicotine, or who try quitting and find they cannot. Unfortunately, many people who try to quit, even those who are quite sure that they are ready and able to do so, start smoking again. Even people who quit for a time often start again in a year or two. For these people, an alternative other than a never-ending cycle of failed quit attempts should be attempted.

E-Cigarettes

In Sweden, most people who successfully switch over to smokeless tobacco (ST) take some time making the full transition. At first, it might seem that we have just added another habit in addition to smoking when we are really on the path to quitting smoking, which is time-consuming process. If we find ourselves using ST or e-cigarettes at times, right direction. Since we promote using alternative sources to reduce the amount of traditional smoking, we would not consider it progress if we only used them when we could not smoke anyway. On the other hand, it is not going to hurt much to use them only at those times (there is no point in being miserable craving a cigarette if we are not going to quit entirely), and maybe then we'll start using them at times we would have smoked. Though many people have successfully switched, there is no guarantee that we will either find either of these substitutes satisfying enough, or that we will necessarily quit smoking, but we think that in the interests of a healthier life, we should at the very least try them and see if they work for us. There is U.S. data that shows many people have used ST to quit smoking, and probably did it without even knowing how much safer it was. If we talk to ST users, we will find that many switched from cigarettes. There has even been a clinical trial that successfully got smokers to switch. Although, switching from smoking to one of these alternatives will not work for everyone, for many people they have been just the answer they were looking for regarding using ST as a cessation measure by using e-cigarettes, and also gaining the experiences of former smokers currently using e-cigarettes (Rodu & Phillips 2008; Godshall 2009). Modern smokeless tobacco comes in many forms and flavors. To help decide on where we might like to start at snusauthority.com. They are going through the popular products and letting us know how they taste and feel. The Swedish snus brands, Snustopia is a good place for information. The good news is that if it doesn't work, we have not really lost anything. When we do try it, make sure to really give it our best shot.

Beneficial Effects of Nicotine

Almost everyone in Western society tries nicotine sometime during their childhood or adolescence, but relatively few of them adopt it as a habit. It has been reported that nicotine provides the benefits that some people get from caffeine or ritalin. It helps them focus and be more productive, overcoming attention-deficit-type problems. Nicotine provides relief from stress, anxiety, or panic. For people suffering from some severe mental illnesses, nicotine seems to provide great relief, which probably explains why a large fraction of psychiatric (schizophrenia) patients smoke. Nicotine is also suspected as the reason for the lower incidence of PD among smokers. And for those who have it, nicotine reduces the associated symptoms. Unfortunately, because nicotine is so stigmatized, there is less information about it than we might want. We do not have sufficient scientific evidence on all of its possible benefits. Many people recognize that they get immediate psychological benefits from nicotine (anything from being able to focus in school to not feeling severe distress) and, keep using it.

References

Anthony, J. C., Warner, L. A., Kessler, R. C., 1994. Comparative epidemiology of dependence on tobacco, alcohol, controlled substances, and inhalants: basic findings from the National Comorbidity Survey. *Experimental and Clinical Psychopharmacology.* 2(3), 244–268.

Barlas F. M., Higgins W. B., Pflieger J. C., Diecker K. 2011 *Department of Defense Health Related Behaviors Survey of Active Duty Military Personnel* [PDF—3.60MB]. U.S. Department of Defense, TRICARE Management Activity, Defense Health Cost Assessment and Program Evaluation, and the United States Coast Guard 2013.

Benowitz 1996; Pharmacology of Nicotine: addiction and therapeutics. *Annual Reviews in Pharmocology and Toxicology 36*:597-613. Abstract.

Benowitz N. L., Brunetta P. G. Smoking hazards and cessation. In: Broaddus VC, Mason R. J., Ernst JD, et al., eds. *Murray and Nadel's Textbook of Respiratory Medicine.* 6th ed. Philadelphia, PA: Elsevier Saunders; 2016: chap 46.

Breslau N., Novak S. P., Kessler R. C. Daily smoking and the subsequent onset of psychiatric disorders. *Psychological Medicine.* 2004a;34(2):323–33.

Breslau N., Novak S. P., Kessler R. C. Psychiatric disorders and stages of smoking. *Biological Psychiatry.* 2004b;55(1):69–76.

Buchting F. O., Emory K. T., Scout, Kim Y., Fagan P., Vera L. E., Emery S. Transgender Use of Cigarettes, Cigars, and E-Cigarettes in a National Study. *American Journal of Preventive Medicine* 2017; doi: 10.1016/j.amepre.2016.11.022.

Carboni, E., Bortone, L., Giua, C., Di Chiara, G., 2000. Dissociation of physical abstinence signs from changes in extracellular DA in the nucleus accumbens and in the prefrontal cortex of nicotine dependent rats. *Drug and Alcohol Dependence.* 58(1–2), 93–102.

Centers for Disease Control and Prevention. *Office of Minority Health and Health Equity. Asian American Populations* [last updated 2013 Jul 2].

Centers for Disease Control and Prevention. Current Cigarette Smoking Among Adults—United States, 2005–2015. *Morbidity and Mortality Weekly Report* 2016;65 (44):1205–11.

Centers for Disease Control and Prevention. Current Cigarette Smoking Among Adults—United States, 2005–2013. *Morbidity and Mortality Weekly Report* 2014;69 (47):1108–12.

Centers for Disease Control and Prevention. Disparities in Adult Cigarette Smoking–United States, 2002-2005 and 2010-2013. *Morbidity and Mortality Weekly Report* 2016:65(30): 753-8.

Centers for Disease Control and Prevention. Quick Stats: Current Smoking Among Men Aged 25–64 Years, by Age Group and Veteran Status—National Health Interview

Survey (NHIS), United States, 2007–2010[PDF – 863KB]. *Morbidity and Mortality Weekly Report* 2012;61(45):929.

Centers for Disease Control and Prevention. Tobacco Use Among Middle and High School Students—United States, 2011–2015. *Morbidity and Mortality Weekly Report* 2016;65(14):361–7.

Centers for Disease Control and Prevention. Trends in Smoking Before, During, and After Pregnancy—Pregnancy Risk Assessment Monitoring System, United States, 40 Sites, 2000–2010. *Morbidity and Mortality Weekly Report* 2013;62(SS06)1–19.

Centers for Disease Control and Prevention. Vital Signs: Current Cigarette Smoking Among Adults Aged ≥18 Years with Mental Illness—United States, 2009–2011. *Morbidity and Mortality Weekly Report* 2013;62(05):81–7.

Dierker, L. C., Avenevoli, S., Merikangas, K. R., Flaherty, B. P., Stolar, M., 2001. Association between psychiatric disorders and the progression of tobacco use behaviors. *Journal of the American Academy of Child and Adolescent Psychiatry.* 40(10), 1159–1167.

Flay, B. R., d'Avernas, J. R., Best, J. A., Kersell, M. W., Ryan, K. B., 1983. Cigarette smoking: why young people do it and ways of preventing it. *Pediatric and Adolescent Behavioral Medicine: Issues in Treatment*. McGrath P. J., Firestone P., editors. New York: Springer; pp. 132–83.

Giovino, G. A., Henningfield, J. E., Tomar, S. L., Escobedo, L. G., Slade, J., 1995. Epidemiology of tobacco use and dependence. *Epidemiologic Reviews*. 17(1), 48–65.

Hildebrand BE, Nomikos GG, Hertel P, Schilström B, Svensson TH. Reduced DA output in the nucleus accumbens but not in the medial prefrontal cortex in rats displaying a Mechamylamine-precipitated nicotine withdrawal syndrome. *Brain Research*. 1998; 779(1–2):214–25.

Imperato, A., Mulas, A., Di Chiara, G., 1986. Nicotine preferentially stimulates DA release in the limbic system of freely moving rats. *European Journal of Pharmacology.* 132(2–3), 337–338.

Institute of Medicine. *Combating Tobacco in Military and Veteran Populations*. Washington: The National Academies Press, 2009.

Kandel, D. B., Chen, K., 2000. Extent of smoking and nicotine dependence in the United States: 1991–1993. *Nicotine & Tobacco Research.* 2(3), 263–274.

Kaplan, R. C., Bandiwala, S. I., Barnhart, J. M., Castañeda, S. F., Gellman, M. D., Lee, D. J., Pérez-Stable, E. J., Talavera. G. A., Youngblood. M. E., Giachello, A. L., 2014. Smoking among U.S. Hispanic/Latino Adults: The Hispanic Community Health Study/Study of Latinos. *American Journal of Preventive Medicine* 46(5), 496–506.

King, B. A., Dube, S. R., Tynan, M. A., 2012. Current Tobacco Use among Adults in the United States: Findings from the National Adult Tobacco Survey. *American Journal of Public Health* 102(11), e93–e100.

Kopstein, A. 2001. Tobacco Use in America: Findings from the 1999 National Household Survey on Drug Abuse. Rockville (MD): US Department of Health and Human Services, Substance Abuse and Mental Health Services, Office of the Assistant Secretary; *Analytic Series*: A-15, DHHS Publication No. SMA 02-3622.

Martin, Laura J., MD, MPH, ABIM Board Certified in *Internal Medicine and Hospice and Palliative Medicine*, Atlanta GA. Also reviewed by David Zieve, MD, MHA, Isla Ogilvie, PhD, and the A.D.A.M. Editorial team.

Mayhew, K. P., Flay, B. R., Mott, J. A., 2000. Stages in the development of adolescent smoking. *Drug and Alcohol Dependence*. 59(Suppl 1), S61–S81.

Mdodo, R., Frazier, E.L., Dube, S. R., Mattson, C. L., Sutton, M. Y., Brooks, J. T., Skarbinski, J., 2015. Cigarette Smoking Prevalence Among Adults With HIV Compared With the General Adult Population in the United States: Cross-Sectional Surveys. *Annals of Internal Medicine* 162, 335–344.

Rakel, R. E., Houston, T., 2016. Nicotine addiction. In: Rakel RE, Rakel DP, eds. *Textbook of Family Medicine*. 9th ed. Philadelphia, PA: Elsevier Saunders; Chapter 49.

Rossetti, Z. L., Hmaidan, Y., Gessa, G. L., 1992. Marked inhibition of mesolimbic DA release: a common feature of ethanol, morphine, cocaine, and amphetamine abstinence in rats. *European Journal of Pharmacology*. 221(2–3), 227–234.

Schroeder, S. A., 2009. *How to mainstream behavioral health into national health policy*. PowerPoint presentation at the NASMHPD Summer 2009 Commissioners Meeting; July 19, St Louis.

Schroeder, SA. 2009. A 51-year-old woman with bipolar disorder who wants to quit smoking. *JAMA*. 301(5), 522-531.

Siegel 2006; False claims about secondhand smoke being used to promote smoking bans and misleading policy makers. *The rest of the story: Tobacco news and commentary*.

Tilashalski K, Rodu B, & Cole P. 2005. Seven year follow-up of smoking cessation with smokeless tobacco. *Journal of Psychoactive Drugs 37*: 105-108. Abstract.

U.S. Department of Health and Human Services, Health Resources and Services Administration. *Guide for HIV/AIDS Clinical Care*, 2014.

U.S. Department of Health and Human Services. AIDS.gov: *HIV and Smoking* [last updated 2014 Aug 12].

U.S. Department of Health and Human Services. *The Health Consequences of Smoking—50 Years of Progress: A Report of the Surgeon General*. Atlanta: U.S. Department of Health and Human Services, Centers for Disease Control and Prevention, National Center for Chronic Disease Prevention and Health Promotion, Office on Smoking and Health, 2014.

U.S. Department of Health and Human Services. *Tobacco Use Among U.S. Racial/Ethnic Minority Groups—African Americans, American Indians and Alaska Natives, Asian Americans and Pacific Islanders, Hispanics: A Report of the Surgeon General*.

Atlanta, Georgia: U.S. Department of Health and Human Services, Centers for Disease Control and Prevention, National Center for Chronic Disease Prevention and Health Promotion, Office on Smoking and Health, 1998.

U.S. Preventive Services Task Force. Behavioral and pharmacotherapy interventions for tobacco smoking cessation in adults, including pregnant women: U.S. Preventive Services Task Force reaffirmation recommendation statement. *Ann Intern Med*. 2015 Sep 22.

Whelan, 2006. Movement. American *Council on Science and Health.*

Xu, X., Bishop, E. E., Kennedy, S. M., Simpson, S. A., Pechacek, T. F., 2015. Annual Healthcare Spending Attributable to Cigarette Smoking: An Update. *American Journal of Preventive Medicine* 48(3), 326–333.

Acknowledgments

The author expresses sincere thanks to his friends, professional colleagues, and students for their moral support and encouragement to write this urgently-needed and timely-released book on "Nicotinism and Emerging Role of E-Cigarettes" by Nova Sciences Publishers, New York, U.S.A for the normal health and well-being of global community for a better quality of life.

This book is intended primarily for the young adolescents, those are highly vulnerable to nicotinism and its deleterious consequences later in their entire life. The information provided is particularly beneficial for young adolescents who are trapped in a vicious circle of nicotinism by smoking tobacco during their critical period of physical and mental development.

Indeed! "Nicotinism" is a serious and life-threatening clinical condition as it compromises the general mitochondrial bioenergetics of human body and significantly impacts the overall quality of our life by triggering CB formation and by inhibiting charnolophagy in the most susceptible cell as a basic molecular mechanism of intracellular detoxification and sanitation to sustain normal function. If nicotinism does not kill, it can reduce at least 10 years of our lifespan. Generally, smokers die 10 years earlier than nonsmokers. Hence, it is highly prudent to understand the basic molecular mechanism(s) of nicotinism and its prevention and treatment, as described elegantly in this book.

Tobacco smoking can have deleterious impact on our health. In addition to serious health hazards, the victims of nicotinism and their families suffer a significant loss of economy and productivity; hence it is highly crucial to prevent its global prevalence by providing specific guidelines to younger generation and by introducing novel therapeutic interventions. In addition to specific guidelines for its effective prevention, helpful instructions may be provided for pregnant women to stop smoking during pregnancy, as it can have deleterious consequences on the developing fetus.

Special emphasis has been laid on the basic molecular pharmacology in various experimental models of nicotinism, including cell cultures, slice cultures, 3D embryos, cerebral organoids, genetically-manipulated mouse models, and Zebra fish models for the development of novel therapeutic drugs, employing computer-based omics and molecular imaging biotechnology for the safe and effective treatment of nicotinism.

In general, this book provides basic concepts and mechanisms in nicotine addiction and novel biomarkers as targets for developing safe and effective interventions for its prevention and treatment. The emerging role of e-cigarettes in minimizing the potential harmful effects of tobacco smoking has been highlighted. In addition, a comparative analysis of cigarette smoking vs vaping is provided to highlight the relative benefits and risk of two kinds of smoking.

It is envisaged that the entire medical community as well as public will be benefited by going through the clinically-significant and thought-provoking contents of this manuscript. In addition to the entire scientific community, public (particularly young adolescent population) across the globe will enjoy going through the interesting contents of this highly informative, thought-provoking, and interesting book.

The unique feature of this book is that it provides a novel concept and basic molecular mechanism of nicotine-induced CB formation and charnolosome induction in the most vulnerable cells of human body and their pathophysiological significance by inhibiting the argyrophilic nucleolar organizer (AgNOR) involved in the ribosomal and ultimately protein synthesis, highly essential for the normal growth and survival of a cell. The basic molecular mechanism of nicotine-induced stem cell-specific CB and charnolosome (CS) formation is described in detail to elucidate their pathophysiological significance in multi-drug resistant (MDR) malignancies due to enhanced release of glutathione, metallothioneins, heat shock protein (HSP-70), BCl-2, SOD, and catalase. Hence, it will be promising to develop novel charnolopharmacotherapeutics involving CB prevention/inhibition, charnolophagy induction, and charnolosome stabilization as a basic molecular mechanism of intracellular detoxification in nicotine addiction to remain healthy. However, it remains uncertain whether cigarette smoking induces relatively more inhibition in AgNOR as compared to e-cigarettes (vaping). Further studies in this direction will determine the safety aspects of conventional smoking vs vaping.

Although, every effort has been made to confer most recent, accurate, and precise information regarding nicotinism and its harmful and beneficial effects, certain specialized topics could not be covered in sufficient detail because of limited time and space allocated to write this book. Although, clinically-significant topics regarding nicotinism are described in sufficient detail, it is possible that the most recent contribution by an eminent researcher, scientist, or a physician might have been inadvertently omitted because of the author's own lack of knowledge, experience, and expertise.

The author extends sincere and heartiest thanks to President Nadya Columbus and her efficient team of the Nova Science Publishers, New York, U.S.A. for the constant and consistent support, commitment, partnership, and promptness to publish this urgently needed book in time for the welfare of particularly global young adolescent community and smoking pregnant women.

The author apologies for any mistake and/or omission, and humbly requests the entire global community to kindly go through its most interesting, informative, and thought-provoking contents for augmenting basic knowledge and wisdom, and ignore several limitations it may have. Any helpful criticism and valuable suggestion for further improvement will be gratefully acknowledged.

Respectfully submitted,

Sushil Sharma, PhD, DMRIT

Abbreviations

AAD	Alcohol Abuse Disorder
AD	Alzheimer's disease
ADD	Average Daily Dose
ADI	Acceptable Daily Intake
ADNFLE	Autosomal Dominant Nocturnal Frontal Lobe Epilepsy
AGEP	Advanced Glycation Products
ALI	Air-Liquid Interface
ANDS	Alternative Nicotine Delivery Systems
ANOVA	Analysis of Variance
AOPP	Advanced Oxidation Products (AOPP),
ATTUD	Association for the Treatment of Tobacco Use and Dependence
Avenic Cigarettes	Average Nicotine Cigarettes
BC	Biochemical Confirmation
BMI	Body Mass Index
BOEs	Biomarkers of Exposure
CAD	Cannabis Abuse Disorder
CAD	Cocaine Abuse Disorder
CAD	Coronary Artery Disease
CAP	Cholinergic Anti-Inflammatory Pathway
CB	Charnoly Body
CBT	Cognitive-Behavioral Therapy
CCs	Combustible Cigarettes
CCs:	Combustible Cigarettes
CDC	Center for Disease Control and Prevention
CHARON	Chemical Analysis of Aerosol Online
CHD	Coronary heart Disease
CHTP	Carbon-Heated Tobacco Product

CIPN	Chemotherapy-Induced Peripheral Neuropathy
CMBEL	Compromised Mitochondrial Bioenergetics Levels (0-3)
CO	Carbon Monoxide
CPS	Charnolophagosome
CPs	Charnolopharmaceutics
CS	Charnolosome
CS	Cigarette Smoking
CSE	Cigarette Smoke Extract
CSF	Cancer Slope Factor
CTLA4	Cytotoxic T-Lymphocyte Antigen 4
DAD	Drug Abuse Disorder
DAergic	Dopaminergic
Denic Cigarettes	Deniconized Cigarettes
DIP-EI/MS	Electron Ionization Mass Spectrometry by using a Direct Insertion Probe
DSM	Diagnostic and Statistical Manual of Mental Disorders (IV)
EC	Exposure Air Concentration
e-Cigarettes	Electronic Cigarettes
EDRS	Ecstasy and Related Drugs Reporting System P
EGF	Epidermal Growth Factor
ENDS	E-Cigarettes and other Electronic Nicotine Delivery Systems
ENDS	Electronic Nicotine Delivery Systems
EPA	Environmental Protection Agency
ERN	Extended-Release Nicotinic Acid
ETS	Environmental Tobacco Smoke
ETS	Environmental Tobacco Smoke
FAPA	Flowing Atmospheric-Pressure Afterglow Plasma Ion Source
FST	Forced Swimming Test
FTND	Fagerström test for Nicotine Dependence
FTND	Fagerström Test for Nicotine Dependence (CO) measurements
FTQ	Fonds de Solidarité
GATS	Global Adult Tobacco Survey
GD	Grave's Disease
GEE	Generalized Estimating Equations
GO	Grave's Orbitopathy
GTS	Green Tobacco Sickness
GSD	Geometric Standard Deviations
GWAS	Genome Wide Association Studies
GWAS	Genome-Wide Association Study
HDL	High Density Lipoprotein

HDL-C	High Density Lipoprotein-Cholesterol
Hinic Cigarettes	High Nicotine Cigarettes
HONC	Hooked on Nicotine Checklist
Hp	Helicobacter Pylori
HPHCs	Harmful and Potentially Harmful Constituents
HPHCs	Harmful and Potentially Harmful Constituents
HPHCs	Harmful/Potentially Harmful Constituents
HQ	Hazard Quotient
HRMS	High-Resolution Mass Spectrometry
HSP	Heat Shock Protein
HS-SPME	Headspace Solid-Phase Micro-Extraction
IAQ	Indoor Air Quality
ICD	International Classification of Diseases
ICTL	Intracellular Toxicity Levels (0-3)
IDRS	Illicit Drug Reporting System
IRS	Infrared Spectroscopy
IUR	Inhalation Unit Risk
LADD	Lifetime Average Daily Dose
LC-MS	Liquid Chromatography-Tandem Mass Spectrometry
LCR	Life-time Cancer Risk
LDCT	Lung Cancer Screening with Low-Dose Computed Tomography
LDL	Low Density Lipoprotein
LED	Light Emitting Diode
LLNCs	Very Low Nicotine Content Cigarettes (Nicotine <250 µg/cigarette)
LOD	Limits of Detection
Lox	Lipoxygenase
LPB	lipopolysaccharide Binding Protein
LPB	Lipoprotein Binding Protein
Lp-ntPET	Linear Parametric Neurotransmitter PET
LPS	Lipopolysaccharides
LRP	Lung Resistance Related Protein
LSUT	Lung Screen Uptake Trial
MAD	Morphine Abuse Disorder
MDDs	Major Depressive Disorders
MDR	Multi-Drug Resistant
MEAD	Methamphetamine Abuse disorder
MIPs	Molecularly Imprinted Polymers
MNWS	Minnesota Nicotine Withdrawal Scale
MOFs	Metal Organic Frameworks

MRI	Magnetic Resonance Imaging
MRS	Magnetic Resonance Spectroscopy
MTG	MitoTracker Green
nAChR	Alpha-4 Nicotinic Acetylcholine Receptor
NAD	Nicotine Abuse Disorder
Nef2	Nuclear Factor Erythroid 2-Related Factor
NIDA	National Institute on Drug Addiction
NIMH-RDCI	National Institute of Mental Health-Research Domain Criteria Initiative
NIOSH	National Institute for Occupational Safety and Health
NMR	Nuclear Magnetic Resonance
NMR	Nuclear Magnetic Resonance
NMR	Nicotine Metabolite Ratio
NNAL	4-(Methylnitrosamino)-1-(3-Pyridyl)-1-Butanol
NNAL	4-(Methylnitrosamino)-1-(3-Pyridyl)-1-Butanol (NNAL: A Pulmonary Carcinogen), VOCs: Volatile Organic Compounds
NNC	Normal Nicotine Content Cigarettes
NNCs	Normal Nicotine Content (NNC) Cigarettes (Nicotine: 1 mg/cigarette)
NNN	N-Nitrosonor Nicotine
NNK	4-(Methylnitrosamino)-1-(3-pyridyl)-1-butanone
NNN	N'-Nitrosonor Nicotine
NRT	Nicotine Replacement Therapy
NSCLS	Non-Small Cell Lung Cancer Cells
OSHA	Occupational Safety and Health Administration
OHE	Oral Health Education
OPLS-DA	Orthogonal Projection to Latent Structures Discriminant Analysis
OTC-NRT	Over the Counter-Nicotine Replacement
PA	Passive Avoidance
PAH	Polycyclic Aromatic Hydrocarbons
PAH	Polycyclic Aromatic Hydrocarbons
PC	Proxy Confirmation
PD	Parkinson's disease
PEL	Permissible exposure limit
PET	Positron Emission Tomography
PM	Particulate Matter
PPA	Point Prevalence of Abstinence
PROMIS®	Patient Reported Outcomes Measurement Information System

PTPN22	Protein Tyrosine Phosphatase
PTR-ToF-MS	Proton-Transfer-Reaction Time-of-Flight Mass Spectrometer
PV/VG	Propylene Glycol/Vegetable Glycerin
PVD	Peripheral Vascular Disease
PWID	People Who Inject Drugs
QSU	Questionnaire of Smoking Urges
RdD	Reference Dose
REL	Recommended exposure limit
RfC	Reference Concentration
RI	Reflection Index
ROC	Receiver Operator Characteristics
ROI	Regions of Interest
RPU	Regular psychostimulant users
rtfMRI	Real Time Functional Magnetic Resonance Imaging
SHS	Secondhand Smoking
SI	Stiffness Index
SIDS	Sudden Infant Death Syndrome
SNP	Single Nucleotide Polymorphism
SNPs	Single-Nucleotide Polymorphisms
SPD	Serious Psychological Distress
SPECT	Single Photon Emission Tomography
SR	Self-Reported
SRNT	Society for Research on Nicotine and Tobacco
ST	Smokeless Tobacco
STS-CPs	Spatio-temporally-Specific Charnolopharmaceuticals
SUDs	Substance Use Disorders
TCP	Tobacco Cessation Products
TG	Triglyceride
TGA	Thermogravimetric Analysis
THS	Tobacco Heating System
TMRE	Tetra-methylrhodamine ethyl ester
TP	Transformation products
TSNA	Tobacco specific nitrosamines
TSRH	Thyroid Stimulating Hormone Receptor
TUDs	Tobacco Use Disorders
UHPLC-QTOF-MS	Ultrahigh-Performance Liquid Chromatography-Quadrupole Time-of-Flight Mass Spectrometry.
UPLC	Ultra-Performance Liquid Chromatography
USPSTF	US Preventive Services Task Force
UV/VIS Analysis	Ultraviolet/Visible Analysis

Abbreviations

VLDL	Very Low Density Lipoproteins
VLNC	Very Low Nicotine Content Cigarettes
VOCs	Volatile Organic Compounds
WHO	Word Health Organization
WISDM	Wisconsin Inventory of Smoking Dependence Motives
ZSDS	Zung Self-Rating Depression Scale

Section 1: Concepts and Mechanism

Chapter 1

Basic Molecular Mechanisms of Nicotinism

Abstract

This chapter illustrates basic pathophysiology of nicotine addiction, physiological and pharmacological role of nicotinic acetylcholine receptors (nAChRs) in tobacco smoking behavior, and neuro-substrates of nicotine reinforcement. The chapter also highlights the neurophysiological and neuropharmacological significance of brain regional neurotransmitters in nicotine addiction. Particularly, the clinical significance of glutamatergic, GABAergic, opioid, endocannabinoids, serotonergic and NEergic systems are described in relation to nicotine dependence to further elucidate the neurochemical correlates and the basic molecular mechanism of nicotinism and nicotine withdrawal. The involvement of various neurotransmitters receptors and their role in alleviating behavioral symptoms of nicotine withdrawal are also described briefly, in addition to molecular imaging studies and psychiatric comorbidities in nicotinism.

Keywords: nicotinic acetyl choline receptors (nAChRs), nicotine reinforcement, glutamate, GABA, opioids, endocannabinoids, serotonin, norepinephrine, nicotine dependence, withdrawal, molecular imaging, psychiatric comorbidities

Introduction

It is now well-established that positive reinforcement from nicotine plays a significant role in the initiation of smoking, and negative reinforcement, particularly relief from withdrawal, is a contributor to the persistence of smoking and relapse. Measures of nicotine's reinforcing effects, especially the most common measure—self-reported number of cigarettes smoked per day—are related to other indices of addiction, including the risk of relapse. However, other measures of nicotine's reinforcing effects, especially those reflecting persistence in smoking behavior, may provide even stronger markers of addiction for predicting clinical outcomes and for testing the efficacy of new treatments or tobacco products. Such measures may also be useful as endophenotypes of dependence for future research into the etiology of addiction, including the influence of a person's genetic composition. Therefore, the development of these markers for nicotine and smoking reinforcement is critical for future research examining the etiology and treatments for nicotine addiction and for tobacco product testing.

Nicotine addiction not only results from the pharmacodynamic effects of nicotine but also from associative learning and conditioning. Nicotine serves not only as a US, but can also serve as a CS and a modifier of associative processes. Motivational influences on persistent smoking are more linked to negative reinforcement than to positive reinforcement.

Interoceptive (internal) cues of negative affect have been linked to craving and relapse, whereas positive affective states are less likely to lead to relapse. Exteroceptive (environmental) cues also play a significant role in eliciting craving and relapse. Reactivity to both internal and environmental cues may provide another measure of nicotine addiction. Hence, factors such as age, gender, and psychiatric comorbid history are important to consider in future research, because they have an important role in moderating responses to nicotine. Because of the importance of learning in the development and maintenance of nicotine addiction, this is an area that requires further research.

This chapter describes basic pathophysiology of nicotine addiction, physiological and pharmacological role of nAChRs in nicotinism, and neuro-substrates of nicotine reinforcement. The chapter also highlights the clinical significance of brain regional neurotransmitters in nicotine addiction. Particularly, the significance of glutamatergic, GABAergic, opioid, endocannabinoids, serotonergic, NEergic systems are described in relation to nicotine dependence to further elucidate the basic molecular mechanism of nicotinism and neurochemical correlates and nicotine withdrawal. The involvement of various neurotransmitters receptors and their role in behavioral symptoms of nicotine withdrawal are also described, in addition to molecular imaging studies and psychiatric comorbidities in nicotinism.

Pathophysiology of Nicotine Addiction

Because nicotine is one of the primary constituents responsible for tobacco addiction, research to promote an understanding of the neurobiology of tobacco addiction focuses on the mechanisms mediating nicotine addiction. Dependence on nicotine is characterized by both the persistence of a drug-seeking behavior and the emergence of withdrawal symptoms on abrupt cessation of nicotine administration (Wikler 1973; Levine 1974; Stewart et al., 1984; Ludwig 1986; O'Brien et al., 1990; Hughes and Hatsukami 1992; Koob et al., 1993; Markou et al., 1993, 1998; APA 1994; Kenny and Markou 2001).

Therefore, both the neuro-substrates (brain structures, pathways, and systems) mediating the reinforcing effects of acute administration of nicotine and those mediating its withdrawal syndrome are relevant to drug dependence. The physiological systems that develop adaptations to repeated nicotine administration and lead to the emergence of withdrawal signs on cessation of nicotine administration are likely to intersect with systems that mediate the acute effects of nicotine (Markou et al., 1998; Kenny and Markou 2001). That is, drug dependence develops as a neurobiological adaptation to chronic drug exposure.

This chapter first describes the systems and pathways mediating the reinforcing effects of nicotine and then discusses the neuro-adaptations that occur because of chronic nicotine exposure. These neurobiological adaptations mediate the tolerance to and effects of withdrawal from nicotine that are interlinked in most theoretical conceptualizations. It is hypothesized that the sensitization to the locomotor-activating effects of drugs, including effects observed after repeated nicotine administrations, reflect a progressive augmentation in the motivation to self-administer the drug (Robinson and Berridge 1993). (The locomotor-activating effects consist of increased locomotor responses to repeated drug-challenge injections). However, no direct evidence suggests that sensitization to the locomotor-activating effects of nicotine reflects any aspect of dependence on nicotine. Therefore, sensitization is not covered in this section. If sensitization to the reinforcing effects of nicotine develops, it will be relevant to early phases of tobacco use involving the acquisition of tobacco smoking as a persistent behavior. The primary focus has been on the comorbidity of nicotine dependence and psychiatric disorders in the context of shared substrates that mediate nicotine dependence and depression-like aspects of psychiatric disorders (Markou et al., 1998; Markou and Kenny 2002; Paterson and Markou 2007).

Nicotinic Acetylcholine Receptors

Nicotine, an alkaloid in concentrations of ~1-3% in tobacco, is an agonist at the nicotinic acetylcholine receptors (nAChRs) expressed both in the peripheral nervous system and the CNS (Browne 1990; Henningfield et al., 1996; Vidal 1996; Holladay et al., 1997; Paterson and Norberg 2000). Similar to other ligand-gated ion channels, neuronal nAChRs are composed of five membrane-spanning subunits that combine to form a functional receptor (Lindstrom et al., 1996; Role and Berg 1996; Albuquerque et al., 1997; Lèna and Changeux 1998, 1999; Dani 2000; Gotti et al., 2006). Neuronal nAChR subunits are arranged in different combinations to form nAChRs with distinct pharmacologic and kinetic properties. The neuronal α subunit exists in nine isoforms (α2 through α10), whereas the neuronal β subunit exists in three isoforms (β2, β3, and β4) (Arneric et al., 1995; Wonnacott 1997; Elgoyhen et al., 2001). Study of oocyte expression systems injected with pairwise combinations of different neuronal α and β subunits indicated that these subunits combine with a stoichiometry of 2α:3β to produce a functional neuronal nicotinic hetero-oligomeric receptor (Deneris et al., 1991; Conroy and Berg 1995; Colquhoun and Patrick 1997). In contrast, α7, α8, and α9 subunits form homo-oligomeric complexes composed of five α subunits and no β subunits (Chen et al., 1998). Only the α7 pentamer is expressed in the CNS.

Neuronal nAChRs in rats are divided broadly into three classes: (1) those with a high-affinity binding site for racemic nicotine —the nAChRs containing α4, of which the α4β2 combination is the most abundant (Flores et al., 1992; Picciotto et al., 1995); (2) those with a high affinity for the radioiodine [^{125}I] α-bungarotoxin that correspond to the homomeric α7 nAChRs (Clarke 1992); and (3) those with a high affinity for neuronal bungarotoxin—the α3-containing nAChRs (Schulz et al., 1991). The precise molecular combinations of nAChR subunits that constitute active brain nAChRs *in vivo* have been inferred from their pharmacologic profile (Sershen et al., 1997; Kaiser et al., 1998; Luo et al., 1998; Sharples et al., 2000). However, nAChR subunits expressed by individual neurons in specific brain regions have also been identified (Lèna et al., 1999; Sheffield et al., 2000).

The predominant role of nAChRs in the brain is the modulation of neurotransmitter release, because nAChRs are situated primarily on presynaptic terminals (Wonnacott 1997). Nevertheless, nAChRs are also found at somato-dendritic, axonal, and postsynaptic sites (Sargent 1993). As a result of actions at the nAChR sites, nicotine stimulates the release of most neurotransmitters throughout the brain (Araujo et al., 1988; Toide and Arima 1989; McGehee and Role 1995; Gray et al., 1996; Role and Berg 1996; Wilkie et al., 1996; Albuquerque et al., 1997; Alkondon et al., 1997; Kenny et al., 2000; Grady et al., 2001). Therefore, various transmitter systems are involved in the rewarding effects of nicotine and in the adaptations that occur in response to chronic exposure to nicotine, which give rise to physical tolerance and dependence and withdrawal symptoms.

Neuro-Substrates of Nicotine Reinforcement

The meso-cortico-limbic brain system in the midbrain of mammals is composed of interconnected brain structures, which is involved in the effects of drugs of abuse (Koob 2008). Among the main components of this system are the DAergic neurons originating in the ventral tegmental area (VTA) and projecting to the nucleus accumbens

(NA) and the frontal cortex. The activity of these VTA DA neurons is regulated by the release of the excitatory neurotransmitter glutamate from neuronal projections originating from several sites, including the nucleus accumbens and the frontal cortex as the author has described in his recently published book "Fetal Alcohol Spectrum Disorder: Concepts, Mechanisms, and Clinical Management" released by Nova Science Publishers, New York, U.S.A. (2017) . Other inputs that also regulate activity of the mesolimbic system are (1) γ-aminobutyric acid (GABA) inhibitory interneurons located within the VTA and the nucleus accumbens (NA) and (2) cholinergic projections from brainstem nuclei to the VTA. These projections release the endogenous neurotransmitter acetylcholine, which acts on excitatory nAChRs located on glutamate and GABA neuronal terminals in the VTA. A critical role of the meso-cortico-limbic system and its connections in several behavioral and affective responses to drugs of abuse has been demonstrated. For further details please refer the Source: Markou 2006. Neural pathways for γ-aminobutyric acid, glutamate, DA, and excitatory neurotransmitters. Reprinted with permission from Wiley-Blackwell, © 2006.

DA and Nicotinic Acetylcholine Receptors

Just like other drugs of abuse, the mesolimbic DAergic system and nAChRs within that system are involved in the reinforcing properties of nicotine (Watkins et al., 2000; Picciotto and Corrigall 2002; Balfour 2004). Acute administration of nicotine increased the firing rate of DAergic neurons in the VTA (Grenhoff et al., 1986; Pidoplichko et al., 1997) and elevated dialysate levels of DA in the shell of the nucleus accumbens (Imperato et al., 1986; Damsma et al., 1989; Mifsud et al., 1989; Benwell and Balfour 1992; Pontieri et al., 1996; Nisell et al., 1997; Carboni et al., 2000). These effects of nicotine may occur through excitatory actions at nAChRs on the mesolimbic DAergic neurons in both the VTA and the nucleus accumbens and at nAChRs located on local neuronal circuitry within these brain regions (McGehee and Role 1996; Nisell et al., 1997; Teng et al., 1997). The nAChRs in the VTA plays an important role than those in the nucleus accumbens in the effects of nicotine on the release of DA from the nucleus accumbens (Nisell et al., 1994a,b, 1997).

The nAChRs located within the VTA are involved in nicotine reinforcement. I.V nicotine self-administration is a procedure that allows the assessment of the reinforcing effects of nicotine by measuring the number of infusions a rat chooses to receive i.v through an indwelling catheter by pressing a lever during 1-hr daily sessions. Each of four factors decreased i.v nicotine self-administration in rats (Picciotto and Corrigall 2002). The factors were (a) injections of the competitive nAChR antagonist DHβE into the VTA (Williams and Robinson 1984) but not the nucleus accumbens (Corrigall et al., 1994), (b) development of lesions of the mesolimbic DAergic projections from the VTA to the nucleus accumbens (Corrigall et al., 1992), (c) development of cholinergic lesions of the brainstem pedunculopontine tegmental nucleus that project to the VTA (Lança et al., 2000), and (d) systemic administration of DA receptor antagonists (Corrigall and Coen 1991b). These studies suggested an involvement of the nAChR subtypes containing α4β2 in both the nicotine-induced release of DA and nicotine reinforcement (Picciotto et al., 1998; Schilström et al., 1998b; Watkins et al., 1999; Grillner and Svensson 2000; Sharples et al., 2000). In addition, mutant mice with hypersensitive α4 nAChRs demonstrated a 50-fold increase in sensitivity to the reinforcing effects of nicotine measured by a place-preference procedure which assesses the rewarding effects of a drug by measuring the preference a rat exhibits for a compartment previously associated with the effects of a drug instead of a compartment associated with an injection of saline (Tapper et al., 2004).

The place-preference finding further indicated a critical role of α4 nAChRs in nicotine reinforcement (Tapper et al., 2004). The α7 homomeric receptors may be involved in the reinforcing effects of nicotine. Methyllycaconitine, an antagonist with limited selectivity for the α7 nAChR, decreased the i.v nicotine self-administration procedure in rats (Markou and Paterson 2001), although another study with rats showed no effects of this antagonist on nicotine - induced hyperactivity or nicotine self-administration (Grottick et al., 2000). Finally, both the α4β2 and α7 subtypes have been implicated in the effects of nicotine on memory (Levin et al., 1999; Bancroft and Levin 2000) and the anxiolytic effects of nicotine, which also contribute to persistent tobacco use (Cheeta et al., 2001; Gordon 1999; USDHHS 1988).

Glutamate in Nicotine Addiction

Other mechanisms by which nicotine may elevate striatal DA levels include increases in excitatory glutamatergic inputs from the frontal cortex to the nucleus accumbens and/or excitatory glutamatergic inputs to VTA DAergic neurons projecting to the striatum. Nicotine increases the release of glutamate by agonist actions at excitatory presynaptic nAChRs on glutamatergic terminals in various brain sites, including the VTA (Fu et al., 2000; Grillner and Svensson 2000; Mansvelder and McGehee 2000), nucleus accumbens (Reid et al., 2000), prefrontal cortex (Gioanni et al., 1999), and hippocampus (Gray et al., 1996). In the VTA, nicotine acts at presynaptic α7 nAChRs located on glutamate neurons (neurons that release glutamate as the primary neurotransmitter). Activation of these α7 nAChRs on glutamate neurons (Mansvelder and McGehee 2000) increases the release of glutamate in the VTA. This activity stimulates the release of DA in the nucleus accumbens (Nisell et al., 1994a,b; Schilström et al., 1998a,b; Fu et al., 2000; Mansvelder and McGehee 2000). This increased release of glutamate acts at metabotropic and ionotropic glutamate receptors located on postsynaptic DAergic neurons (neurons that have DA as the primary neurotransmitter). Activation of these glutamate receptors leads to excitation of the DAergic neurons that results in increased release of DA in terminal brain sites where these neurons project, such as the nucleus accumbens (NA), the amygdala, and the frontal cortex.

It has been shown that ionotropic antagonists of NMDA receptors blocked (prevented) tolerance to the locomotor depressant effects of acute nicotine administration (Shoaib and Stolerman 1992; Shoaib et al., 1994) and blocked sensitization to the locomotor stimulant effects of chronic nicotine administration (Shoaib and Stolerman 1992). Blockade of the postsynaptic metabotropic glutamate receptor subtype 5 (mGluR5) with 2-methyl-6-(phenyl-ethynyl)pyridine (MPEP) decreased i.v. nicotine self-administration in rats and mice (Paterson et al., 2003) and decreased the motivation to self-administer nicotine (Paterson and Markou 2005). These effects were mediated by decreasing the nicotine-stimulated release of DA in the mesolimbic system. At doses that blocked nicotine self-administration, MPEP had no effect on response for food (Paterson et al., 2003). The progressive-ratio schedule of reinforcement, which increases the response requirements after each earned reward, allows the assessment of the motivation for reinforcers, such as nicotine or food, by evaluating the maximal number of responses emitted by the rat (i.e., breaking point) to receive a single i.v infusion of nicotine or a single food reward. In this schedule, MPEP had a greater effect on motivation for nicotine than on motivation for food, even when the magnitudes of reinforcer value were equated to support equal breaking points for nicotine and food under baseline conditions (Paterson and Markou 2005). This selectivity of the MPEP effects for nicotine reinforcement versus food reinforcement suggested that MPEP selectively blocks the reinforcing effects of nicotine without affecting motor performance or food reinforcement, suggesting a potential role of ionotropic glutamate receptors in the effects of nicotine. Animals that self-administered nicotine chronically exhibited an increase in ionotropic glutamate receptor subunits in brain regions, such as the VTA and the frontal cortex, that are implicated in the reinforcing effects of nicotine (Wang et al., 2007).

γ-Aminobutyric Acid in Nicotine Addiction

It is now well-established that GABA is the major inhibitory transmitter in the brain and is involved in the reinforcing effects of acute nicotine administration. Several factors inhibit the release of mesolimbic DA, including inhibitory GABAergic neurotransmission on ascending afferents to DAergic VTA neurons from the pedunculopontine tegmental nucleus (Walaas and Fonnum 1980; Yim and Mogenson 1980), descending GABA-ergic inputs from the ventral pallidum and the nucleus accumbens, GABA interneurons within the VTA, and medium spiny GABAergic neurons in the nucleus accumbens (Walaas and Fonnum 1979; Heimer and Alheid 1991; Churchill et al., 1992; Dewey et al., 1992;

Kalivas et al 1992; Klitenick et al., 1992; Sugita et al., 1992; Engberg et al., 1993). As suggested by neuroanatomy and electrophysiological studies, interactions between the GABAergic, DArgic, and glutamatergic systems in the VTA are complex (Mansvelder and McGehee 2000; Mansvelder et al., 2002). Glutamate afferents to the VTA excite DAergic neurons, and GABA-ergic afferents to the VTA inhibit DAergic neurons. Excitatory nAChRs are located on both glutamate and GABA-ergic neurons. The nAChRs on GABAergic neurons desensitize quickly to chronic administration of nicotine, but the nAChRs on glutamatergic neurons require higher doses of nicotine for desensitization, which leads to a nicotine-induced increase in the release of DA in the nucleus accumbens, the terminal area of VTA neurons (Schilström et al., 1998b; Mansvelder and McGehee 2000). Similar transmitter interactions may also occur in other brain regions.

Increased GABA-ergic transmission abolishes both the nicotine-induced increases in DA in the nucleus accumbens and the reinforcing effects of nicotine (Dewey et al., 1999; Brebner et al., 2002). Systemic injections of γ-vinyl GABA (Vigabatrin) increased GABA levels and decreased nicotine self-administration in rats (Paterson and Markou 2002). Vigabatrin is an irreversible inhibitor of GABA transaminase, the primary enzyme involved in GABA metabolism (Jung et al., 1977; Lippert et al., 1977). Systemic injections of Vigabatrin also abolished the expression and acquisition of nicotine-induced conditioned place preference (Dewey et al., 1998). The administration of Vigabatrin also lowered nicotine-induced increases in DA in the nucleus accumbens in both untreated rats and those receiving long-term treatment with nicotine in a dose-and time-dependent manner measured by in vivo microdialysis. In addition, Vigabatrin abolished nicotine - induced increases in striatal DA in primates, as determined by PET neuroimaging (Brebner et al., 2002).

The use of receptor-selective agonists in animals have suggested the involvement of $GABA_B$ receptors in the reinforcing effects of nicotine. Systemic injections or microinjections of Baclofen or CGP44532 [(3-Amino-2[S]-Hydroxypropyl)-Methylphosphinic Acid]—two $GABA_B$ receptor agonists—into the nucleus accumbens shell, the VTA, or the pedunculopontine tegmental nucleus that sends cholinergic, GABA-ergic, and glutamatergic projections to the VTA decreased the reinforcing effects of nicotine (Shoaib et al., 1998; Corrigall et al., 2000, 2001; Fattore et al., 2002; Paterson et al., 2004). However, injections into the caudate-putamen did not have these effects. The decreases in nicotine self-administration persisted even after administration of CGP44532 for 14 days, indicating tolerance to this effect of the $GABA_B$ receptor agonist with this duration of treatment (Paterson et al., 2005b); that is, the reduction in nicotine self-administration persisted over time. The issue of tolerance is important because long-term administration of drug therapies is necessary to achieve smoking cessation. However, in studies of rats, Vigabatrin and $GABA_B$ receptor agonists also decreased response for food, although at doses higher than the threshold doses for inducing decreases in nicotine self-administration (Paterson and Markou 2002; Paterson et al., 2004, 2005b). These effects on response for food may reflect nonspecific effects on performance by GABA-ergic compounds or specific effects on food intake. The possibility of effects on food intake is intriguing, because weight gain associated with abstinence from smoking is often a concern for smokers, especially women, who want to quit smoking cigarettes. Thus, enhanced GABAergic neurotransmission through the activation of $GABA_B$ receptors blocks the reinforcing effects of nicotine. However, a single dose of Baclofen had no effect on either the number of cigarettes smoked or the craving for nicotine (Cousins et al., 2001). Nevertheless, other clinical studies show that long-term administration of Baclofen reduced abuse of cocaine and alcohol, as well as cue-induced brain activation (Ling et al., 1998; Addolorato et al., 2000, 2002a, b). Hence, long-term treatment with these GABA-ergic drugs may be required to reduce tobacco smoking.

Opioid, Endocannabinoid, and Serotonergic Systems in Nicotine Addiction

The data on the role of opioid systems in the rewarding effects of nicotine remain uncertain. Nicotine did not induce a conditioned place preference in µ-opioid receptor *NULL-mutant mice, but it did so in wild-type animals (Berrendero et al., 2002). Similarly, nicotine induced a conditioned place preference in wild-type but not in preproenkephalin *NULL-mutant mice. A nicotine-induced elevation in DA overflow in the nucleus accumbens was absent in *NULL mutants (Berrendero et al., 2005). However, systemic or intra-VTA administration of the opiate receptor antagonist Naltrexone or the opiate receptor agonist d-Ala^2,N-Me-Phe^4-Gly-ol-enkephalin, respectively, had limited or no effects on nicotine self-administration in rats (Corrigall and Coen 1991a; Corrigall et al., 2000).

In humans, acute and short-term nicotine administration leads to the release of β-Endorphins, endogenous opioid peptides that have reinforcing effects (Davenport et al., 1990; Boyadjieva and Sarkar 1997). Furthermore, in humans, the acute administration of Naltrexone decreased the reinforcing value of nicotine in a procedure involving choice between puffs on nicotinized versus denicotinized cigarettes (i.e., compared with placebo, Naltrexone significantly reduced the number of nicotine cigarette choices) (Rukstalis et al., 2005). This result is consistent with a previous finding that acute administration of Naltrexone decreased the total number of choice cigarettes smoked (e.g., subjects were given a choice to smoke four cigarettes in a two-hrs. time period) (Epstein and King 2004). However, a randomized, double-blind trial of Naltrexone for smoking cessation found only a nonsignificant trend toward increased cessation rates, and the effect disappeared at 12 months after cessation (Covey et al., 1999). Other clinical trials examining the effects of Naltrexone versus placebo in smokers who were assigned nicotine patches to aid cessation have also observed no significant effects of Naltrexone on improving treatment outcomes (King et al., 2006; O'Malley et al., 2006). Thus, the possible involvement of the opiate system in the reinforcing effects of nicotine remains uncertain, and the use of opiate antagonists as treatments for dependence on tobacco smoking appears unwarranted. A Cochrane review in 2001 concluded that opioid antagonists failed to increase long-term abstinence from smoking on the basis that the limited evidence was insufficient to support a conclusive finding on whether Naltrexone is an aid to smoking cessation (David et al., 2006). Although one study suggested an effect of gender, women benefited more than men from treatment with Naltrexone (King et al., 2006).

The evidence is much stronger for the role of serotonin in the reinforcing effects of nicotine. Acute administration of nicotine elevated extracellular serotonin in the nucleus accumbens (Schiffer et al., 2001) and the VTA (Singer et al., 2004). Serotonin was also implicated in a neurochemical sensitization to nicotine, relevant to nicotine dependence. The administration of the serotonin ($5HT_2$) receptor agonist (±)-2,5-Dimethoxy-4-Iodoamphetamine (Olausson et al., 2001) or the $5HT_{2C}$ receptor agonist (S)-2-(Chloro-5-Fluoro-Indol-1-yl)-1-Methylethyl-amine Fumarate (Di Matteo et al., 2004) blocked the increased overflow of serotonin observed after a nicotine challenge in nicotine-treated rats. In addition, nicotine increased serotonin overflow in cortical areas (Toth et al., 1992; Ribeiro et al., 1993; Summers and Giacobini 1995; Singer et al., 2004) and in the dorsal hippocampus (Singer et al., 2004). In contrast, Balfour and Ridley (2000) found a decrease in the serotonin overflow after acute administration of nicotine. However, Singer et al (2004) used anesthetized rats, and Balfour and Ridley (2000) used in vivo microdialysis in conscious rats. In addition, administration of nicotine for at least 20 days was associated with decreased serotonin levels in the dorsal hippocampus (Benwell and Balfour 1979; Balfour and Ridley 2000). However, nicotine administration for 14 days was associated with increased serotonin levels (Takada et al., 1995). Nicotine infusion into the ventromedial nuclei or the lateral hypothalamic area increased the release of serotonin in this area (Yang et al., 1999; Ramos et al., 2004), suggesting that acute administration of nicotine increases serotonin levels but that long-term administration leads to decreases in serotonin levels that may mediate the affective aspects of nicotine dependence and withdrawal (Harrison et al., 2001).

Studies provide conflicting evidence on the role of cannabinoid subtype 1 (CB_1) receptors in modulating the reinforcing effects of nicotine. CB_1 knockout mice (i.e., mice genetically engineered to lack CB_1 receptors) self-administered nicotine (Cossu et al., 2001) but did not exhibit conditioned place preference to nicotine (Castañe et al., 2002). Furthermore, the CB_1 receptor antagonist Rimonabant (SR141716) decreased nicotine seeking behavior and self-administration of nicotine induced by the presentation of conditioned cues and also attenuated a nicotine -induced release of DA in the nucleus accumbens (Cohen et al., 2002, 2005; De Vries et al., 2005). Thus, the data from studies of rodents on the role of the cannabinoid system are inconclusive and so are the clinical data (Le Foll and Goldberg 2005). However, an analysis of data pooled from three clinical trials of Rimonabant compared with a placebo showed modest success at the end of treatment (Cinciripini et al., 2006).

Norepinephrine (NE) in Nicotine Addiction

There is also evidence to suggest a role of NE in the effects of nicotine. Acute nicotine administration increased extracellular NE in the nucleus accumbens, the hippocampus, and the cortex in rats (Brazell et al., 1991; Mitchell et al., 1993; Summers and Giacobini 1995; Benwell and Balfour 1997; Schiffer et al., 2001). Nicotine -evoked hippocampal release of NE was attenuated by α-bungarotoxin but was unaffected by either of the nAChR antagonists Mechamylamine or DHβE, implicating α7 nAChRs, rather than α4β2 nAChRs associated with the release of NE in this region of the brain (Fu et al., 1999). However, NE release from hippocampal synaptosomes in rats was sensitive to mechamylamine, DHβE, and methyllycaconitine suggesting that its release may be unspecific to α7 nAChRs (Clarke and Reuben 1996). Additional studies suggest the role of NE in nicotine's effects. I.V self-administration of nicotine increased NE in the amygdala and the hypothalamic paraventricular nucleus (Fu et al., 2001, 2003). *In vitro* studies indicated that nicotine increased release of NE in (1) prefrontal cortex slices of rats (Rao et al., 2003) and (2) locus coeruleus neurons of fetal rats grown in cultures (Gallardo and Leslie 1998).

Consistent with these neurochemical findings, short-term or long-term administration of Reboxetine, the selective NE reuptake inhibitor, decreased nicotine self-administration in rats (Rauhut et al., 2002). However, Reboxetine also decreased sucrose-maintained response, although to a lesser degree than nicotine-maintained response. Reboxetine acts as a noncompetitive nAChR antagonist, in addition to blocking NE reuptake (Miller et al., 2002). Thus, it remains uncertain that the effects of Reboxetine on nicotine self-administration are attributable to its effects on NE reuptake rather than to its actions as a nAChR antagonist.

Bupropion, a smoking cessation aid, also inhibited reuptake of NE, as well as DA (Ferris et al., 1983). Administration of Bupropion increased extracellular concentrations of DA and epinephrine in the nucleus accumbens, hypothalamus, and prefrontal cortex (Nomikos et al., 1989, 1992; Li et al., 2002). Bupropion decreased the firing rates of DAergic neurons in the nucleus accumbens and NE-ergic neurons in the locus coeruleus but had no effect on firing of 5-HT-ergic dorsal raphe neurons (neurons located in the dorsal raphe firing) (Cooper et al., 1994).

Despite the demonstrated effects of Bupropion on neurotransmitter and receptor systems that mediate the effects of nicotine, Bupropion had inconsistent effects on nicotine self-administration in rats. Some studies showed a decrease in nicotine self-administration in fixed-ratio schedules of reinforcement but had no effects in a progressive-ratio schedule (Glick et al., 2002; Bruijnzeel and Markou 2003). In contrast, another study indicated that repeated daily administration of Bupropion increased nicotine self-administration in a fixed-ratio schedule, but this was not significant (Shoaib et al., 2003). Finally, Rauhut et al (2003) showed that low doses of Bupropion increased and high doses decreased nicotine self-administration and response for sucrose, suggesting a robust effect of nicotine on NE-ergic neurotransmission, but Bupropion, which inhibits the reuptake of both DA and NE, had inconsistent effects on nicotine self-administration in rodents. Thus, other properties of Bupropion, such as relief from withdrawal symptoms, may contribute to its efficacy as an aid to smoking cessation.

Nicotine Dependence and Withdrawal

Nicotine Withdrawal Syndrome in Rodents

Smoking cessation leads to an aversive withdrawal syndrome lasting 1-4 weeks after cessation (Shiffman et al., 2004b). It has affective, behavioral, somatic, and cognitive components. The nicotine withdrawal syndrome is considered an important motivational factor that contributes to the perpetuation of nicotine dependence and continuing behaviors related to tobacco smoking (Markou et al., 1998; Kenny and Markou 2001). Withdrawal signs are often opposite to the acute effects of the drug (e.g., improved concentration versus poor concentration), reflecting the finding that the development of nicotine dependence leads to changes in brain function to counteract the acute effects of nicotine (e.g., increase in receptor number). One of the first and most widely used measures developed to investigate the neurobiology of the nicotine withdrawal syndrome and nicotine dependence is the frequency of somatic signs reliably observed in rats, but less reliably observed in mice (Malin et al., 1992; Epping-Jordan et al., 1998; Hildebrand et al., 1999; Isola et al., 1999; Carboni et al., 2000; Malin 2001; Semenova and Markou 2003; Salas et al., 2004). The most prominent somatic signs in rats are abdominal constrictions (writhes), gasps, ptosis, facial fasciculation, and eye blinks. These somatic signs are both centrally and peripherally mediated (Hildebrand et al., 1999; Carboni et al., 2000; Watkins et al., 2000; Malin 2001; Cryan et al., 2003).

The somatic components of nicotine withdrawal are unpleasant. However, avoidance of the negative affect and depression-like components of withdrawal may play a more important role in nicotine dependence than do the somatic aspects of withdrawal (Hughes 1992; Kenny and Markou 2001). In rodents, a valid and reliable measure of the affective and motivational aspects of drug withdrawal is the elevation of brain-reward thresholds observed after cessation of long-term administration of nicotine (Epping-Jordan et al., 1998; Harrison et al., 2001; Cryan et al., 2003; Semenova and Markou 2003). Elevations of reward thresholds are an operational measure of "diminished interest or pleasure" in rewarding stimuli (i.e., anhedonia), which is a symptom of nicotine withdrawal and a cardinal symptom of depression (APA 1994). Similar threshold elevations are observed during withdrawal from all major drugs of abuse in rodents (Kokkinidis et al., 1980; Markou and Koob 1991; Schulteis et al., 1994, 1995; Paterson et al., 2000; Spielewoy and Markou 2003). Several dissociations have been identified between the threshold elevations and the somatic signs of nicotine withdrawal, and these observations are similar to those in clinical studies, suggesting that the various aspects of withdrawal are mediated by different substrates (Epping-Jordan et al., 1998; Watkins et al., 2000; Harrison et al., 2001; Semenova and Markou 2003). Other rodent models that may be relevant to the disruption of behavioral performance in humans involve (a) disruptions induced by termination of administration of nicotine on behavioral responses maintained by food (Carroll et al., 1989); (b) increases in the acoustic startle response in rats (Helton et al., 1993); and (c) decreases in pre-pulse inhibition (i.e., decrease in the adaptation response to a stronger stimuli after presentation of a prior weaker stimuli) in mice (Semenova et al., 2003).

It has been demonstrated that rats with threshold elevations reflecting a reward deficit associated with nicotine withdrawal can become conditioned to previously neutral environmental stimuli (Kenny and Markou 2005). Nicotine -dependent rats were presented with a light and tone CS and received injections of the nicotinic receptor antagonist DHβE for four consecutive days before an assessment of brain-reward thresholds, which led to elevations of brain-reward thresholds in the nicotine-dependent rats. When the rats were presented with just the light and tone CS on the test day, thresholds were again elevated, reflecting a conditioned state of negative affect, which may lead to a relapse to tobacco smoking to alleviate this conditioned state of negative affect. This finding may explain the relapse observed months or even years after a person last smoked a cigarette.

Subsequent data suggest that the experience of nicotine withdrawal in male adolescent rats may differ from that in adult rats. The evidence for this hypothesis was threefold. First, male adolescent rats displayed fewer somatic signs of nicotine withdrawal than did adult males. Second, although male adolescent rats displayed a conditioned place aversion produced by nicotine withdrawal, it was less robust than that seen in adult males. Third, adolescent male rats did not display the decreases in brain-reward function seen in adult rats experiencing withdrawal (O'Dell et al., 2006, 2007).

Neurochemical Correlates of Nicotine Withdrawal

Several experimental approaches have been used to investigate the neuronal substrates of nicotine dependence and withdrawal. *In vivo* microdialysis studies provide information about the neurochemical changes occurring in specific brain sites with nicotine dependence. The precipitation of nicotine withdrawal in nicotine-treated rats, but not in controls, with administration of drugs that probe various transmitter systems and receptors suggests that chronic exposure to nicotine induces adaptations in specific transmitter systems and receptors. The combination of the *in vivo* microdialysis with the precipitated nicotine withdrawal indicated that the circuits mediating the acute effects of nicotine develop adaptations with nicotine dependence that lead to the withdrawal syndrome.

During nicotine withdrawal precipitated by systemic or intra-VTA administration of the nAChR antagonist Mechamylamine in nicotine-treated rats, dialysate levels of DA were decreased in the nucleus accumbens (Fung et al., 1996; Hildebrand et al., 1998; Carboni et al., 2000) and in the central nucleus of the amygdala (Panagis et al., 2000). These Mechamylamine injections into the VTA also produced, in a dose-dependent manner, most of the somatic signs of nicotine withdrawal (Hildebrand et al., 1999). This finding suggests the involvement of nAChRs in the VTA in the expression of the somatic signs of nicotine withdrawal. Similar decreases in levels of DA in the nucleus accumbens were observed in rats allowed to self-administer nicotine for 25 days, beginning 24-48 hrs. after the last session for self-administration of nicotine (Rahman et al., 2004). Decreases in DA levels in the nucleus accumbens were also associated with withdrawal from other drugs of abuse, such as ethanol, morphine, cocaine, and amphetamine (Rossetti et al., 1992). In contrast, the increases in dialysate DA levels observed in the frontal cortex (Hildebrand et al., 1998; Carboni et al., 2000) were similar to those observed during withdrawal from other drugs of abuse (Imperato et al., 1986). Thus, it appears that common substrates are involved in the mediation of the withdrawal signs associated with different drugs of abuse that involve alterations in DAergic neurotransmission in the nucleus accumbens and the frontal cortex.

The smoking cessation aid Bupropion, an atypical antidepressant, acts at least partly by inhibiting the neuronal uptake of DA, which thereby increases DAergic neurotransmission (Nomikos et al., 1992). Bupropion reverses both the threshold elevations and the somatic signs associated with nicotine withdrawal in rats (Cryan et al., 2003), although its effects on nicotine self- administration were inconsistent (Glick et al., 2002; Bruijnzeel and Markou 2003; Shoaib et al., 2003), suggesting that a decrease in mesolimbic DAergic neurotransmission mediates aspects of nicotine withdrawal.

Another transmitter system that may be involved in nicotine dependence and withdrawal is the NE-ergic system. However, to date, the role of this system in nicotine dependence has not been investigated as extensively as that of the DAergic system. Acute administration of nicotine elevated extracellular NE levels in the nucleus accumbens (Schiffer et al., 2001), hippocampus (Brazell et al., 1991; Mitchell et al., 1993; Benwell and Balfour 1997), cortex (Summers and Giacobini 1995), amygdala, and hypothalamic paraventricular nucleus (Fu et al., 2001), indicating that nicotine withdrawal may be characterized by a decrease in NE-ergic neurotransmission. This hypothesis was supported by evidence for the beneficial effects on smoking cessation of nortriptyline, a NE reuptake inhibitor (Hughes et al., 2004b) and the ameliorative effects of the α2-adrenoceptor agonist Clonidine on nicotine withdrawal in double-blind, placebo-controlled studies (Covey and Glassman 1991). There is limited evidence to suggest that other neurotransmitter systems such as 5-HT, endocannabinoid, or opioid may also be involved in withdrawal. A few studies suggested the involvement of the opioid system. For example, Naloxone precipitated somatic signs of withdrawal in nicotine -dependent rats (Malin et al., 1993; Watkins et al., 1999). Some studies also demonstrated the involvement of the 5-HTergic system.

Receptors and Behavioral Signs of Nicotine Withdrawal

It has been demonstrated that administration of a variety of nAChR antagonists induces behavioral signs of withdrawal in addition to the neurochemical effects of withdrawal in nicotine-treated rats. Systemic or intra-VTA administration of Mechamylamine or systemic or intra-ventricular administration of chlorisondamine induced somatic signs and/or elevation of reward threshold in nicotine-dependent rats only (Hildebrand et al., 1999; Watkins et al., 2000). Administration of the nAChR antagonist DHβE, which is selective for high-affinity nAChRs containing α4 (Harvey and Luetje 1996), induced threshold elevations (Epping-Jordan et al., 1998; Bruijnzeel and Markou 2004) but did not induce increases in somatic signs in nicotine-dependent rats (Epping-Jordan et al., 1998) suggesting that the threshold elevations are not due to nonspecific performance effects of the antagonists and that nAChRs are involved in the VTA in both the somatic and affective aspects of nicotine withdrawal.

In addition, work in knockout mice demonstrated a role of β4 but not β2 nAChRs in the somatic signs of withdrawal (Salas et al., 2004; Jackson et al., 2008). β2 nAChRs are critical for the reinforcing effects of nicotine (Picciotto and Corrigall 2002) and for the affective signs of nicotine withdrawal, as reflected in anxiety-like behavior and conditioned place aversion (Jackson et al., 2008). The α7 homomeric nAChRs may be involved in the reinforcing effects of nicotine (Markou and Paterson 2001) and in some somatic aspects but not in the affective aspects of nicotine withdrawal (Markou and Paterson 2001; Jackson et al., 2008). Specifically, administration of the α7 nAChR antagonist methyllycaconitine did not precipitate either the typical somatic signs of nicotine withdrawal or the reward deficits reflected in threshold elevations in nicotine-dependent rats (Markou and Paterson 2001). However, in α7 knockout mice, no hyperalgesia was noticed during nicotine withdrawal, an effect seen in wild-type mice during nicotine withdrawal (Jackson et al., 2008). However, α7 knockout mice showed normal levels of somatic and affective signs of nicotine withdrawal. Thus, the role of α7 nAChRs may be limited to somatic signs, including hyperalgesia, of nicotine withdrawal. Finally, α4 nAChRs is involved in the reinforcing effects of nicotine (Tapper et al., 2004). Although, their exact role in nicotine withdrawal has not been delineated, it may influence both affective and somatic withdrawal effects (Salas et al., 2004; Gonzales et al., 2006; Jorenby et al., 2006; Jackson et al., 2008). Overall, the observation that nAChR antagonists precipitate the behavioral and neurochemical signs of withdrawal in nicotine-dependent rats, but not in controls, suggested that chronic exposure to nicotine induces a compensatory reduction in the endogenous cholinergic tone that leads to the nicotine withdrawal syndrome.

Because glutamate stimulates DA release, decreased glutamate transmission may mediate nicotine withdrawal (Schilström et al., 1998a; Mansvelder and McGehee 2000). Systemic or intra-VTA administration of the mGluR subtype 2/3 (mGluR2/3) agonist LY314582 led to withdrawal-like threshold elevations in nicotine-dependent rats but not in control rats (Kenny et al., 2003). These mGluR2/3 receptors are found primarily pre-synaptically (i.e., on the transmitting neuron at the synaptic terminal that extends to the synapse, and the released transmitters target the postsynaptic neuron), where they inhibit glutamate transmission (Cartmell and Schoepp 2000; Kenny and Markou 2004). The increased sensitivity of nicotine-dependent rats to an agonist at the presynaptic inhibitory mGluR2/3 suggests that nicotine dependence is characterized by increased inhibition of glutamate transmission through these receptors, resulting in decreases in the release of glutamate when nicotine is no longer present to stimulate glutamate release. Consistent with this hypothesis, the mGluR2/3 antagonist LY341495 reversed the threshold elevations in rats that had spontaneous nicotine withdrawal (Kenny et al., 2003). Similarly, activity decreased in postsynaptic α-amino-3-hydroxy-5-methyl-4-isoxazole proprionic/kainate receptors, although no adaptations in mGluR5 receptors were observed in nicotine-dependent rats (Kenny et al., 2003). This result was somewhat surprising considering the important role found for this receptor in the reinforcing effects of nicotine (Paterson et al., 2003; Paterson and Markou 2005), indicating that decreased glutamate neurotransmission resulting from adaptations in presynaptic and postsynaptic receptors may contribute to the affective aspects of nicotine withdrawal. These data on the lack of adaptations in mGluR5 activity highlight that not all systems involved in the reinforcing effects of nicotine develop changes with long-term exposure to nicotine, which was also supported by data demonstrating that there are no changes in GABA ergic transmission, $GABA_B$ receptor activity, or α7 nAChR activity in nicotine-dependent rats, despite the important role of the GABA$_B$ receptor and the α7 nAChR in the reinforcing effects of nicotine (Markou and Paterson 2001; Paterson and Markou 2002; Paterson et al., 2004, 2005a,b).

It has been demonstrated that activated nAChRs are permeable to both sodium ions and Ca^{2+}, which lead to activation of the neurons and thus the release of many transmitters (Wonnacott et al., 2005). The widespread brain activation induced by acute or long-term administration of nicotine is shown by the expression of C-FOS in areas such as the amygdala, bed nucleus of the stria terminalis, lateral septum, hypothalamic nuclei, striatum, parts of the cortex, superior colliculus, optic tract, interpeduncular nucleus, supra-mammillary nucleus, periaqueductal gray matter, nucleus of the solitary tract, and locus coeruleus (Merlo Pich et al., 1999). C-FOS–related antigens are C-FOS proteins that heterodimerize with C-JUN proteins to produce complexes of activator protein-1 and transcriptionally regulate large numbers of genes related to plasticity (Dobranzki et al., 1991; Merlo Pich et al., 1997). Another protein researchers have studied extensively is the cyclic adenosine monophosphate–response element binding protein (CREB), because it is part of the signaling cascade for several receptors, including nAChRs (Nestler 2001). Acute treatment with nicotine had no effect on levels of total CREB or phosphorylated CREB (p-CREB). However, 18 hrs. after withdrawal from long-term administration of nicotine, concentrations of CREB and p-CREB decreased in the shell but not in the core of the nucleus accumbens (Pluzarev and Pandey 2004) and in the medial and basolateral amygdala but not in the central amygdala (Pandey et al., 2001). The high Ca^{2+} permeability of nAChRs also causes stimulation of additional intracellular messenger systems such as calmodulin-dependent protein kinases, including Ca^{2+}calmodulin-dependent protein kinase II (CaMKII), which is the most abundant kinase in the brain (Schulman and Hanson 1993). Acute administration of nicotine in mice induced increases in CaMKII expression in the spinal cord that was involved in the antinociceptive effects of nicotine (Damaj 2000). These are a few examples of the molecular changes observed after acute or long-term administration of nicotine and on withdrawal from long-term administration, suggesting that nicotine induces changes in molecular mechanisms involved in long-term plasticity. Such molecular mechanisms may also mediate several aspects of dependence on nicotine.

Neuroimaging Studies in Nicotine Addiction

Clinical neuroimaging studies have confirmed findings from basic research in rodents and have provided additional information about brain sites and processes involved in tobacco addiction in humans that cannot readily be investigated in animals (e.g., hedonic responses and craving). Similar to other drugs of abuse, nicotine decreases global glucose metabolism in the brain, as determined by PET with [^{18}F]-fluorodeoxyglucose (Stapleton et al., 2003). Long-term exposure to tobacco smoke also inhibits MAOA and MAOB activity (Volkow et al., 1999). Congruent with the suggested role of mesolimbic DA in the rewarding effects of nicotine in rodents, PET studies with [^{11}C]raclopride indicated that cigarette smoking increased DA levels in the striatum of smokers (Brody et al., 2004b) and that the hedonic response of the smoker to cigarette smoking was proportional to the DA released in the striatum (Barrett et al., 2004). Other areas activated by nicotine or smoking are the prefrontal cortex, ventral putamen, anterior cingulated cortex, superior parietal cortex, and thalamus (Kumari et al., 2003; Rose et al., 2003b; Brody et al., 2004b; Fallon et al., 2004; Jacobsen et al., 2004; Brody 2006). Smoking-associated images during inductions of craving that often lead to smoking increased the functional MRI signal in reward circuits such as the right posterior amygdala, posterior hippocampus, VTA, and medial thalamus (Due et al., 2002). Long-term administration of Bupropion attenuated cue-induced craving and blunted activation of the perigenual and ventral anterior cingulate cortex (Brody et al., 2004a). Functional MRI was used to compare the effects of nicotine on the brains of patients with schizophrenia and the brains of control participants. Nicotine -induced activation of the anterior cingulate cortex and bilateral thalamus was greater in patients with schizophrenia than in control participants during performance of a cognitive task (Jacobsen et al., 2004), suggesting that nicotine may improve cognitive performance in patients with schizophrenia by enhancing the thalamo-cortical functional connectivity (Jacobsen et al., 2004). Relevant to the high prevalence of smoking among patients with depression, smokers showed cortical responses suggesting vulnerability to depression in a study that used tryptophan depletion to increase the depressed mood in smokers (Pergadia et al., 2004).

Psychiatric Comorbidity in Nicotinism

Antidepressant and Antipsychotic Drugs and Nicotine Withdrawal

Another experimental approach used to identify systems that mediate nicotine withdrawal and dependence is a study of pharmacologic manipulations that reverse spontaneous nicotine withdrawal. Inferences can be made regarding the underlying abnormality associated with withdrawal through the mechanisms associated with the pharmacotherapy. On the basis of the phenomenological similarities among depression, the depression-like aspects of nicotine withdrawal, and the negative symptoms of schizophrenia, it has been hypothesized that overlapping neurobiologic substrates may mediate these depressive symptoms and that antidepressant and atypical antipsychotic treatments would alleviate the depression-like symptoms of nicotine withdrawal (Markou et al., 1998; Markou and Kenny 2002). Such common substrates mediating nicotine dependence and psychiatric disorders may explain the high prevalence of tobacco smoking among psychiatric populations. Compared with the percentage of smokers in the general population (20- 30%), a higher percentage of mentally ill patients were smokers (26-88%, depending on the mental illness) (Lasser et al., 2000), particularly those with schizophrenia, depression, or addiction to alcohol or other drugs (Hughes et al., 1986; Glassman et al., 1990; Breslau 1995).

Depression and Nicotine Dependence

Although the estimates vary across age, population, and criteria for tobacco dependence, most estimates suggest that the incidence of major depressive disorder among smokers is ~2 to 3 times that among nonsmokers (Hughes et al., 1986; Glassman et al., 1988, 1990; Kandel et al., 2001; Fergusson et al., 2003). A history of major depression increased the risk for progression to daily smoking and Nicotine dependence, and a history of daily smoking and Nicotine dependence increased the risk for major depression (Breslau et al., 1993b, 1998). A depressed mood is one of the symptoms of tobacco withdrawal syndrome experienced by persons who attempt to stop smoking (West et al., 1984; Hughes and Hatsukami 1992; APA 1994). Therefore, tobacco smoking may be a self-medication for either the depression that preceded the drug use or the smoking-induced depression (Pomerleau et al., 1978; Waal-Manning and de Hamel 1978; Hughes et al., 1986; Glassman 1993; Markou et al., 1998).

In particular, 5HT and the $5HT_{1A}$ receptors are involved in the mode of action of several antidepressants used clinically (Markou et al., 1998) and may play a role in nicotine withdrawal (Kenny and Markou 2001). Systemic administration of $5HT_{1A}$ receptor agonists, such as 8-hydroxy-2-dipropylaminotetralin (8-OH-DPAT), exacerbated the increased startle response observed during nicotine withdrawal, whereas $5HT_{1A}$ receptor antagonists (e.g., WAY-100635) alleviated this increased response (Rasmussen et al., 1997, 2000). In addition, the responsiveness of dorsal raphe nucleus neurons to 8-OH-DPAT increased during nicotine withdrawal (Rasmussen and Czachura 1997). Thus, nicotine withdrawal may increase the inhibitory influence of somatodendritic $5HT_{1A}$ autoreceptors in the raphe nuclei, and thereby decrease the release of serotonin in the forebrain and limbic brain sites (Benwell and Balfour 1979, 1982; Ridley and Balfour 1997). This is supported by the observation that a 5-HTergic antidepressant treatment involving the coadministration of the selective 5-HT reuptake inhibitor Fluoxetine and the $5HT_{1A}$ receptor antagonist p-MPPI [4-(2'-methoxy-phenyl)-1-[2'-(n-2''-pyridinyl)-p-Iodobenzamido]ethyl-piperazine] reversed the elevation in thresholds of brain-stimulation reward observed in rats with nicotine withdrawal, but the treatment did not block the somatic signs of withdrawal (Harrison et al., 2001). Consistent with this finding, the $5HT_{1A}$ receptor partial agonist Buspirone has shown limited efficacy in smoking cessation trials and may reduce the severity of withdrawal in persons attempting to stop smoking (West et al., 1991; Hilleman et al., 1992, 1994; Schneider et al., 1996). Thus, the depression-like aspects of Nicotine withdrawal may be mediated by a decrease in monoaminergic neurotransmission.

Consistent with the hypothesis that shared substrates mediate nicotine dependence and depression, clinical trials indicate that two of the antidepressant drug treatments are efficacious for smoking cessation. The atypical antidepressant Bupropion, which primarily inhibits the reuptake of DA, was more effective than a placebo in clinical trials to achieve smoking cessation (Fiore et al., 2008), and Bupropion has been approved for this use by the U.S. FDA. Preclinical research suggests that Bupropion reverses both the depression-like and somatic aspects of nicotine withdrawal (Cryan et al., 2003), although its effects on the rewarding effects of nicotine are inconsistent (Bruijnzeel and Markou 2003). In addition, the tricyclic antidepressant Nortriptyline, which primarily inhibits the reuptake of Norepinephrine, is recommended by WHO and the U.S. Public Health Service as a smoking cessation aid, suggesting that similar monoaminergic mechanisms are involved in both depression and nicotine dependence (Fiore et al., 2008).

Schizophrenia and Nicotine Dependence

It has been estimated that >80- 90% of patients with schizophrenia smoke compared with 20-30% of the general population (Masterson and O'Shea 1984; Goff et al., 1992; de Leon et al., 1995; Hughes 1996; Diwan et al., 1998). Persons with schizophrenia are commonly heavy smokers (>1.5 packs of cigarettes per day); smoke high-tar cigarettes, which are also high in nicotine content; and extract more nicotine from cigarettes than do smokers without schizophrenia (Masterson and O'Shea 1984; Hughes et al., 1986; Olincy et al., 1997).

The mesolimbic DAergic system and its efferent and afferent connections to other brain sites and systems, particularly DA-glutamate interactions, are implicated in both the reinforcing effects of nicotine and schizophrenia (Snyder 1976; Carlsson 1977). Abnormalities in these systems may render patients with schizophrenia more susceptible to the rewarding effects of nicotine (Chambers et al., 2001). These patients may use nicotine to counteract the cognitive and/or depression-like symptoms of schizophrenia that are not effectively treated with most antipsychotic drugs (Markou and Kenny 2002). Nicotine administration through tobacco smoking ameliorated visuospatial cognitive deficits of patients with schizophrenia (George et al., 2002) that involve the prefrontal cortex (Funahashi and Kubota 1994; Goldman-Rakic 1995; Callicott et al., 1998; Kikuchi-Yorioka and Sawaguchi 2000; Manoach et al., 2000).

Two forms of sensory-gating deficits (the inability to ignore or filter out irrelevant sensory information) that patients with schizophrenia exhibit may be influenced by actions on α7 or other nAChRs (Freedman et al., 1997; Adler et al., 1998). The two deficits are (a) auditory P50 gating, a form of sensory blocking, and (b) pre-pulse inhibition of the startle response. Thus, smoking may be a form of self-medication to compensate for these gating deficits. In support of this hypothesis, one study found that acute nicotine treatment reversed disruptions in pre-pulse inhibition induced in mice by the administration of the N-Methyl-d-Aspartate receptor antagonist phencyclidine, which mimics human psychosis (Spielewoy and Markou 2003). Nicotine administration may be a form of self-medication for the depression-like negative symptoms of schizophrenia. The atypical antipsychotic drug Clozapine treats the negative symptoms of schizophrenia most effectively and has decreased tobacco smoking in some persons without any encouragement to reduce smoking (George et al., 1995). In addition, long-term pretreatment with Clozapine attenuated the severity of the nicotine withdrawal syndrome in rats (Semenova and Markou 2003).

References

Addolorato, G., Caputo, F., Capristo, E., Colombo, G., Gessa, G. L., Gasbarrini, G., 2000. Ability of Baclofen in reducing alcohol craving and intake. II: preliminary clinical evidence. *Alcoholism, Clinical and Experimental Research*. 24(1), 67–71.

Adler, L. E., Olincy, A., Waldo, M., Harris, J. G., Griffith, J., Stevens, K., Flach, K., Nagamoto, H., Bickford, P., Leonard, S., et al., 1998. Schizophrenia, sensory gating, and nicotinic receptors. *Schizophrenia Bulletin*. 24(2), 189–202.

al'Absi, M., Hatsukami, D., Davis, G. L., Wittmers, L. E., 2004. Prospective examination of effects of smoking abstinence on cortisol and withdrawal symptoms as predictors of early smoking relapse. *Drug and Alcohol Dependence*. 73(3), 267–278.

al'Absi M, Hatsukami D, Davis GL. Attenuated adrenocorticotropic responses to psychological stress are associated with early smoking relapse. *Psychopharmacology*. 2005;181(1):107–17.

Albuquerque, E. X., Alkondon, M., Pereira, E .F. R., Castro, N. G., Schrattenholz, A., Barbosa, C. T. F., Bonfante-Cabarcas, R., Aracava, Y., Eisenberg, H. M., Maelicke, A., 1997. Properties of neuronal nicotinic acetylcholine receptors: pharmacological characterization and modulation of synaptic function. *Journal of Pharmacology and Experimental Therapeutics*. 280(3), 1117–1136.

Alkondon, M., Pereira, E. F. R., Barbosa, C. T. F., Albuquerque, E. X., 1997. Neuronal nicotinic acetylcholine receptor activation modulates γ-aminobutyric acid release from CA1 neurons of rat hippocampal slices. *Journal of Pharmacology and Experimental Therapeutics*. 283(3), 1396–1411.

Araujo, D. M., Lapchak, P. A., Collier, B., Quirion, R., 1988. Characterization of N-[^{3}H]methylcarbamylcholine binding sites and effect of N-methylcarbamylcholine on acetylcholine release in rat brain. *Journal of Neurochemistry.* 51(1), 292–299.

Arneric, S. P., Sullivan, J. P., Williams, M., 1995. Neuronal nicotinic acetylcholine receptors: novel targets for central nervous system therapeutics. *Psychopharmacology: The Fourth Generation of Progress.* Bloom FE, Kupfer DJ, editors. New York: Raven Press. pp. 95–110.

Balfour, D. J. K., Ridley, D. L., 2000. The effects of nicotine on neural pathways implicated in depression: a factor in nicotine addiction? *Pharmacology, Biochemistry, and Behavior.* 66(1), 79–85.

Balfour, D. J. K., Wright, A. E., Benwell, M. E. M., Birrell, C. E., 2000. The putative role of extra-synaptic mesolimbic DA in the neurobiology of nicotine dependence. *Behavioural Brain Research.* 113(1–2), 73–83.

Balfour, D. J. K., 2004. The neurobiology of tobacco dependence: a preclinical perspective on the role of the DA projections to the nucleus accumbens. *Nicotine & Tobacco Research.* 6(6), 899–912.

Bancroft, A., Levin, E. D., 2000. Ventral hippocampal α4β2 nicotinic receptors and chronic nicotine effects on memory. *Neuropharmacology.* 39(13), 2770–2778.

Barrett, S. P., Boileau, I., Okker, J., Pihl, R. O., Dagher, A., 2004. The hedonic response to cigarette smoking is proportional to DA release in the human striatum as measured by positron emission tomography and [^{11}C]raclopride. *Synapse.* 54(2), 65–71.

Benwell, M. E. M., Balfour, D. J. K., 1979. Effects of nicotine administration and its withdrawal on plasma corticosterone and brain 5-hydroxyindoles. *Psychopharmacology.* 63(1), 7–11.

Benwell, M. E. M., Balfour, D. J. K., 1997. Regional variation in the effects of nicotine on catecholamine overflow in rat brain. *European Journal of Pharmacology.* 325(1), 13–20.

Benwell, M. E. M., Balfour, D. J. K., 1992. The effects of acute and repeated nicotine treatment on nucleus accumbens DA and locomotor activity. *British Journal of Pharmacology.* 105(4), 849–856.

Benwell, M. E. M. Balfour, D. J. K., 1982. The effects of nicotine administration on 5-HT uptake and biosynthesis in rat brain. *European Journal of Pharmacology.* 84(1–2), 71–77.

Berrendero, F., Kieffer, B. L., Maldonado, R., 2002. Attenuation of nicotine-induced antinociception, rewarding effects, and dependence in μ-opioid receptor knock-out mice. *Journal of Neuroscience.* 22(24), 10935–10940.

Boyadjieva, N. I., Sarkar, D. K., 1997. The secretory response of hypothalamic β-endorphin neurons to acute and chronic nicotine treatments and following nicotine withdrawal. *Life Sciences.* 61(6), PL59–66.

Brebner, K., Childress, A. R., Roberts, D. C., 2002. A potential role for GABA$_B$ agonists in the treatment of psychostimulant addiction. *Alcohol and Alcoholism.* 37(5), 478–484.

Breslau, N., Fenn, N., Peterson, E. L., 1993a. Early smoking initiation and nicotine dependence in a cohort of young adults. *Drug and Alcohol Dependence.* 33(2), 129–137.

Breslau, N., Johnson, E. O., Hiripi, E., Kessler, R., 2001. Nicotine dependence in the United States: prevalence, trends, and smoking persistence. *Archives of General Psychiatry.* 58(9), 810–816.

Breslau, N., Johnson, E. O., 2000. Predicting smoking cessation and major depression in nicotine -dependent smokers. *American Journal of Public Health.* 90(7), 1122–1127.

Breslau, N., Kilbey, M. M., Andreski, P., 1994. DSM-III-R nicotine dependence in young adults: prevalence, correlates and associated psychiatric disorders. *Addiction.* 89(6), 743–754.

Breslau, N., Kilbey, M. M., Andreski, P., 1993b. Nicotine dependence and major depression: new evidence from a prospective investigation. *Archives of General Psychiatry.* 50(1), 31–35.

Breslau, N., Kilbey, M. M., Andreski, P., 1991. Nicotine dependence, major depression, and anxiety in young adults. *Archives of General Psychiatry.* 48(12), 1069–1074.

Brody, A. L., Mandelkern, M. A., Lee, G., Smith, E., Sadeghi, M., Saxena, S., Jarvik, M. E., London, E. D., 2004a. Attenuation of cue-induced cigarette craving and anterior cingulate cortex activation in Bupropion-treated smokers: a preliminary study. *Psychiatry Research.* 130(3), 269–281.

Brody, A. L., Olmstead, R. E., London, E. D., Farahi, J., Meyer, J. H., Grossman, P., Lee, G. S., Huang, J., Hahn, E. L., Mandelkern, M. A., 2004b. Smoking-induced ventral striatum DA release. *American Journal of Psychiatry.* 161(7), 1211–1218.

Brody, C. L., Hamer, D. H., Haaga, D. A. F., 2005. Depression vulnerability, cigarette smoking, and the serotonin transporter gene. *Addictive Behaviors.* 30(3), 557–566.

Browne, C. L., 1990. *The Design of Cigarettes.* 3rd ed. Charlotte (NC): Hoechst Celanese Corporation.

Bruijnzeel, A. W., Markou, A., 2004. Adaptations in cholinergic transmission in the ventral tegmental area associated with the affective signs of nicotine withdrawal in rats. *Neuropharmacology.* 47(4), 572–579.

Bruijnzeel, A. W., Markou, A., 2003. Characterization of the effects of Bupropion on the reinforcing properties of nicotine and food in rats. *Synapse.* 50(1), 20–28.

Callicott, J. H., Ramsey, N. F., Tallent, K., Bertolino, A., Knable, M. B., Coppola, R., Goldberg, T., van Gelderen, P., Mattay, V. S., Frank, J. A., et al., 1998. Functional magnetic resonance imaging brain mapping in psychiatry: biological issues illustrated in a study of working memory in schizophrenia. *Neuropsychopharmacology.* 18(3), 186–196.

Carboni, E., Bortone, L., Giua, C., Di Chiara, G., 2000. Dissociation of physical abstinence signs from changes in extracellular DA in the nucleus accumbens and in the prefrontal cortex of nicotine dependent rats. *Drug and Alcohol Dependence.* 58(1–2), 93–102.

Carlsson, A., 1977. Does DA play a role in schizophrenia? *Psychological Medicine.* 7(4), 583–97.

Carroll, M. E., Lac, S. T., Asencio, M., Keenan, R. M., 1989. Nicotine dependence in rats. *Life Sciences.* 45(15), 1381–1388.

Cartmell, J., Schoepp, D. D., 2000. Regulation of neurotransmitter release by metabotropic glutamate receptors. *Journal of Neurochemistry.* 75(3), 889–907.

Castañe, A., Valjent, E., Ledent, C., Parmentie, M., Maldonado, R., Valverde, O., 2002. Lack of CB1 cannabinoid receptors modifies nicotine behavioural responses, but not nicotine abstinence. *Neuropharmacology.* 43(5), 857–867.

Chambers, R. A., Krystal, J. H., Self, D. W., 2001. A neurobiological basis for substance abuse comorbidity in schizophrenia. *Biological Psychiatry.* 50(2), 71–83.

Cheeta, S., Tucci, S., File, S. E., 2001. Antagonism of the anxio-lytic effect of nicotine in the dorsal raphé nucleus by dihydro-β-erythroidine. *Pharmacology, Biochemistry, and Behavior.* 70(4), 491–496.

Chen, D., Dang, H., Patrick, J. W., 1998. Contributions of N-linked glycosylation to the expression of a functional α7-nicotinic receptor in *Xenopus* oocytes. *Journal of Neurochemistry.* 70(1), 349–357.

Churchill, L., Dilts, R. P., Kalivas, P. W., 1992. Autoradiographic localization of γ-aminobutyric acid$_A$ receptors within the ventral tegmental area. *Neurochemical Research.* 17(1), 101–106.

Clarke, P. B. S., Reuben, M., 1996. Release of [^{3}H]-noradrenaline from rat hippocampal synaptosomes by nicotine: mediation by different nicotinic receptor subtypes from striatal [^{3}H]-DA release. *British Journal of Pharmacology.* 117(4), 595–606.

Clarke, P. B. S. 1992. The fall and rise of neuronal α-bungarotoxin binding proteins. *Trends in Pharmacological Sciences.* 13(11), 407–413.

Colquhoun, L. M., Patrick, J. W., 1997. α3, β2, and β4 form hetero-trimeric neuronal nicotinic acetylcholine receptors in *Xenopus* oocytes. *Journal of Neurochemistry.* 69(6), 2355–2362.

Conroy, W. G., Berg, D. K., 1995. Neurons can maintain multiple classes of nicotinic acetylcholine receptors distinguished by different subunit compositions. *Journal of Biological Chemistry.* 270(9), 4424–4431.

Cooper, B. R., Wang, C. M., Cox, R. F., Norton, R., Shea, V., Ferris, R. M., 1994. Evidence that the acute behavioral and electrophysiological effects of Bupropion (Wellbutrin) are mediated by a noradrenergic mechanism. *Neuropsychopharmacology.* 11(2), 133–141.

Corrigall, W. A., Coen, K. M., Adamson, K. L., Chow, B. L. C., Zhang, J., 2000. Response of nicotine self-administration in the rat to manipulations of mu-opioid and γ-aminobutyric acid receptors in the ventral tegmental area. *Psychopharmacology.* 149(2), 107–114.

Corrigall, W. A., Coen, K. M., Adamson, K. L., 1994. Self-administered nicotine activates the mesolimbic DA system through the ventral tegmental area. *Brain Research.* 653(1–2), 278–284.

Corrigall, W. A., Coen, K. M., Zhang., Adamson, K. L., 2001. GABA mechanisms in the pedunculopontine tegmental nucleus influence particular aspects of nicotine self-administration selectively in the rat. *Psychopharmacology.* 158(2), 190–197.

Corrigall, W. A., Coen, K. M., 1991a. Opiate antagonists reduce cocaine but not nicotine self-administration. *Psychopharmacology.* 104(2), 167–170.

Corrigall, W. A., Coen, K. M., 1991. Selective DA antagonists reduce nicotine self-administration. *Psychopharmacology.* 104(2), 171–176.

Corrigall, W. A., Franklin, K. B. J., Coen, K. M., Clarke, P. B. S., 1992. The mesolimbic DAergicsystem is implicated in the reinforcing effects of nicotine. *Psychopharmacology.* 107(2–3), 285–289.

Cossu, G., Ledent, C., Fattore, L., Imperato, A., Bohme, G. A., Parmentier, M., Fratta, W., 2001. Cannabinoid CB_1 receptor knockout mice fail to self-administer morphine but not other drugs of abuse. *Behavioral Brain Research.* 118(1), 61–65.

Cousins, M. S., Stamat, H. M., de Wit, H., 2001. Effects of a single dose of Baclofen on self-reported subjective effects and tobacco smoking. *Nicotine & Tobacco Research.* 3(2), 123–129.

Covey, L. S., Glassman, A. H., Stetner, F., Becker, J., 1993. Effect of history of alcoholism or major depression on smoking cessation. *American Journal of Psychiatry.* 150(10), 1546–1547.

Covey, L. S., Glassman, A. H., Stetner, F., 1999. Naltrexone effects on short-term and long-term smoking cessation. *Journal of Addictive Diseases.* 18(1), 31–40.

Crooks, P. A., Dwoskin, L. P., 1997. Contribution of CNS nicotine metabolites to the neuropharmacological effects of nicotine and tobacco smoking. *Biochemical Pharmacology.* 54(7), 743–753.

Damaj, M. I., 2000. The involvement of spinal Ca^{2+}/calmodulin-protein kinase II in nicotine -induced antinociception in mice. *European Journal of Pharmacology.* 404(1–2), 103–110.

Damsma, G., Day, J., Fibiger, H. C., 1989. Lack of tolerance to nicotine -induced DA release in the nucleus accumbens. *European Journal of Pharmacology.* 168(3), 363–368.

Dani, J. A., 2000. Properties underlying the influence of nicotinic receptors on neuronal excitability and epilepsy. *Epilepsia.* 41(8), 1063–1065.

Davenport, K. E., Houdi, A. A., Van Loon, G. R., 1990. Nicotine protects against μ-opioid receptor antagonism by β-funaltrexamine: evidence for nicotine-induced release of endogenous opioids in brain. *Neuroscience Letters.* 113(1), 40–46.

David, S., Lancaster, T., Stead, L. F., 2006. Opioid antagonists for smoking cessation. *Cochrane Database of Systematic Reviews.* Art. No.: CD003086.

de Leon, J., Dadvand, M., Canuso, C., White, A. O., Stanilla, J. K., Simpson, G. M., 1995. Schizophrenia and smoking: an epidemiological survey in a state hospital. *American Journal of Psychiatry.* 152(3), 453–455.

De Vries, T. J., de Vries, W., Janssen, M. C., Schoffelmeer, A. N., 2005. Suppression of conditioned nicotine and sucrose seeking by the cannabinoid-1 receptor antagonist SR141716A. *Behavioural Brain Research.* 161(1), 164–168.

Deneris, E. S., Connolly, J., Rogers, S. W., Duvoisin, R., 1991. Pharmacological and functional diversity of neuronal nicotinic acetylcholine receptors. *Trends in Pharmacological Sciences.* 12(1), 34–40.

Dewey, S. L., Brodie, J. D., Gerasimov, M., Horan, B., Gardner, E. L., Ashby, C. R. Jr., 1999. A pharmacologic strategy for the treatment of nicotine addiction. *Synapse.* 31(1), 76–86.

Dewey, S. L., Morgan, A. E., Ashby, C. R. Jr., Horan, B., Kushner, S. A., Logan, J., Volkow, N. D., Fowler, J. S., Gardner, E. L., Brodie, J. D., 1998. A novel strategy for the treatment of cocaine addiction. *Synapse.* 30(2), 119–129.

Dewey, S. L., Smith, G. S., Logan, J., Brodie, J. D., Yu, D. W., Ferrieri, R. A., King, P. T., MacGregor, R. R., Martin, T. P., Wolf, A. P., et al., , 1992. GABAergic inhibition of endogenous DA release measured *in vivo* with [^{11}C]raclopride and positron emission tomography. *Journal of Neuroscience.* 12(10), 3773–3780.

Di Matteo, V., Pierucci, M., Esposito, E., 2004. Selective stimulation of serotonin$_{2c}$ receptors blocks the enhancement of striatal and accumbal DA release induced by nicotine administration. *Journal of Neurochemistry.* 89(2), 418–429.

Diwan, A., Castine, M., Pomerleau, C. S., Meador-Woodruff, J. H., Dalack, G. W., 1998. Differential prevalence of cigarette smoking in patients with schizophrenic vs mood disorders. *Schizophrenia Research.* 33(1–2), 113–118.

Dobrzanzki, P., Noguchi, T., Kovary, K., Rizzo, C. A., Lazo, P. S., Bravo, R., 1991. Both products of the *fosB* gene, FosB and its short form, FosB/SF, are transcriptional activators in fibroblasts. *Molecular and Cellular Biology.* 11(11), 5470–5478.

Due, D. L., Huettel, S. A., Hall, W. G., Rubin, D. C., 2002. Activation in mesolimbic and visuospatial neural circuits elicited by smoking cues: evidence from functional magnetic resonance imaging. *American Journal of Psychiatry.* 159(6), 954–960.

Elovainio, M., Kivimäki, M., Viikari, J., Ekelund, K., Keltikangas-Järvinen, L., 2005. The mediating role of novelty seeking in the association between the type 4 DA receptor gene polymorphism and cigarette-smoking behavior. *Personality and Individual Differences.* 38(3), 639–645.

Engberg, G., Kling-Petersen, T., Nissbrandt, H., 1993. GABA$_B$- receptor activation alters the firing pattern of DA neurons in the rat substantia nigra. *Synapse.* 15(3), 229–238.

Epping-Jordan, M. P., Watkins, S. S., Koob, G. F., Markou, A., 1998. Dramatic decreases in brain reward function during nicotine withdrawal. *Nature.* 393(6680), 76–79.

Epstein, A. M., King, A. C., 2004. Naltrexone attenuates acute cigarette smoking behavior. *Pharmacology, Biochemistry, and Behavior.* 77(1), 29–37.

Fallon, J. H., Keator, D. B., Mbogori, J., Turner, J., Potkin, S. G., 2004. Hostility differentiates the brain metabolic effects of nicotine. *Brain Research Cognitive Brain Research.* 18(2), 142–148.

Fattore, L., Cossu, G., Martellotta, M. C., Fratta, W., 2002. Baclofen antagonizes intravenous self-administration of nicotine in mice and rats. *Alcohol and Alcoholism.* 37(5), 495–498.

Ferguson, J. A., Patten, C. A., Schroeder, D. R., Offord, K. P., Eberman, K. M., Hurt, R. D., 2003. Predictors of 6-month tobacco abstinence among 1224 cigarette smokers treated for Nicotine dependence. *Addictive Behaviors.* 28(7), 1203–1218.

Ferris, R. M., Cooper, B. R., Maxwell, R. A., 1983. Studies of Bupropion's mechanism of antidepressant activity. *Journal of Clinical Psychiatry.* 44(5 Pt 2), 74–78. [PubMed]

Fiore, M. C., Jaén, C. R., Baker, T. B., Bailey, W. C., Benowitz, N. L., Curry, S. J., Dorfman, S. F., Froelicher, E. S., Goldstein, M. G., Healton, C. G., et al., 2008. *Treating Tobacco Use and Dependence: 2008 Update, Clinical Practice Guideline.* Rockville (MD): U.S. Department of Health and Human Services, Public Health Service.

Flores, C. M., Rogers, S. W., Pabreza, L. A., Wolfe, B. B., Kellar, K. J., 1992. A subtype of nicotinic cholinergic receptor in rat brain is composed of α4 and β2 subunits and is up-regulated by chronic nicotine treatment. *Molecular Pharmacology.* 41(1), 31–37.

Freedman, R., Coon, H., Myles-Worsley, M., Orr-Urtreger, A., Olincy, A., Davis, A., Polymeropoulos, M., Holik, J., Hopkins, J., Hoff, M., et al., 1997. Linkage of a neurophysiological deficit in schizophrenia to a chromosome 15 locus. *Proceedings of the National Academy of Sciences of the United States of America.* 94(2), 587–592.

Fu, Y., Matta, S. G., Brower, V. G., Sharp, B. M., 2001. Norepinephrine secretion in the hypothalamic paraventricular nucleus of rats during unlimited access to self-administered nicotine: an *in vivo* microdialysis study. *Journal of Neuroscience.* 21(22), 8979–8989.

Fu, Y., Matta, S. G., Gao, W., Brower, V. G., Sharp, B. M., 2000. Systemic nicotine stimulates DA release in nucleus accumbens: re-evaluation of the role of *N*-methyl-d-aspartate receptors in the ventral tegmental area. *Journal of Pharmacology and Experimental Therapeutics.* 294(2), 458–465.

Fu, Y., Matta, S. G., Kane, V. B., Sharp, B. M., 2003. Norepinephrine release in amygdala of rats during chronic nicotine self-administration: an in vivo microdialysis study. *Neuropharmacology.* 45(4), 514–523.

Fu, Y., Matta, S. G., Sharp, B. M., 1999. Local α-bungarotoxin-sensitive nicotinic receptors modulate hippocampal norepinephrine release by systemic nicotine. *Journal of Pharmacology and Experimental Therapeutics.* 289(1), 133–139.

Funahashi, S., Kubota, K., 1994. Working memory and prefrontal cortex. *Neuroscience Research.* 21(1), 1–11.

Fung, Y. K., Schmid, M. J., Anderson, T. M., Lau, Y. S., 1996. Effects of nicotine withdrawal on central DAergic systems. *Pharmacology, Biochemistry, and Behavior.* 53(3), 635–640.

Gallardo, K. A., Leslie, F. M., 1998. Nicotine-stimulated release of [3H]norepinephrine from fetal rat locus coeruleus cells in culture. *Journal of Neurochemistry.* 70(2), 663–670.

George, T. P., Sernyak, M. J., Ziedonis, D. M., Woods, S. W., 1995. Effects of clozapine on smoking in chronic schizophrenic out-patients. *Journal of Clinical Psychiatry.* 56(8), 344–346.

George, T. P., Vessicchio, J. C., Termine, A., Sahady, D. M., Head, C. A., Pepper, W. T., Kosten, T. R., Wexler, B. E., 2002. Effects of smoking abstinence on visuospatial working memory function in schizophrenia. *Neuropsychopharmacology.* 26(1), 75–85.

Gioanni, Y., Rougeot, C., Clarke, P. B. S., Lepousé, C., Thierry, A. M., Vidal, C., 1999. Nicotinic receptors in the rat prefrontal cortex: increase in glutamate release and facilitation of mediodorsal thalamo-cortical transmission. *European Journal of Neuroscience.* 11(1), 18–30.

Glassman, A. H., Covey, L. S., Dalack, G. W., Stetner, F., Rivelli, S. K., Fleiss, J., Cooper, T.B., 1993. Smoking cessation, clonidine, and vulnerability to nicotine among dependent smokers. *Clinical Pharmacology and Therapeutics.* 54(6), 670–679.

Glassman, A. H., Helzer, J. E., Covey, L. S., Cottler, L. B., Stetner, F., Tipp, J. E., Johnson, J., 1990. Smoking, smoking cessation, and major depression. *JAMA: the Journal of the American Medical Association.* 264(12), 1546–1549.

Glassman, A. H., Stetner, F., Walsh, B. T., Raizman, P. S., Fleiss, J. L., Cooper, T. B., Covey, L. S., 1988. Heavy smokers, smoking cessation, and clonidine: of a double-blind, randomized trial. *JAMA: the Journal of the American Medical Association.* 259(19):2863–6.

Glassman, A. H., 1993. Cigarette smoking: for psychiatric illness. *American Journal of Psychiatry.* 150(4), 546–553.

Glick, S. D., Maisonneuve, I. M., Kitchen, B. A., 2002. Modulation of nicotine self-administration in rats by combination therapy with agents blocking α3β4 nicotinic receptors. *European Journal of Pharmacology.* 448(2–3), 185–191.

Goff, D. C., Henderson, D. C., Amico, E., 1992. Cigarette smoking in schizophrenia: relationship to psychopathology and medication side effects. *American Journal of Psychiatry.* 149(9), 1189–94.

Goldman-Rakic, P. S., 1995. Cellular basis of working memory. *Neuron.* 14(3), 477–485.

Gordon, J., 1999. AR-R17779: A high affinity, subtype-selective full agonist of the alpha-7 nicotinic acetylcholine receptor. *Paper presented at the 2nd International Symposium on Nicotinic Acetylcholine Receptors.* Series AR-R17779: A high affinity, subtype-selective full agonist of the alpha-7 nicotinic acetylcholine receptor; Annapolis (MD).

Gotti, C., Zoli, M., Clementi, F., 2006. Brain nicotinic acetylcholine receptors: native subtypes and their relevance. *Trends in Pharmacological Sciences.* 27(9), 482–491.

Gourlay, S. G., Benowitz, N. L., 1997. Arteriovenous differences in plasma concentration of nicotine and catecholamines and related cardiovascular effects after smoking, nicotine nasal spray, and intravenous nicotine. *Clinical Pharmacology and Therapeutics.* 62(4), 453–463.

Grady, S. R., Meinerz, N. M., Cao, J., Reynolds, A. M., Picciotto, M. R., Changeux, J. P., McIntosh, J. M., Marks, M. J., Collins, A. C., 2001. Nicotinic agonists stimulate acetylcholine release from mouse interpeduncular nucleus: a function mediated by a different nAChR than DA release from striatum. *Journal of Neurochemistry.* 76(1), 258–268.

Gray, R., Rajan, A. S., Radcliffe, K. A., Yakehiro, M., Dani, J. A., 1996. Hippocampal synaptic transmission enhanced by low concentrations of nicotine. *Nature.* 383(6602), 713–716.

Grenhoff, J., Aston-Jones, G., Svensson, T. H., 1986. Nicotinic effects on the firing pattern of midbrain DA neurons. *Acta Physiologica Scandinavica.* 128(3), 351–358.

Grillner, P., Svensson, T. H., 2000. Nicotine-induced excitation of midbrain DA neurons in vitro involves ionotropic glutamate receptor activation. *Synapse.* 38(1), 1–9.

Grottick, A. J., Trube, G., Corrigall, W. A., Huwyler, J., Malherbe, P., Wyler, R., Higgins, G. A., 2000. Evidence that nicotinic α7 receptors are not involved in the hyperlocomotor and rewarding effects of nicotine. *Journal of Pharmacology and Experimental Therapeutics.* 294(3), 1112–1119.

Harrison, A. A., Liem, Y. T. B., Markou, A., 2001. Fluoxetine combined with a serotonin-1A receptor antagonist reversed reward deficits observed during nicotine and amphetamine withdrawal in rats. *Neuropsychopharmacology.* 25(1), 55–71.

Harvey, S. C., Luetje, C. W., 1996. Determinants of competitive antagonist sensitivity on neuronal nicotinic receptor β subunits. *Journal of Neuroscience.* 16(12), 3798–806.

Heimer, L., Alheid, G. F., 1991. Piecing together the puzzle of basal forebrain anatomy. *Advances in Experimental Medicine and Biology*. 295, 1–42.

Heishman, S. J., Taylor, R. C., Henningfield, J. E., 1994. Nicotine and smoking: a review of effects on human performance. *Experimental and Clinical Psychopharmacology*. 2(4), 345–395.

Helton, D. R., Modlin, D. L., Tizzano, J. P., Rasmussen, K., 1993. Nicotine withdrawal: a behavioral assessment using schedule controlled responding, locomotor activity, and sensorimotor reactivity. *Psychopharmacology*. 113(2), 205–210.

Henningfield, J. E., Keenan, R. M., Clarke, P. B. S., 1996. Nicotine. Pharmacological Aspects of Drug Dependence: Toward an Integrated Neurobehavioral Approach. *Handbook of Experimental Pharmacology*. Schuster CR, Kuhar M, editors. New York: Springer; Vol. 118, pp. 271–314.

Hildebrand, B. E., Nomikos, G. G., Hertel, P., Schilström, B., Svensson, T. H., 1998. Reduced DA output in the nucleus accumbens but not in the medial prefrontal cortex in rats displaying a Mechamylamine-precipitated nicotine withdrawal syndrome. *Brain Research*. 779(1–2), 214–225.

Hildebrand, B. E., Panagis, G., Svensson, T. H., Nomikos, G. G., 1999. Behavioral and biochemical manifestations of meca-mylamine-precipitated nicotine withdrawal in the rat: role of nicotinic receptors in the ventral tegmental area. *Neuropsychopharmacology*. 21(4), 560–574.

Hilleman, D. E., Mohiuddin, S. M., DelCore, M. G., 1994. Comparison of fixed-dose transdermal nicotine, tapered-dose trans-dermal nicotine, and buspirone in smoking cessation. *Journal of Clinical Pharmacology*. 34(3), 222–224.

Holladay, M. W., Dart, M. J., Lynch, J. K., 1997. Neuronal nicotinic acetylcholine receptors as targets for drug discovery. *Journal of Medicinal Chemistry*. 40(26), 4169–4194.

Hughes, J. R., Gulliver, S. B., Fenwick, J. W., Valliere, W. A., Cruser, K., Pepper, S., Shea, P., Solomon, L. J., Flynn, B. S., 1992. Smoking cessation among self-quitters. *Health Psychology*. 11(5), 331–334.

Hughes, J. R., Hatsukami, D. K., Mitchell, J. E., Dahlgren, L. A., 1986. Prevalence of smoking among psychiatric outpatients. *American Journal of Psychiatry*. 143(8), 993–997.

Hughes, J. R., Hatsukami, D. K., 1992. The nicotine withdrawal syndrome: a brief review and update. *International Journal of Smoking Cessation*. 1(2), 21–26.

Hughes, J. R., Oliveto, A. H., Riggs, R., Kenny, M., Liguori, A., Pillitteri, J. L., MacLaughlin, M. A., 2004. Concordance of different measures of nicotine dependence: two pilot studies. *Addictive Behaviors*. 29(8), 1527–1539.

Hughes, J. R., 1996. The future of smoking cessation therapy in the United States. *Addiction*. 91(12), 1797–802.

Imperato, A., Mulas, A., Di Chiara, G., 1986. Nicotine preferentially stimulates DA release in the limbic system of freely moving rats. *European Journal of Pharmacology.* 132(2–3), 337–338.

Isola, R., Vogelsberg, V., Wemlinger, T. A., Neff, N. H., Hadjicon-stantinou, M., 1999. Nicotine abstinence in the mouse. *Brain Research.* 850(1–2), 189–196.

Jackson, K. J., Martin, B. R., Changeux, J. P., Damaj, M. I., 2008. Differential role of nicotinic acetylcholine receptor subunits in physical and affective nicotine withdrawal signs. *Journal of Pharmacology and Experimental Therapeutics.* 325(1), 302–312.

Jacobsen, L. K., D'Souza, D. C., Mencl, W. E., Pugh, K. R., Skudlarski, P., Krystal, J. H., 2004. Nicotine effects on brain function and functional connectivity in schizophrenia. *Biological Psychiatry.* 55(8), 850–858.

Jorenby, D. E., Hays, J. T., Rigotti, N. A., Azoulay, S., Watsky, E. J., Williams, K. E., Billing, C. B., Gong, J., Reeves, K. R., 2006. *Varenciline* Phase 3 Study Group. Efficacy of Varenicline, an alpha4beta2 nicotinic acetylcholine receptor partial agonist, vs placebo or sustained-release Bupropion for smoking cessation. *JAMA: the Journal of the American Medical Association.* 296(1), 56–63.

Jung, M. J., Lippert, B., Metcalf, B. W., Böhlen, P., Schechter, P. J., 1977. γ-Vinyl GABA (4-amino-hex-5-enoic acid), a new selective irreversible inhibitor of GABA-T: effects on brain GABA metabolism in mice. *Journal of Neurochemistry.* 29(5), 797–802.

Kaiser, S. A., Soliakov, L., Harvey, S. C., Luetje, C. W., Wonnacott, S., 1998. Differential inhibition by α-conotoxin-MII of the nicotinic stimulation of [^{3}H]DA release from rat striatal synaptosomes and slices. *Journal of Neurochemistry.* 70(3), 1069–1076.

Kalivas, P. W., Striplin, C. D., Steketee, J. D., Klitenick, M. A., Duffy, P., 1992. Cellular mechanisms of behavioral sensitization to drugs of abuse. *Annals of the New York Academy of Sciences.* 654, 128–135.

Kandel, D. B., Huang, F. Y., Davies, M., 2001. Comorbidity between patterns of substance use dependence and psychiatric syndromes. *Drug and Alcohol Dependence.* 64(2), 233–241.

Kenny, P. J., File, S. E., Neal, M. J., 2000. Evidence for a complex influence of nicotinic acetylcholine receptors on hippo-campal serotonin release. *Journal of Neurochemistry.* 75(6), 2409–2414.

Kenny, P. J., Gasparini, F., Markou, A., 2003. Group II metabotropic and α-amino-3-hydroxy-5-methyl-4-isoxazole propionate (AMPA)/kainate glutamate receptors regulate the deficit in brain reward function associated with nicotine withdrawal in rats. *Journal of Pharmacology and Experimental Therapeutics.* 306(3), 1068–1076.

Kenny, P. J., Markou, A., 2005. Conditioned nicotine withdrawal profoundly decreases the activity of brain reward systems. *Journal of Neuroscience.* 25(26), 6208–6212.

Kenny, P. J., Markou, A., 2001. Neurobiology of the nicotine withdrawal syndrome. *Pharmacology, Biochemistry, and Behavior.* 70(4), 531–549.

Kenny, P. J., Markou, A., 2001. The ups and downs of addiction: role of metabotropic glutamate receptors. *Trends in Pharmacological Sciences.* 25(5), 265–272.

Kikuchi-Yorioka, Y., Sawaguchi, T., 2000. Parallel visuospatial and audiospatial working memory processes in the monkey dorsolateral prefrontal cortex. *Nature Neuroscience.* 3(11), 1075–1076.

King, A., de Wit, H., Riley, R. C., Cao, D., Niaura, R., Hatsukami, D., 2006. Efficacy of Naltrexone in smoking cessation: a preliminary study and an examination of sex differences. *Nicotine & Tobacco Research.* 8(5), 671–682.

Klitenick, M. A., DeWitte, P., Kalivas, P. W., 1992. Regulation of somatodendritic DA release in the ventral tegmental area by opioids and GABA: an *in vivo* microdialysis study. *Journal of Neuroscience.* 12(7), 2623–2632.

Kokkinidis, L., Zacharko, R. M., Predy, P. A., 1980. Post-amphetamine depression of self-stimulation responding from the substantia nigra: reversal by tricyclic antidepressants. *Pharmacology, Biochemistry, and Behavior.* 13(3), 379–383.

Koob, G. F., Markou, A., Weiss, F., Schultheis, G., 1993. Opponent process and drug dependence: neurobiological mechanisms. *Seminars in Neuroscience.* 5(3), 351–358.

Koob, G. F., 2008. Neurobiology of addiction. The American Psychiatric Publishing. Textbook of Substance Abuse Treatment. 4th Edition. Galanter M, Kleber HD, editors. Arlington (VA): *American Psychiatric Publishing.* pp. 3–16.

Kumari, V., Gray, J. A., ffytche, D. H., Mitterschiffthaler, M. T., Das, M., Zachariah, E., Vythelingum, G. N., Williams, S. C. R., Simmons, A., Sharma, T., 2003. Cognitive effects of nicotine in humans: an fMRI study. *Neuroimage.* 19(3), 1002–1013.

Lança, A. J., Adamson, K. L., Coen, K. M., Chow, B. L. C., Corrigall, W. A., 2000. The pedunculopontine tegmental nucleus and the role of cholinergic neurons in nicotine self-administration in the rat: a correlative neuroanatomical and behavioral study. *Neuroscience.* 96(4), 735–742.

Lasser, K., Boyd, J. W., Woolhandler, S., Himmelstein, D. U., McCormick, D., Bor, D. H., 2000. Smoking and mental illness: a population-based prevalence study. *JAMA: the Journal of the American Medical Association.* 284(20), 2606–2610.

Le Foll, B., Goldberg, S. R., 2005. Control of the reinforcing effects of nicotine by associated environmental stimuli in animals and humans. *Trends in Pharmacological Sciences.* 26(6), 287–293.

Léna, C., Changeux, J. P., 1998. Allosteric nicotinic receptors, human pathologies. *Journal of Physiology Paris.* 92(2), 63–74.

Léna, C., de Kerchove, d'Exaerde, A., Cordero-Erausquin, M., Le Novère, N., del Mar Arroyo-Jimenez, M., Changeux, J. P., 1999. Diversity and distribution of nicotinic acetylcholine receptors in the *locus ceruleus* neurons. *Proceedings of the National Academy of Sciences of the United States of America.* 96(21), 12126–12131.

Levin, E. D., Bettegowda, C., Blosser, J., Gordon, J., 1999. AR-R17779, and α7 nicotinic agonist, improves learning and memory in rats. *Behavioral Pharmacology.* 10(6–7), 675–680.

Levine, D. G., 1974. "Needle freaks": compulsive self-injection by drug users" *American Journal of Psychiatry.* 131(3), 297–300.

Li, S. X. M., Perry, K. W., Wong, D. T., 2002. Influence of fluoxetine on the ability of Bupropion to modulate extracellular DA and norepinephrine concentrations in three mesocorticolimbic areas of rats. *Neuropharmacology.* 42(2), 181–190.

Ling, W., Shoptaw, S., Majewska, D., 1998. Baclofen as a cocaine anti-craving medication: a preliminary clinical study. *Neuropsychopharmacology.* 18(5), 403–404.

Lippert, B., Metcalf, B. W., Jung, M. J., Casara, P., 1977. 4-Amino-hex-5-enoic acid, a selective catalytic inhibitor of 4-aminobutyric-acid aminotransferase in mammalian brain. *European Journal of Biochemistry.* 74(3), 441–445.

Ludwig, A. M., 1986. Pavlov's "bells" and alcohol craving. *Addictive Behaviors.* 11(2), 87–91.

Luo, S., Kulak, J. M., Cartier, G. E., Jacobsen, R. B., Yoshikami, D., Olivera, B. M., McIntosh, J. M., 1998. α-Conotoxin AuIB selectively blocks α3β4 nicotinic acetylcholine receptors and nicotine -evoked norepinephrine release. *Journal of Neuroscience.* 18(21), 8571–8579.

Malin, D. H., Lake, J. R., Carter, V. A., Cunningham, J. S., Wilson, O. B., 1993. Naloxone precipitates nicotine abstinence syndrome in the rat. *Psychopharmacology.* 112(2–3), 339–342.

Malin, D. H., Lake, J. R., Newlin-Maultsby, P., Roberts, L. K., Lanier, J. G., Carter, V. A., Cunningham, J. S., Wilson, O. B., 1992. Rodent model of nicotine abstinence syndrome. *Pharmacology, Biochemistry, and Behavior.* 43(3), 779–784.

Malin, D. H., 2001. Nicotine dependence: studies with a laboratory model. *Pharmacology, Biochemistry, and Behavior.* 70(4), 551–559.

Manoach, D. S., Gollub, R. L., Benson, E. S., Searl, M. M., Goff, D. C., Halpern, E., Saper, C. B., Rauch, S. L., 2000. Schizophrenic subjects show aberrant fMRI activation of dorsolateral prefrontal cortex and basal ganglia during working memory performance. *Biological Psychiatry.* 48(2), 99–109.

Mansvelder, H. D., Keath, J. R., McGehee, D. S., 2002. Synaptic mechanisms underlie nicotine -induced excitability of brain reward areas. *Neuron.* 33(6), 905–919.

Mansvelder, H. D., McGehee, D. S., 2000. Long-term potentiation of excitatory inputs to brain reward areas by nicotine. *Neuron.* 27(2), 349–357.

Markou, A., Kenny, P. J., 2002. Neuroadaptations to chronic exposure to drugs of abuse: relevance to depressive symptomatology seen across psychiatric diagnostic categories. *Neurotoxicity Research.* 4(4), 297–313.

Markou, A., Koob, G. F., 1991. Postcocaine anhedonia: an animal model of cocaine withdrawal. *Neuropsychopharmacology.* 4(1), 17–26.

Markou, A., Kosten, T. R., Koob, G. F., 1998. Neurobiological similarities in depression and drug dependence: a self-medication hypothesis. *Neuropsychopharmacology.* 18(3), 35–74.

Markou, A., Paterson, N. E., 2001. The nicotinic antagonist methyl-lycaconitine has differential effects on nicotine self-administration and nicotine withdrawal in the rat. *Nicotine & Tobacco Research.* 3(4), 361–373.

Markou, A., Weiss, F., Gold, L. H., Caine, S. B., Schultheis, G., Koob, G. F., 1993. Animal models of drug craving. *Psychopharmacology.* 112(2–3), 163–182.

Markou, A., 2006. Pathways and systems involved in Nicotine dependence. *Understanding Nicotine and Tobacco Addiction.* Novartis Foundation Symposium 275. Bock G, Goode J, editors. Hoboken (NJ): John Wiley & Sons. pp. 132–52.

Masterson, E., O'Shea, B., 1984. Smoking and malignancy in schizophrenia. *British Journal of Psychiatry.* 145, 429–432.

McGehee, D. S., Role, L. W., 1995. Physiological diversity of nicotinic acetylcholine receptors expressed by vertebrate neurons. *Annual Review of Physiology.* 57, 521–546.

McGehee, D. S., Role, L. W., 1996. Presynaptic ionotropic receptors. *Current Opinion in Neurobiology.* 6(3), 342–349.

Merlo Pich, E., Chiamulera, C., Carboni, L., 1999. Molecular mechanisms of the positive reinforcing effect of nicotine. *Behavioural Pharmacology.* 10(6–7), 587–596.

Merlo Pich, E., Pagliusi, S. R., Tessari, M., Talabot-Ayer, D., Hooft van Huijsduijnen, R., Chiamulera, C., 1997. Common neural substrates for the addictive properties of nicotine and cocaine. *Science.* 275(5296), 83–86.

Mifsud, J. C., Hernandez, L., Hoebel, B. G., 1989. Nicotine infused into the nucleus accumbens increases synaptic DA as measured by in vivo microdialysis. *Brain Research.* 478(2), 365–367.

Miller, D. K., Wong, E. H. F., Chesnut, M. D., Dwoskin, L. P., 2002. Reboxetine: functional inhibition of monoamine transporters and nicotinic acetylcholine receptors. *Journal of Pharmacology and Experimental Therapeutics.* 302(2), 687–695.

Nestler, E. J., 2000. Genes and addiction. *Nature Genetics.* 26(3), 277–281.

Nisell, M., Marcus, M., Nomikos, G. G., Svensson, T. H., 1997. Differential effects of acute and chronic nicotine on DA output in the core and shell of the rat nucleus accumbens. *Journal of Neural Transmission.* 104(1), 1–10.

Nisell, M., Nomikos, G. G., Svensson, T. H., 1994a. Infusion of nicotine in the ventral tegmental area or the nucleus accumbens of the rat differentially affects accumbal DA release. *Pharmacology and Toxicology.* 75(6), 348–352.

Nisell, M., Nomikos, G. G., Svensson, T. H., 1994. Systemic nicotine -induced DA release in the rat nucleus accumbens is regulated by nicotinic receptors in the ventral tegmental area. *Synapse.* 16(1), 36–44.

Nomikos, G. G., Damsma, G., Wenkstern, D., Fibiger, H. C., 1989. Acute effects of Bupropion on extracellular DA concentrations in rat striatum and nucleus accumbens studied by in vivo microdialysis. *Neuropsychopharmacology.* 2(4), 273–279.

Nomikos, G. G., Damsma, G., Wenkstern, D., Fibiger, H. C., 1992. Effects of chronic Bupropion on interstitial concentrations of DA in rat nucleus accumbens and striatum. *Neuropsychopharmacology.* 7(1), 7–14.

O'Brien, C. P., Childress, A. R., McLellan, T., Ehrman, R., 1990. Integrating systematic cue exposure with standard treatment in recovering drug dependent patients. *Addictive Behaviors.* 15(4), 355–365.

O'Dell, L. E., Bruijnzeel, A. W., Ghozland, S., Markou, A., Koob, G. B., 2004. Nicotine withdrawal in adolescent and adult rats. *Annals of the New York Academy of Sciences.* 1021, 167–174.

O'Malley, S. S., Cooney, J. L., Krishnan-Sarin, S., Dubin, J. A., McKee, S. A., Cooney, N. L., Blakeslee, A., Meandzija, B., Romano-Dahlgard, D., Wu, R., et al., , 2006. A controlled trial of Naltrexone augmentation of nicotine replacement therapy for smoking cessation. *Archives of Internal Medicine.* 166(6), 667–674.

Olausson, P., Åkesso, P., Engel, J. A., Söderpalm, B., 2001. Effects of 5-HT$_{1A}$ and 5-HT$_2$ receptor agonists on the behavioral and neurochemical consequences of repeated nicotine treatment. *European Journal of Pharmacology.* 420(1), 45–54.

Olincy, A., Young, D. A., Freedman, R., 1997. Increased levels of the nicotine metabolite cotinine in schizophrenic smokers compared to other smokers. *Biological Psychiatry.* 42(1), 1–5.

Panagis, G., Hildebrand, B. E., Svensson, T. H., Nomikos, G. G., 2000. Selective *c-fos* induction and decreased DA release in the central nucleus of amygdala in rats displaying a *Mechamylamine*-precipitated nicotine withdrawal syndrome. *Synapse.* 35(1), 15–25.

Panday, S., Reddy, S. P., Ruiter, R. A. C., Bergstrom, E., DeVries, H., 2007. Nicotine dependence and withdrawal symptoms among occasional smokers. *Journal of Adolescent Health.* 40(2), 144–50.

Paterson, N. E., Bruijnzeel, A. W., Kenny, P. J., Wright, C. D., Froestl, W., Markou, A., 2005a. Prolonged nicotine exposure does not alter GABA$_B$ receptor-mediated regulation of brain reward function. *Neuropharmacology.* 49(7), 953–962.

Paterson, N. E., Froestl, W., Markou, A., 2005b. Repeated administration of the GABA$_B$ receptor agonist CGP44532 decreased nicotine self-administration, and acute administration decreased cue-induced reinstatement of nicotine -seeking in rats. *Neuropsychopharmacology.* 30(1), 119–28.

Paterson, N. E., Froestl, W., Markou, A., 2004. The GABA$_B$ receptor agonists Baclofen and CGP44532 decreased nicotine self-administration in the rat. *Psychopharmacology.* 172(2),179–86.

Paterson, N. E., Markou, A., 2002. Increased GABA neurotransmission via administration of gamma-vinyl GABA decreased nicotine self-administration in the rat. *Synapse.* 44(4), 252–253.

Paterson, N. E., Markou, A., 2005. The metabotropic glutamate receptor 5 antagonist MPEP decreased break points for nicotine, cocaine and food in rats. *Psychopharmacology.* 179(1), 255–261.

Paterson NE, Myers C, Markou A. Effects of repeated withdrawal from continuous amphetamine administration on brain reward function in rats. *Psychopharmacology.* 2000;152(4):440–6.

Paterson, N. E., Semenova, S., Gasparini, F., Markou, A., 2003. The mGluR5 antagonist MPEP decreased nicotine self-administration in rats and mice. *Psychopharmacology.* 167(3), 257–264.

Pergadia, M., Spring, B., Konopka, L. M., Twardowska, B., Shirazi, P., Crayton, J. W., 2004. Double-blind trial of the effects of tryptophan depletion on depression and cerebral blood flow in smokers. *Addictive Behaviors.* 29(4), 665–671.

Picciotto, M. R., Corrigall, W. A., 2002. Neuronal systems underlying behaviors related to nicotine addiction: neural circuits and molecular genetics. *Journal of Neuroscience.* 22(9), 3338–3341.

Picciotto, M. R., Zoli, M., Léna, C., Bessis, A., Lallemand, Y., LeNovère, N., Vincent, P., Pich, E. M., Brûlet, P., Changeux, J. P., 1995. Abnormal avoidance learning in mice lacking functional high-affinity nicotine receptor in the brain. *Nature.* 374(6517), 65–67.

Picciotto, M. R., Zoli, M., Rimondini, R., Léna, C., Marubio, L. M., Pich, E. M., Fuxe, K., Changeux, J. P., 1998. Acetylcholine receptors containing the β2 subunit are involved in the reinforcing properties of nicotine. *Nature.* 391(6663), 173–177.

Pidoplichko, V. I, DeBiasi, M., Williams, J. T., Dani, J. A., 1997. Nicotine activates and desensitizes midbrain DA neurons. *Nature.* 390(6658), 401–404.

Pluzarev, O., Pandey, S. C., 2004. Modulation of CREB expression and phosphorylation in the rat nucleus accumbens during nicotine exposure and withdrawal. *Journal of Neuroscience Research.* 77(6), 884–891.

Pomerleau, O., Adkins, D., Pertschuk, M., 1978. Predictors of outcome and recidivism in smoking cessation treatment. *Addictive Behaviors.* 3(2), 65–70.

Pontieri, F. E., Tanda, G., Orzi, F., Di Chiara, G., 1996. Effects of nicotine on the nucleus accumbens and similarity to those of addictive drugs. *Nature.* 382(6588), 255–257.

Rahman, S., Zhang, J., Engleman, E. A., Corrigall, W. A., 2004. Neuroadaptive changes in the mesoaccumbens DA system after chronic nicotine self-administration: a microdialysis study. *Neuroscience.* 129(2), 415–424.

Ramos, E. J. B., Meguid, M. M., Zhang, L., Miyata, G., Fetissov, S. O., Chen, C., Suzuki, S., Laviano, A., 2004. Nicotine infusion into rat ventromedial nuclei and effects on monoaminergic system. *Neuroreport.* 15(14), 2293–2297.

Rasmussen, K., Calligaro, D. O., Czachura, J. F., Dreshfield-Ahmad, L. J., Evans, D. C., Hemrick-Luecke, S.K., Kallman, M. J., Kendrick, W. T., Leander, J. D., Nelson, D. L., et al., 2000. The novel 5-hydroxytryptamine$_{1A}$ antagonist LY426965: effects on nicotine withdrawal and interactions with fluoxetine. *Journal of Pharmacology and Experimental Therapeutics.* 294(2), 688–700.

Rasmussen, K., Czachura, J. F., 1997. Nicotine withdrawal leads to increased sensitivity of serotonergic neurons to the 5-HT$_{1A}$agonist8-OH-DPAT. *Psychopharmacology.* 133(4), 343–346.

Rasmussen, K., Kallman, M. J., Helton, D. R., 1997. Serotonin-1A antagonists attenuate the effects of nicotine withdrawal on the auditory startle response. *Synapse.* 27(2), 145–152.

Rauhut, A. S., Mullins, S. N., Dwoskin, L. P., Bardo, M. T., 2002. Reboxetine: attenuation of intravenous nicotine self-administration in rats. *Journal of Pharmacology and Experimental Therapeutics.* 303(2), 664–672.

Reid, M. S., Fox, L., Ho, L. B., Berger, S. P., 2000. Nicotine stimulation of extracellular glutamate levels in the nucleus accumbens: neuropharmacological characterization. *Synapse.* 35(2), 129–136.

Ribeiro, E. B., Bettiker, R. L., Bogdanov, M., Wurtman, R.J., 1993. Effects of systemic nicotine on serotonin release in rat brain. *Brain Research.* 621(2), 311–318.

Ridley, D. L., Balfour, D. J. K., 1997. The influence of nicotine on 5-HT overflow in the dorsal hippocampus of the rat. *British Journal of Pharmacology.* 112(Suppl), 301P.

Role, L. W., Berg, D. K., 1996. Nicotinic receptors in the development and modulation of CNS synapses. *Neuron.* 16(6), 1077–1085.

Rose, J. E., Behm, F. M., Westman, E. C., Mathew, R. J., London, E. D., Hawk, T. C., Turkington, T.G., Coleman, R.E., 2003b. PET studies of the influences of nicotine on neural systems in cigarette smokers. *American Journal of Psychiatry.* 160(2), 323–333.

Rossetti, Z. L., Hmaidan, Y., Gessa, G. L., 1992. Marked inhibition of mesolimbic DA release: a common feature of ethanol, morphine, cocaine, and amphetamine abstinence in rats. *European Journal of Pharmacology.* 221(2–3), 227–234.

Rukstalis, M., Jepson, C., Strasser, A., Lynch, K. G., Perkins, K., Patterson, F., Lerman, C., 2005. Naltrexone reduces the relative reinforcing value of nicotine in a cigarette smoking choice paradigm. *Psychopharmacology.* 180(1), 41–48.

Salas, R., Pieri, F., De Biasi, M., 2004. Decreased signs of nicotine withdrawal in mice null for the β4 nicotinic acetylcholine receptor subunit. *Journal of Neuroscience.* 24(45), 10035–10039.

Schiffer, W. K., Gerasimov, M. R., Marsteller, D. A., Geiger, J., Barnett, C., Alexoff, D. L., Dewey, S. L., 2001. Topiramate selectively attenuates nicotine -induced increases in monoamine release. *Synapse.* 42(3), 196–198.

Schilström, B., Nomikos, G. G., Nisell, M., Hertel, P., Svensson, T. H., 1998a. *N*-methyl-d-aspartate receptor antagonism in the ventral tegmental area diminishes the systemic nicotine -induced DA release in the nucleus accumbens. *Neuroscience.* 82(3), 781–789.

Schilström, B., Svensson, H. M., Svensson, T. H., Nomikos, G. G., 1998b. Nicotine and food induced DA release in the nucleus accumbens of the rat: putative role of α7 nicotinic receptors in the ventral tegmental area. *Neuroscience.* 85(4), 1005–1009.

Schneider, N. G., Olmstead, R. E., Steinberg, C., Sloan, K., Daims, R. M., Brown, H. V., 1996. Efficacy of buspirone in smoking cessation: a placebo-controlled trial. *Clinical Pharmacology and Therapeutics.* 60(5), 568–575.

Schulman, H., Hanson, P. I., 1993. Multifunctional Ca^{2+}/calmodulin-dependent protein kinase. *Neurochemistry Research.* 18(1), 65–77.

Schulteis, G., Markou, A., Cole, M., Koob, G.F., 1995. Decreased brain reward produced by ethanol withdrawal. *Proceedings of the National Academy of Sciences of the United States of America.* 92(13), 5880–5884.

Schulz, T. G., Ruhnau, P., Hallier, E., 2001. Lack of correlation between CYP2A6 genotype and smoking habits. *Advances in Experimental Medicine and Biology.* 500, 213–215.

Semenova, S., Bespalov, A., Markou, A., 2003. Decreased prepulse inhibition during nicotine withdrawal in DBA/2J mice is reversed by nicotine self-administration. *European Journal of Pharmacology.* 472(1–2), 99–110.

Semenova, S., Markou, A., 2003. Clozapine treatment attenuated somatic and affective signs of nicotine and amphetamine withdrawal in subsets of rats exhibited hyposensitivity to the initial effects of clozapine. *Biological Psychiatry.* 54(11), 1249–1264.

Sershen, H., Balla, A., Lajtha, A., Vizi, E. S., 1997. Characterization of nicotinic receptors involved in the release of nor-adrenaline from the hippocampus. *Neuroscience.* 77(1), 121–130.

Sharples, C. G. V., Kaiser, S., Soliakov, L., Marks, M. J., Collins, A. C., Washburn, M., Wright, E., Spencer, J. A., Gallagher, T., Whiteaker, P., et al., 2000. UB-165: a novel nicotinic agonist with subtype selectivity implicates the α4β2 subtype in the modulation of DA release from rat striatal synaptosomes. *Journal of Neuroscience.* 20(8), 2783–2791.

Sheffield, E. B., Quick, M. W., Lester, R. A. J., 2000. Nicotinic acetylcholine receptor subunit mRNA expression and channel function in medial habenula neurons. *Neuropharmacology.* 39(13), 2591–2603.

Shiffman, S., West, R. J., Gilbert, D. G., 2004b. SRNT Work Group. Recommendation for the assessment of tobacco craving and withdrawal in smoking cessation trials. *Nicotine & Tobacco Research.* 6(4), 599–614.

Shoaib, M., Benwell, M. E. M., Akbar, M. T., Stolerman, I. P., Balfour, D. J. K., 1994. Behavioural and neurochemical adaptations to nicotine in rats: influence of NMDA antagonists. *British Journal of Pharmacology.* 111(4), 1073–1080.

Shoaib, M., Sidhpura, N., Shafait, S., 2003. Investigating the actions of Bupropion on dependence-related effects of nicotine in rats. *Psychopharmacology.* 165(4), 405–412.

Shoaib, M., Stolerman, I. P., 1992. MK801 attenuates behavioral adaptation to chronic nicotine administration in rats. *British Journal of Pharmacology.* 105(3), 514–515.

Shoaib, M., Swanner, L. S., Beyer, C. E., Goldberg, S. R., Schindler, C. W., 1998. The GABAB agonist Baclofen modifies cocaine self-administration in rats. *Behavioural Pharmacology.* 9(3), 195–206.

Singer, S., Rossi, S., Verzosa, S., Hashim, A., Lonow, R., Cooper, T., Sershen, H., Lajtha, A., 2004. Nicotine-induced changes in neurotransmitter levels in brain areas associated with cognitive function. *Neurochemical Research.* 29(9), 1779–1792.

Snyder, S. H., 1976. DA and schizophrenia. *Psychiatric Annals.* 6(1), 53–65.

Spielewoy, C., Markou, A., 2003. Withdrawal from chronic phencyclidine treatment induces long-lasting depression in brain reward function. *Neuropsychopharmacology.* 28(6), 1106–1116.

Stapleton, J. M., Gilson, S. F., Wong, D. F., Villemagne, V. L., Dannals, R. F., Grayson, R. F., Henningield, J. E., London, E. D., 2003. Intravenous nicotine reduces cerebral glucose metabolism: a preliminary study. *Neuropsychopharmacology.* 28(4), 765–772.

Stewart, J., de Wit, H., Eikelboom, R., 1984. Role of unconditioned and conditioned drug effects in the self-administration of opiates and stimulants. *Psychological Review.* 91(2), 251–268.

Sugita, S., Johnson, S. W., North, R. A., 1992. Synaptic inputs to $GABA_A$ and $GABA_B$ receptors originate from discrete afferent neurons. *Neuroscience Letters.* 134(2), 207–211.

Summers, K. L., Giacobini, E., 1995. Effects of local and repeated systemic administration of (–)nicotine on extracellular levels of acetylcholine, norepinephrine, DA, and serotonin in rat cortex. *Neurochemical Research.* 20(6), 753–759.

Takada, K., Swedberg, M. D., Goldberg, S. R., Katz, J. L., 1989. Discriminative stimulus effects of intravenous *l*-nicotine and nicotine analogs or metabolites in squirrel monkeys. *Psychopharmacology.* 99(2), 208–212.

Tapper, A. R., McKinney, S. L., Nashmi, R., Schwarz, J., Deshpande, P., Labarca, C., Whiteaker, P., Marks, M. J., Collins, A. C., Lester, H. A., 2004. Nicotine activation of α4* receptors: sufficient for reward, tolerance, and sensitization. *Science.* 306(5698), 1029–1032.

Teng, L., Crooks, P. A., Buxton, S. T., Dwoskin, L. P., 1997. Nicotinic-receptor mediation of S(-)nornicotine -evoked [^{3}H] overflow from rat striatal slices preloaded with [^{3}H]do-pamine. *Journal of Pharmacology and Experimental Therapeutics.* 283(2), 778–787.

Toide, K., Arima, T., 1989. Effects of cholinergic drugs on extracellular levels of acetylcholine and choline in rat cortex, hippocampus and striatum studied by brain dialysis. *European Journal of Pharmacology.* 173(2–3), 133–141.

Toth, E., Sershen, H., Hashim, A., Vizi, E. S., Lajtha, A., 1992. Effect of nicotine on extracellular levels of neurotrans-mitters assessed by microdialysis in various brain regions: role of glutamic acid. *Neurochemical Research.* 17(3), 265–271.

Vidal, C., 1996. Nicotinic receptors in the brain: molecular biology, function, and therapeutics. *Molecular and Chemical Neuropathology.* 28(1–3), 3–11.

Volkow, N. D., Fowler, J. S., Ding, Y. S., Wang, G. J., Gatley, S. J., 1999. Imaging the neurochemistry of nicotine actions: studies with positron emission tomography. *Nicotine & Tobacco Research.* 1(Suppl 2), S127–S132.

Waal-Manning, H. J., de Hamel, F. A., 1978. Smoking habit and psy-chometric scores: a community study. *New Zealand Medical Journal.* 88(619), 188–191.

Walaas, I., Fonnum, F., 1980. Biochemical evidence for γ-aminobutyrate containing fibres from the nucleus accumbens to the substantia nigra and ventral tegmental area in the rat. *Neuroscience.* 5(1), 63–72.

Walaas, I., Fonnum, F., 1979. The distribution and origin of glutamate decarboxylase and choline acetyltransferase in ventral pallidum and other basal forebrain regions. *Brain Research.* 177(2), 325–336.

Wang, F., Chen, H., Steketee, J. D., Sharp, B. M., 2007. Upregulation of ionotropic glutamate receptor subunits within specific mesocorticolimbic regions during chronic nicotine self-administration. *Psychopharmacology.* 32(1), 103–109.

Watkins, S. S., Epping-Jordan, M. P., Koob, G. F., Markou, A., 1999. Blockade of nicotine self-administration with nicotinic antagonists in rats. *Pharmacology, Biochemistry, and Behavior.* 62(4), 743–751.

Watkins, S. S., Stinus, L., Koob, G. F., Markou, A., 2000. Reward and somatic changes during precipitated nicotine withdrawal in rats: centrally and peripherally mediated effects. *Journal of Pharmacology and Experimental Therapeutics.* 292(3), 1053–1064.

West, R., Hajek, P., McNeill, A., 1991. Effect of buspirone on cigarette withdrawal symptoms and short-term abstinence rates in a smokers clinic. *Psychopharmacology.* 104(1), 91–96.

West, R. J., Jarvis, M. J., Russell, M. A. H., Carruthers, M. E., Feyera-bend, C., 1984. Effect of nicotine replacement on the cigarette withdrawal syndrome. *British Journal of Addiction.* 79(2), 215–219.

Wilkie, G. I., Hutson, P., Sullivan, J. P., Wonnacott, S., 1996. Pharmacological characterization of a nicotinic autoreceptor in rat hippocampal synaptosomes. *Neurochemical Research.* 21(9),1141–8.

Williams, M., Robinson, J. L., 1984. Binding of the nicotinic cholinergic antagonist, dihydro-β-erythroidine, to rat brain tissue. *Journal of Neuroscience;* 4(12), 2906–2911.

Wonnacott, S., Sidhpura, N., Balfour, D. J. K., 2005. Nicotine: from molecular mechanisms to behaviour. *Current Opinion in Pharmacology.* 5(1), 53–59.

Wonnacott, S., 1997. Presynaptic nicotinic ACh receptors. *Trends in Neurosciences.* 20(2), 92–98.

Yim, C. Y., Mogenso, G. J., 1980. Electrophysiological studies of neurons in the ventral tegmental area of Tsai. *Brain Research.* 181(2), 301–313.

Chapter 2

Nicotinism in Chronic Diseases and Its Clinical Management (Emerging Concepts and Mechanisms)

Abstract

It is now well-established that multidrug resistant (MDR) and chronic pain-associated diseases including malignancies, rheumatoid arthritis, gout, trigeminal neuralgia, fibromyalgia, and numerous others are directly or indirectly linked to nicotinism. This chapter describes the prevalence of nicotine abuse in these diseases involving chronic pain and agony. These clinical conditions are also linked to genetic predisposition of an individual. Although genes can act as loaded guns, life-style (cigarette smoking and alcohol abuse) and environment may serve as a trigger to aggravate chronic obstructive pulmonary diseases (COPD) such as asthma, emphysema, and bronchitis among tobacco smokers. Indeed! COPDs are abrogated by cigarette smoking. A patient suffering from chronic pain becomes victim to smoking tobacco, which may deteriorate the clinical prognosis in tobacco smoking patients. The brain response to cigarette-related cues and tobacco cessation efforts become challenging in chronic pain because of complex mental health issues (such as persistent depression) in these patients. A significant association of life adversity with smoking relapse after a quit attempt has been observed in specific group of patients. In addition, maternal smoking during pregnancy has deleterious consequences on the offspring's initial response to cigarettes and alcohol abuse, as noticed in lung screen uptake trials (LSUT). The incidence of tobacco abuse among veterans admitted for the treatment of COPD and mental disorders was quite high. Furthermore, the prevalence of cannabis abuse with or without cigarette smoking was directly associated with increased body mass index among adolescents. Social anxiety motivated cigarette and marijuana abuse among adolescents, whereas the cannabis abuse was associated with increased risk of psychiatric disorders. Cocaine craving was accompanied with cognitive decline and chronic nicotine abuse induced a reinforcing effect in nonhuman primates. The pro-inflammatory cytokines (IL-6 and IL-10) were significantly elevated in the cord blood samples of intrauterine crack/cocaine-exposed newborn infants. The clinical significance of these findings is yet to be established. Smoking was a major risk factor in patients with chronic low back pain. Recently, various genetic models of nicotinism and alcoholism have been proposed for screening medications to treat addiction. Cigarette smoking and organizational justice was linked to psychological distress. Experimental evidence suggests that nicotine is addictive not only to humans, its self-administration was also observed in squirrel monkeys, as they developed physical tolerance and psychological dependence. In addition, smoking is a serious health hazard among prison inmates. Serious smoking related cardiovascular health issues have been noticed among female inmates, which require further investigations. Certain similarities and differences in smoking history among African American and Whites have been noticed. Several protective strategies have been implemented for the safe and effective clinical management of nicotinism and associated illnesses. For example, protective effects of elafin have been reported in asthma patients. Validity of the PROMIS smoking assessment toolkit has been authenticated. It has been demonstrated that Varenicline as smoking cessation drug impairs extinction and enhances reinstatement across repeated cycles of nicotine self-administration in rats. Furthermore, oral health education and nicotine replacement therapy have been proposed for the clinical management of nicotinism, as described briefly in this chapter.

Keywords: chronic multidrug resistant malignancies, rheumatoid arthritis, gout, chronic pain, trigeminal neuralgia, fibromyalgia, Chronic Obstructive Pulmonary Diseases (COPD), pro-inflammatory cytokines, cocaine, marijuana, nicotine, Lung Screen Uptake Trials (LSUT). PROMIS, Varenicline, smoking cessation

Introduction

More than 7000 chemical compounds have been identified in the tobacco plant leaves those are used for manufacturing cigarettes. In addition, the manufacturers also include some other chemicals to enhance the flavor and over all taste and fragrance of the cigarette smoke. Out of these 7000 chemical compounds some of them have been shown to have therapeutic potential, some of them have harmful effects, and some of them might be neither harmful nor beneficial to human health. At least, 70 chemical compounds have been identified as carcinogenic in the cigarette smoke which also contains charcoal, tar, carbon monoxide (CO), cyanide (-CN), cadmium, and arsenic. Chronic application of tar on the skin of experimental animals (nude mice) caused skin cancer, indicating that tar is also responsible for inducing cancer.

An increased prevalence of tobacco smoking has been noticed in patients suffering from chronic multidrug resistant (MDR) diseases associated with persistent pain. These diseases include: malignancies, rheumatoid arthritis, gout, trigeminal neuralgia, fibromyalgia, chronic back pain, and numerous other conditions those are directly or indirectly linked to nicotinism. These clinical conditions may also be linked to genetic predisposition of an individual, such as chronic obstructive pulmonary diseases (COPD) (asthma, emphysema, and bronchitis). These chronic conditions may be abrogated by cigarette smoking. Complex mental health issues (such as persistent depression) were reported in patients suffering from chronic pain. Tobacco smoking may compromise the clinical prognosis of these patients. An association of life adversity with smoking relapse after a quit attempt was noticed in some patients. Deleterious consequences were noticed on the offspring's initial response to cigarettes and alcohol abuse by maternal smoking during pregnancy as noticed in lung screen uptake trials (LSUT). In addition, the pro-inflammatory cytokines (IL-6 and IL-10) were significantly elevated in the cord blood samples of intrauterine crack/cocaine-exposed newborn infants. However, the clinical significance of these findings remains uncertain.

The incidence of tobacco abuse among veterans admitted for the treatment of COPD and mental disorders was quite high. The prevalence of cannabis abuse with or without cigarette smoking was directly associated with increased body mass index among adolescents. Furthermore, social anxiety motivated cigarette and marijuana abuse among adolescents, whereas the cannabis abuse was associated with increased risk of psychiatric disorders and cocaine craving induced cognitive decline. Chronic abuse of nicotine induced a reinforcing effect in nonhuman primates. Various genetic models of nicotinism and alcoholism have been proposed for screening medications to treat nicotine addiction. Psychological distress was linked to cigarette smoking and organizational justice system. Experimental studies demonstrated that nicotine is addictive not only to humans, its self-administration is also observed in squirrel monkeys. Serious health hazards have been noticed among prison inmates who were smoking. Smoking related cardiovascular health issues were noticed particularly among female inmates, which require further investigations. In addition, certain similarities and differences have been noticed in smoking habits among African American and Whites.

Recently, several protective strategies were implemented for the safe and effective clinical management of nicotinism and associated illnesses. This chapter describes the prevalence of nicotine abuse in chronic MDR diseases involving chronic pain and agony and their alleviation by therapeutic intervention. For example, protective effects of elafin were reported in asthma patients; validity of the PROMIS smoking assessment toolkit; and Varenicline as smoking cessation drug impaired extinction and enhanced reinstatement across repeated cycles of nicotine self-administration in rats. Furthermore, oral health education and nicotine replacement therapy have been proposed for the clinical management of nicotinism as described in this chapter.

Smoking and Chronic Pain

Previous studies have demonstrated a direct relationship between smoking and addiction to opioids in patients with chronic non-malignant pain. This could be explained by a susceptibility in some patients to develop addiction. Another explanation could be that nicotine influences both pain and the opioid system. Therefore, Plesner et al., (2016) investigated whether smoking, former smoking ± nicotine use and nicotine dependence in patients with chronic non-malignant pain were associated with opioid use and addiction to opioids. All (98) patients aged 18 or more were invited to participate in this study. The prevalence of current smokers was twice as high as in the general population. The prevalence of patients using opioids was 54% and the prevalence of addiction to opioids was 6%. No significant differences in addiction were observed between the different smoking groups, but smokers and former smokers using nicotine tended to use opioids more frequently and at higher doses than never smokers and former smokers not using nicotine, supporting the evidence that smoking is associated with chronic pain and that use of nicotine substitution in chronic non-malignant patients are relevant both in a clinical setting, but also in future studies of the association between smoking habits, pain, and opioid use.

Tobacco Cessation and Mental Health

It has been noticed that persons with mental health, abuse tobacco at alarming rates, yet misperceptions remain about the effect of quitting on mental health outcomes. Krebs et al., (2016) recently examined the relationship between tobacco cessation and changes in severity of mental illness. Participants were $N = 577$ veterans with a history of mental health treatment in a tobacco cessation study. The effects of abstinence and time on Behavior and Symptom Identification Scale-24 scores and subscales were examined. Abstinence at both 2 and 6 months post-baseline was related to lower Behavior and Symptom Identification Scale-24 scores and improvement on three Behavior and Symptom Identification Scale-24 subscales, indicating that tobacco treatment may be recommended to all mental health patients to improve their physical and mental health status.

Brain Responses to Cigarette-Related Cues

Decreased sensitivity to pleasant stimuli has been associated with a higher vulnerability to nicotine dependence in youths and with difficulty quitting in adult smokers. Recently, Engelmann et al., (2016) demonstrated that smokers exhibiting lower brain reactivity to non-cigarette-related pleasant images than to cigarette-related ones have lower chances of achieving long-term abstinence during a quit attempt. They tested whether individual differences in brain responses to cigarette-related and pleasant stimuli require a long history of smoking to develop by measuring the late positive potential (LPP) to cigarette cues, emotional, and neutral stimuli in 45 young, light smokers (ages

18-25). These investigators utilized k-means cluster analysis to categorize smokers into two groups based on the magnitude of their LPPs. Group 1 was characterized by larger LPPs to pleasant pictures than cigarette-related pictures whereas Group 2 exhibited the opposite pattern, indicating that individual differences in brain responses to cigarette-related and pleasant cues do not require a long smoking history to develop.

Association of Life Adversity with Smoking Relapse after a Quit Attempt

Multiple cross-sectional studies have linked adverse childhood events and adult adversities to current smoking, lifetime smoking, and former smoking. Lemieux et al., (2016) recently studied 123 participants, 86 of whom were habitual smokers, from pre-quit ad libitum smoking to four weeks post-quit. Thirty-seven non-smokers were also tested as a comparison group. Subjects provided biological samples for confirmation of abstinence status and self-report history of adversities such as abuse, neglect, family dysfunction, incarceration, and child-parent separation. They also completed mood and smoking withdrawal symptom measures. Within non-smokers and smokers who relapsed within the first month of a quit attempt, but not abstainers, females had higher adversity scores than males. Cigarette craving, which was independent from depressive affect, increased for low adversity participants, but not those with no adversity nor high adversity, indicating that sex and relapse status interact to predict adversity and that craving for nicotine may be an additional mediator of relapse, providing further evidence of an adversity and smoking relationship. These investigators recommended further studies to clarify how adversity complicates smoking cessation and impacts smoking behavior.

Effects of Maternal Smoking during Pregnancy on Offspring's Initial Responses to Cigarettes and Alcohol

When examining the effects of prenatal exposure to maternal smoking during pregnancy (MSDP) on later offspring substance use, it is highly prudent to consider familial environments confounded with MSDP. In this context, Bidwell et al., (2016) examined the effect of MSDP on offspring's initial reactions to cigarettes and alcohol, which are indicators of future substance-abuse related problems. They tested these effects using two propensity score approaches (1) by controlling for confounding using the MSDP propensity score and (2) examining effects of MSDP across the MSDP risk distribution by grouping individuals into quantiles based on their MSDP propensity score. This study used data from 829 unrelated mothers with a lifetime history of smoking to determine the propensity for smoking only during their first trimester (MSDP-E) or throughout their entire pregnancy (MSDP-T). Propensity score analyses focused on the offspring (N = 1616 female twins) of a large subset of these mothers. They examined the effects of levels of MSDP-E/T on offspring initial reactions to their first experiences with alcohol and cigarettes, across the distribution of liability for MSDP-E/T. MSDP-E/T proved to be a significant predictors of offspring reactions to alcohol and cigarettes, but the effects were confounded by the familial liability for MSDP. The MSDP effects that emerged were heterogeneous across the MSDP familial risk distribution, suggesting the importance of properly accounting for correlated familial risk factors when examining the effects of MSDP on substance abuse-related outcomes.

Lung Screen Uptake Trial (LSUT)

It was recognized that participation in low-dose CT (LDCT) lung cancer screening offered in the trial context has been poor, especially among smokers from socio-economically deprived communities; a group for whom the risk-benefit ratio is improved due to their high risk of lung cancer. Hence, attracting high risk participants is essential to the success and equity of any future screening program. In a study, Quaife et al (2016) investigated whether low and biased uptake of screening can be improved by employing a targeted invitation strategy. A randomized controlled trial was used to test the hypothesis whether targeted invitation are effective at improving engagement with an offer of lung cancer screening for high risk candidates. Two thousand patients aged 60-75 years and recorded as a smoker within the last 5 years, were identified from primary care records and received either intervention invitation (which take a targeted, stepped and low burden approach to information provision prior to the appointment) or control invitation. The primary outcome was uptake of a nurse-led 'lung health check' hospital appointment, during which patients were offered a spirometry test, an exhaled carbon monoxide (CO) reading, and an LDCT. Initial data on demographics (i.e., age, sex, ethnicity, deprivation score) and smoking status were collected in primary care and analyzed to explore differences between attenders and non-attenders with respect to invitation group. Those who attended the lung health check had further data on smoking collected during their appointment (including pack-year history, nicotine dependence and confidence to quit). Secondary outcomes included willingness to be screened, uptake of LDCT and measures of informed decision-making to ensure the latter is not compromised by either invitation strategy. If effective at improving informed uptake of screening and reducing bias in participation, this invitation strategy could be adopted by local screening pilots or a national program.

Tobacco Use among Veterans Admitted for COPD

Usually, smokers admitted for COPD are not given smoking cessation medications at discharge. The reasons behind this remains uncertain, and may reflect an interplay of patient characteristics, health disparities, and the receipt of inpatient tobacco control processes. Recently, Melzer et al., (2016) assessed disparities in treatment for tobacco abuse following discharge of COPD and examined the inpatient tobacco control processes. Smokers aged ≥ 40 years, admitted for treatment of a COPD exacerbation within the VA Veterans Integrated Service Network 20, identified using ICD-9 discharge codes and admission diagnoses from 2005-2012. The outcome was any tobacco cessation medication dispensed within 48 hrs. of discharge. These investigators assessed potential predictors up to 1 year prior to admission and created the final logistic regression model using manual model building, clustered by site in 1511 subjects. A total of 16.9% were dispensed a medication at discharge. In the adjusted model, several predictors were associated with decreased odds of receiving medications: older age, higher comorbidity score, and history of psychosis, hypertension, and treatment with steroids in the past year. Inpatient tobacco control processes were associated with increased odds of receiving medications: brief counseling at discharge and receipt of smoking cessation medications. Few patients were treated with tobacco cessation medications at discharge. These investigators found evidence for disparities in treatment, but also beneficial effects of inpatient tobacco control measures and recommended on using novel processes of care to improve medications and minimize disparities.

Protective Effects of Elafin against Asthma

It is known that elafin inhibits serine proteases, such as human neutrophil elastase and proteinase 3, to prevent excessive damage during inflammation. However, the relationship between elafin and asthma remains uncertain. Therefore, Tsai et al., (2016) used gene expression microarray technology to evaluate smoking- and asthma-related biomarkers in a discovery-driven protocol. They identified candidate genes, e.g., proteinase inhibitor 3 (PI3), related to asthma and smoking and evaluated their potential as biomarkers for asthma. They used human genome microarray data sets from smoking- and asthma-related gene expression data sets and performed real-time QPCR to validate and estimate differences in gene expression. They also recruited adult patients with asthma and age- and sex-matched control patients who were administered a questionnaire and evaluated for lung function and plasma elafin levels, which were encoded by the PI3 gene. Six altered candidate genes, PI3, protein kinase C, phosphoserine phosphatase, IQ motif-containing GTPase activating protein 1, interleukin 13 receptor α 1, and signal transducing adaptor molecule SH3 domain and ITAM motif 2, were identified across the four asthma- and four smoking-related data sets. An *in vitro* study of human airway epithelial cells (A549) and a human monocytic cell line (THP-1) demonstrated that PI3 messenger RNA levels are altered by nicotine. Elafin concentration was higher in controls than in patients with asthma. The plasma elafin concentration in the highest quartile (≥ 12.69 ng/mL) was inversely associated with asthma compared with the lowest quartile (<5.82 ng/mL) after adjusting for age, sex, smoking status, waist-to-hip ratio, percentage predicted forced expiratory volume in 1 second, cockroaches in the home, incense burning, and family history. This study demonstrated that high elafin levels identified in smoking- and asthma-related microarray data sets and an epidemiologic study reduced the risk of asthma.

Prevalence and Severity of Mental Disorders in Military Personnel

Provision and need for mental health services among military personnel are a major concern across nations. Two recent comparisons suggest higher rates of mental disorders in US and UK military personnel compared with civilians. However, these findings may not apply to other nations. Previous studies have been focused on the effects of military service rather than the individual effects of military service and deployment. Recently, Trautmann et al., (2016) compared German military personnel with and without a history of deployment to sociodemographically matched civilians regarding prevalence and severity of 12-month DSM-IV mental disorders. A total of 1439 deployed soldiers (DS), 779 never deployed soldiers (NS) and 1023 civilians were assessed with an adapted version of the Munich Composite International Diagnostic interview across the same timeframe. Data were weighted using propensity score ology to assure comparability of the three samples. Compared with adjusted civilians, the prevalence of any 12-month disorder was lower in NS and did not differ in DS. Significant differences between military personnel and civilians regarding prevalence and severity of individual diagnoses appeared only for alcohol and nicotine dependence with lower values in both military samples. Elevated rates of panic/agoraphobia and posttraumatic stress disorder were observed in DS with high combat exposure compared with civilians. Rates and severity of mental disorders in the German military were comparable with civilians for internalizing and lower for Substance Abuse Disorders (SUDs). A higher risk of some disorders was reduced to DS with high combat exposure. This finding had great significance for mental health service provision and suggested need for targeted interventions. Differences to previous US and UK studies suggested that higher prevalence in military personnel might result from divergent study, deployment characteristics, military structures, and occupational factors, which might yield valuable targets to improve military mental health.

Cannabis Use and Body Mass Index (BMI) among Adolescents

Research conducted on the association between cannabis abuse and BMI has revealed mixed findings. It is possible that individual differences in decision-making (DM) abilities may influence these associations. Ross et al., (2016) recently analyzed the influence of quantity of cannabis use, DM performance, and the interaction of these variables on BMI and clinical classifications of weight among adolescents (ages 14 to 18 years; 56% male; 77% Hispanic). The sample consisted primarily of cannabis abusers (n = 238) without a history of developmental disorders, birth complications, neurological conditions, or history of mood, thought, or attention deficit/hyperactivity disorder at screening. Few participants also engaged frequently in other drug abuse (except for alcohol and nicotine). More lifetime cannabis abuse was associated with a higher BMI and greater likelihood of being overweight/obese. Interactions between DM and cannabis abuse on BMI were insignificant, and it was not directly associated with BMI, suggesting that among adolescents, cannabis abuse was associated with a greater BMI regardless of DM abilities and this association was not accounted for by other factors including; depression, alcohol abuse, nicotine abuse, race, ethnicity, or IQ.

Social Anxiety in Cigarette and Marijuana Abuse Motives among Adolescents

Nicotine and Marijuana are two of the most widely used substances among adolescents in the US. Symptoms of social anxiety (SA) usually emerge during early adolescence, and elevated levels are associated with increased substance-related problems despite inconsistent links to frequency of use. Substance use motives, and coping motives, play an important role in understanding the increased risk for abuse among those with elevated SA. Importantly, work to date has been conducted with adult samples. In a study, Cloutier et al., (2016) examined whether similar patterns would emerge among adolescents. This research included 56 adolescents (ages 12-17 years; 41% girls) with a history of lifetime marijuana and cigarette smoking. Consistent with the adult literature, SA was not positively associated with frequency of abuse across either substance. Further, SA was positively associated with conformity abuse motives and unrelated to social or enhancement motives for both substances. However, SA was unrelated to coping abuse motives for either marijuana or cigarette smoking, emphasizing the need for future research to improve developmentally-sensitive models of SUDs behaviors and their etiology.

Cannabis Abuse and Risk of Psychiatric Disorders

With rising rates of marijuana abuse in the general population and an increasing number of states legalizing recreational marijuana abuse and authorizing medical marijuana programs, there are renewed clinical and policy concerns regarding the mental health effects of cannabis abuse. To examine associations between cannabis abuse and risk of mental health and SUDs in the general population, Blanco et al., (2016) utilized a nationally representative sample of US adults aged 18 years or older, which was interviewed 3 years apart in the National Epidemiologic Survey on Alcohol and Related Conditions (wave 1, 2001-2002; wave 2, 2004-2005). The primary analyses were limited to 34 653 respondents. They used multiple regression and propensity score to estimate the strength of independent associations between cannabis abuse at wave 1 and incident and prevalent psychiatric disorders at wave 2. Psychiatric disorders were measured with a structured interview (Alcohol Use Disorder and Associated Disabilities Interview Schedule-DSM-IV). In both analyses, the same set of wave 1 confounders was used, including sociodemographic characteristics, family history of SUDs, disturbed family environment, childhood parental loss, low self-esteem, social deviance, education, recent trauma, past and present psychiatric disorders, and respondent's history of divorce. In the regression analysis of 34 653 respondents (14 564 male [47.9% weighted]; mean [SD] age, 45.1 [17.3] years), cannabis abuse in wave 1 (2001-2002), which was reported by 1279 respondents, was associated with SUDs in wave 2 (2004-2005) (any SUD: any alcohol abuse disorder (AAD): any cannabis abuse disorder (CAD): any other drug abuse disorder (DAD): and nicotine dependence: but not any mood disorder or anxiety disorder. The same general pattern of was observed in the regression analyses of wave 2 prevalent psychiatric disorders and in the propensity score-matched analysis of incident and prevalent psychiatric disorders. Based on this study, these investigators concluded that cannabis abuse is associated with an increased risk for SUDs. Hence, physicians and policy planners should take these associations of CAD under serious consideration.

Cocaine Craving by Cognitive Strategies among Cocaine Abusers

Emphasis on the negative consequences of drug abuse is a critical component of cognitive behavioral therapy (CBT) skills to regulate craving. Despite the relative success of CBT for treating SUDs, effective human lab models of CBT are lacking. Recent reports indicated that the regulation of craving (ROC) task provides a valid model of craving regulation for nicotine, alcohol, and METH abuse. Strickland et al., (2016) recently examined ROC in an online sample of regular cocaine abusers (n = 44) recruited from Amazon.com's Mechanical Turk. In the ROC task, cognitive regulation strategies were manipulated by instructing participants to think about either the positive or negative consequences of consuming cocaine. Participants were subsequently presented with cocaine images while engaging in each cognitive regulation strategy and asked to report current craving that was compared to neutral look conditions. Food images served as a control. A cocaine purchase task was also completed to assess economic demand for cocaine and its relationship with cocaine craving. The use of negative appraisal strategies that model those used in CBT attenuated craving for cocaine. Cocaine craving was also stimulus-specific, with greater smoked cocaine craving reported by individuals with a history of smoked cocaine abuse. This online extension of the ROC task provided evidence as a model of CBT cocaine-craving regulation and suggested that this model may be used to examine the mechanisms underlying the effectiveness of CBT for cocaine abuse and the relationship between craving regulation and drug-abuse behavior.

Nicotine Self-Administration in Squirrel Monkeys

The primary psychoactive agent in tobacco, are not well-established in lab animals. Hence, Desai et al., (2016) examined the use of a fading procedure to establish robust and consistent i.v. nicotine self-administration under second-order schedule conditions in squirrel monkeys. These investigators first developed self-administration behavior in two groups of male squirrel monkeys using a second-order fixed-interval 5-min schedule with fixed-ratio 5 units (FI 5-min (FR5: S)). Comparable performances were maintained by i.v. cocaine (0.032 mg/kg/injection (inj); group A, n = 3) and the combination of food delivery (20-30 % condensed milk) and 0.01 mg/kg/inj i.v. nicotine (group B, n = 3). Subsequently, the concentration of condensed milk was gradually reduced to zero in the second group and self-administration behavior was maintained by i.v. nicotine alone. Self-administration of i.v. nicotine (0.001-0.032 mg/kg/inj) and, in additional experiments, the minor tobacco alkaloid anatabine (0.01-0.18 mg/kg/inj) was studied in both groups. Nicotine and anatabine had reinforcing effects in both groups. However, optimal doses of nicotine and anatabine maintained higher rates of i.v. self-administration behavior in subjects trained with the fading procedure than in subjects provided with a history of cocaine-maintained responding. These findings illustrated conditions under which i.v. nicotine self-administration can be established in squirrel monkeys and the influence of prior experimental history in the expression of reinforcing effects of nicotine and anatabine.

Reinforcing Effect of Nicotine in Nonhuman Primates

Despite the high prevalence of nicotine abuse in humans, robust nicotine self-administration has been difficult to demonstrate in lab animals. Hence, Kohut and

Bergman (2016) conducted analysis of nicotine self-administration to study its reinforcing effects in nonhuman primates. Adult rhesus macaques (N = 6) self-administered nicotine (0.001-0.1 mg/kg; i.v) under a fixed-ratio (FR) 1 schedule of reinforcement during daily 90-min sessions. The demand function relating drug intake and response cost was determined by increasing the FR across sessions during the availability of each of several doses of nicotine (0.0032-0.032 mg/kg/inj). The reinforcing effects of 0.01 mg/kg/inj cocaine and 1 g banana-flavored food pellets were also determined. Finally, the nicotine demand function was re-determined after ~8 months of daily i.v. nicotine self-administration. I.v. nicotine self-administration followed an inverted U-shaped pattern, with the peak number of injections maintained by 0.0032 mg/kg/inj. Self-administration of each reinforcer (food pellets, IV cocaine, and IV nicotine) decreased as FR size increased. The exponential model showed that demand elasticity for nicotine was (1) dose-dependent and lowest for 0.0032 mg/kg/inj; (2) for 0.0032 mg/kg/inj, similar to that of food pellets and higher than cocaine; and (3) decreased after 8 months of daily nicotine self-administration, indicating that, though high levels of nicotine self-administration can be achieved under simple FR schedules in nonhuman primates, its reinforcing effectiveness was dose-related but limited and could increase as a function of time.

Cytokines (IL-6 and IL-10) Levels in the Cord Blood of Intrauterine Crack/Cocaine-Exposed Newborns

It is known that prenatal cocaine exposure (PCE) is associated with neurobehavioral problems during childhood and adolescence. Early activation of the inflammatory response may contribute to such changes. Therefore, Mardini et al., (2016) compared inflammatory markers (IL-6 and IL-10) both in umbilical cord blood and in maternal peripheral blood at delivery between newborns with history of crack/cocaine exposure in utero and non-exposed newborns. In this study, 57 newborns with a history of crack/cocaine exposure in utero (EN) and 99 non-exposed newborns (NEN) were compared for IL-6 and IL-10 levels. Sociodemographic and perinatal data, maternal psychopathology, consumption of nicotine and other substances were collected in cases and controls. After adjusting for potential confounders, mean IL-6 was higher in EN than in NEN Mean IL-10 was also higher in EN than in NEN. Adjusted postpartum measures of IL-6 were higher in mothers with a history of crack/cocaine abuse, with no differences for IL-10. There was no correlation between maternal and neonatal cytokine levels, suggesting that IL-6 and IL-10 could be utilized as early biomarkers of PCE in newborns to elucidate neurobiological pathways underlying neurodevelopmental changes for early intervention.

Risk Factors in Patients with Low Back Pain

Low back pain is one of the most common reasons for physician visits in the US and is a major complaint seen by orthopedic surgeons. Patients with chronic low back pain experience recurring debilitating pain and disability, decreasing their quality of life. In a recent study, Shemory et al., (2016) employed a commercially available software, Explorys (Explorys, Inc, Cleveland, Ohio), to mine electronic health care database consisting of the medical records of >26 million patients. According to the available medical history data, 1.2 million patients had a diagnosis of low back pain (4.54%). This information was used to determine the incidence of low back pain in patients with a history of nicotine dependence, obesity (body mass index, >30 kg/m^2), depressive disorders, and alcohol abuse. Relative risk was then calculated for the modifiable risk factors. Patients with nicotine dependence, obesity, depressive disorders, and alcohol abuse had a relative risk of 4.489, 6.007, 5.511, and 3.326 for low back pain, respectively, compared with patients without the defined risk factor. A significant difference was observed in the incidence of low back pain between all 4 groups with the risk factors evaluated and the general population. By determining treatable patient risk factors for low back pain, physicians can monitor at-risk patients and focus on prevention and control of debilitating disease, suggesting that these approaches can decrease the number of patients with low back pain.

Genetic Model of Alcoholism for Screening Medications to Treat Addiction

Recently, Bell et al., (2016) wrote a review to up-to-date pharmacological, genetic, and behavioral findings from the alcohol-preferring P rat and summarize similar previous work. The primary focus was on how the P rat meets criteria for a valid animal model of alcoholism with its use as an animal model of polysubstance abuse, including alcohol, nicotine, and psychostimulants. Pharmacologically and genetically, the focus was on the neurotransmitter and neuropeptide systems that have received the most attention including: cholinergic, DArgic, GABAergic, glutamatergic, serotonergic, noradrenergic, corticotrophin releasing hormone, opioid, and neuropeptide Y. These researchers studied the P rats behavioral and neurochemical phenotypes, and its genotype, in the context of the clinical literature and also discussed future directions for expanding the use of genetic model of alcoholism to identify molecular targets for treating drug addiction in general.

Cigarette Smoking and Organizational Justice System with Psychological Distress

Recently, Inue et al., (2016) examined the modifying effect of cigarette smoking (i.e., smokers vs. non-smokers) on the association of organizational justice system (i.e., procedural justice and interactional justice) with serious psychological distress (SPD) in Japanese employees. As many as 2838 participants from two factories completed a self-administered questionnaire comprising the scales on organizational justice (Organizational Justice Questionnaire), smoking status, psychological distress (K6 scale), demographic and occupational characteristics (i.e., gender, age, education, family size, history of depression, chronic physical conditions, occupation, and work form), and other health-related behaviors (i.e., drinking habit and physical activity). After adjusting for demographic and occupational characteristics as well as other health-related behaviors, low procedural justice and low interactional justice were associated with SPD (defined as K6 ≥ 13). Furthermore, marginally significant interaction effect of procedural justice with smoking status was observed. Specifically, the association of low procedural justice with SPD was greater among smokers for low vs. high procedural justice subgroup than among non-smokers. On the other hand, interaction effect of interactional justice with smoking status was not significant. Cigarette smoking had a harmful effect on the association of the lack of procedural justice with SPD in Japanese employees.

Cardiovascular Health Promotion among Female Inmates

Female inmates in the US tend to be overweight, physically inactive, experience high stress, and have a history of nicotine and other drug dependence. Thus, they bear an increased risk of cardiovascular (CV) disease than the general population. However, few evidence-based health interventions exist for this particular population. Nair et al., (2016) recently conducted a study to test proof of concept, feasibility, and potential efficacy of a multiple health behavior change intervention that integrated CV-health promotion education delivered during a physical activity (PA) program (indoor cycling). They used a 2-group design with two measurement time-points: baseline and 8-week end of treatment. N = 120 incarcerated women (18-59 years of age) who were medically cleared for participation in PA were enrolled. Indoor cycling instructors were trained to deliver five health education topics over an 8-week period during twice-weekly cycling classes. Topics matched the American Heart Association recommendations for CV health: (a) nutrition, (b) PA promotion, (c) weight management, (d) stress management, and (e) smoking cessation and relapse prevention. Modes of intervention included instructor advice, written and audio/video clips reviewed during class. CV-related and mental health measures were assessed at both time-points. These investigators suggested that future research in this area has potential to impact the health of female inmates, a high-risk population. Moreover, multiple health behavior change intervention represented a community approach to health promotion that could generalize to other underserved populations who may benefit from similar interventions.

Smoking History among African American and Whites in the US

Characterizing smoking history patterns summarizes life course exposure for birth cohorts, essential for evaluating the impact of tobacco control on health. Limited attention has been given to patterns among African Americans. Therefore, Holford et al., 2016 estimated life course smoking histories of African Americans and whites beginning with the 1890 birth cohort. Estimates of smoking initiation and cessation probabilities, and intensity could be used as a baseline for studying smoking intervention strategies that target smoking exposure. US National Health Interview Surveys conducted from 1965 to 2012 yielded information on current smoking behavior among African Americans and whites. Additional detail for smokers including age at initiation, age at cessation and smoking intensity were available in some surveys and these were used to construct smoking histories for participants up to the date that they were interviewed. Age-period-cohort models with constrained natural splines provided estimates of current, former and never-smoker prevalence in cohorts beginning in 1890. This approach yielded yearly estimates of initiation, cessation and smoking intensity by age for each birth cohort. Smoking initiation probabilities were lower among African Americans compared to whites, and cessation probabilities also were generally lower. Higher initiation led to higher smoking prevalence among whites in younger ages, but lower cessation led to higher prevalence at older ages in blacks, when adverse health effects of smoking became most apparent. These estimates provided could be used to better understand the effects of changes in smoking behavior. A novel approach of estimating smoking histories was applied to data from the National Health Interview Surveys, which provided the smoking history in this population following publication of the Surgeon General's Report in 1964, suggesting that the existing disparities in smoking-related disease may be due to the lower cessation rates in African Americans compared to whites. However, the number of cigarettes smoked was also lower among African Americans. Based on these findings, these investigators recommended further work to determine mechanisms by which smoking duration and intensity could account for racial disparities in smoking-related diseases.

Clinical Management of Nicotinism

Oral Health Education versus Nicotine Replacement Therapy for Tobacco Cessation

India has millions of tobacco abusers. It is the leading cause of deaths due to oral cancer and hence needs effective strategies to curb it. Recently, Raja et al., (2016) evaluated and compared the effectiveness of Oral Health Education (OHE) and nicotine replacement therapy (NRT) in tobacco cessation. The clinical trial consisted of factory workers (n = 40) providing history of tobacco consumption (smoking/smokeless) within past 30 days. They were divided into OHE (n = 20) and NRT (n = 20) groups. Baseline evaluation (demographic, smoking/ smokeless behavior) was done. Fagerström test was used for nicotine dependence (FTND) and to assess the level of nicotine addiction. Follow up was done at an interval of 1week, 2 weeks, 1 month, 2 months and 3 months to assess the reduction in the FTND score. "Nano-CheckTM Rapid Nicotine test" was used for the qualitative detection of cotinine in human urine. In both OHE and NRT group there was a significant reduction in mean Fagerström score at every follow up but when both the groups were compared, mean Fagerström score reduction was more in NRT than OHE at all time interval though it was not significant. Based on this study, these investigators concluded that NRT is better than OHE when both the groups were compared. However, any intervention given to tobacco abusers (either NRT or OHE) was helpful for the patients interested in quitting tobacco.

Treatment of Tobacco Use and Dependence

It is now well-recognized that smoking cessation is crucial for reducing cancer risk and premature mortality. The US Preventive Services Task Force (USPSTF) has recommended annual lung cancer screening with low-dose computed tomography (LDCT), and the Center for Medicare and Medicaid Services recently approved lung screening as a benefit for patient's ages 55 to 77 years who have a 30 pack-year history. The Society for Research on nicotine and Tobacco (SRNT) and the Association for the Treatment of Tobacco Use and Dependence (ATTUD) developed the guideline based on literature review to present the evidence for smoking-cessation health benefits in this high-risk group and to provide recommendations for integrating evidence-based smoking-cessation treatment with lung cancer screening. Unfortunately, data on lung cancer screening participants were scarce at the time this guideline was written. Fucito et a (2016) recently summarized the evidence on the benefits of smoking cessation and the efficacy of smoking-cessation interventions for smokers ages 55 to 77 years to provide smoking-cessation interventions for smokers who seek lung cancer screening. It was concluded that smokers who present for lung cancer screening should be encouraged to quit smoking at each visit. Access to evidence-based smoking-cessation interventions should be provided to all smokers regardless of scan, and motivation to quit should not be a necessary precondition for treatment. Follow-up contacts to support smoking-cessation efforts should be arranged for smokers. In addition, evidence-based behavioral strategies should be used to motivate smokers who are unwilling to try quitting/reducing smoking or to try evidence-based treatments that may lead to eventual cessation.

Validity of the PROMIS Smoking Assessment Toolkit

The Patient Reported Outcomes Measurement Information System (PROMIS®) Smoking Initiative developed six item banks for assessing smoking behaviors and biopsychosocial correlates of smoking among daily and nondaily adult cigarette smokers. Recently, Edelen et al., (2016) presented new validity evidence for the item banks including correlations of the item banks to the existing legacy measures of smoking (Fagerström Test of Nicotine Dependence (FTND), Questionnaire of Smoking Urges (QSU), and the Wisconsin Inventory of Smoking Dependence Motives (WISDM)). Using data from a follow-up sample (N = 491) and a community sample (N = 369) of adult daily and nondaily smokers, these investigators replicated the findings from Edelen et al., (2014a) and examined the correlations of legacy smoking measures with the new item bank scores. Preliminary validity findings were replicated with the new data. Correlations among the banks were moderate and bank score associations with measures of smoking behavior, quitting history, and other PROMIS measures followed expected patterns (e.g., nicotine dependence was associated with smoking quantity and time to first cigarette of the day; health and psychosocial expectancies were related to quitting recency and interest). Correlations of bank scores with legacy measures were moderate to strong. The PROMIS nicotine dependence scores were associated with the legacy instruments. These analyses provided evidence for the validity of the PROMIS Smoking item banks in two independent samples.

Varenicline Impairs Extinction and Enhances Reinstatement across Repeated Cycles of Nicotine Self-administration in Rats

Varenicline is a partial nicotine receptor agonist prescribed as a smoking cessation medication. Repeated (or long-term) use of Varenicline has been proposed as a treatment option for tobacco addiction. However the effect of repeated Varenicline use on motivation for nicotine remains unknown. Hence, Macnamara et al., (2016) used i.v. nicotine self-administration paradigm in rats to evaluate the consequences of Varenciline treatment across repeated cycles of administration, extinction and reinstatement. Rats acquired nicotine self-administration across 20 days before undergoing 6 days of extinction, where each extinction session was preceded by a single injection of Varenicline or saline. This was followed by a single Varenicline-free nicotine-primed reinstatement test. All rats reacquired nicotine self-administration for 10 days followed by a second cycle of extinction. During this period, rats either received a second cycle of Varenicline (VAR-VAR) or saline (SAL-SAL), or the alternative treatment (SAL-VAR, VAR-SAL), followed by a final reinstatement test. Treatment with Varenicline increased responding across the first cycle of extinction, but did not affect responding in the reinstatement test. Across the second cycle, Varenicline increased responding across extinction, and, rats treated with Varenicline across cycle 1 and saline across cycle 2 (Group VAR-SAL) exhibited more reinstatement than rats in any other group. The effect of VAR on nicotine seeking behavior was not due to its effects on locomotor activity. Instead, these findings suggested that a history of VAR can increase vulnerability to reinstatement/relapse when its treatment is discontinued.

References

Bahadir, A., Iliaz, S., Yurt, S., Ortakoylu, M. G., Bakan, N. D., Yazar, E., 2016. Factors affecting dropout in the smoking cessation outpatient clinic. *Chron Respir Dis.* 2016 Feb 4.

Bell, R. L., Hauser, S., Rodd, Z. A., Liang, T., Sari, Y., McClintick, J., Rahman, S., Engleman, E. A., A 2016. Genetic Animal Model of Alcoholism for Screening Medications to Treat Addiction. *Int Rev Neurobiol.* 126, 179-261.

Bidwell, L. C., Palmer, R. H., Brick, L., Madden, P. A., Heath, A. C., Knopik, V. S., 2016. A Propensity Scoring Approach to Characterizing the Effects of Maternal Smoking during Pregnancy on Offspring's Initial Responses to Cigarettes and Alcohol. *Behav Genet.* 46(3), 416-430.

Blanco, C., Hasin, D. S., Wall, M. M., Flórez-Salamanca, L., Hoertel, N., Wang, S., Kerridge, B. T., Olfson, M., 2016. Cannabis Use and Risk of Psychiatric Disorders: Prospective Evidence from a US National Longitudinal Study. *JAMA Psychiatry.* 73(4), 388-395.

Cloutier, R. M., Blumenthal, H., Mischel, E. R., 2016. An Examination of Social Anxiety in Marijuana and Cigarette Use Motives among Adolescents. *Subst Use Misuse.* 51(3),408-418.

Crooks, P. A., Dwoskin, L. P., 1997. Contribution of CNS nicotine metabolites to the neuropharmacological effects of nicotine and tobacco smoking. *Biochemical Pharmacology.* 54(7), 743–753.

Desai, R. I., Sullivan, K. A., Kohut, S. J., Bergman, J., 2016. Influence of experimental history on nicotine self-administration in squirrel monkeys. *Psychopharmacology* (Berl). 2016 Apr 4.

Edelen, M. O., Huang, W., Stucky, B. D., 2016. Additional validity evidence for the PROMIS Smoking Assessment Toolkit. *Addict Behav.* 58, 80-84.

Engelmann, J. M., Versace, F., Gewirtz, J. C., Cinciripini, P. M., 2016. Individual differences in brain responses to cigarette-related cues and pleasant stimuli in young smokers. *Drug Alcohol Depend.* Apr 25.

Fucito, L. M., Czabafy, S., Hendricks, P. S., Kotsen, C., Richardson, D., Toll, B.A. 2016. Association for the Treatment of Tobacco Use and Dependence (ATTUD)/Society for Research on nicotine and Tobacco (SRNT) Synergy Committee. Pairing smoking-cessation services with lung cancer screening: A clinical guideline from the Association for the Treatment of Tobacco Use and Dependence and the Society for Research on nicotine and Tobacco. *Cancer.* 122(8), 1150-1159.

Green, S. H., Bayer, R., Fairchild, A. L., 2016. Evidence, Policy, and e-cigarettes--Will England Reframe the Debate? *N Engl J Med.* 374(14), 1301-1303.

Grizzell, J. A.; Echeverria, V. (Jun 2014). "New insights into the mechanisms of action of cotinine and its distinctive effects from nicotine." *Neurochemical Research 27: 2032–2046.*

Henningfield, J. E., Zeller, M., 2006. "Nicotine psychopharmacology research contributions to United States and global tobacco regulation: a look back and a look forward." *Psychopharmacology 184 (3–4), 286–291.*

Henningfield, J. E., Zeller, M., 2009. "Nicotine psychopharmacology: policy and regulatory." Handb Exp Pharmacol. *Handbook of Experimental Pharmacology 192 (192), 511–534.*

Hewitt, G. F. 1941. The history of nicotine. *J. Chem. Educ.*, 18 (7), p 303.

Holford, T. R., Levy, D. T., Meza, R., 2016. Comparison of Smoking History Patterns among African American and White Cohorts in the United States Born 1890 to 1990. *Nicotine Tob Res.* 18 Suppl 1, S16-29.

Huh, J., Cerrada, C. J., Kirkpatrick, M. G., Dunton, G., Leventhal, A. M., 2016. Social contexts of momentary craving to smoke among Korean American emerging adults. *Addict Behav.* 56, 23-29.

Inoue, A., Kawakami, N., Eguchi, H., Tsutsumi, A., 2016. Modifying effect of cigarette smoking on the association of organizational justice with serious psychological distress in Japanese employees: a cross-sectional study. *Int Arch Occup Environ Health.* Apr7.

Kohut, S. J., Bergman, J., 2016. Reinforcing effectiveness of nicotine in nonhuman primates: effects of nicotine dose and history of nicotine self-administration. *Psychopharmacology* (Berl). Apr 14.

Krebs, P., Rogers, E., Smelson, D., Fu, S., Wang, B., Sherman, S., 2016. Relationship between tobacco cessation and mental health outcomes in a tobacco cessation trial. *J Health Psychol.* May 4.

Lang, J. 1997. "The Divine Origin of Tobacco." *Winds of Change*, 12(3), 55-59. (http://wocmag.org/1997/s97cont.html).

Lemieux, A., Olson, L., Nakajima, M., Schulberg, L., al'Absi, M. 2016. Life adversity is associated with smoking relapse after a quit attempt. *Addict Behav.* 60, 71-77.

Little, M. A., Ebbert, J. O., 2016. The safety of treatments for tobacco use disorder. *Expert Opin Drug Saf.* 15(3), 333-341.

Macnamara, C. L., Holmes, N. M., Westbrook, R. F., Clemens, K. J., 2016. *Varenciline* impairs extinction and enhances reinstatement across repeated cycles of nicotine self-administration in rats. *Neuropharmacology.* 105, 463-470.

Mardini, V., Rohde, L. A., Cereser, K. M., Gubert, Cde. M., Silva, E. G., Xavier, F., Parcianello, R., Röhsig, L. M., Pechansky, F., Pianca, T. G., Szobot, C. M., 2016. IL-6 and IL-10 levels in the umbilical cord blood of newborns with a history of crack/cocaine exposure in utero: a comparative study. *Trends Psychiatry Psychother.* 38(1), 40-49.

Melsens, L. H. Frédéric., 1843. "Note sur la Nicotine," [Note on Nicotine] *Annales de chimie et de physique*, third series, 9, 465-479.

Melzer, A. C., Feemster, L. C., Collins, M. P., Au, D. H., 2016. Predictors of Pharmacotherapy for Tobacco Use Among Veterans Admitted for COPD: The Role of Disparities and Tobacco Control Processes. *J Gen Intern Med.* (in press).

MMWR, 1993. *Green Tobacco Sickness in Tobacco Harvesters* – Kentucky, 1992. Vol 42, No 13;237 April 9, 1993. Online: <http://www.cdc.gov/mmwr/preview/mmwrhtml/00020119.htm> (accessed: 28 August, 2008).

Motlagh, F., Ibrahim, F., Menke, J. M., Rashid, R., Seghatoleslam, T., Habil, H., 2016. Neuroelectrophysiological approaches in heroin addiction research: A review of literatures. *J Neurosci Res.* 94(4), 297-309.

Mucchietto V, Crespi A, Fasoli F, Clementi F, Gotti C., 2016. Neuronal Acetylcholine Nicotinic Receptors as New Targets for Lung Cancer Treatment. *Curr Pharm Des.* 22(14), 2160-2169.

Nair, U. S., Jordan, J. S., Funk, D., Gavin, K., Tibbetts, E., Collins, B. N., 2016. Integrating health education and physical activity programming for cardiovascular health promotion among female inmates: A proof of concept study. *Contemp Clin Trials.* 48, 65-69.

Naughton, F., Riaz, M., Sutton, S., 2016. Response Parameters for SMS Text Message Assessments among Pregnant and General Smokers Participating in SMS Cessation Trials. *Nicotine Tob Res.* 18(5), 1210-1214.

Nichols, D. E., 2016. Psychedelics. *Pharmacol Rev.* 68(2), 264-355.

Peters, R., Poulter, R., Warner, J., Beckett, N., Burch, L., Bulpitt, C., 2008. "Smoking, dementia and cognitive decline in the elderly, a systematic review." *BMC Geriatr 8, 36.*

Pinner, A. 1893. "Ueber Nicotin. Die Constitution des Alkaloïds." [About nicotine. The Constitution of the Alkaloids] *Berichte der deutschen chemischen Gesellschaft.* 26, 292–305.

Pinner, A., 1893. "Ueber Nicotin. I. Mitteilung." [About nicotine. I. Communication] *Archiv der Pharmazie* 231 (5–6), 378–448.

Pinner, A., Wolffenstein, R., 1891. "Ueber Nicotin." [About nicotine] *Berichte der deutschen chemischen Gesellschaft* 24, 1373–1377.

Plesner, K., Jensen, H. I., Højsted, J., 2016. Smoking history, nicotine dependence and opioid use in patients with chronic non-malignant pain. *Acta Anaesthesiol Scand.* 60(7), 988-994.

Quaife, S. L., Ruparel, M., Beeken, R. J., McEwen, A., Isitt, J., Nolan, G., Sennett, K., Baldwin, D. R., Duffy, S. W., Janes, S. M., Wardle, J., 2016. The Lung Screen Uptake Trial (LSUT): protocol for a randomised controlled demonstration lung cancer screening pilot testing a targeted invitation strategy for high risk and 'hard-to-reach' patients. *BMC Cancer.* 16(1), 281.

Rabin, R. L., Sugarman, S. D. (eds) 2001. *Regulating Tobacco.* Oxford University Press, USA.

Raja, M., Saha, S., Krishna-Reddy, V., Mohd, S., Narang, R., Sood, P., 2016. Effectiveness of oral health education versus nicotine *replacement therapy* for tobacco cessation- a parallel randomized clinical trial. *J Clin Exp Dent.* 8(1), e64-70.

Rang, H. P et al., 2007. *Rang and Dale's Pharmacology* 6th Edition, Elsevier, page 598.

Ross, J. M., Graziano, P., Pacheco-Colón, I., Coxe, S., Gonzalez, R., 2016. Decision-Making does not Moderate the Association between Cannabis Use and Body Mass Index among Adolescent Cannabis Users. *J Int Neuropsychol Soc.* 22, 1-6.

Salín-Pascual RJ1, Rosas M, Jimenez-Genchi A, Rivera-Meza BL, Delgado-Parra V (September 1996). "Antidepressant effect of transdermal nicotine patches in nonsmoking patients with major depression." *J Clin Psychiatry.* 59 (9): 387–9.

Schindler, C. W., Scherma, M., Redhi, G. H., Vadivel, S. K., Makriyannis, A., Goldberg, S. R., Justinova, Z., 2016. Self-administration of the anandamide transport inhibitor AM404 by squirrel monkeys. *Psychopharmacology* (Berl). 233(10), 1867-1877.

Shemory, S. T., Pfefferle, K. J., Gradisar, I. M., 2016. Modifiable Risk Factors in Patients with Low Back Pain. *Orthopedics.* Apr 7, 1-4.

Srinivasan, R., Henley, B. M., Henderson, B. J., Indersmitten, T., Cohen, B. N., Kim, C. H., McKinney, S., Deshpande, P., Xiao, C., Lester, H. A., 2016. Smoking-Relevant nicotine Concentration Attenuates the Unfolded Protein Response in DAergic Neurons. *J Neurosci.* 36(1), 65-79.

Strickland J. C., Reynolds A. R., Stoops W. W., 2016. Regulation of Cocaine Craving by Cognitive Strategies in an Online Sample of Cocaine Users. *Psychol Addict Behav.* 2016 Apr 14.

Sutherland, R., Sindicich, N., Entwistle, G., Whittaker, E., Peacock, A., Matthews, A., Bruno, R., Alati, R., Burns, L., 2016. Tobacco and e-cigarettes use amongst illicit drug users in Australia. *Drug Alcohol Depend.* 159, 35-41.

Talati, A., Keyes, K. M., Hasin, D. S., 2016. Changing relationships between smoking and psychiatric disorders across twentieth century birth cohorts: clinical and research. *Mol Psychiatry.* 21(4), 464-471.

Trautmann, S., Goodwin, L., Höfler, M., Jacobi, F., Strehle, J., Zimmermann, P., Wittchen, H. U., 2016. Prevalence and severity of mental disorders in military personnel: a standardised comparison with civilians. *Epidemiol Psychiatr Sci.* 2016 Apr 18, 1-10.

Tsai, Y. S., Tseng, Y. T., Chen, P. S., Lin, M. C., Wu, C. C., Huang, M. S., Wang, C. C., Chen, K. S., Lin, Y. C., Wang, T. N., 2016. Protective effects of elafin against adult asthma. *Allergy Asthma Proc.* 37(2), 15-24.

Vilardaga, R., Rizo, J., Kientz, J. A., McDonell, M. G., Ries, R. K., Sobel, K., 2016. User Experience Evaluation of a Smoking Cessation App in People with Serious Mental Illness. *Nicotine Tob Res.* 18(5),1032-1038.

Chapter 3

Nicotinisms: Emerging Concepts and Mechanisms

Abstract

Several concepts and mechanisms have emerged recently to understand and clinically manage nicotinism. Factors affecting dropout in the smoking cessation in outpatient clinics have been investigated. It is now recognized that neuronal acetylcholine nicotinic receptors (nAChRs) may be a drug discovery target for lung cancer treatment. A relationship between smoking and psychiatric disorders has been established in relation to psychedelics serotonergic hallucinogens. In male adult rats, the effect of nicotine self-administration and withdrawal on concurrently available chow and sucrose intake and the effect of Varenicline on self-administration of alcohol and/or nicotine in rat model of co-abuse was investigated. It has been demonstrated that the squirrel monkeys are able to self-administer anandamide transport inhibitor, AM404. In addition, social contexts of craving to smoke among Korean American adults have been investigated. Several electrophysiological similarities were observed between heroin addiction and nicotinism. It has been demonstrated that smoking-relevant nicotine concentration can attenuate the unfolded protein response in DAergic neurons. Some investigators highlighted the importance of safety of treatment for tobacco abuse disorders. Recently, tobacco and e-cigarettes abuse was reported amongst illicit drug abusers in Australia. Pregnant and general smokers participated in SMS cessation trials and smoking cessation was evaluated in patients with serious mental illness. Quit line counseling and text messaging were implemented for smoking cessation. Predictors of 10-year smoking abstinence in smokers abstinent for 1 year after treatment were evaluated. Cigarette smoking and nicotine dependence was observed particularly among HIV-positive patients in Vietnam, which influenced remarkably on their adherence to antiretroviral therapy. In addition, gender differences were noticed in the smoking and expectancies of consuming e-cigarettes among males and females. Recently, some false beliefs about smokeless tobacco abuse have been highlighted, which need further evaluation. Although adolescent population may consider tobacco smoking as glamourous in the beginning, it becomes a socio-economic stigma later on, when they become chronically-addicted to nicotine.

Keywords: acetylcholine nicotinic receptors, psychedelics serotonergic hallucinogens, Varenicline, heroin, DArgic neurons, quit-line counseling and text messaging, antiretroviral therapy, nicotinism, HIV-positive patients, gender differences, e-cigarettes

Introduction

The clinical management of nicotinism is currently a significant challenge. Several concepts and mechanisms and factors affecting dropout in the smoking cessation have been proposed. There is now evidence to suggest that neuronal acetylcholine nicotinic receptors may be considered as novel drug discovery target for lung cancer treatment. In addition, relationship between smoking and psychiatric disorders has been established to understand the behavior of psychedelics serotonergic hallucinogens in nicotine addicts.

Recently, the effect of nicotine self-administration and withdrawal on chow and sucrose intake and the effect of Varenicline on self-administration of alcohol and/or nicotine was evaluated in rat model. In addition, it was demonstrated that the squirrel monkeys are able to self-administer Anandamide transport inhibitor, AM404.

A study investigated social contexts of craving to smoke among Korean American adults. Several electrophysiological similarities were observed between heroin addiction and nicotinism. Smoking-relevant nicotine concentration could attenuate the unfolded protein response in DAergic neurons. Some investigators emphasized the importance of safety of treatment for tobacco abuse disorders. Tobacco and e-cigarettes abuse has been reported amongst illicit drug abusers in Australia. In SMS cessation trials, pregnant and general smokers participated and smoking cessation was evaluated in patients with serious mental illness. Recently, Quit-line counseling and text messaging have been implemented for smoking cessation programs. In another study, predictors of 10-year smoking abstinence in smokers abstinent for 1 year after treatment were evaluated. Cigarette smoking and nicotine dependence was observed particularly among HIV-positive patients in Vietnam, which influenced remarkably on their adherence to antiretroviral therapy.

Although adolescent population may consider tobacco smoking glamorous in the beginning, it becomes a serious socio-economic stigma later on, when they become addicted to nicotine. In addition, gender differences have been noticed among smokers and expectancies of consuming e-cigarettes among males and females and some false beliefs about smokeless tobacco abuse have been highlighted in this chapter, which need further evaluation.

This chapter highlights concepts and mechanisms to clinically manage nicotinism, factors affecting dropout in the smoking cessation in outpatient clinics, clinical significance of neuronal acetylcholine Nicotinic receptors (nAChRs) as a drug discovery target for lung cancer treatment, relationship between smoking and psychiatric disorders in relation to serotonergic hallucinogens, nicotine self-administration and withdrawal on concurrently available lab chow and sucrose intake and the effect of Varenicline on self-administration of alcohol and/or nicotine in rat model, and self-administration of Anandamide transport inhibitor, AM404 by squirrel monkeys. The chapter also describes social contexts of craving to smoke among Korean Americans, electrophysiological similarities between Heroin addiction and nicotinism, attenuation of the unfolded protein response in DAergic neurons by nicotine, importance of safety of treatment for tobacco abuse disorders, tobacco and e-cigarettes abuse among illicit drug abusers in Australia, Quit line counseling and text messaging smoking cessation, and cigarette smoking and nicotine dependence among HIV-positive patients in Vietnam, influencing adherence to antiretroviral therapy. In addition, gender differences in smoking and expectancies of consuming e-cigarettes among males and females and false beliefs about smokeless tobacco abuse are highlighted. Although adolescent population may consider tobacco smoking as glamorous in the beginning, it becomes a serious socio-economic stigma later in life, when they become totally addicted to nicotine as briefly described in this chapter.

Factors Affecting Dropout in the Smoking Cessation Outpatient Clinic

Bahadir et al., (2016) recently investigated the prevalence of discontinuation in the smoking cessation outpatient clinic (SCC) and examined the causes of noncompliance. They included 1324 smokers in this study. Patients were divided into two groups, as those who discontinued (dropped out) follow-up (group 1) and those who stayed in follow-up (group 2). A total of 540 (40.8%) patients were in group 1. The mean age, smoking pack-years, and Fagerström scores of group 1 were lower than group 2. The choice of treatment was also different between groups. Motivational/behavioral therapy and nicotine replacement therapy (NRT) were more common in group 1 compared with group 2. No difference among groups in gender, having household smokers, history of antidepressant treatment, previous quit attempts, and educational status was observed. Almost 40% of these patients did not come to their follow-up SCC visit. Younger age, lower Fagerström score, low amount of daily cigarette consumption, and being treated only with behavioral therapy or NRT were identified as the primary causes of the dropout group, which may facilitate implementation of personalized treatment at the first appointment.

Neuronal Acetylcholine Nicotinic Receptors as Targets for Lung Cancer Treatment

Lung cancer is the leading cause of cancer-related deaths worldwide. Recently, Muchietto et al., (2016) reported that smoking accounts for ~ 70% of the non- small cell lung cancer (NSCLC) and 90% of the cases of small-cell lung cancer (SCLC), although some patients develop lung cancer without a history of smoking. Nicotine is the most active addictive component of tobacco smoke. Although, nicotine does not initiate tumorigenesis in humans and rodents, it alters the pathophysiology of lung cells by inducing the secretion of growth factors, neurotransmitters and cytokines, and promotes tumor growth and metastases by inducing cell cycle progression, migration, invasion, angiogenesis and the evasion of apoptosis. Most of these effects are a result of nicotine binding and activation of cell-surface neuronal nicotinic acetylcholine receptors (nAChRs) and downstream signaling cascades, and are blocked by nAChR subtype-selective antagonists. Recent genome-wide association studies have revealed single nucleotide polymorphisms of nAChR subunits that influence nicotine dependence and lung cancer. These investigators described the molecular basis of nAChR structural and functional diversity in normal and cancer lung cells, and the genetic alterations facilitating smoking-induced lung cancers. They also summarized current knowledge of the intracellular pathways induced by nicotine and other compounds in tobacco smoke

Serotonergic Hallucinogens (Psychedelics)

Psychedelics (serotonergic hallucinogens) are powerful psychoactive drugs that alter perception and mood and affect numerous cognitive processes. They are generally considered physiologically safe and do not lead to dependence or addiction. They were employed in many sociocultural and ritual contexts in early days. After the discovery of (5R, 8R)-(+)-Lysergic Acid-N, N-Diethylamide (LSD)-25 and the identification of serotonin in the brain, research focused on whether LSD and other psychedelics had a serotonergic action. Today there is a consensus that psychedelics are agonists or partial agonists at brain 5-HT$_{2A}$ receptors, with importance on those expressed on apical dendrites of neocortical pyramidal cells in layer V. Several rodent models have been developed to help unravel the neurochemical correlates of 5-HT2A receptor activation in the brain, and a variety of imaging techniques have been developed to identify key brain areas that are directly affected by psychedelics. Several double-blind placebo-controlled phase 2 studies of psilocybin-assisted psychotherapy in patients with cancer-related psychosocial distress have demonstrated relief of anxiety and depression. Two small pilot studies of psilocybin-assisted psychotherapy have shown benefit in treating both alcohol and nicotine addiction. Recently, blood oxygen level-dependent functional MRI and magnetoencephalography were employed for *in vivo* neuroimaging after administration of a psychedelic, and indicated that i.v. psilocybin and LSD produce significant reduction in oscillatory power in areas of the brain's default mode network.

Relationship between Smoking and Psychiatric Disorders

As the risks of tobacco use become recognized and smoking becomes stigmatized, new smokers may be driven to smoking by biological or genetic vulnerabilities rather than social desirability. Given that genetic risk for deviant proneness is shared across other psychiatric and addictive disorders, Talati et al., (2016) predicted that as rates of smoking decreased through the latter half of the twentieth century, associations between smoking and psychopathology would increase. Participants (N = 25 412) from a US study-the National Epidemiologic Survey on Alcohol and Related Conditions, NESARC- were interviewed using the Alcohol Use Disorder and Associated Disabilities Interview Schedule-DSM-IV Version (AUDADIS-IV) and classified into one of five birth cohort decades (1940s to 1980s) and three smoking history (nonsmokers, never-dependent smokers and ever-dependent smokers) groups. They found that the prevalence of smoking decreased across the five birth cohorts, but associations of smoking with drug and AUDs, attention-deficit hyperactivity disorder, bipolar disorder and antisocial personality disorder, each increased in more recently born cohorts, even after adjusting for demographic and socioeconomic changes. For drug and AUDs, increases were observed among smokers both with and without a history of nicotine dependence; for other outcomes, increases were entirely driven by nicotine-dependent smokers, suggesting that smokers have high psychiatric vulnerability, and may benefit from mental health screenings. Hence, differentiating between casual and dependent smokers may further help prioritize those at greatest risk. However, potential variation in psychiatric comorbidity based on cohort of birth when defining groups of smokers to minimize confounding must be known.

Self-Administration of the Anandamide Transport Inhibitor AM404 by Squirrel Monkeys

It is now well established that N-(4-Hydroxyphenyl)-Arachidonamide (AM404) is an anandamide transport inhibitor and reduces rewarding and relapse-inducing effects of nicotine in several animal models of tobacco dependence. However, its reinforcing/rewarding effects remain uncertain. Hence, Schindler et al., (2016) investigated whether AM404 maintains self-administration behavior or reinstates extinguished drug seeking in squirrel monkeys. In monkeys with a history of anandamide or cocaine self-administration, they substituted injections of AM404 (1-100 µg/kg/injection). Using a 10-response, fixed-ratio schedule, self-administration behavior was maintained by AM404. Dose-response curves had inverted U shapes, with peak response rates occurring at 10 µg/kg/injection. In anandamide-experienced monkeys, self-administration of another anandamide transport inhibitor VDM11 was also demonstrated.

In addition to supporting self-administration, priming injections of AM404 (0.03-0.3 mg/kg) reinstated drug-seeking behavior previously reinforced by cannabinoids (Δ (9)-tetrahydrocannabinol (THC) or anandamide) or cocaine. Both AM404 self-administration and reinstatement of drug seeking by AM404 were reduced by the cannabinoid CB1 receptor antagonist/inverse agonist Rimonabant (0.3 mg/kg). Moreover, the reinforcing effects of AM404 were potentiated with the fatty acid amide hydrolase (FAAH) inhibitor URB597 (0.3 mg/kg) suggesting a major role of anandamide in these effects. Finally, AM404 (0.3 mg/kg) potentiated the reinforcing effects of anandamide but not those of cocaine. Thus, AM404 reinforced self-administration behavior and induced reinstatement of drug-seeking behavior in abstinent monkeys. These effects were mediated by cannabinoid CB1 receptors. Hence, compounds that promote actions of endo-cannabinoids in the brain by inhibiting their membrane transport may have a potential for abuse.

Social Contexts of Momentary Craving to Smoke among Korean American Emerging Adults

Korean American emerging adult (KAEA) smokers represent a culturally and developmentally unique population constituted of primarily light, intermittent smokers. Sociocultural contexts might play a significant role in contributing to acute cigarette craving and motivation to smoke in this population; yet, there is limited evidence to support this hypotheses. Huh et al., (2016) recently tested whether and how social contexts are associated with the craving among KAEA smokers. Seventy-eight daily KAEA smokers, who smoke 4+ cigs/day, participated in a 7-day ecological momentary assessment (EMA) trial, in which participants responded to both signal-contingent (random) and event-contingent (smoking) prompts to answer surveys on their mobile phones (prompt-level n = 1377; 603 random +774 smoking prompts). Nicotine dependence was measured at baseline; and cigarette craving, negative affect, presence of others smoking, social contexts were measured with EMA. Modeling of within-participant variation and covariation showed that being with Korean friends (vs. alone) was associated with increased incidence of momentary craving. This association between Korean friends and craving disappeared when adjusted for the presence of others smoking, which was a strong predictor of momentary craving. The positive association between Korean friends and craving was amplified immediately prior to smoking (vs. non-smoking random) instances. Being with Korean friends might serve as a culturally-specific salient smoking cue, which might have been learned throughout their smoking history. These data also showed that increased craving associated with Korean friends may represent social settings that involve cigarette smoking. Hence, addressing cigarette abuse as a group behavior might be a fruitful intervention strategy.

Neuroelectrophysiology of Heroin Addiction

Neuroelectrophysiological properties have been used in human heroin addiction studies. These studies vary in their approach, experimental conditions, paradigms, and outcomes. However, it is essential to integrate previous findings and experimental for a better understanding of current issues and challenges in designing such studies. Recently, Motlagh et al., (2016) examined methodologies and experimental conditions of neuroelectrophysiological research among heroin addicts during withdrawal, abstinence, and methadone maintenance treatment. Their findings showed decrements in attentional processing and dysfunctions in brain response inhibition as well as brain activity abnormalities induced by chronic heroin abuse. Chronic heroin addiction caused increased β and $\alpha 2$ power activity, latency of P300 and P600, and diminished P300 and P600 amplitude. These findings confirmed that EEG band power and coherence were associated with craving indices and heroin abuse history. First symptoms of withdrawal could be seen in high-frequency EEG bands, and the severity of these symptoms was associated with brain functional connectivity. EEG spectral changes and event-related potentials (ERP) have been associated with abstinence length and tend to normalize within 3-6 months of abstinence. Based on these findings, these investigators suggested a longitudinal study with a multimodality approach for monitoring EEG and ERP attributes of heroin addicts from early stages of withdrawal until long-term abstinence to control the confounding effects, such as nicotine abuse and other comorbid and premorbid conditions.

Smoking-Relevant Nicotine Concentration Attenuates the Unfolded Protein Response in DAergic Neurons

Retrospective epidemiological studies show an inverse correlation between susceptibility to Parkinson's disease (PD) and a person's history of tobacco use. Animal models of PD suggest nicotine as a neuroprotective agent and nicotinic acetylcholine (ACh) receptors (nAChRs) as targets for neuroprotection, but the underlying mechanism(s) of neuroprotection remains unknown. Hence, Sriniwas et al., (2016) cultured mouse ventral midbrain neurons for 3 weeks. Ten to 20% of neurons were DAergic, revealed by tyrosine hydroxylase (TH) immunoreactivity. They evoked mild ER stress with tunicamycin (Tu), producing modest increases in the nuclear ATF6, phosphorylated eukaryotic initiation factor 2α, nuclear XBP1, and the downstream proapoptotic effector nuclear C/EBP homologous protein. They incubated cultures for 2 weeks with 200 nm nicotine, the approximate steady-state concentration between cigarette smoking and vaping, or during nicotine patch use. Nicotine incubation suppressed Tu-induced ER stress and the unfolded protein response (UPR). Study of mice with fluorescent nAChR subunits showed that the cultured TH+ neurons displayed α4, α6, and β3 nAChR subunit expression and ACh-evoked currents. Gene expression profile in cultures from TH-eGFP mice showed that the TH+ neurons also express several other genes associated with DA release. Nicotine also upregulated ACh-induced currents in DA neurons by ~2.5-fold. Thus, nicotine, at a concentration too low to activate an appreciable fraction of plasma membrane nAChRs, induced UPR suppression and nAChR upregulation. Therefore, one mechanism of neuroprotection by nicotine is pharmacological chaperoning, leading to UPR suppression. Therefore, measuring this pathway may help in assessing neuroprotection. Yet PD cannot be cured or prevented. However, many retrospective epidemiological studies reveal that PD is diagnosed less frequently in tobacco abusers. Existing programs attempting to develop nicotinic drugs that might exert this neuroprotective effect are asking whether agonists, antagonists, partial agonists, or channel blockers may have some promise. The underlying rationale resembles the previous development of Varenicline for smoking cessation. These investigators studied whether, nicotine produces neuroprotective effects in cultured DAergic neurons. They showed that nicotine, through nicotinic receptors, does protect DAergic neurons against ER stress. However, the mechanism is probably "inside-out": pharmacological chaperoning in the ER. This cellular-level insight could help to guide neuroprotective strategies.

Safety of Treatment for Tobacco Used Disorders

Tobacco continues to be a leading cause of preventable morbidity and mortality in the world. First-line pharmacotherapies for the treatment of tobacco abuse disorder include nicotine replacement therapy (NRT), Bupropion sustained-release (SR), and Varenicline. Little and Ebbert (2016) recently provided evidence on the safety of first-line pharmacotherapies for the treatment of tobacco use disorder (TUDs). They identified randomized clinical trials up to July 2015 and reviewed through searches of PUBMED using the terms nicotine replacement therapy, Bupropion SR, Varenicline, smoking, and tobacco cessation. They highlighted that NRT has few contraindications and side effects and can be recommended to almost all TUDs. However, Bupropion SR should be used with caution in patients with bipolar disorder or liver or kidney disease, and alternative treatments should be considered for patients with a history of seizures or who are at risk for seizures. The only contraindication for Varenicline is an allergy to the medication, and nausea is the most common side effect. Varenicline can even be used safely in patients with cardiovascular disease. It can also be used in patients with stable psychiatric disease by close clinical monitoring.

Table 1. Safety of Treatment for Tobacco Use Disorders

S.No	Intervention	Adverse Effects	Contraindications
1	Nicotine Replacement Therapy	Minimum	None
2	Bupriopion		Bipolar disorders
			Liver or Kidney Disease
			Seizures
3	Varenicilline	Nausea	Allergy to Medication
			Close Clinical Monitoring of Psychiatric Patients

Tobacco and E-Cigarettes Use Amongst Illicit Drug Users in Australia

To examine the rates and patterns of tobacco and e-cigarettes use amongst two samples of illicit drug users in Australia. Sutherland et al., (2016) obtained data from the 2015 Illicit Drug Reporting System (IDRS) and the 2015 Ecstasy and Related Drugs Reporting System (EDRS). These studies comprised cross-sectional samples of 888 people who inject drugs (PWID) and 763 regular psychostimulant users (RPU). Tobacco was consumed by the majority of both samples, however, use in the 6 months preceding interview was significantly higher amongst PWID than RPU. Inversely, PWID were less likely to have a history of e-cigarettes use: 31.5% of PWID reported lifetime use of e-cigarettes vs. 57.0% of RPU and 18.1% reported use in the 6 months preceding interview vs. 33.7% of RPU. PWID were more than three times as likely as RPU to report using e-cigarettes as a smoking cessation tool, but were less likely to use e-liquids that contained nicotine. Higher levels of poly drug use, daily tobacco use, recent use of synthetic cannabinoids and employment status were associated with e-cigarettes use. The use of e-cigarettes was relatively common amongst Australian samples of PWID and RPU. Majority of PWID reported using e-cigarettes as a smoking cessation tool, whereas RPU were using them for experimental or recreational purposes.

Pregnant and General Smokers Participating in SMS Cessation Trials

Despite a substantial increase in use of SMS text messages for collecting smoking-related data, there is limited knowledge on the parameters of response. Naughton et al., (2016) recently assessed response rates, response speed, and impact of reminders and predictors of response to text message assessments among smokers. Data were from two

SMS cessation intervention trials using clinical samples of pregnant (n = 198) and general smokers (n = 293) sent text message assessments during 3-month cessation programs. Response rates were calculated using data from the host web-server. Changes in response over time, impact of reminders and potential demographic (age, gender, ethnicity, parity, and deprivation) and smoking (nicotine dependence, determination to quit, prenatal smoking history, smoking status at follow-up) predictors of response were analyzed. Mean response rates were 61.9% (pregnant) and 67.8% (general) with aggregated median response times of 0.35 (pregnant) and 0.64 (general) hrs. Response rate reduced over time for general smokers only. Text message reminders had a significant effect on response, with observed mean increases of 13.8% (pregnant) and 17.7% (general). Age and deprivation weakly predicted response among pregnant smokers and nonsmoking status at 4 weeks follow-up predicted response among general smokers, indicating that text message assessments within trial-based cessation programs yield rapid responses from a sizable proportion of smokers, which can be increased using text reminders. While few sources of nonresponse bias were identified for general smokers, older and more deprived pregnant women were less likely to respond. This study demonstrated that most pregnant and general smokers enrolled in a cessation trial will respond to a small number of questions about their smoking sent by text message, mostly within 1 hr. of being sent the assessment text message. For those who do not initially respond, suggested that 24- and 48-hrs. Text message reminders increase response a small but meaningful amount. However, older age and higher deprivation among pregnant smokers and relapse among general smokers reduced the chance of response.

Evaluation of a Smoking Cessation in Patients with Serious Mental Illness

Smoking rates among people with serious mental illness are 3 to 4 times higher than the general population, yet currently there are no smoking cessation apps specifically designed to address this need. Recently, Vilardaga et al., (2016) reported the usability of a User Experience (UX) evaluation of a National Cancer Institute smoking cessation app, QuitPal, and provide user centered design data that can be used to tailor smoking cessation apps for this population. Two hundred forty hrs. of field experience with QuitPal, 10 hrs. of recorded interviews and task performances, usage logs and a self-reported usability scale, revealed the usability of this study. Participants were five individuals recruited from a community mental health clinic with a reported serious mental illness history. Performance, self-reports, usage logs and interview data were triangulated to identify critical usability errors and UX themes emerging from this population. These data suggested that QuitPal has below average levels of usability, elevated time on task performances and required considerable amounts of guidance. UX themes provided information to tailor smoking cessation apps for this population, such as the importance of breaking down "cessation" into smaller steps and use of a reward system. This was the first study to evaluate the UX of a smoking cessation app among people with serious mental illness. This study will inform future research efforts to expand the effectiveness and reach of smoking cessation apps for this highly nicotine-dependent yet under-served population. This study can also inform future research efforts to expand the effectiveness and reach of smoking cessation apps for people with serious mental illness, a highly nicotine dependent yet under-served population.

Effect of Nicotine Self-Administration and Withdrawal on Concurrently Available Chow and Sucrose Intake in Adult Male Rats

It is known that carbohydrate intake, preference, and taste thresholds may be altered in current and former cigarette smokers, which may cause weight gain and risk for obesity in individuals who quit smoking. Attempts to model these effects in rodents have primarily used noncontingent nicotine administration. Hence, Bunney et al., (2016) conducted a study to characterize changes in chow and sucrose intake in rats during a 23-hrs. access model of i.v. nicotine self-administration (NSA), in which rats lever-pressed for chow, sucrose, and nicotine under concurrent fixed-ratio (FR) 1 schedules. Male rats were assigned to one of three groups that differed in food and drug availability. The nicotine C+S group had concurrent access to nicotine, chow, and sucrose. The Saline C+S group had access to saline, chow, and sucrose. The nicotine C-Only group had access to nicotine and chow, but not sucrose. Changes in food intake and weight gain were assessed during baseline, NSA, and nicotine withdrawal (i.e., saline extinction). Weight gain was slowed during NSA and increased during withdrawal, but did not differ between the nicotine groups. NSA produced a decrease in both chow and sucrose intake. Gradual tolerance to nicotine's effects on sucrose, but not chow intake, occurred. During withdrawal, chow and sucrose intake increased, with a larger percent increase in sucrose intake compared to chow. The proportion of total food intake from sucrose was greater at the end of withdrawal compared to baseline, indicating a history of nicotine intake changed dietary preference, and that sucrose intake was more resistant to nicotine's appetite suppressant effects and withdrawal from nicotine produces a greater increase in sweet food intake alongside general increases in chow intake. Hence, changes in overall food intake in current and ex-smokers may lead to increased risk for obesity and other health problems, potentially limiting the benefit of quitting smoking.

Quit-Line Counseling and Text Messaging for Smoking Cessation.

Recently, Boal et al., (2016) determined whether comprehensive quit-line services combined with text-messaging improve smoking cessation rates beyond those achieved by offering comprehensive quit line services alone. The study sample consisted of callers to the Alere Wellbeing, Inc, commercial quit line in 2012. A quasi-experimental design was implemented using propensity score matching to create the intervention and control groups. The intervention group consisted of those who were offered and accepted a text message intervention in addition to usual quit-line services, while the control group consisted of those who were not offered the text message intervention. Analyses utilized baseline data collected at intake, program use data (e.g., call history and text message use), and reports of smoking behaviors and program satisfaction collected 6 months after intake. Similar rates of 7-day abstinence were reported regardless of whether participants received combined multi-call quit-line services plus text messaging (25.3%) or multi-call quit line services in isolation (25.5%), though those who received combined services reported higher treatment satisfaction. Among those who received combined services, the number of text messages sent predicted 7-day abstinence such that those who sent more text messages were less likely to report 7-day abstinence. Hence, text messaging may not confer additional benefits over and above those received through multi-modal, multi-call quit-line programs. These investigators recommended future research to investigate whether text-messaging improve quit rates when combined with less intensive services such as single-call phone counseling. While the impact of quit-line and text- messaging services for smoking cessation have been examined in isolation, no study has explored the impact of combined services on smoking outcomes. This study examined the role of text-messaging in combination with quit-line services including multi-call phone counseling, access to an interactive website and nicotine replacement therapy.

Predictors of 10-Year Smoking Abstinence in Smokers Abstinent for 1 Year after Treatment

To identify factors predicting long-term relapse to smoking in people attending smoking treatment services who have maintained at least 1 year abstinence, Álvarez Gutiérrez et al., (2016) conducted an observational, prospective study with multiple logistic regression used to model predictors of relapse between 1 and 10 years from cessation using variables measured pre-cessation. Among smokers receiving behavioral support for cessation, in some cases with nicotine patches or Bupropion, 366 remained abstinent after 1 year of follow-up and were included into the study. Predictive measures (disease history, psychological disorder, age of starting smoking, years of smoking, cigarette dependence and smoking cessation treatment used) were obtained at the time of the quit attempt, and 'failure' (defined as reported smoking, loss to follow-up, died or an expired air carbon monoxide reading of > 5 parts per million) was assessed 10 years later. At follow-up, abstinence status was confirmed in 50.5% (n = 185) of participants, while 21.0% (n = 77) reported that they had resumed smoking, and 28.5% (n = 104) were lost to follow-up (also counted as having resumed smoking). In the multiple regression model, the main factor that predicted relapse had a psychological disorder. Having a psychological disorder at the time of stopping smoking remained a risk factor for relapse to smoking, even after >1 year of abstinence.

Cigarette Smoking and Nicotine Dependence on Adherence to Antiretroviral Therapy among HIV-Positive Patients in Vietnam

Cigarette smoking has been recognized as an indicator for inferior adherence to antiretroviral therapy (ART) among HIV-positive patients. Given the limited body of work on this issue, Nguyen et al., (2016) explored the relationship between cigarette smoking, nicotine dependence, and ART adherence. A cross-sectional study of 1050 HIV-positive patients was conducted. Adherence to ART during the last 30 days was measured by the 100-point visual analog scale (VAS). Smoking history and nicotine dependence (Fagerström Test of Nicotine Dependence) were self-reported by participants. Multiple logistic regression was performed to examine the association of current smoking and nicotine dependence with ART nonadherence. Using the established VAS cut point of 95 to indicate adequate adherence, the prevalence of ART nonadherence was 30.9%. ~35.5% of the sample reported current smoking. No association between smoking status and ART nonadherence was found. However, participants with greater nicotine dependence were more likely to be nonadherent. Also, female patients, receiving ART, and currently feeling anxiety had a higher likelihood of ART nonadherence. Additionally, current smokers reporting pain were more likely to be nonadherent. Conversely, protective factors included living with a spouse/partner and having more than a high school education. Given the high prevalence of suboptimal adherence and current smoking among HIV-positive patients, screening for smoking status and nicotine dependence during ART treatment may help to improve patients' adherence to medication. Based on the findings of this study, these investigators indicated that more efforts should be targeted to women, patients with mental health problems, and ART clinics in rural areas.

Tobacco Smoking: From 'Glamour' to 'Stigma'

In a narrative review, Castaldelli-Maia et al., (2016) explored the history of tobacco smoking, its associations and portrayal of its use with luxury and glamour in the past, and its subsequent transformation into a mass consumption industrialized product encouraged by advertising and films. Then, they described the next phase where tobacco has become an unwanted product. However, the number of smokers is still increasing, especially in new markets, and increasingly younger individuals are being attracted to it, despite the well-known health consequences of tobacco use in the entire world. They also explored current smoking behaviors, looking at trends in the prevalence of consumption throughout the world, discrimination against smokers, light and/or intermittent smokers, and the e-cigarettes. They placed these changes in the context of neuroscience, which may help explain why the cognitive effects of smoking can be reinforcers for its consumption despite strong anti-smoking pressure in Western countries.

Gender Differences in Smoking Behavior

It has been recognized that while the overall prevalence of smoking has declined, nondaily smoking is on the rise. Among daily smokers (DS) men tend to smoke more cigarettes per day and have higher dependence. Unfortunately little is known about gender differences in nondaily smokers (NDS). Recently, Allen et al., (2016) utilized secondary-data analysis data from a cross-sectional online survey. Participants reported on smoking behavior (e.g., cigarettes per day, history of quit attempts) and nicotine dependence motives as assessed by the Brief Wisconsin Inventory of Dependence Motives via the primary and secondary subscales (i.e., core features of tobacco dependence such as craving and accessory motives such as weight control, respectively). Participants were 1175 DS (60% women) and 1201 NDS (56% women). Two interactions between group and gender were noted suggesting that the NDS had greater gender differences in past quit attempts and reported change in smoking behavior over the past year. Further, among the NDS group, men scored higher than women on both the primary and secondary dependence motives subscales. There were no differences in dependence motives in the DS group. Gender differences in smoking behavior and dependence motives varied between NDS and DS. Specifically, gender differences in smoking behavior and smoking dependence motives was larger among NDS compared to DS. Hence, additional research is needed to explore how these relationships may relate to smoking cessation in NDS.

Gender Differences in Use and Expectancies of E-Cigarettes

Given the rapid increase in e-cigarettes use, it is important to understand factors that may contribute to their initiation and maintenance. Because gender differences in tobacco use, product preferences, and expectancies are well established, similar gender differences may exist with e-cigarettes. In a recent study, Piñeiro et al., (2016) identified gender differences among e-cigarettes users in patterns of use, reasons for initiation and maintenance, and outcome expectancies regarding e-cigarettes. Participants (N = 1815) completed an online survey. These investigators assessed sociodemographic, smoking and e-cigarettes history and use, and expectancies about e-cigarettes. They found gender differences in type of e-cigarettes used, flavors used, nicotine dosage, and source of information about e-cigarettes, place of purchase, and use of e-cigarettes where smoking was prohibited. In addition, males were more likely to report initiating e-cigarettes use to quit smoking due to health concerns, whereas females were more likely to report initiation based on recommendations from family and friends. Males reported higher attributions for maintenance of e-cigarettes use related to positive reinforcement (enjoyment), whereas females reported higher negative reinforcement attributions (stress reduction or mood management). Males reported more positive expectancies about e-cigarettes, including taste, social facilitation, and energy, whereas women rated e-cigarettes higher for weight control. Males also reported greater addiction-related e-cigarettes expectancy than females. Many of the gender differences with e-cigarettes paralleled those previously found with cigarette smoking. Although effect sizes associated with these differences were small, these findings may help advance research and intervention development with respect to e-cigarettes initiation, maintenance and cessation.

Effect of Varenicline on Self-Administration of Alcohol and/or Nicotine in Rat Model of Model of Co-Abuse

Alcohol and nicotine (in the form of tobacco) are often taken together, with increased negative health consequences. Co-use may modify intake of one or both of the drugs, or the effects of drugs used to treat nicotine or alcohol addiction. Varenicline is prescribed as an aid to enhance quitting smoking. More recently it has been shown to reduce alcohol intake in humans and lab animals. There is little work investigating the role of co-exposure to alcohol and nicotine in the effects of Varenicline. In pilot clinical studies, it has been reported that smoking enhances Varenicline effectiveness as a treatment for alcohol misuse, but this relationship has not been systematically investigated. To help resolve this, Funk et al., (2016) examined if the effects of Varenicline on alcohol and nicotine self-administration (SA) in rats are modified when the two drugs are taken together. Rats were trained on alcohol SA, and some were implanted with i.v. catheters for nicotine SA. Groups of animals then lever-pressed for alcohol or nicotine alone, and another group lever-pressed for alcohol and nicotine, using a two lever choice procedure. Varenicline did not affect alcohol SA, whereas Varenicline reduced nicotine SA modestly. Access to both alcohol and nicotine reduced SA of either drug, but did not change the effects of Varenicline. In rats with a history of alcohol SA, Varenicline reduced reinstatement of extinguished alcohol seeking induced by exposure to an alcohol prime combined with cues previously associated with alcohol.

Normative Beliefs about Smokeless Tobacco Abuse

It has been recently realized that evaluation of consumer responses to modified risk tobacco products (MRTPs) are urgently needed. Adkison et al., (2016) recently reported a relationship between normative beliefs and future intentions to use tobacco. They sought to (1) develop a measure of normative beliefs about smokeless tobacco (ST) and establish the underlying factor structure, (2) evaluate the structure with confirmatory factor analysis utilizing an independent sample of youth, and (3) establish the measure's concurrent validity. Respondents (smokers and nonsmokers aged 15-65; N = 2991) completed a web-based survey that included demographic characteristics, tobacco abuse history and dependence, and a measure of attitudes about ST adapted from the Normative Beliefs about Smoking scale. A second sample of youth (aged 14-17; N = 305) completed a similar questionnaire. Based on this study, they reported that exploratory factor analysis produced the anticipated three-factor solution and accounted for nearly three-quarters of the variance in the data reflecting (1) perceived prevalence of ST use, (2) popularity of ST among successful/elite, and (3) approval of ST use by parents/peers. Confirmatory factor analysis with data from the youth sample demonstrated good model fit. Logistic regression demonstrated that the scales effectively discriminate between ST users and nonusers and are associated with interest in trying snus, suggesting that assessment of MRTPs for regulatory purposes, which allows messages of reduced risk, should include measurement of social norms. Furthermore, surveillance efforts that track use of new MRTPs should include measures of social norms to determine how norms change with prevalence of use.

Relapse Prevention Trial in Longer-Term Abstinence after Short-term Smoking Cessation Treatment from Specialists and Nonspecialists

It has been realized that smokers receiving support in specialist centers tend to have a higher short-term quit rate, compared with those receiving support in other settings from professionals for whom smoking cessation is only a part of their work. Hence, Song et al., (2016) investigated the difference in longer-term abstinence after short-term smoking cessation treatment from specialist and nonspecialist smoking cessation services. They conducted analysis of data from a randomized controlled trial of self-help booklets for the prevention of smoking relapse. The trial included 1088 short-term quitters from specialist stop smoking clinics and 316 from nonspecialist cessation services (such as general practice, pharmacies, and health trainer services). The difference in prolonged smoking abstinence from months 4 to 12 between specialist and nonspecialist services was compared. Multivariable logistic regression analyses were conducted to investigate the association between continuous smoking abstinence and the type of smoking cessation services, adjusted for possible confounding factors (including demographic, socioeconomic, and smoking history variables). The proportion of continuous abstinence from 4 to 12 months was higher in short-term quitters from specialist services compared with those from nonspecialist services. After adjusting for a range of participant characteristics and smoking variables, the specialist service was associated with a higher rate of longer-term smoking abstinence, indicating that people who receive support to stop smoking from a specialist are at lower risk of relapse than those receiving support from a nonspecialist advisor.

References

Adkison, S. E., O'Connor, R. J., Bansal-Travers, M., Cummings, K. M., Rees, V. W., Hatsukami, D. K. Validation of a Measure of Normative Beliefs About Smokeless Tobacco Use. *Nicotine & Tob Res.* 2016 May;18(5):801-8.

Allen, A. M., Scheuermann, T. S., Nollen, N., Hatsukami, D., Ahluwalia, J. S., 2016. Gender Differences in Smoking Behavior and Dependence Motives among Daily and Nondaily Smokers. *Nicotine & Tob Res.* 18(6), 1408-1413.

Álvarez Gutiérrez, F. J., Ferrer Galván, M., Ruiz Bernal, A., Medina Gallardo, J.F., Romero Romero, B., Sáez Díaz, A., Romero Falcón, A. 2016. Predictors of 10-year smoking abstinence in smokers abstinent for 1 year after treatment. *Addiction.* 111(3),545-551.

Boal, A. L., Abroms, L. C., Simmens, S., Graham, A. L., Carpenter, K. M., 2016. Combined Quitline Counseling and Text Messaging for Smoking Cessation: A Quasi-Experimental Evaluation. *Nicotine Tob Res.* 18(5),1046-1053.

Bunney, P. E., Burroughs, D., Hernandez, C., LeSage, M. G., 2016. The effects of nicotine self-administration and withdrawal on concurrently available chow and sucrose intake in adult male rats. *Physiol Behav.* 154, 49-59.

Castaldelli-Maia, J. M., Ventriglio, A., Bhugra, D., 2016. Tobacco smoking: From 'glamour' to 'stigma.' A comprehensive review. *Psychiatry Clin Neurosci.* 70(1), 24-33.

Funk, D., Lo, S., Coen, K., Lê, A. D., 2016. Effects of *Varenciline* on operant self-administration of alcohol and/or nicotine in a rat model of co-abuse. *Behav Brain Res.* 296, 157-162.

Nguyen, N. T., Tran, B. X., Hwang, L. Y., Markham, C. M., Swartz, M. D., Vidrine, J. I., Phan, H. T., Latkin, C. A., Vidrine, D. J., 2016. Effects of cigarette smoking and nicotine dependence on adherence to antiretroviral therapy among HIV-positive patients in Vietnam. *AIDS Care.* 28(3), 359-364.

Piñeiro, B., Correa, J. B., Simmons, V. N., Harrell, P. T., Menzie, N. S., Unrod, M., Meltzer, L. R., Brandon, T. H., 2016. Gender differences in use and expectancies of e-cigarettes: Online survey. *Addict Behav.* 52, 91-97.

Song, F., Maskrey, V., Blyth, A., Brown, T. J., Barton, G. R., Aveyard, P., Notley, C., Holland, R., Bachmann, M. O., Sutton, S., Brandon, T. H., 2016. Differences in Longer-Term Smoking Abstinence after Treatment by Specialist or Nonspecialist Advisors: Secondary Analysis of Data From a Relapse Prevention Trial. *Nicotine Tob Res.* 18(5), 1061-1066.

Chapter 4

Nicotinism:
Its Prevention and Treatment

Abstract

In this chapter a brief description of nicotinism among smokers with a history of childhood abuse and cigarette smoking among APOE carriers and Alzheimer's disease (AD) is presented. In addition, smoking status confirmation by proxy, dual trajectories of cigarette smoking and smokeless tobacco abuse are described. A brief description of smoking patterns and cessation attempts, reliability and stability of puff topography variables in non-daily smokers, and nicotine patch for the treatment of nicotine gum addiction is also highlighted. Particularly, the chapter emphasizes that individuals with childhood physical, psychological, and verbal abuse are more vulnerable to nicotinism and its withdrawal symptoms. It has been reported that persons with APOE carrier gene are more susceptible to nicotine-induced AD and nicotine patch can be utilized for the safe and effective treatment of nicotine gum addiction. Furthermore, three CYP2A6 inhibitors: two furanocoumarins, xanthotoxin (15 mg/kg) and bergapten (25 mg/kg), and the coumarin umbelliferone (25 mg/kg) have been reported to prolong the antidepressive and procognitive effects of nicotine, suggesting that these natural products may offer a novel approach for the treatment of nicotinism as antidepressant and memory improvement agents in nicotine addicts. It has been recommended that anti-tobacco program derived in the area of knowledge, attitude and behavior should constitute modification of educational programs regarding techniques and instruments to further explore adolescent's gender predispositions to nicotinism.

Keywords: childhood abuse, nicotinism, puff topography, APOE carrier, Alzheimer's disease, nicotine patch, nicotine gum addiction, coumarin derivatives, gender predisposition

Introduction

Recent studies have highlighted that the incidence of nicotinism is more prevalent among smokers with a history of childhood abuse as compared to those who did not had history of childhood abuse. Primarily three main types of childhood abuse were included: (i) physical, (ii) psychological, and (iii) verbal. However, it remains unknown, which particular type of childhood abuse is more responsible for nicotinism in later life. Whether these three types of childhood abuses exert additive or synergistic effect also remains unknown. The unresolved issue is the association of nicotinism with the prevalence of Alzheimer's disease (AD). It has been now resolved that those who are APOE carriers and smoking cigarettes are more likely to have increased incidence of AD neuropathology as assessed by estimating cortical amyloid deposition, glucose metabolism, and neurocognition.

This chapter describes the prevalence of nicotinism among smokers with a history of childhood abuse, cigarette smoking among APOE carriers and (AD), dual trajectories of cigarette smoking and smokeless tobacco abuse. A description of smoking patterns and cessation attempts, reliability and stability of puff topography variables in non-daily smokers, and nicotine patch for the treatment of nicotine gum addiction is provided. The chapter also highlights that individuals with childhood physical, psychological, and verbal abuse are more vulnerable to nicotinism and its withdrawal symptoms, persons with APOE carrier gene are more susceptible to nicotine -induced AD, and smoking status confirmation by proxy and nicotine patch can be utilized for the safe and effective treatment of nicotinisms and nicotine gum addiction.

Nicotinism among Smokers with a History of Childhood Abuse

Earlier studies have found that those with a history of childhood abuse are more likely to smoke cigarettes than those without a history of abuse. Mechanisms underlying this greater prevalence are unclear. Hence, Smith et al., (2013) examined whether current smokers with a history of childhood abuse reported greater levels of nicotine dependence and more severe nicotine withdrawal symptoms. These investigators analyzed data from a 2-wave, national, random-digit-dial survey of adult cigarette smokers (n = 751) and examined whether childhood physical, emotional, and sexual abuse were associated with greater levels of nicotine dependence. Among those who made a quit attempt (n = 368), they examined whether abuse was associated with more severe withdrawal symptoms recalled during the 14 months between surveys. For both dependence and withdrawal, they tested a mediation pathway through current serious mental illness (SMI). All 3 types of childhood abuse were associated with more severe withdrawal symptoms. These associations were partially mediated by SMI. Sexual abuse and physical abuse were directly associated with dependence, whereas emotional abuse was indirectly associated with dependence through SMI. All 3 forms of childhood abuse were associated with both dependence and withdrawal. The greater prevalence of smoking found among those with a history of childhood abuse may be explained by heightened vulnerability to nicotine dependence and withdrawal and may be partially due to comorbid mental illness.

Cigarette Smoking among APOE Carriers and Alzheimer's Disease

It has been recognized that chronic cigarette smoking is associated with increased risk for Alzheimer's disease (AD). Recently, Durazzo et al. (2016). Recently conducted a study to determine if smoking history moderated the associations of age and APOE genotype (the most robust risk factors for AD) on brain amyloid deposition, glucose metabolism, and neurocognition in cognitively-normal elders. These investigators grouped 264 participants according to their APOE ε4 carrier status (ε4 carrier: APOE4+; non-ε4 carrier: APOE4-) and smoking status (smokers: at least 1 year of smoking during lifetime; never-smokers: no history of smoking). ~89% of the smoking sample was former-smokers. They tested for interactions of smoking status with APOE ε4 carrier status and age on measures of cortical amyloid deposition, glucose metabolism, and neurocognition. (1) smoking status interacted with APOE ε4 carrier status, where smoker APOE4+ showed lower glucose metabolism and poorer auditory-verbal learning and memory than never-smoking APOE4-, never-smoking APOE4+, and smoking APOE4-; (2) smoking status interacted with age on measures of semantic fluency, processing speed/set-shifting and global neurocognition; smokers, irrespective of APOE ε4 carrier status, demonstrated poorer performance with increasing age than never-smokers; and (3) smoking APOE4+ and never-smoking APOE4+ showed greater cortical amyloid deposition than never-smoking APOE4- and smoking APOE4, indicating that consideration of smoking history is essential to better understand the factors associated with neurobiological and neurocognitive abnormalities in elders, and the risk for development of AD-related neuropathology.

Reliability and Stability of Puff Topography Variables in Non-Daily Smokers

Puff topography variables, often measured using the Clinical Research Support System device, have traditionally been studied in regular, daily smokers and have been shown to be highly stable. However, more recent research has focused on non-daily smokers. Hence, Gass et al., (2016) examined puff topography stability (cross-cigarette agreement over time) and reliability (within-cigarette consistency) in non-daily smokers across six lab sessions. A sum of 107 non-daily smokers attended six lab sessions over the course of 3 months. At each session, they smoked one cigarette through the Clinical Research Support System pocket, in addition to completing questionnaires about their smoking history and dependence. Puff topography measurements were highly reliable and puff behavior was highly stable across sessions. Adding sessions substantially improved reliability estimates. Aspects of puffing behavior observed in session, including puff volume, puff duration, time of puff peak, and total cigarette volume were related to level of smoke exposure, measured by expired carbon monoxide. Instability in puffing behavior was not predicted by recent or long-term smoking patterns. This study concluded that puff topography appeared to be a stable and routinized aspect of smoking in non-daily smokers. The feasibility of assessing puff topography in this population is supported by the high reliabilities observed, though reliability improved by having more than one session.

Smoking Status Confirmation by Proxy

Biochemical confirmation (BC) of self-report is the gold standard of evidence for abstinence in smoking cessation research, but difficulty in obtaining samples may bias estimates of quit rates. Proxy confirmation (PC) has not been validated in cessation trials. Regan et al., (2016) recently assessed the feasibility and validity of PC in a cessation trial for hospitalized smokers. They enrolled 402 daily cigarette smokers during a hospital admission. At enrollment, participants provided demographics, smoking history, and named proxies to confirm their smoking status at follow-up. Participants provided self-reported (SR) 7-day tobacco abstinence by telephone at 6 months post-discharge. SR quitters were asked to mail a saliva sample for BC. Incentives were offered for survey completion ($20) and returned samples ($50). They called proxies for all those with SR to obtain PC. Quit rates were calculated with missing data indicating smoking. They assessed associations of nonresponse with baseline characteristics using chi-squared tests and logistic regression and calculated the sensitivity and specificity of PC in detecting smokers as determined by BC. All patients named at least one proxy. Response rates were 82% for SR, 84% for PC, and 69% for BC. Observed participant characteristics were unrelated to provision of sample for BC. Estimated quit rates were 35% for SR, 27% for SR + PC, 21% for SR + BC and 27% for SR + BC or PC. Sensitivity of PC was not higher than SR (73% vs. 77%); specificity was lower (84% vs. 100%), indicating that PC was feasible but not superior to self-report in a cessation trial.

Smoking Patterns, and Cessation Attempts

Although, associations between reports of minority stressors and smoking behaviors among lesbian, gay, and bisexual populations; there is very limited information about how minority stressors are related to smoking behaviors and cessation attempts among transgender women. Hence, Gamarel et al., (2016) performed a study (1) to examine the associations between transgender-based discrimination and smoking patterns among a sample of transgender women; and (2) to identify barriers to smoking cessation in a sample of transgender women with a history of smoking. A community sample of 241 transgender women completed a one-time survey. Binary and multinomial logistic regression models examined associations between minority stressors and (1) smoking behaviors and (2) cessation attempts. Both models adjusted for income, education, race/ethnicity, recent sex work, HIV status, depression, alcohol use, and current hormone use. Overall, 83% of participants indicated that they had smoked a cigarette in the last month. Of these women, 62.3% reported daily smoking and 51.7% reported an unsuccessful quit attempt. Discrimination was associated with currently smoking. Discrimination was positively associated with unsuccessful cessation compared to successful cessation. Discrimination was also positively associated with never attempting compared to unsuccessful cessation, indicating that smoking cessation may be driven by unique transgender-related minority stressors, such as discrimination. Based on this study, these investigators recommended future research to address stigmatizing contexts when understanding and providing tailored intervention addressing smoking among transgender women.

Dual Trajectories of Cigarette Smoking and Smokeless Tobacco Abuse

Identifying trajectories of tobacco abuse is critical for understanding its natural history and targeting interventions, but research on trajectories of smokeless tobacco and dual use of smokeless tobacco and cigarettes is very limited. Macy et al., (2016) recently conducted a study to identify tobacco use trajectories from adolescence to midlife and tested correlates of trajectory group membership. They included all male participants in this study who reported cigarette smoking or smokeless tobacco use in 1987, 1993, 1999, 2005, or 2011 (N = 2230). Group-based trajectory analyses were conducted with zero-inflated Poisson models. Analysis of covariance was used to test adolescent health beliefs associated with trajectory group membership. Five smoking trajectory groups were identified: (1) consistent abstinence from cigarettes; (2) late onset intermittent, then cessation; (3) early onset regular, then cessation; (4) delayed onset regular, then cessation; and (5) consistent regular. Four smokeless tobacco trajectory groups were identified: (1) early onset, then cessation; (2) consistent abstinence from smokeless tobacco; (3) late onset, escalating; and (4) consistent regular. The proportion of participants in trajectory groups representing dual use was low. Adolescent beliefs favorable to smoking and smokeless tobacco were associated with membership in consistent regular use groups. The prevalence of dual use of cigarettes and smokeless tobacco was low, and there was some evidence to suggest switching between tobacco products. Participants who held more positive beliefs about smoking and smokeless

Nicotine Patch for the Treatment of Nicotine Gum Addiction

Some long-term nicotine gum users are addicted to nicotine and may need assistance to stop. There is no experimental evidence on the use of nicotine patches for this purpose. Mendelsohn (2016) reported a case of a 45-year old man presented with a 30-year history of high-dose nicotine gum use (up to 200mg nicotine per day). He was highly nicotine dependent and had failed repeatedly to stop using nicotine gum use in the past. Within a week of commencing nicotine patches he was able to cease nicotine gum with minimal discomfort and remained nicotine-free for 6 months, with abstinence confirmed biochemically. His severe sweating disorder rapidly resolved with cessation of the gum, indicating that nicotine patches may be an effective treatment for long-term nicotine gum addiction.

Coumarins-Mediated Modulation of the Behavioral Effects of Nicotine

Nicotine, a dominant alkaloid found in tobacco, is responsible for physical tolerance and dependence, as well as addiction to cigarette smoking; consequently, smoking cessation is a very difficult process. Hepatic cytochrome P-450 2A6 (CYP2A6) is involved in the 70-80% of the initial metabolism of nicotine and its co-metabolites. As this metabolism is slowed by inhibitors of CYP2A6, this kind of enzymatic inhibition has been proposed as a novel target for smoking cessation. In a study, Budzynska et al., (2016) demonstrated that nicotine administered alone improved memory acquisition and consolidation as well as exerted antidepressive activity in animal models. These effects persisted for 24 hrs. However, these effects were completely extinguished 48 hrs. after administration. These researchers investigated if the coumarins prolong the behavioral effects of nicotine in the forced swimming test (FST)-animal models of depression, and passive avoidance (PA) test-memory and learning. This study revealed that three CYP2A6 inhibitors: two furanocoumarins, xanthotoxin (15 mg/kg) and bergapten (25 mg/kg), and the coumarin umbelliferone (25 mg/kg), prolonged the antidepressive and procognitive effects of nicotine, indicating that these natural products may offer a novel approach for the treatment of nicotinism as antidepressant and memory improvement involved in nicotine dependence.

The Effects of Anti-Tobacco Health Education Program with Respect to Nicotinism among Boys and Girls

It is being recognized that health education used for increasing the effectiveness of intervention actions should cover a number of factors which exert an effect on learning. Kanicka et al., (2013) conducted a study with a primary objective to recognize the extent to which gender may determine the effects of an anti-tobacco health education program. The intervention study covered 859 first-year school children. The sample was selected by means of two-stage stratified sampling with consideration of two groups: an intervention group and a control group. In the group of girls, the 2-year educational program resulted in an increase in knowledge concerning the negative effects of cigarette smoking by 21%, and being familiar with anti-tobacco actions and campaigns carried out in Poland by 24.5%. Among boys, an increase was observed only with respect to the knowledge of anti-tobacco actions and campaigns - by 10.7%. Considering the attitudes of girls after the completion of the program, changes were noted with respect to three from among the six elements analyzed. However, among boys, after completion of the project, no changes were noted in any of the analyzed elements of attitude. In girls who participated in the anti-nicotine program, the percentage of smokers did not increase, while an increase in this percentage was observed among girls of the control group and boys in both groups, indicating that different effects of the 2-year anti-tobacco program obtained in the area of knowledge, attitude and behavior should constitute a premise for the modification of educational programs from the aspect of the variety of techniques and instruments which would be adequate for adolescents' predispositions resulting from their gender.

References

Budzynska, B., Skalicka-Wozniak, K., Kruk-Slomka, M., Wydrzynska-Kuzma, M., Biala, G., 2016. In vivo modulation of the behavioral effects of nicotine by the coumarins xanthotoxin, bergapten, and umbelliferone. *Psychopharmacology* (Berl). 233(12), 2289-300.

Durazzo, T. C., Mattsson, N., Weiner, M. W., 2016. Alzheimer's Disease Neuroimaging Initiative. Interaction of Cigarette Smoking History With APOE Genotype and Age on Amyloid Level, Glucose Metabolism, and Neurocognition in Cognitively Normal Elders. *Nicotine Tob Res*. 18(2), 204-211.

Gamarel, K. E., Mereish, E. H., Manning, D., Iwamoto, M., Operario, D., Nemoto, T., 2016. Minority Stress, Smoking Patterns, and Cessation Attempts: Findings from a Community-Sample of Transgender Women in the San Francisco Bay Area. *Nicotine Tob Res*. 18(3), 306-313.

Gass, J. C., Germeroth, L. J., Wray, J. M., Tiffany, S. T., 2016. The Reliability and Stability of Puff Topography Variables in Non-Daily Smokers Assessed in the Laboratory. *Nicotine Tob Res*. 18(4), 484-490.

Kanicka, M., Poniatowski, B., Szpak, A., Owoc, A., 2013. Differences in the effects of anti-tobacco health education programme in the areas of knowledge, attitude and behavior, with respect to nicotinism among boys and girls. *Ann Agric Environ Med.* 20(1), 173-177.

Macy, J. T., Li, J., Xun, P., Presson, C. C., Chassin, L., 2016. Dual Trajectories of Cigarette Smoking and Smokeless Tobacco Use From Adolescence to Midlife Among Males in a Midwestern US Community Sample. *Nicotine Tob Res*. 18(2), 186-195.

Mendelsohn, C. P., 2016. Three Decades of High-Dose Nicotine Gum Dependence Treated With Nicotine Patches. *Nicotine Tob Res.* 18(5), 1220-1221.

Regan, S., Reid, Z. Z., Kelley, J. H., Reyen, M., Korotkin, M., Japuntich, S. J., Viana, J. C., Levy, D. E., Rigotti, N. A., 2016. Smoking Status Confirmation by Proxy: Validation in a Smoking Cessation Trial. *Nicotine Tob Res.* 18(1), 34-40.

Smith, P. H., Homish, G. G., Saddleson, M. L., Kozlowski, L. T., Giovino, G. A., 2013. Nicotine withdrawal and dependence among smokers with a history of childhood abuse. *Nicotine Tob Res.* 15(12), 2016-2021.

Chapter 5

Pharmacogenomics of Nicotinism

Abstract

This chapter describes recent update on the pharmacogenomics of nicotinism. Recently, pharmacogenomics, pharmacokinetics, and metabolism of nicotine and cotinine were evaluated in African American smokers. Another study established the longitudinal effects of CYP2A6 in young adolescent smokers and iNOS and TNF-α were proposed in nutritional intervention against nicotine-induced pancreatic islet cell damage. Particularly, metabolomic profiling of pre-term neonatal urinary renal development and acute kidney injury were observed in children exposed to intrauterine nicotine. In addition, ethnic differences in cytochrome P450-(2A6) induced nicotine metabolism and smoking have been established. Alcohol and nicotine codependence were associated with changes in DNA methylation in the promoter regions of addiction-related genes. The nicotine metabolism was altered in young adult daily menthol and nonmenthol smokers. Notably, a remarkable heritability was noticed in the initiation and persistence of smoking and nicotine dependence. To date, the only candidate genes with consistent evidence of an association with smoking behavior or nicotine dependence are CYP2A6 and 5HTT and SNPs in the CHRNA5/A3/B4 gene cluster. It has been demonstrated that withdrawal symptoms remain persistent and severe for several months after an attempt to stop smoking, and there was a significant heterogeneity in these symptoms. Thus, features such as severity, variability, and the course of withdrawal symptoms conferred intense risk for relapse. Recent studies also identified biochemical differences among smokers. Potential biomarkers of nicotinism have been proposed. These biomarkers can be screened in urine and saliva samples by utilizing atmospheric pressure solid analysis probe (ASAP) and high resolution mass spectrometry with quadrupole and time of flight (ASAP-MS-Q-TOF) detector. It has been identified that maternal smoking significantly alters the cytokine profile and circulating immunoglobulin levels of newborn infants. Another promising biomarkers of tobacco exposure include quantification of 8-hydroxy-2'-deoxy-guanosine (a mitochondrial DNA oxidation product involved in CB formation, charnolophagy, and CS destabilization) and cotinine (a major metabolism of nicotine), which can be estimated from human urine by solid-phase extraction liquid chromatography with tandem mass spectrometry (LC-MS/MS). These biomarkers can be utilized to quantitatively assess the levels of tobacco exposure to the newborn infant as well as tobacco smoking mother for their health and well-being.

Keywords: pharmacogenomics, nicotinism, pharmcokinetics, nicotine exposure biomarkers, 8-hydroxy-2'-deoxy-guanosine (8-OH, 2dG), charnoly body, charnolophagy, charnolosome destabilization, cotinine, cytochrome P450-(2A6), metalomics, CYP2A6, 5HTT, single nucleotide polymorphism (SNPs) CHRNA5/A3/B4 gene cluster, solid-phase extraction liquid chromatography with tandem mass spectrometry (LC-MS/MS), atmospheric pressure solid analysis probe (ASAP) and high resolution mass spectrometry with quadrupole and time of flight (ASAP-MS-Q-TOF) detector

Introduction

Recent studies were performed to establish the pharmacogenomics of nicotinism. A study evaluated pharmacogenomics, pharmacokinetics, and metabolism of nicotine and cotinine in African American smokers. Another study established the longitudinal effects of CYP2A6 in young adolescent smokers and proposed iNOS and TNF-α in nutritional intervention against nicotine -induced pancreatic islet cell damage.

Metabolomic profiling of pre-term neonatal urinary renal developmental and acute kidney injury in children exposed to intrauterine nicotine and ethnic differences in P450-(2A6) induced nicotine metabolism and smoking and association of Alcohol and nicotine codependence with changes in DNA methylation in the promoter regions of addiction-related genes were established. The nicotine metabolism was altered in young adult daily menthol and nonmenthol smokers.

Recent studies established a remarkable heritability in the initiation and persistence of smoking and nicotine dependence. In addition, CYP2A6 and 5HTT and SNPs in the CHRNA5/A3/B4 gene cluster were established as promising candidate genes with evidence of an association with smoking behavior or nicotine dependence. Nicotine withdrawal symptoms were persistent and often severe for several months even after an attempt to stop smoking and there was a great heterogeneity in the symptoms. Severity, variability, and the course of withdrawal symptoms conferred intense risk for relapse. Moreover, biochemical differences were also noticed among smokers.

Recently, potential biomarkers of nicotinism were proposed, which can be screened in urine and saliva samples by ASAP-MS-Q-TOF. Maternal smoking significantly altered the cytokine profile and circulating immunoglobulin levels of newborn infants. Promising biomarkers of tobacco exposure included 8-hydroxy-2'-deoxy-guanosine (a mitochondrial DNA oxidation product involved in CB formation, charnolophagy, and CS destabilization) and cotinine (a major metabolism of nicotine) which can be estimated from human urine by LC-MS/MS. These biomarkers can be utilized to quantitatively assess the levels of tobacco exposure to the newborn infant as well as tobacco smoking mother, as described systematically in this chapter.

Pharmacogenomics, Pharmacokinetics, and Metabolism of Nicotine and Cotinine in African American Smokers

The rate of nicotine metabolism, determined primarily by CYP2A6 activity, influences tobacco dependence and smoking-induced disease risk. The prevalence of CYP2A6 gene variants differs by race, with greater numbers in African Americans compared with Caucasians. Recently, Benowitz et al., (2016) studied nicotine disposition kinetics and metabolism by the CYP2A6 genotype and enzymatic activity, as measured by the nicotine metabolite ratio (NMR), in African American smokers. Participants received i.v. infusions of deuterium-labeled nicotine and cotinine. Plasma and urine concentrations of nicotine and metabolites were measured and pharmacokinetic parameters were estimated. Pharmacokinetic parameters and urine metabolite excretion data were analyzed by CYP2A6 genotype and by NMR. A number of gene variants were associated with markedly reduced nicotine and cotinine clearances. NMR was correlated with nicotine and cotinine clearances. Participants with higher NMR excreted significantly greater nicotine C-oxidation and lower non-C-oxidation products compared with lower NMR participants. Based on these findings, these investigators concluded that CYP2A6 genotype, NMR, and nicotine pharmacokinetic data may inform studies of individual differences in smoking behavior and biomarkers of nicotine exposure.

CYP2A6 Longitudinal Effects in Young Smokers

In a recent study, Cannon et al., (2016) sought to identify time-dependent within-participant effects of CYP2A6 genotypes on smoking frequency and nicotine dependence in young smokers. Predicted nicotine metabolic rate based on CYP2A6 diplotypes (CYP2A6 diplotype predicted rate [CDPR]) was partitioned into Normal, Intermediate, and Slow categories using a metabolism metric. Growth-curve models characterized baseline and longitudinal CDPR effects with data from eight longitudinal assessments during a 6-year period (from approximately age 16-22) in young smokers of European descent (N = 296, 57% female) who had smoked less than 100 cigarettes lifetime at baseline and more than that amount by Year 6. Phenotypes were number of days smoked during the previous 30 days and a youth version of the Nicotine Dependence Syndrome Scale (NDSS). A zero-inflated Poisson growth-curve model was used to account for the preponderance of zero days smoked. At baseline, Intermediate CDPR was a risk factor relative to both Normal and Slow CDPR for smoking frequency and the NDSS. Slow CDPR was associated with the highest probability of smoking discontinuation at baseline. However, due to CDPR time trend differences, by young adulthood these baseline effects had been reordered such that the greatest risks for smoking frequency and the NDSS were associated with Normal CDPR, indicating that reduced metabolism CYP2A6 genotypes are associated with both risk and protective effects in novice smokers. However, differences in the time-by-CDPR effects result in a reordering of genotype effects such that normal metabolism becomes the risk variant by young adulthood, as has been reported in older smokers.

INOS and TNF-α in Nutritional Intervention against Nicotine-Induced Pancreatic Islet Cell Damage

It is well established that nicotine is the more abundant and most significant components of cigarette smoke. Epidemiological evidence has suggested an association between cigarette smoking and pancreatic injury. Although effects of smoking on endocrine pancreas are still controversial. Bhattacharjee et al., (2016) examined the impact and underlying mechanisms of action of Folic acid and Vitamin B_{12} on nicotine-induced damage in pancreatic islets of rats. These investigators treated male Wistar rats with nicotine (3mg/kg body weight/day, i.p) with or without Folic acid (36µg/kg body weight/day, orally) and Vitamin B_{12} (0.63µg/kg body weight/day, orally) for 21days. Supplementation with Folic acid and Vitamin B_{12} suppressed the nicotine-induced changes in HbA1c, Insulin, TNF-α, IL-6, generation of reactive oxygen species (ROS), and attenuated the changes in the biomarkers of oxidative stress. Folic acid and Vitamin B_{12} also counteracted the increased expression of protein and mRNA contents of TNF-α and iNOS produced by nicotine. Further, Folic acid and Vitamin B_{12} in combination limited the nicotine-induced changes in cell cycle and excessive apoptosis of the pancreatic β-cells and also attenuated nicotine-induced loss of mitochondrial membrane potential ($\Delta\Psi$) suggesting that Folic acid and Vitamin B_{12} may be possible nutritional intervention against cellular oxidative stress, which is a critical step in nicotine-mediated islet injury, and improves islet cell functional status by scavenging free radicals and by inhibiting the generation of pro-inflammatory mediators, involved in CB formation, charnolophagy, and CS destabilization.

Metabolomic Profiling of Pre-term Neonatal Urinary Renal Developmental and Acute Kidney Injury

Acute kidney injury (AKI) staging has been developed in the adult and pediatric populations, but these do not yet exist for the neonatal population. Recently, Mercier et al., (2017) utilized metabolomics to uncover biomarkers of normal and AKI-associated renal function in preterm infants. The study comprised 20 preterm infants with an AKI diagnosis who were matched by gestational age and gender to 20 infants without an AKI diagnosis. Urine samples from pre-term newborn infants collected on day 2 of life were analyzed using broad-spectrum NMR metabolomics. Multivariate analysis were used to identify metabolite profiles that differentiated AKI and no AKI, and to identify a metabolomics profile correlating with gestational age in infants with and without AKI. There was a clear distinction between the AKI and no-AKI profiles. Two previously identified biomarkers of AKI, hippurate and homovanillate, differentiated AKI from no-AKI profiles. Pathway analysis revealed similarities to cholinergic neurons, prenatal nicotine exposure on pancreatic β cells, and amitraz-induced inhibition of Insulin secretion. Additionally, a pH difference was noted. Both pH and the metabolites were associated with AKI; however, only the metabotype was a significant predictor of AKI. Pathways for the no-AKI group that correlated uniquely with gestational age included aminoacyl-t-RNA biosynthesis, whereas pathways in the AKI group yielded potential metabolite changes in pyruvate metabolism. Metabolomics was able to differentiate the urinary profiles of neonates with and without an AKI diagnosis and metabolic developmental profiles correlated with gestational age. Further studies in larger cohorts are needed to validate these findings.

Nicotine Metabolism and Smoking: Ethnic Differences in the Role of P450

It is known that nicotine is the primary addictive agent in tobacco, and P450 2A6 (gene name: CYP2A6) is the primary catalyst of nicotine metabolism. Murphy (2017) proposed >20 years ago that individuals who metabolize nicotine poorly would smoke less, either fewer cigarettes per day or less intensely per cigarette, compared to smokers who metabolize nicotine more efficiently. These poor metabolizers would then be less likely to develop lung cancer due to their lower exposure to the many carcinogens delivered with nicotine in each puff of smoke. Numerous studies have reported that smokers who carry reduced activity or null CYP2A6 alleles do smoke less. Yet only in Asian populations, both Japanese and Chinese, which have a high prevalence of genetic variants, has a link between CYP2A6, smoking dose, and lung cancer been established. In other ethnic groups, it has been challenging to confirm a direct link between P450 2A6-mediated nicotine metabolism and the risk of lung cancer. This challenge is due in part to the difficulty in accurately quantifying smoking dose and accurately predicting or measuring P450-2A6-mediated nicotine metabolism. Biomarkers of nicotine metabolism and smoking exposure, including the ratio of trans-3-hydroxycotine to cotinine, a measure of P450 2A6 activity and plasma cotinine, or urinary total nicotine equivalents (the sum of nicotine and six metabolites) as measures of exposure are useful for addressing this challenge. However, to take full advantage of these biomarkers in the study of ethnic/racial differences in the risk of lung cancer requires the complete characterization of nicotine metabolism across ethnic/racial groups. Variation in metabolism pathways, other than those catalyzed by P450 2A6, can impact biomarkers of both nicotine metabolism and dose. This is obviously important for smokers with low levels of UGT2B10-catalyzed nicotine and cotinine glucuronidation because the UGT2B10 genotype influences plasma cotinine levels. Cotinine is not glucuronidated in 15% of African American smokers (compared to 1% of Whites) due to the prevalence of a UGT2B10 splice variant. This variant contributes significantly to the higher plasma cotinine levels per cigarette in this group and may also influence the accuracy of the 3HCOT to cotinine ratio as a measure of P450 2A6 activity.

Alcohol and Nicotine Co-Dependence-Associated Changes in DNA Methylation in Promoter Regions of Addiction-Related Genes

It is now realized that altered DNA methylation in addiction-related genes may modify the susceptibility to alcohol or drug dependence (AD or ND). Hence, Xu et al., (2017) profiled peripheral blood DNA methylation levels of 384 CpGs in the promoter regions of 82 addiction-related genes in 256 African Americans (AAs) (117 cases with AD-ND codependence and 139 controls) and 196 European Americans (103 cases with AD-ND codependence and 93 controls) using Illumina's Golden Gate DNA methylation array assays. AD-ND co-dependence-associated DNA methylation changes were analyzed using linear mixed-effects models with consideration of batch effects and covariates age, sex, and ancestry proportions. Seventy CpGs (in 41 genes) showed significant associations with AD-ND codependence in both AAs and EAs. One CpG (HTR2B cg27531267) was hypomethylated in AA cases ($P = 7.2 \times 10^{-5}$), while 17 CpGs in 16 genes (including HTR2B cg27531267) were hypermethylated in EA cases ($5.6 \times 10^{-9} \leq P \leq 9.5 \times 10^{-5}$). Nevertheless, 13 single nucleotide polymorphisms (SNPs) nearby HTR2B cg27531267 and the interaction of these SNPs and cg27531267 did not show significant effects on AD-ND codependence in either AAs or EAs, indicating that DNA methylation changes in addiction-related genes could be potential biomarkers for AD-ND co-dependence. Future studies need to explore whether DNA methylation alterations influence the risk of AD-ND co-dependence or the other way around.

The Prototoxin LYPD6B Modulates Heteromeric α3β4-Containing Nicotinic Acetylcholine Receptors

Prototoxins are a diverse family of membrane-tethered molecules expressed in the nervous system that modulate nicotinic cholinergic signaling, but their functions and specificity have yet to be completely explored. In a recent study, Ochoa et al., (2016) tested the selectivity and efficacy of leukocyte antigen, PLAUR (plasminogen activator, urokinase receptor) domain-containing (LYPD)-6B on α3β4-, α3α5β4-, and α7-containing nicotinic acetylcholine receptors (nAChRs). To constrain stoichiometry, fusion proteins encoding concatemers of human α3, β4, and α5 (D and N variants) subunits were expressed in Xenopus laevis oocytes and tested with or without LYPD6B. These investigators used the 2-electrode voltage-clamp to quantify responses to acetylcholine (ACh): agonist sensitivity (EC50), maximal agonist-induced current (IMAX), and time constant (τ) of desensitization. For β4-α3-α3-β4-α3 and β4-α3-β4-α3-α3, LYPD6B decreased EC50 from 631 to 79 µM, reduced IMAX by at least 59%, and decreased τ. For β4-α3-α5D-β4-α3 and β4-α3-β4-α-α5D, LYPD6B decreased IMAX by 63 and 32%, respectively. Thus, LYPD6B acted only on (α3)3(β4)2 and (α3)2(α5D)(β4)2 and did not affect the properties of (α3)2(β4)3, α7, or (α3)2(α5N)(β4)2 nAChRs. Based on these findings they concluded that LYPD6B acts as a mixed modulator that enhances the sensitivity of (α3)3(β4)2 nAChRs to ACh while reducing ACh-induced whole-cell currents. LYPD6B also negatively modulates α3β4 nAChRs that include the α5D common human variant, but not the N variant associated with nicotine dependence.

Nicotine Metabolism in Young Adult Daily Menthol and Nonmenthol Smokers

Menthol cigarette smoking may increase the risk for tobacco smoke exposure and inhibit nicotine metabolism in the liver. Nicotine metabolism is primarily mediated by the enzyme CYP2A6 and the nicotine metabolite ratio (NMR = Trans 3' hydroxyl cotinine/cotinine) is a phenotypic proxy for CYP2A6 activity. No studies have examined differences in this biomarker among young adult daily menthol and nonmenthol smokers. Fagan et al., (2016) recently compared biomarkers of tobacco smoke exposure among young adult daily menthol and nonmenthol smokers. Saliva cotinine and carbon monoxide were measured in a multiethnic sample of daily smokers aged 18-35 (n = 186). Nicotine, cotinine, the cotinine/cigarette per day ratio, Tran's 3' hydroxyl cotinine, the NMR, and expired carbon monoxide were compared. The geometric means for nicotine, cotinine, and the cotinine/cigarette per day ratio did not significantly differ between menthol and nonmenthol smokers. The NMR was significantly lower among Menthol compared with nonmenthol smokers after adjusting for race/ethnicity, gender, body mass index, and cigarette smoked per day. White menthol smokers had significantly higher cotinine/cigarettes per day ratio than white nonmenthol smokers in the adjusted model. White menthol smokers had a lower NMR in the unadjusted model and the differences remained marginally significant in the adjusted model. These investigators did not observe these differences in Native Hawaiians and Filipinos. Young adult daily Menthol smokers had slower rates of nicotine metabolism than nonmenthol smokers. Hence, further studies are needed to determine the utility of this biomarker for smoking cessation treatment assignments.

Initiation and Persistence of Smoking and Nicotine Dependence Show Strong Heritability

Most coefficients of reported heritability range from less than 0.3 to >0.8 and vary on the basis of the smoking behavior phenotype examined and the social or environmental factors such as prevalence of smoking. The balance of evidence suggests that the risk of smoking initiation is influenced by both genetic and environmental factors, whereas the risk of smoking persistence may have a stronger genetic component. Although some genetic influences on smoking initiation and persistence are common, there are also separate and unique genetic influences for initiation and for persistence. Studies also suggest that the ability to stop smoking is under a strong genetic influence, and some consider this phenotype to be the key behavioral phenotype for nicotine dependence. Molecular genetic studies have been conducted to examine the specific genetic factors and biologic mechanisms involved in nicotine addiction. Most of the candidate gene studies have focused on genetic variation in nAChRs, relevant neurotransmitter pathways, or genes for nicotine-metabolizing enzymes. Candidate gene studies are association-based studies comparing prevalence of candidate gene variants in two unrelated groups—for example, nicotine-dependent versus nondependent persons. Examples of candidate gene variants that have been examined include nAChR subunits, such as CHRNA4 and CHRNA5; DA receptors D2 and D4 (DRD2 and DRD4) and DA transporter (DAT) genes; tryptophan hydroxylase, which is associated with serotonin biosynthesis; serotonin transporter 5HTTLPR, which is associated with genes that code for serotonin reuptake; MAOA and DβH genes, which affect NEergic pathways; genes in the endogenous opioid pathway (e.g., OPRM1); and genes involved in the metabolism of nicotine (e.g., CYP2A6).

To date, the only candidate genes with consistent evidence of an association with smoking behavior or nicotine dependence are CYP2A6 and 5HTT and SNPs in the CHRNA5/A3/B4 gene cluster. More research has been conducted on the effects of CYP2A6. Variants of P-450 CYP2A6 associated with *NULL or reduced activity are associated with reduced levels of the CYP2A6 enzyme and slower rates of nicotine metabolism, leading to higher plasma levels of nicotine for a given dose of nicotine. Persons who carry these variants with *NULL or reduced activity tend to have lower risk for becoming smokers, reduced cigarette consumption, and possibly higher likelihood of successful smoking cessation than that for persons with wild-type genotypes and higher rates of nicotine metabolism. Research in this area will be greatly enhanced when there is agreement in the field on phenotypes for smoking initiation, trajectory toward nicotine dependence, and nicotine dependence. One area of research that has provided promising evidence is the pharmacogenetics of treatment to aid in smoking cessation, which included examining genetic variations in drug-metabolizing enzymes and variations in drug targets to predict responses to treatment. It is important to recognize that although genes may play an important role in the various aspects of smoking behavior, the risk for smoking exists in persons without the gene variants, and it is predominantly exposure, rather than the host, that leads to smoking- related illnesses.

Studying recovery from smoking can provide valuable information on the nature of tobacco addiction and the factors that affect it. Relapse to smoking occurs at a high rate, and most smokers who ultimately relapse resume smoking early after the attempt to stop smoking. The risk for relapse is particularly high among those who lapse or engage in a single episode of smoking after their first day of cessation. The pattern of return to smoking varies across individuals. However, on average, a second lapse occurs within 24 hrs. Of the first lapse, and lapse to relapse occurs three to five weeks after the cessation attempt. Several multidimensional factors may be associated with relapse. These factors include the expectations that the effects from smoking will be rewarding, confidence in the ability to stop smoking, educational status, and degree of tobacco dependence. Situational indicators suggest that temptations to smoke and smoking lapse and relapse are associated with alcohol use and environmental signals such as the sight of others smoking and the availability of cigarettes.

Evidence supports the relationship of tobacco withdrawal syndrome with vulnerability to relapse. Studies show three important findings for many smokers: (1) withdrawal symptoms are persistent and often severe for several months after an attempt to stop smoking, (2) the heterogeneity in withdrawal symptoms is great, and (3) features such as the severity, variability, and the course of withdrawal symptoms confer increased risk for relapse. Craving and negative affect are the withdrawal symptoms most predictive of relapse, including urges to smoke that are experienced immediately after awakening in the morning. Research suggests complex interrelationships within and across the different types of influences. Future research is needed to elucidate these interactions.

Identification of Biochemical Differences in Smokers

Determining perturbed biochemical functions associated with tobacco smoking should be helpful for establishing causal relationships between exposure and adverse events. Recently, Kaluarachchi et al., (2016) conducted a multiplatform comparison of serum of smokers (n = 55) and never-smokers (n = 57) using nuclear magnetic resonance spectroscopy, UPLC-MS and statistical modeling revealed clustering of the classes, distinguished by metabolic biomarkers. The identified metabolites were subjected to metabolic pathway enrichment, modeling adverse biological events using available databases. Perturbation of metabolites involved in chronic obstructive pulmonary disease, cardiovascular diseases and cancer were identified and discussed. Combining multiplatform metabolic phenotyping with knowledge-based mapping provided mechanistic insights into disease development, which can be applied to next-generation tobacco and nicotine products for comparative risk assessment.

Biomarkers of Nicotinism

Screening of Tobacco Biomarkers in Urine and Saliva by ASAP-MS-Q-TOF

Recently, Carrizo et al., (2016) developed a new screening for direct analysis of tobacco smoke biomarkers in the saliva and urine. Single run analysis using Atmospheric pressure Solid Analysis Probe (ASAP) and high resolution mass spectrometry with quadrupole and time of flight detector has been applied directly to some urine and saliva samples, providing a fast, efficient and sensitive identification. The procedure was applied to saliva and urine samples from heavy tobacco smokers for exposure studies. Nicotine itself, nicotine metabolites (i.e., cotinine, trans-3'-hydroxycotinine, nicotine -N-glucuronide) and other related tobacco smoke toxic compounds (i.e., NNK 4-[methyl (nitroso) amino]-1-(3-pyridinyl)-1-butanone, anatabine) were found in the analyzed samples. The identification of compounds was confirmed by ultrahigh performance liquid chromatography with MS-triple quadrupole detector after sample treatment. Different temporal trends and biomarkers behavior were found in time series related samples. Both were compared for screening of these biological matrices.

Maternal Smoking and Newborn Cytokine and Immunoglobulin Levels

It is now recognized that prenatal smoking exposure may lead to permanent changes in neonatal inflammation and immune response that have lifelong increased risks for atopy and respiratory disorders. Recently, Chahal et al., (2016) assessed the effect of maternal smoking on neonatal biomarkers of inflammation and immune response among 3459 singletons and twins in the Upstate KIDS Study. The following inflammatory biomarkers were measured using newborn dried blood spots (DBSs): interleukin (IL)-1α, IL-1 receptor antagonist, IL-6, IL-8, C-reactive protein, and TNFα. Immunoglobulins (IgE, IgA, IgM, and IgG subclasses) were also assessed. These investigators used generalized estimating equations to calculate mean differences (β) in biomarker levels by timing of pregnancy smoking, cigarette load, and secondhand smoke exposure after adjusting for sociodemographic and lifestyle factors including maternal body mass index.

Of the 344 (12%) women reporting smoking during pregnancy, about 40% continued throughout pregnancy and 13% reported smoking more than 1 pack per day. After covariate adjustment and Bonferroni correction for multiple comparisons, maternal smoking throughout pregnancy remained significantly associated with increased levels of IL-8. No significant associations were found with cigarette load or secondhand smoke exposure. Higher IgG3 levels were also associated with maternal smoking throughout pregnancy, although the association became nominally significant after adjustment for covariates, suggesting that maternal smoking throughout pregnancy was associated with increased IL-8 levels in newborns. Importantly, neonates of women who stopped smoking anytime in pregnancy did not have increased IL-8 levels. This study evaluated a range of inflammatory biomarkers and immunoglobulins in association with maternal smoking and timing/duration of smoking along with secondhand smoke exposure. By using DBSs, these investigators presented data from a large cohort of children born in Upstate New York. These findings suggested that early differences in immunoregulation of neonates exposed to maternal smoking for full duration in utero may be detected at birth.

Quantification of 8-Hydroxy-2'-Deoxy-Guanosine and Cotinine in Human Urine by LC-MS/MS: Correlation with Tobacco Exposure Biomarkers

It is now being recognized that cigarette smoke can increase oxidative DNA damage. The main component in cigarette smoke is nicotine. Nicotine is metabolized to cotinine, which can be regarded as a biomarker for measuring exposure to tobacco smoke. Chen et al., (2016) developed a sensitive, simple, and robust method based on on-line solid-phase extraction liquid chromatography with tandem mass spectrometry (on-line SPE LC-MS/MS) for the simultaneous determination of 8-OHdG and cotinine. The matrix effects of 8-OHdG and cotinine were measured at 97.1 and 91.7 %, with values for CV at 4.4 and 4.2%, respectively. The limits of detection of 8-OHdG and cotinine were 10.0 and 5.5 pg mL (-1), and the limits of quantification were 40.0 and 20.0 pg mL (-1), respectively. The total run time was 12 min. These investigators quantified 8-OHdG and cotinine in the urine of 80 male subjects. The levels of 8-OHdG and cotinine in smokers were significantly higher than that in non-smokers. Furthermore, 4-(Methylnitrosamino)-1-(3-Pyridyl)-1-Butanol and its glucuronide conjugate (defined as total NNAL) were the nitrosation metabolites of nicotine. The urinary levels of 8-OHdG and cotinine were well correlated with urinary levels of total NNAL. This was the first study to focus on the future risk of oxidative stress from exposure to cigarette smoke based on the relationship between 8-OHdG levels, cotinine levels, and total NNAL concentrations in the urine samples.

Biomarkers of Tobacco in Smokers' Urine

The most common tobacco smoke biomarkers in the urine include: nicotine, nor nicotine, anatabine, and anabasine. These biomarkers of tobacco smoke can be estimated to evaluate the therapeutic benefits of various antidotes prescribed form the clinical management of nicotinism.

Biomarkers of Tobacco Exposure

Since 2009, the FDA Center for Tobacco Products (CTP) has had the authority to regulate the manufacturing, distribution, and marketing of tobacco products in order to reduce the death and disease caused by tobacco use. Biomarkers of exposure pertain to actual human exposure to chemicals arising from tobacco use and could play an important role across a number of FDA regulatory activities, including assessing new and modified-risk tobacco products and identifying and evaluating potential product standards. On August 3-4, 2015, FDA/CTP hosted a public workshop focused on biomarkers of exposure with participants from government, industry, academia, and other organizations. The workshop was divided into four sessions focused on: (i) approaches to evaluating and selecting biomarkers; (ii) biomarkers of exposure and relationship to disease risk; (iii) currently used biomarkers of exposure and biomarkers in development; and (iv) biomarkers of exposure and the assessment of smokeless tobacco and electronic nicotine delivery systems. Chang et al., (2016) synthesized the main findings from the workshop and highlighted research areas that could further strengthen the science around biomarkers of tobacco exposure and help determine their application in tobacco product regulation.

References

Benowitz, N. L., Dt Helen, G., Dempsey, D. A., Jacob, P., Tyndate, R. F., 2016. Disposition Kinetics and Metabolism of Nicotine and Cotinine in African American smokers: Impact of CYP2A6 Genetic Variation and Enzymatic Activity. *Pharmacogenet Genomics*. 26(7), 340–350.

Cannon, D. S., Medina, T. R., Mermelstein, R. J., Hedeker, D., Bakian, A. V., Coon, H., Cook, E. H., Hamil, C., Weiss, R. B., 2016. CYP2A6 Longitudinal Effects in Young Smokers. *Nicotine Tob Res*. 18(2), 196-203.

Cannon, D. S., Medina, T. R., Mermelstein, R. J., Hedeker, D., Bakian, A. V., Coon, H., Cook, E. H., Hamil, C., Weiss, R. B., 2016. CYP2A6 Longitudinal Effects in Young Smokers. *Nicotine Tob Res*. 18(2), 196-203.

Carrizo, D., Nerín, I., Domeño, C., Alfaro, P., Nerín, C. 2016. Direct screening of tobacco indicators in urine and saliva by Atmospheric Pressure Solid Analysis Probe coupled to quadrupole-time of flight mass spectrometry (ASAP-MS-Q-TOF-). *J Pharm Biomed Anal.* 124, 149-156.

Chahal, N., McLain, A. C., Ghassabian, A., Michels, K. A., Bell, E. M., Lawrence, D. A., Yeung, E. H. 2016. Maternal Smoking and Newborn Cytokine and Immunoglobulin Levels. *Nicotine Tob Res.* 2016 Dec 23.

Chen, C. Y., Jhou, Y. T., Lee, H. L., Lin, Y. W. 2016. Simultaneous, rapid, and sensitive quantification of 8-hydroxy-2'-deoxyguanosine and cotinine in human urine by on-line solid-phase extraction LC-MS/MS: correlation with tobacco exposure biomarkers NNAL. *Anal Bioanal Chem.* 408(23), 6295-306.

Fagan, P., Pokhrel, P., Herzog, T. A., Pagano, I. S., Franke, A. A., Clanton, M. S., Alexander, L. A., Trinidad, D. R., Sakuma, K. L., Johnson, C. A., Moolchan, E. T., 2016. Nicotine Metabolism in Young Adult Daily Menthol and Nonmenthol Smokers. *Nicotine Tob Res.* 18(4), 437-446.

Kaluarachchi, M. R., Boulangé, C. L., Garcia-Perez, I., Lindon, J. C., Minet, E. F., 2016. Multiplatform serum metabolic phenotyping combined with pathway mapping to identify biochemical differences in smokers. *Bioanalysis.* 8(19), 2023-2043.

Mercier, K., McRitchie, S., Pathmasiri, W., Novokhatny, A., Koralkar, R., Askenazi, D., Brophy, P. D., Sumner, S., 2017. Preterm neonatal urinary renal developmental and acute kidney injury metabolomic profiling: an exploratory study. *Pediatr Nephrol.* 32(1), 151-161.

Murphy, S. E., Sipe, C. J., Choi, K., Raddatz, L. M., Koopmeiners, J. S., Donny, E. C., Hatsukami, D. K., 2017. Low cotinine glucuronidation in higher serum and saliva cotinine in African American compared to White smokers. *Cancer Epidemiol Biomarkers Prev.* Mar 6.

Murphy, S. E., 2017. *Nicotine* Metabolism and Smoking: Ethnic Differences in the Role of P450 2A6. *Chem Res Toxicol.* 30(1), 410-419.

Murphy, S. E., 2017. *Nicotine* Metabolism and Smoking: Ethnic Differences in the Role of P450 2A6. *Chem Res Toxicol.* 30(1), 410-419.

Ochoa, V., George, A. A., Nishi, R., Whiteaker, P., 2016. The prototoxin LYPD6B modulates heteromeric α3β4-containing nicotinic acetylcholine receptors, but not α7 homomers. *FASEB J.* 30(3),1109-1119.

Xu, H., Wang, F., Kranzler, H. R., Gelernter, J., Zhang, H., 2017. Alcohol and nicotine codependence-associated DNA methylation changes in promoter regions of addiction-related genes. *Sci Rep.* 7, 41816.

Chapter 6

Molecular Biomarkers of Nicotinism (Prevention and Treatment)

Abstract

Molecular biomarkers of nicotinism have been proposed recently for the personalized clinical and therapeutic evaluation of nicotine addiction. Reduced nicotine content cigarettes have been introduced to minimize the nicotine burden in tobacco smokers. An animal model of tobacco smoking demonstrated that even reduced nicotine content cigarettes exert significant influence on the nicotinic acetylcholine receptors (nAChRs). Even tenfold reduction of nicotine content in tobacco smoke was unable to spare the central cholinergic system in adolescent mice. A study evaluated developmental aspects of the cholinergic system in nicotinism and established that smoking during pregnancy induces deleterious consequences on the normal growth and development of fetus. Particularly, dendritic cell-mediated adaptive immunity involved in inflammation was significantly enhanced by nicotine. A study investigated nicotine-mediated basic molecular mechanisms of resistance to anticancer chemotherapy and reversal of the resistance by quitting tobacco smoking. Cigarette smoking was implicated to perionditis, whereas ellagic acid increased osteocalcin and alkaline phosphatase after tooth extraction in nicotine-treated rats. Several studies have demonstrated that nicotine-induced impaired aortic endothelial function through induction of protein, E-selectin. Furthermore, nicotine induced leukocyte adhesion and expression of VCAM and ICAM in endothelial cells to promote atherosclerosis. Tobacco smoking induced several biomarkers of mitochondrial oxidative stress. More importantly, cigarette smoke promoted multiple drug resistance (MDR) and expansion of cancer stem cell population by inducing metallothioneins (MTs)-mediated inhibition of charnoly body (CB) formation and by cancer stem cell-specific charnolosomes (CScsc) destabilization. The CScsc is highly rich in MTs and its endocytosis transforms norproliferating cells into malignant cells to induce MDR malignancies. In addition, nicotine influenced CD38 autoimmunity to promote insulin-resistant (type-2) diabetes. The metabotropic glutamate receptor-5 binding was significantly influenced by nicotine abstinence. Recently, nicotine gum has been introduced in the market for tobacco smoking avoidance and serious efforts are currently being made for the personalized theranostics of nicotinism, as described systematically in this book. In addition, genome-wide association studies (GWAS) have been introduced to evaluate nicotine metabolites in three ancestries. A smokescreen as a targeted genotyping array biotechnology has been developed for the personalized theranostics of nicotinism and drug addiction, in general.

Keywords: molecular biomarkers, reduced nicotine content cigarettes, mitochondrial oxidative stress, nicotine acetyl choline receptor (nAChR), metallothioneins (MTs), multidrug resistance, CD38 autoimmunity, insulin-resistant (type-2) diabetes, ellagic acid, E-selectin., VCAM, ICAM, platelets, endothelial cells, genome-wide association studies (GWAS), cancer stem cell-specific charnolosome (CScsc), smokescreen, target genotyping array, personalized theranostics, nicotinism

Introduction

Recently, several molecular biomarkers of nicotinism have been proposed for the personalized theranostics of nicotine addiction. Reduced nicotine content cigarettes have been introduced to minimize the nicotine burden in tobacco smokers. However, an animal model of tobacco smoking demonstrated that even reduced nicotine content cigarettes can have significant influence on the nicotine acetyl choline receptors (nAChRs). Even tenfold reduction of nicotine content in tobacco smoke could not spare the central cholinergic system in adolescent mice.

A study evaluated developmental aspects of the cholinergic system in nicotinism and established that smoking during pregnancy can have deleterious consequences on the normal growth and development of the fetus. In addition, the dendritic cell-mediated adaptive immunity involved in inflammation was significantly enhanced by nicotine. A recent study investigated nicotine-mediated basic molecular mechanisms of resistance to anticancer agents and reversal of the resistance by quitting tobacco smoking. Furthermore, cigarette smoking was implicated to perionditis, whereas ellagic acid increased osteocalcin and alkaline phosphatase after tooth extraction in nicotine-treated rats, indicating the therapeutic potential of ellagic acid in nicotine-induced perionditis.

Several recent studies have demonstrated nicotine-induced impaired aortic endothelial function through induction of protein, E-selectin. Nicotine induced leukocyte adhesion and expression of VCAM and ICAM in endothelial cells to promote atherosclerosis. In addition, the biomarker analysis has revealed that tobacco smoking induces several biomarkers of mitochondrial oxidative stress. The author reported that cigarette smoke promoted multiple drug resistance (MDR) and expansion of cancer stem cell-like population by inducing metallothioneins (MTs)-mediated inhibition of CB formation and by cancer stem cell-specific charnolosomes (CScsc) destabilization.

The CScsc is highly rich in MTs and its endocytosis transforms non-proliferating cells into malignant cell to induce MDR malignancies. In addition, nicotine significantly influenced CD38 autoimmunity to promote insulin-resistant (type-2) diabetes.

A recent study established that the metabotropic glutamate receptor-5 binding is significantly influenced by nicotine abstinence. Nicotine gum was introduced for tobacco smoking avoidance and serious efforts are being made for the personalized theranostics of tobacco dependence. In addition, genome-wide association studies have been performed to evaluate nicotine metabolites in three ancestries and a smokescreen as a targeted genotyping array biotechnology has been developed for the personalized theranostics of nicotinism and drug addiction, as described systematically in this chapter.

Effect of Reduced Nicotine Content in Cigarettes in an Animal Model of Tobacco Smoke

The tobacco industry has gradually decreased nicotine content in cigarette smoke but the impact of this reduction on health is still controversial. Since the central cholinergic system is the primary site of action of nicotine, Abreu-Villaça et al., (2016) investigated the effects of exposure of adolescent mice to tobacco smoke containing either high or low levels of nicotine on the central cholinergic system and the effects associated with cessation of exposure. From postnatal day (PN) 30 to 45, male and female Swiss mice were exposed to tobacco smoke (whole body exposure, 8h/day, 7 days/week) generated from 2R1F (HighNic group: 1.74 mg nicotine/cigarette) or 4A1 (LowNic group: 0.14 mg nicotine/cigarette) research cigarettes, whereas control mice were exposed to ambient air. Cholinergic biomarkers were assessed in the cerebral cortex and midbrain by the end of exposure (PN45), at short- (PN50) and long-term (PN75) deprivation. Nicotinic cholinergic receptor upregulation was observed with either type of cigarette in the cortex. Upregulation was detected only in HighNic mice and remained significant in females at short-term deprivation in the mid brain. The high-affinity choline transporter was reduced in the cortex: of HighNic mice by the end of exposure; of both HighNic and LowNic females at short-term deprivation; of LowNic mice at long-term deprivation. These decrements were separable from effects on choline acetyltransferase and acetylcholinesterase activities, suggesting cholinergic synaptic impairment. These investigators demonstrated central cholinergic alterations in an animal model of tobacco smoke exposure during adolescence. This system was sensitive even to tobacco smoke with very low nicotine content.

Developmental Aspects of the Cholinergic System

Beyond its importance in sustaining or modulating different aspects of the activity of the CNS, the cholinergic system plays important roles during development. In a study, Abreu-Villaça et al., (2011) focused on the developmental aspects associated with major components of the cholinergic system: Acetylcholine, choline acetyltransferase, vesicular acetylcholine transporter, high-affinity choline transporter, and acetylcholinesterase, nicotinic and muscarinic receptors. These investigators described when and where each one of these components was first identified in the CNS and the changes in their levels that occur during the course of prenatal and postnatal development. They also described how these components are relevant to many events that occur during the development of the CNS, including progenitor cells proliferation and differentiation, neurogenesis, gliogenesis, neuronal maturation and plasticity, axonal pathfinding, regulation of gene expression and cell survival. The evidence regarding the developmental aspects of the cholinergic system came mostly from studies that used agonists, such as nicotine, and antagonists, such as Hemicholinium-3. Studies using immunohistochemistry and genetically altered mice also provided valuable information.

Smoking during Pregnancy

It is well-known that smoking during pregnancy is a serious public health problem. Throughout this period, cessation is crucial. Everybody agrees that pregnancy is an appropriate moment to try to quit. Continuing smoking is a major risk for both the pregnant woman and her developing baby. Tobacco contains numerous toxics which easily pass through the placenta. All healthcare teams should be committed to helping pregnant women stop smoking and should train themselves to provide advice and support. The healthcare structures should implement consensual preventive and curative actions. In a report, Adler et al., (2005) suggested many diagnostic and curative tools for global care of pregnant smoking women. Their partners, whether smokers or not, should play an important role. In addition to psychological support, nicotinic substitutes are indispensable tools for helping pregnant women stop smoking.

Ahijevych, (2009) wrote a chapter on biological models for studying and assessing tobacco use to provide and to some of the common concepts and biomarkers in this arena to inform intervention research by nurse scientists. An overview of selected biomarkers of tobacco exposure in individuals included exhaled carbon monoxide, cotinine (the immediate metabolite of nicotine), and measurement of an individual's puffing pattern termed smoking topography. Common tobacco contents discussed included tobacco specific nitrosamines (TSNA) and polycyclic aromatic hydrocarbons (PAH) some of which increase disease risk including cancer. Exemplars of additives to cigarettes by the tobacco industry were described including Menthol, one additive marketed by the industry. In addition, genetics and tobacco addiction has emerged as a rapidly expanding field. Illustrative of this area are twin studies, nicotinic receptors, CYP2A6 polymorphisms, and genes that impact DA receptors.

Nicotine-Induced Activation of Dendritic Cell-Mediated Adaptive Immunity

It is known that antigen-presenting cells (APCs) such as monocytes and dendritic cells (DCs) stimulate T-cell proliferation and activation in the course of adaptive immunity. This cellular interaction plays a crucial role in the growth of atherosclerotic plaques. Nicotine has been shown to increase the growth of atherosclerotic lesions. Therefore, Aicher et al., (2003) investigated whether nicotine can stimulate APCs and their T cell-stimulatory capacity using human monocyte-derived DCs and murine bone marrow-derived DCs as APCs. These investigators reported that nicotine dose-dependently (10^{-8} to 10^{-4} mol/L) induced DC expression of costimulatory molecules (i.e., CD86, CD40), MHC class II, and adhesion molecules (i.e., LFA-1, CD54). Moreover, nicotine induced a 7.0-fold increase in secretion of the proinflammatory T (H) 1 cytokine interleukin-12 by human DCs. These effects were abrogated by the nicotinic receptor antagonist α-bungarotoxin and mechamylamine, respectively. The effects of nicotine were mediated in part by the phosphorylation of the PI3 kinase downstream target Akt and the mitogen-activated kinases ERK and p38 MAPK. Nicotine-stimulated APCs had a greater capacity to stimulate T-cell proliferation and cytokine secretion, as documented by mixed lymphocyte reactions and ovalbumin-specific assays with Ovalbumin-transgenic DO10.11 mice. In a murine model of atherosclerosis, nicotine significantly enhanced the recruitment of DCs to atherosclerotic lesions in vivo. Nicotine activated DCs and augmented their capacity to stimulate T-cell proliferation and cytokine secretion. These effects of nicotine may contribute to its influence on the progression of atherosclerotic lesions.

Mechanisms of Resistance to Anticancer Agents and the Reversal of the Resistance

It is well-established that MDR from overexpression of P-glycoprotein (Pgp) and multidrug resistance protein (MRP or MRP1) that function as ATP-dependent efflux pumps. Lung resistance related protein (LRP) is also involved in MDR. In earlier studies, Akiyama et al., (1999) isolated the human canalicular multispecific organic anion transporter (cMOAT) gene that is responsible for the defects in Dubin-Johnson syndrome. CMOAT is homologous to MRP1 and is involved in drug resistance. Human cMOAT cDNA transfected LLC-PK1 cells, LLC/cMOAT-1, had increased resistance to Vincristine (VCR), 7-ethyl-10-hydroxycamptothecin (SN-38), and cisplatin. The multidrug resistance (MDR)-reversing agents, Cyclosporin A (CsA) and PAK-104P, almost completely reversed the resistance to VCR, SN-38 and Cisplatin of LLC/cMOAT-1 cells by interacting with the substrate binding site of cMOAT. Treatment of human colorectal carcinoma SW-620 cells with Sodium butyrate (NaB) induced LRP in the cells and conferred resistance to Adrianycin (ADM), VCR, VP-16, Gramicidin D and Taxol. Two LRP-specific ribozymes inhibited the NaB-induced expression of LRP in SW-620 cells and abolished their acquisition of the MDR phenotype. The accumulation of ADM, VCR and Taxol was not decreased in NaB-treated cells, suggesting that ATP-binding cassette transporters are not involved in the MDR of NaB-treated cells. ADM was primarily located in the nuclei of untreated and the cytoplasm of NaB-treated cells. The accumulation level of ADM in the nuclei isolated from untreated cells or those from treated cells in the presence of anti-LRP polyclonal antibody was higher than that from treated cells in the absence of the antibody. Efflux of ADM from nuclei isolated from NaB-treated cells was enhanced compared with those from untreated cells and NaB-treated cells transfected with a LRP-specific ribozyme. The polyclonal antibody against LRP inhibited the enhanced efflux of ADM from nuclei isolated from NaB-treated cells. These findings indicated that LRP is involved in resistance to ADM, VCR, VP-16, Taxol and Gramicidin D, and has an important role in the transport of ADM from the nucleus to the cytoplasm.

Ellagic Acid Increases Osteocalcin and Alkaline Phosphatase after Tooth Extraction in Nicotine-Treated Rats

To examine the effect of nicotine (Ni) on bone socket healing treated with Ellagic acid (EA) after tooth extraction in rat, Al-Obaidi et al., (2016) divided thirty-two Sprague Dawley (SD) male rats into four groups. The group 1 was administrated with distilled water intragastrically and injected sterile saline subcutaneously. The group 2 was administrated with EA orally and injected with sterile saline subcutaneously. The groups 3 & 4 were subcutaneously exposed to Ni for 4 weeks twice daily before tooth extraction procedure, and maintained Ni injection until the animals were sacrificed. After one month Ni exposure, the group 4 was fed with EA while continuing Ni injection. All the groups were anesthetized, and the upper left incisor was extracted. Four rats from each group were sacrificed on 14(Th) and 28(Th) days. Tumor necrosis factor alpha (TNFα), Interleukin-1 beta (IL-1β) and Interleukin-6 (IL-6) were applied to assess in serum rat at 14th and 28(Th) days. Superoxide dismutase (SOD) and thiobarbituric acid reactive substances (TBRAS) levels were assessed to evaluate the antioxidant status and lipid peroxidation accordingly after tooth extraction in homogenized gingival maxilla tissue of rat at 14(th) and 28(th) days. The socket hard tissue was stained by eosin and hematoxylin (H&E); immunohistochemical technique was used to assess the healing process by osteocalcin (OCN) and alkaline phosphatase (ALP) biomarkers. Ni-induced rats administered with EA compound (Group 4) dropped the elevated concentration of pro-inflammatory cytokines significantly when compared to Ni-induced rats (Group 3) Ni-induced rats administrated with EA compound (Group 4) showed significant production of SOD and recession in TBRAS level when compared to Ni-induced rats (Group 3). The immunohistochemistry analysis have revealed that OCN and ALP have presented stronger expression in Ni-induced rats treated with EA (Group 4), as against Ni-induced rats (Group 3), indicating that Ni-induced rats, treated with EA have exert positive effect on the trabecular bone formation after tooth extraction in nicotinic rats could be due to the antioxidant activity of EA which lead to upregulate OCN and ALP proteins which are responsible for osteogenesis.

Nicotine-Mediated Induction of E-Selectin in Aortic Endothelial Cells

It is known that smoking is highly correlated with enhanced likelihood of atherosclerosis by inducing endothelial dysfunction. In endothelial cells, various cell-adhesion molecules including E-selectin, are upregulated upon exposure to nicotine, the addictive component of tobacco smoke; however, the molecular mechanisms underlying this induction are poorly understood. In a study, Alamanda et al., (2012) demonstrated that nicotine-induced E-selectin transcription in human aortic endothelial cells (HAECs) could be significantly blocked by α7-nAChR subunit inhibitor, α-BT, Src-kinase inhibitor, PP2, or siRNAs against Src or β-Arrestin-1 (β-Arr1). Further, chromatin immunoprecipitations showed that E-selectin is an E2F1 responsive gene and nicotine stimulation increased recruitment of E2F1 on E-selectin promoter. Inhibiting E2F1 activity using RRD-251, a disruptor of the Rb-Raf-1 kinase interaction, could significantly inhibit the nicotine-induced recruitment of E2F1 to the E-selectin promoter as well as E-selectin expression. Stimulation of HAECs with nicotine resulted in increased adhesion of U937 monocytic cells to HAECs and could be inhibited by pre-treatment with RRD-251. Similarly, depletion of E2F1 or Src using RNAi blocked the increased adhesion of monocytes to nicotine-stimulated HAECs, suggesting that nicotine-stimulated adhesion of monocytes to endothelial cells is dependent on the activation of α7-nAChRs, β-Arr1 and cSrc regulated increase in E2F1-mediated transcription of E-selectin gene. Therefore, agents such as RRD-251 that can target activity of E2F1 may have potential therapeutic benefit against cigarette smoke induced atherosclerosis.

Nicotine-Induced Leukocyte Adhesion and Expression of VCAM and ICAM, in Endothelial Cells

The pathology of atherosclerotic cardiovascular disease (ASCVD) has been characterized as an inflammatory response to vessel injury. The initial steps of this response involve mononuclear leukocyte (MNL) attachment and infiltration into the vessel wall. Leukocyte adhesion is potentiated by expression of cellular adhesion molecules. Vascular cell adhesion molecule-1 (VCAM) and intracellular adhesion molecule-1 (ICAM) are markers of cellular activation and have the ability to attach leukocytes to the endothelium, which is an initial event in the inflammatory response in the vessel wall. In the recent past, Albaugh et al., (2004) plated Human umbilical vein endothelial cells (HUVEC) in endothelial growth medium (EGM) on plastic coverslips and grown until cells were 75% confluent. Free base nicotine (FBN) was diluted in EGM to a concentration of 10^{-8} M and added to experimental cells. At 3 hr., coverslips were removed and fixed. Immunohistochemical staining (IHCS) was performed using a monoclonal antibody to human ICAM and VCAM. Digital image analysis (DIA) was performed to quantify the expression of ICAM and VCAM. An intensity stain index (ISI) measuring area and intensity of stain/total cellular area was determined. Additional HUVEC grown in a similar manner were either exposed to 10^{-8} M FBN in EGM or EGM control for 4 hrs., then were exposed to MNL suspension for 10 min. Coverslips were removed, rinsed, and fixed. Hematoxylin and eosin staining was performed and cells examined under light microscopy. Leukocyte number per high power field (HPF) was counted and compared to controls. Data were analyzed using analysis of variants (ANOVA) and Student's t-test. Differences were considered significant ($p < 0.05$). ICAM and VCAM expression was absent in control cells. Nicotine exposure at 3 hrs. induced expression of VCAM (ISI = 30.85+/-0.77) and to a lesser extent ICAM (ISI = 16.6+/-1.39) ($p < 0.001$). MNL adhesion was markedly increased in cells exposed to nicotine (79.4+/-16.9/HPF) when compared to control cells (1.8+/-0.91/HPF) exposed to MNL ($p < 0.01$). These data showed nicotine's ability to activate HUVEC as evidenced by induction of ICAM and VCAM expression in vitro. The biological effects of these adhesion molecules were demonstrated by a marked increase in MNL adhesion to HUVEC as demonstrated by leukocyte adhesion assay (LAA). Hence, MNL adhesion and subsequent migration into the intima, if occurring in vivo, may be a vital step in the pathogenesis of ASCVD associated with nicotine exposure.

Smoking and Biomarkers of Oxidative Stress

Generally, biomarker studies of oxidative stress and antioxidant status are employed to determine the risk of developing chronic diseases, such as cancer, cardiovascular diseases or cognitive decline. The influence of lifestyle factors can have a significant influence on the biomarker concentrations; hence these factors, including smoking, should be considered in biomarker-based studies (Mayne 2003). It has been reported that during smoking, free radicals are generated that can induce inflammatory cells to synthesize high levels of reactive oxygen metabolites (Harats et al., 1989; Mezzetti et al., 1995). Therefore smokers are subjected to an increased oxidative stress condition, which can result in redox imbalance (Thompson et al., 1992). As a consequence, biomarkers of oxidative stress, antioxidant and redox status are significantly influenced by smoking behavior (Mohod ET l., 2014; Durazzo et al., 2014). In a recent study, Jansen et al., (2014) determined the influence of smoking on biomarkers of both oxidative stress, redox and antioxidant status in a healthy male population. These investigators determined the influence of smoking on the biomarkers of oxidative stress, antioxidant status and redox status in 48 healthy men with a mean age of 25 yrs. The biomarkers of oxidative stress were the reactive oxygen metabolites (ROM) and the total oxidant status (TOS). The biomarkers for the antioxidant activity were the biological antioxidant potential (BAP), the ferric reducing ability of plasma (FRAP), the total antioxidant status (TAS), the assay for the defense against the oxidation by hypochlorous acid (OXY) and uric acid (UA). The total thiol levels (TTL) were measured as a biomarker for the redox status. The average concentration of ROM was 14% higher in smokers compared with non-smokers, whereas TOS was 4.9% higher. The average concentrations of BAP, FRAP and TAS decreased with smoking with 3.6. Alsouric acid, the main antioxidant in serum and a major contributor to the antioxidant status in serum, decreased by 10.6%, suggesting that in epidemiological studies the effect of smoking should be considered when using oxidative stress and antioxidant biomarkers.

Cigarette Smoke Promotes Drug Resistance and Expansion of Cancer Stem Cell-Like Population by Inhibiting CB Formation through MTs Induction and by Destabilizing Cancer Stem Cell-Specific Charnolosomes (CScsc)

It is well known that many patients continue to smoke cigarettes after being diagnosed with cancer. Although smoking cessation has typically been presumed to possess little therapeutic value for cancer, a growing body of evidence suggests that continued smoking is associated with reduced efficacy of treatment and a higher incidence of recurrence. An et al., (2012), therefore investigated the effect of cigarette smoke condensate (CSC) on drug resistance in the lung cancer and head and neck cancer cell lines A549 and UMSCC-10B, respectively. They showed that CSC significantly increased the cellular efflux of Doxorubicin and Mitoxantrone. This was accompanied by membrane localization and increased expression of the multi-drug transporter ABCG2.

The induced efflux of Doxorubicin was reversed upon addition of the specific ABCG2 inhibitor Fumitremorgin C, confirming the role of ABCG2. Treatment with CSC increased the concentration of phosphorylated Akt, while addition of the PI3K inhibitor LY294002 blocked Doxorubicin extrusion, suggesting that Akt activation is required for CSC-induced drug efflux. In addition, CSC was found to promote resistance to Doxorubicin as determined by MTS assays. This CSC-induced Doxurbicin-resistance was mitigated by mechamylamine, a nicotinic acetylcholine receptor inhibitor, suggesting that nicotine is at least partially responsible for the effect of CSC. Lastly, CSC increased the size of the side population (SP), which has been linked to a cancer stem cell-like phenotype.

CSC promotes chemo-resistance via Akt-mediated regulation of ABCG2 activity, and may also increase the proportion of cancer stem-like cells, contributing to tumor resilience. These findings highlight the importance of smoking cessation following a diagnosis of cancer, and elucidate the mechanisms of continued smoking that may be detrimental to effective treatment of cancer. The author reported that non-specific induction of CB causes alopecia, myelosuppression, and GIT disturbance in multi-drug resistance (MDR) malignancies. Moreover, nicotine inhibits cancer-stem cell CB formation to augment multidrug-resistant (MDR) malignancies. Nicotine-induced MTs render cancer stem cell specific charnolosome (CSscs) highly resistant to anticancer treatment. Endocytosis of cancer stem cell specific charnolosome (CSscs) transforms non-proliferating cell to malignant cell and makes them MDR, and highly invasive and metastatic.

CD38 Autoimmunity and Diabetes

In the recent past, Antonelli and Ferrannini (2004) reported that human CD38 is a protein which catalyzes the synthesis of nicotinic acid adenine dinucleotide (NAADP+) and the conversion of NAD+ to cADPR. Both cADPR and NAADP+ are powerful intracellular Ca^{2+} $[Ca^{2+}]_i$ mobilizers in different cell types. Recently, the presence of CD38 autoantibodies has been found in a significant number (9-15%) of patients with Type 2 or long-standing Type 1 diabetes. These autoantibodies are biologically active, the majority of them (-60%) displaying agonistic properties, i.e., $[Ca^{2+}]_i$ mobilization in lymphocytic cell lines and in pancreatic islets. In cultured rat pancreatic islets, the human autoantibodies inhibit glucose-induced insulin release, whereas, in human pancreatic islets CD38 autoantibodies stimulate glucose-mediated insulin secretion. The clinical phenotype of anti-CD38-positive Type 2 diabetes differs from the LADA (latent autoimmune diabetes of adults) phenotype. When accurately matched for age and obesity, only LADA patients with anti-GAD antibodies, but not GAD-negative/CD38-positive patients, have reduced in vivo beta-cell function in comparison to antibody-negative patients. Transgenic mice overexpressing CD38 show enhanced glucose-induced insulin release, whereas, conversely, CD38 knockout mice display a severe impairment in beta-cell function. Few Japanese diabetic patients carry a missense mutation in the CD38 gene; in Caucasian patients mutations in the CD38 gene have not been found. Collectively, these findings suggest that activation of CD38 represents an alternative signaling pathway for glucose-induced insulin secretion in human pancreatic β-cells. More information, however, is necessary to gauge the role of CD38 autoimmunity in the context of the natural history of human Type 1 or Type 2 diabetes.

Nicotine Abstinence and Metabotropic Glutamate Receptor-5 Binding

It now well recognized that nicotine addiction is a major public health problem and is associated with primary glutamatergic dysfunction. Recently, Akkus et al., (2016) showed marked global reductions in metabotropic glutamate receptor type 5 (mGluR5) binding in smokers and recent ex-smokers (average abstinence duration of 25 weeks). These investigators examined the role of mGluR5 downregulation on nicotine addiction by investigating a group of long-term ex-smokers (abstinence >1.5 years), and explored associations between mGluR5 binding and relapse in recent ex-smokers. Images of mGluR5 receptor binding were acquired in 14 long-term ex-smokers, using positron emission tomography with radiolabeled [^{11}C] ABP688, which binds to an allosteric site with high specificity. Long-term ex-smokers and individuals who had never smoked exhibited no differences in mGluR5 binding in any of the brain regions examined. Long-term ex-smokers revealed significantly higher mGluR5 binding than recent ex-smokers, in the frontal cortex (42%) and thalamus (57%), suggesting that downregulation of mGluR5 is a pathogenetic mechanism underlying nicotine dependence and the high relapse rate in individuals previously exposed to nicotine. Hence, mGluR5 receptor binding appears to be an effective biomarker in smoking and a promising target for the discovery of novel medication for nicotine dependence and other substance-related disorders.

Protective Effect of Ellagic Acid after Tooth Extraction in Nicotine-Treated Rats

To examine the effect of nicotine (Ni) on bone socket healing treated with Ellagic acid (EA) after tooth extraction in rat, Al-Obaidi et al., (2016) divided 32 Sprague Dawley (SD) male rats into four groups. The group 1 was administrated with distilled water intragastrically and injected sterile saline s.c. The group 2 was administrated with EA orally and injected with sterile saline s.c. The groups 3 & 4 were s.c exposed to Ni for

4 weeks twice daily before tooth extraction procedure, and maintained Ni injection until the animals were sacrificed. After one month Ni exposure, the group 4 was fed with EA while continuing Ni injection. All the groups were anesthetized, and the upper left incisor was extracted. Four rats from each group were sacrificed on 14(Th) and 28(Th) days. Tumor necrosis factor alpha (TNFα), Interleukin-1 beta (IL-1β) and Interleukin-6 (IL-6) were assess in serum at 14th and 28(Th) days. Superoxide dismutase (SOD) and thiobarbituric acid reactive substances (TBRAS) levels were assessed to evaluate the antioxidant status and lipid peroxidation after tooth extraction in homogenized gingival maxilla tissue. The socket hard tissue was stained by eosin and hematoxylin (H&E); immunohistochemical technique was used to assess the healing process by osteocalcin (OCN) and alkaline phosphatase (ALP) biomarkers. Ni-induced rats administered with EA compound (Group 4) dropped the elevated concentration of pro-inflammatory cytokines significantly when compared to Ni-induced rats (Group 3). Ni-induced rats administrated with EA compound (Group 4) showed significant production of SOD and recession in TBRAS level when compared to Ni-induced rats (Group 3. The immunohistochemistry analysis has revealed that OCN and ALP have presented stronger expression in Ni-induced rats treated with EA (Group 4), as against Ni-induced rats (Group 3). The results of this study were interpreted to suggest that Ni-induced rats, treated with EA had exerted positive effect on the trabecular bone formation after tooth extraction in nicotinic rats could be due to the antioxidant activity of EA which induced upregulation of OCN and ALP proteins, responsible for osteogenesis.

Nicotine Gum for Cigarette Avoidance

It has been realized that women are more susceptible to the harmful effects of cigarette smoking. Thus, identifying effective harm reduction approaches for women is necessary. Allen et al., (2016) recently examined the gender differences in response to snus versus nicotine gum for cigarette avoidance, as a means of harm reduction. These investigators randomly assigned the participants to use snus or nicotine gum to avoid cigarette smoking. Participants (n = 391; 47% women) were randomized into the snus group (n = 196; 45% women) and the gum group (n = 195; 49% women). Men used more snus whereas women used more gum. During treatment, men in the snus group had higher total nicotine equivalent values whereas women did not vary by group. Overall, fewer men in the snus group completely avoided cigarettes compared to men in the gum group. Among women, there were no differences by randomization in cigarette avoidance. Despite a number of gender differences in response to snus versus nicotine gum, these data suggested that snus may not be an optimal harm reduction approach for either gender.

Personalized (Precision) Medicine for Tobacco Dependence

It is well-recognized that quitting smoking significantly reduces the risk of tobacco-related morbidity and mortality, yet there is a high rate of relapse amongst smokers who try to quit. Recently, Allenby et al., (2016) highlighted that phenotypic biomarkers have the potential to improve smoking cessation outcomes by identifying the best available treatment for an individual smoker. These investigators introduced the nicotine metabolite ratio (NMR) as a reliable and stable phenotypic measure of nicotine metabolism that can guide smoking cessation treatment among smokers who wish to quit. They addressed how the NMR accounts for sources of variation in nicotine metabolism including genotype and other biological and environmental factors such as estrogen levels, alcohol use, body mass index, or menthol exposure. Then, they highlighted clinical trials that validate the NMR as a biomarker to predict therapeutic response to different pharmacotherapies for smoking cessation. This study supported the use of nicotine replacement therapy for slow metabolizers, and non-nicotine treatments such as Varenicline for normal metabolizers. Finally, these investigators discussed future research directions to elucidate mechanisms underlying NMR associations with treatment response, and facilitate the implementation of the NMR as biomarker in clinical practice to guide smoking cessation.

Genome-Wide Association of Nicotine Metabolite Ratio in Three Ancestries

Metabolic enzyme variation and other patient and environmental characteristics influence smoking behaviors, treatment success, and risk of related disease. Population-specific variation in metabolic genes contributes to challenges in developing and optimizing pharmacogenetic interventions. In a study, Baurley et al., (2016) applied a custom genome-wide genotyping array for addiction research (Smokescreen), to three laboratory-based studies of nicotine metabolism with oral or venous administration of labeled nicotine and cotinine, to model nicotine metabolism in multiple populations. The trans-3'-hydroxycotinine/cotinine ratio, the nicotine metabolite ratio (NMR), was the nicotine metabolism measure analyzed. A sum of 312 individuals of self-identified European, African, and Asian American ancestry were genotyped and included in ancestry-specific genome-wide association scans (GWAS) and a meta-GWAS analysis of the NMR. These investigators modeled natural-log transformed NMR with covariates: principal components of genetic ancestry, age, sex, body mass index, and smoking status. African and Asian American NMRs were significantly lower than European American NMRs. Meta-GWAS analysis identified 36 genome-wide significant variants over a 43 kilobase pair region at CYP2A6 with minimum $P = 2.46E-18$ at rs12459249, proximal to CYP2A6. Additional minima were located in intron 4 (rs56113850, $P = 6.61E-18$) and in the CYP2A6-CYP2A7 intergenic region (rs34226463, P = 1.45E-12). Most (34/36) genome-wide significant variants suggested reduced CYP2A6 activity; functional mechanisms were identified and tested in knowledge-bases. Conditional analysis resulted in intergenic variants of possible interest. This meta-GWAS of the NMR identifies CYP2A6 variants, replicates the top-ranked single nucleotide polymorphism from a recent Finnish meta-GWAS of the NMR, identified functional mechanisms, and provided pan-continental population biomarkers for nicotine metabolism. This multiple ancestry meta-GWAS of the lab study-based NMR provided novel evidence and replication for genome-wide association of CYP2A6 single nucleotide and insertion-deletion polymorphisms. These investigators identified three regions of genome-wide significance: proximal, intronic, and distal to CYP2A6. They replicated the top-ranking single nucleotide polymorphism (SNP) from a recent GWAS of the NMR in Finnish smokers, identified a functional mechanism for this intronic variant from in silico analyses of RNA-seq data that was consistent with CYP2A6 expression measured in postmortem lung and liver, and provided additional support for the intergenic region between CYP2A6 and CYP2A7.

Smokescreen: A Targeted Genotyping Array for Addiction Research

It is well-known that addictive disorders are a class of chronic, relapsing mental disorders that are responsible for increased risk of mental and medical disorders and represent the largest, potentially modifiable cause of death. Tobacco dependence is associated with increased risk of disease and premature death. While tobacco control efforts and therapeutic interventions have made good progress in reducing smoking prevalence, challenges remain in optimizing their effectiveness based on patient characteristics, including genetic variation. In order to maximize collaborative efforts to advance addiction research, Baurley et al., (2016) developed a genotyping array called Smokescreen. This custom array was built upon previous work in the analyses of human genetic variation, the genetics of addiction, drug metabolism, and response to therapy, with an emphasis on smoking and nicotine addiction. The Smokescreen genotyping array included 646,247 markers in 23 categories. The array design covered genome-wide common variation (65.67, 82.37, and 90.72% in African (YRI), East Asian (ASN), and European (EUR) respectively); most of the variation with a minor allele frequency ≥0.01 in 1014 addiction genes (85.16, 89.51, and 90.49% for YRI, ASN, and EUR respectively); and nearly all variation from the 1000 Genomes Project Phase 1, NHLBI GO Exome Sequencing Project and HapMap databases in the regions related to smoking behavior and nicotine metabolism: CHRNA5-CHRNA3-CHRNB4 and CYP2A6-CYP2B6. Of the 636 pilot DNA samples derived from blood or cell line biospecimens that were genotyped on the array, 622 (97.80%) passed quality control. In passing samples, 90.08% of markers passed quality control. The genotype reproducibility in 25 replicate pairs was 99.94%. For 137 samples that overlapped with HapMap2 release 24, the genotype concordance was 99.76%. In a genome-wide association analysis of the nicotine metabolite ratio in 315 individuals participating in nicotine metabolism lab studies, they identified genome-wide significant variants in the CYP2A6 region (min p = 9.10E-15) and developed a comprehensive genotyping array for addiction research and demonstrated its validity and utility through pilot genotyping of HapMap and study samples. This array allowed these researchers to perform genome-wide analysis of candidate genes, and pathway-based association analyses of addiction, tobacco-use, treatment response, comorbidities, and associated diseases in a standardized high-throughput platform.

References

Abreu-Villaça, Y., Correa-Santos, M., Dutra-Tavares, A. C., Paes-Branco, D., Nunes-Freitas, A., Manhães, A. C., Filgueiras, C. C., Ribeiro-Carvalho, A. 2016. A ten-fold reduction of nicotine yield in tobacco smoke does not spare the central cholinergic system in adolescent mice. *Int. J. Dev. Neurosci.* 52, 93-103.

Abreu-Villaça, Y., Filgueiras, C. C., Manhães, A. C. 2011. Developmental aspects of the cholinergic system. *Behav Brain Res.* 221(2), 367-378.

Adler, M., Dautzenberg, E., Garelik, D., Nguyen, P. 2005. Cessation of smoking: implementation of effective techniques. Prenatal and hospital pregnancy consultations with smoking women and/or smoking couples. *J Gynecol Obstet Biol Reprod (Paris).* 34 Spec No 1, 3S194-205.

Ahijevych, K. 2009. Biological models for studying and assessing tobacco use. *Annu Rev Nurs* Res. 27, 145-68.

Aicher, A., Heeschen, C., Mohaupt, M., Cooke, J. P., Zeiher, A. M., Dimmeler, S. 2003. Nicotine strongly activates dendritic cell-mediated adaptive immunity: potential role for progression of atherosclerotic lesions. *Circulation.* 107(4), 604-611.

Akiyama, S., Chen, Z. S., Kitazono, M., Sumizawa, T., Furukawa, T., Aikou, T. 1999. Mechanisms for resistance to anticancer agents and the reversal of the resistance. *Hum Cell.* 12(3), 95-102.

Al-Obaidi, M. M., Al-Bayaty, F. H., Al Batran, R., Ibrahim, O. E., Daher, A. M. 2016. Ellagic Acid Increases Osteocalcin and Alkaline Phosphatase After Tooth Extraction in Nicotinic-Treated Rats. *Curr Pharm Des.* 22(16), 2403-2410.

Alamanda, V., Singh, S., Lawrence, N. J., Chellappan, S. P. 2012. Nicotine -mediated induction of E-selectin in aortic endothelial cells requires Src kinase and E2F1 transcriptional activity. *Biochem Biophys Res Commun.* 418(1), 56-61.

Albaugh, G., Bellavance, E., Strande, L., Heinburger, S., Hewitt, C. W., Alexander, J. B. 2004. Nicotine induces mononuclear leukocyte adhesion and expression of adhesion molecules, VCAM and ICAM, in endothelial cells *in vitro*. *Ann Vasc Surg.* 18(3), 302-307.

An, Y., Kiang, A., Lopez, J. P., Kuo, S. Z., Yu, M. A., Abhold, E. L., Chen, J. S., Wang-Rodriguez, J., Ongkeko, W. M. 2012. Cigarette smoke promotes drug resistance and expansion of cancer stem cell-like side population. *PLoS One.* 7(11), e47919.

Antonelli, A., Ferrannini, E., 2004. CD38 autoimmunity: recent advances and relevance to human diabetes. *J Endocrinol Invest.* 2004 Jul-Aug; 27(7):695-707.

Abreu-Villaça Y, Correa-Santos M, Dutra-Tavares AC, Paes-Branco D, Nunes-Freitas A, Manhães AC, Filgueiras CC, Ribeiro-Carvalho A.2016. A tenfold reduction of *Nicotine* yield in tobacco smoke does not spare the central cholinergic system in adolescent mice. *Int J Dev Neurosci.* 52, 93-103.

Akkus, F., Treyer, V., Johayem, A., Ametamey, S. M., Mancilla, B. G., Sovago, J., Buck, A., Hasler, G. 2016. Association of Long-Term Nicotine Abstinence with Normal Metabotropic Glutamate Receptor-5 Binding. *Biol Psychiatry.* 79(6), 474-480.

Al-Obaidi, M. M., Al-Bayaty, F. H., Al Batran, R., Ibrahim, O. E., Daher, A. M. 2016. Ellagic Acid Increases Osteocalcin and Alkaline Phosphatase After Tooth Extraction in Nicotinic-Treated Rats. *Curr Pharm Des.* 22(16), 2403-2410.

Allen, A., Vogel, R. I., Meier, E., Anderson, A., Jensen, J., Severson, H. H., Hatsukami, D. 2016. Gender differences in snus versus nicotine gum for cigarette avoidance among a sample of US smokers. *Drug Alcohol Depend.* 168, 8-12.

Allenby, C. E., Boylan, K. A., Lerman, C., Falcone, M. Precision Medicine for Tobacco Dependence: Development and Validation of the Nicotine Metabolite Ratio. *J Neuroimmune Pharmacol.* 2016 Sep;11(3):471-483.

Baurley, J. W., Edlund, C. K., Pardamean, C. I., Conti, D. V., Krasnow, R., Javitz, H. S., Hops, H., Swan, G. E., Benowitz, N. L., Bergen, A. W., 2016. Genome-Wide Association of the Laboratory-Based Nicotine Metabolite Ratio in Three Ancestries. *Tob Res.* 18(9), 1837-1844.

Baurley, J. W., Edlund, C. K., Pardamean, C. I., Conti, D. V., Bergen, A. W. 2016. Smokescreen: a targeted genotyping array for addiction research. *BMC Genomics.* 17, 145.

Benowitz, N. L., St Helen, G., Dempsey, D. A., Jacob, P. 3rd., Tyndale, R. F. 2016. Disposition kinetics and metabolism of nicotine and cotinine in African American smokers: impact of CYP2A6 genetic variation and enzymatic activity. *Pharmacogenet Genomics.* 26(7), 340-350.

Bhattacharjee, A., Prasad, S. K., Pal, S., Maji, B., Banerjee, A., Das, D., Bose, A., Chatterjee, N., Mukherjee, S., 2016. Possible involvement of iNOS and TNF-α in nutritional intervention against nicotine -induced pancreatic islet cell damage. *Biomed Pharmacother.* 84, 1727-1738.

Cannon, D. S., Medina, T. R., Mermelstein, R. J., Hedeker, D., Bakian, A. V., Coon, H., Cook, E. H., Hamil, C., Weiss, R. B., 2016. CYP2A6 Longitudinal Effects in Young Smokers. *Nicotine Tob Res.* 18(2), 196-203.

Carrizo, D., Nerín, I., Domeño, C., Alfaro, P., Nerín, C. 2016. Direct screening of tobacco indicators in urine and saliva by Atmospheric Pressure Solid Analysis Probe coupled to quadrupole-time of flight mass spectrometry (ASAP-MS-Q-TOF-). *J Pharm Biomed Anal.* 124, 149-156.

Chahal, N., McLain, A. C., Ghassabian, A., Michels, K. A., Bell, E. M., Lawrence, D. A., Yeung, E.H. 2016. Maternal Smoking and Newborn Cytokine and Immunoglobulin Levels. *Nicotine Tob Res.* 2016 Dec 23.

Chang, C. M., Edwards, S. H., Arab, A., Del Valle-Pinero, A. Y., Yang, L., Hatsukami, D. K., 2017. Biomarkers of Tobacco Exposure: of an FDA-Sponsored Public Workshop. *Cancer Epidemiol Biomarkers Prev.* 26(3), 291-302.

Chen, C. Y., Jhou, Y. T., Lee, H. L., Lin, Y. W. 2016. Simultaneous, rapid, and sensitive quantification of 8-hydroxy-2'-deoxyguanosine and cotinine in human urine by on-line solid-phase extraction LC-MS/MS: correlation with tobacco exposure biomarkers NNAL. *Anal Bioanal Chem.* 408(23), 6295-306.

Chen, L. S., Horton, A., Bierut, L. 2016. Pathways to precision medicine in smoking cessation treatments. *Neurosci Lett.* 2016 May 18.

Contreras-Rodríguez, O., Albein-Urios, N., Vilar-López, R., Perales J. C., Martínez-Gonzalez, J. M., Fernández-Serrano, M. J., Lozano-Rojas, O., Clark, L., Verdejo-García, A. 2016. Increased corticolimbic connectivity in cocaine dependence versus pathological gambling is associated with drug severity and emotion-related impulsivity. *Addict Biol.* 21(3), 709-718.

Cox, S., Kośmider, L., McRobbie, H., Goniewicz, M., Kimber, C., Doig, M., Dawkins, L.2016. E-cigarettes puffing patterns associated with high and low nicotine e-liquid strength: effects on toxicant and carcinogen exposure. *BMC Public Health.* 16, 999.

Cravo, A. S., Bush, J., Sharma, G., Savioz, R., Martin, C., Craige, S., Walele, T.2016. A randomised, parallel group study to evaluate the safety profile of an electronic vapour product over 12 weeks. *Regul Toxicol Pharmacol.* 81 Suppl 1, S1-S14.

D'Ruiz, C. D., Graff, D. W., Robinson, E., 2016. Reductions in biomarkers of exposure, impacts on smoking urge and assessment of product use and tolerability in adult smokers following partial or complete substitution of cigarettes with e-cigarettes. *BMC Public Health.* 16, 543.

El Golli, N., Jrad-Lamine, A., Neffati, H., Rahali, D., Dallagi, Y., Dkhili, H., Ba, N., El May, M. V., El Fazaa, S. 2016. Impact of e-cigarettes refill liquid with or without nicotine on liver function in adult rats. *Toxicol Mech.* 26(6), 419-426.

El Golli, N., Dkhili, H., Dallagi, Y., Rahali, D., Lasram, M., Bini-Dhouib, I., Lebret, M., Rosa, J. P., El Fazaa, S., Allal-El Asmi, M. 2016. Comparison between electronic cigarette refill liquid and nicotine on metabolic parameters in rats. *Life Sci.* 146, 131-138.

El-Sherbeeny, N. A., Nader, M. A., Attia, G. M., Ateyya, H., 2016. Agmatine protects rat liver from nicotine-induced hepatic damage via antioxidative, antiapoptotic, and antifibrotic pathways. *Naunyn Schmiedebergs Arch Pharmacol.* 389(12), 1341-1351.

Eugen-Olsen, J., Ladelund, S., Sørensen, L. T., 2016. Plasma suPAR is lowered by smoking cessation: a randomized controlled study. *Eur. J. Clin. Invest.* 46(4), 305-311.

Chapter 7

Harmful Effects of Nicotine and Personalized Theranostics of Nicotinism

Abstract

This chapter describes various harmful effects of nicotine on the developing fetus, environmental exposure and effects on health of children from tobacco-producing regions, secondhand smoke and serum cotinine levels, reduced expression of nucleolar organizer region (AgNOR) of developing Purkinje neurons in SIDS, metabolomic profiling of preterm neonatal urinary renal developmental and acute kidney injury in infants, and the effect of active and passive smoking on serum bilirubin levels. In addition, the chapter highlights association of gambling with drug severity and emotional impulsivity, cigarette smoke inhalation-induced rat testis apoptosis, metabolic activation of biomarkers of tobacco-specific carcinogenic nitrosamines, circulating monoamine precursors and smoking in schizophrenia patients, and salivary stress biomarkers of nicotine abuse and dependence to facilitate personalized (precision) theranostics of nicotinism.

Keywords: nucleolar organizer region; purkinje neurons, sudden infant death syndrome (SIDS), emotional impulsivity, testicular apoptosis, tobacco-specific carcinogenic nitrosamines, schizophrenia, salivary stress biomarkers, nicotine abuse, personalized medicine, smoking cessation

Introduction

Recently, several harmful effects of nicotine in tobacco have been identified by state of the art biotechnology including liquid chromatography-mass spectroscopy (LC-MS).

Nicotine has been reported to induce deleterious changes in the developing fetus. The deleterious effects of environmental exposure of nicotine in children from tobacco-producing regions have been reported. Particularly, developing cerebellar cortex is highly vulnerable to the deleterious consequences of maternal nicotinism. Nicotine directly inhibits nucleolar organizer region (AgNOR) of the developing Purkinje neurons to cause sudden infant death syndrome (SIDS). Nicotine caused reduced expression of metabolomic profiling of preterm neonatal urinary renal development and acute kidney injury in infants. In addition, serum bilirubin levels were significantly influenced by active and passive smoking. Recent studies have also provided evidence of association of gambling with drug severity (smoking) and emotional impulsivity.

This chapter highlights the deleterious consequences of intrauterine nicotine exposure to developing fetus and infants. Experimental studies on rats have demonstrated that cigarette smoke inhalation induces testicular apoptosis to cause infertility in the rats and various metabolic biomarkers are activated by tobacco-specific carcinogenic nitrosamines. Furthermore, circulating monoamine precursors are significantly influenced by smoking in schizophrenia patients. To facilitate personalized (precision) theranostics of nicotinism in the safe and effective clinical, management of smoking; salivary stress biomarkers have been identified, as described in this chapter.

Fetal Exposure to Tobacco

It is well-recognized that fetal exposure to tobacco constituents is a risk factor for negative birth outcomes. Recently, Jacob et al., (2017) determined the relationships between nicotine and cotinine concentrations in amniotic fluid and maternal saliva. As part of a therapeutic trial, 42 pregnant smokers agreed to sample amniotic fluid (8 samples from amniocentesis, 34 at birth). Their smoking characteristics were collected along with the newborns' birth outcomes. The median concentrations [IQR] in amniotic fluid and saliva were 11 [7-31] and 38 [7-174] µg/L for nicotine and 72 [22-123] µg/L and 55 [17-109] µg/L for cotinine, respectively. Multivariate models showed that salivary cotinine concentration predicted amniotic fluid nicotine and cotinine concentrations respectively). Amniotic fluid nicotine or cotinine concentration was not associated with birth weight. In multivariate analysis, the time elapsed since the last cigarette was the only variable associated with increased birth weight. Hence, maternal saliva sampling for the determination of cotinine concentration is of interest to monitor fetal exposure to nicotine of any origin. Nevertheless, the time elapsed since the last cigarette was a better predictor of birth weight than the biomarkers concentration in amniotic fluid or maternal saliva.

Second Hand Smoke and Serum Cotinine Levels

It is well-known that secondhand smoke (SHS) provides additional exposure to nicotine and toxins for smokers, but has been understudied. Recently, Lindsay et al., (2016) determined whether SHS exposure among smokers yields detectable differences in cotinine levels compared with unexposed smokers at the population level. Using the US National Health and Nutrition Examination Survey (NHANES) for the years 1999-2012, these investigators compared serum cotinine levels of 4547 current adult cigarette smokers stratified by self-reported SHS exposure sources (home and/or work) and smoking intensity. A weighted multivariable linear regression model determined the association between SHS exposure and cotinine levels among smokers. Smokers with SHS exposure at home (43.8%) had higher cotinine levels compared with those with no SHS exposure at home after controlling for the number of cigarettes smoked per day and number of days smoked in the previous 5 days, survey year, age, gender and education. Smokers with SHS exposure at work (20.0%) did not have significantly higher cotinine levels after adjustment. The adjusted geometric mean cotinine levels of light smokers (1-9 cigarettes per day) with no SHS exposure, exposure at work only, home only, and both home and work were 52.0, 62.7, 67.2, 74.4 ng/mL, respectively, compared with 219.4, 220.9, 255.2, 250.5 ng/mL among moderate/heavy smokers (≥10 cigarettes per day). These data were interpreted to suggest that smokers living in residences where others smoke inside the home had significantly higher cotinine levels than smokers reporting no SHS exposure, regardless of individual smoking intensity. Hence future research should target the role that SHS exposure may have in nicotine dependence, cessation outcomes, and other health impacts among smokers.

Effect of Active and Passive Smoking on Serum Bilirubin Levels

It has been established that serum bilirubin is an endogenous antioxidant biomarker and its low level is a potential risk factor for smoking related health disorders. Recently, Kim et al., (2016) investigated the association of cigarette smoke with serum total bilirubin among Koreans. Between 2006 and 2011, they examined 4899 Korean adults living in a rural community. After excluding 38 participants with serum bilirubin >2mg/dL, 75 participants who did not report their smoking status or who had liver or bile duct disorders, and 711 participants with liver enzymes exceeding the upper reference values, and performed a cross-sectional analysis on 4075 participants. Participants were classified into four groups: never-smokers without secondhand smoke exposure (SHSE), never-smokers with SHSE, former smokers, and active smokers. Serum total bilirubin concentration was measured using the enzyme. Compared to never-smokers without SHSE, never-smokers with SHSE (β = -0.025 mg/dL), former smokers (β = -0.049

mg/dL), and active smokers (β = -0.149 mg/dL) had significantly lower serum bilirubin levels even after adjusting for demographic factors, study year, alanine aminotransferase, gamma-glutamyl transferase, hemoglobin, lifestyle factors, and chronic diseases. A sex-stratified analysis indicated that for men, former smokers and active smokers were associated with having lower bilirubin compared to never-smokers without SHSE. However, for women, never-smokers with SHSE and active smokers were associated with having lower bilirubin compared to never-smokers without SHSE, suggesting that both active and passive cigarette smoking are associated with low serum bilirubin among Korean adults and that not only active smoking but also passive smoking including SHSE can have an influence on decreasing serum bilirubin levels. With this different point of view, this study supported efforts to create smoke-free environments in order to foster more favorable serum bilirubin profiles, which may improve endothelial function and reduce the risk of cardiovascular disease.

Environmental Exposure and Effects on Health of Children from a Tobacco-Producing Region

Children may be environmentally exposed to several hazards. In order to evaluate the health of children living in a tobacco-producing region, Nascinento et al., (2017) recently evaluated different biomarkers of exposure and effect, as well as hematological parameters. Biomarkers of exposure to the following xenobiotics were assessed: pesticides, nicotine, toxic elements, and organic solvents. Oxidative damage markers malondialdehyde (MDA) and protein carbonyls (PCO), vitamin C, microalbuminuria (mALB) levels, and N-acetyl-β-D-glucosaminidase (NAG) activity were also evaluated. Peripheral blood samples and urine were collected from 40 children (6-12 years), at two different crop periods: in the beginning of pesticide applications (period 1) and in the leaf harvest (period 2). The Wilcoxon signed-rank test for paired data was used to evaluate the differences between both periods. Biomarkers of exposure cotinine in urine and blood chromium (Cr) levels were increased in period 1 when compared to period 2. Moreover, a significantly-reduced plasmatic activity of butyrylcholinesterase (BuChE) was observed in period 2 in relation to period 1. Blood Cr levels were above the recommended by WHO in both evaluations. The biomarkers MDA and PCO as well as the kidney dysfunction biomarker, mALB, presented levels significantly increased in period 1. Additionally, decreased lymphocytes and increased basophils were observed. Cotinine was positively associated with PCO, and Cr was positively associated with PCO and MDA. The increased Cr levels were associated with decreased lymphocytes and increased basophils, illustrating that children environmentally exposed to xenobiotics in rural area may present early kidney dysfunction, hematological alterations, as well as lipid and protein damages, associated with co-exposure to different xenobiotics involved in tobacco cultivation.

Nicotine -Induced Reduced Expression of Nucleolar Organizer Region (AgNOR) of Developing Purkinje Cells in SIDS

It has been very well-established that the nucleolus is an important cellular component involved in the biogenesis of the ribosomes. Recently, Lavezzi et al., (2016) performed a study to validate the role of argyrophilic nucleolar organizer region (AgNOR), specific for the nucleoli detection, in neuropathological studies on sudden fetal and infant death (SIDS). In a wide set of fetuses and infants, aged from 27 gestational weeks to eight postnatal months and dead from both known and unknown causes, an in-depth neuropathological study usually applied at the Lino Rossi Research Center of the Milan University was implemented by the AgNOR evaluation. Peculiar abnormalities of the nucleoli, as partial or total disruption in Purkinje cells (PCs), were observed in victims of SIDS, and not in controls. The observed nucleolar alterations were related to nicotine absorption during pregnancy, suggesting that reduced AgNOR represent early hallmarks of PC degeneration, contributing to the pathophysiology of SIDS. We have shown that exposure to malnutrition, environmental toxins (nicotine, ethanol), and microbial (bacteria, virus, and fungus) infections increase the requirement of energy (ATP) for intracellular detoxification in response to toxic insult. The increased production of energy (ATP) results in the free radical overproduction as a byproduct of oxidative phosphorylation in the electron transport chain. The free radicals (OH, NO) induce lipid peroxidation of polyunsaturated fatty acids in the mitochondrial membranes to cause their degeneration. The degenerated mitochondrial membranes condense together in the form of electron-dense multi-lamellar (usually penta or hepta-lamellar) structures to form Charnoly bodies (CBs). CBs were discovered for the first time in the developing rat cerebellar Purkinje cells (Sharma et al., 1986; Sharma et al., 1987; Sharma et al., 1993; Sharma et al., (2013), Sharma et al., (2013b), Sharma and Ebadi (2014), Sharma et al., (2015), Sharma et al., (2016 a,b), Sharma (2017). The number of ribosomes per unit area was significantly reduced in the Purkinje cells, where CB formation and CS sequestration occurred due to down-regulation of AgNOR. CB as a nonfunctional, pleomorphic structure is an intracellular inclusion and is efficiently phagocytosed by lysosomes to synthesize charnolophagosome (CPS). The CPS is transformed to charnolosome (CS) when the phagocytosed CB is completely hydrolyzed by the lysosomal enzymes. The CS is structurally and functionally highly unstable structure and is liable to permeabilization, sequestration, and/or disintegration in response to further free radical-induced cellular injury. Subsequently, CS budding occurs to form charnolosome bodies (CS bodies). The CS bodies are pinched off from the CS and enter in the nucleus through energy-dependent endonucleosis and releases toxic substances including: cytochrome-C, iron, acetaldehyde, ammonia, hydrogen peroxide, apoptosis-inducing factor, bax, bak, caspase-3) to cause inhibition of AgNOR. AgNOR is involved in the synthesis of ribosomes, required for the normal protein synthesis at the rough endoplasmic reticulum. Thus CS-induced AgNOR down-regulation causes complete shut-down of intracellular protein synthesizing machinery, resulting in cellular apoptosis, and eventually sudden infant death syndrome (SIDS).

Biomarkers of Tobacco in Smokers Urine

The most important biomarkers of tobacco can be detected in smoker's urine. These include: nicotine, nor nicotine, anatabine, and anabasine as illustrated in Figure 6.

Figure 6. Biomarkers of tobacco in smokers urine.

Charnolopharmacotherapeutics of Nicotinism

Three Major Types of Addiction

As described earlier, there are primarily three major types of addictions including: (a) food addiction (b) sex addiction and (c) drug addiction. Out these three, drug addiction has devastating consequences involving poor quality of life, socio-economic stigma, early morbidity, and mortality. In fact a chronic drug addict suffers from early morbidity and mortality due to compromised mitochondrial bioenergetics of neural progenitor cells and cardiac progenitor cells derived from induced pluripotent cells. Drugs of abuse, including nicotine induce charnoly body (CB) formation. Simultaneously, charnolophagy is induced as a cytoprotective mechanism. Charnolophagy is highly orchestrated energy-driven process involved in intracellular detoxification. A lysosome containing phagocytosed CB is named as charnolophagosome (CSP). The charnolophagosome (CPS) is transformed to charnolosome (CS), when the entire CB is completely hydrolyzed by the lysosomal enzymes. The charnolosome (CS) is single layered, highly labile organelle. It is efficiently eliminated from the cell by energy (ATP)-driven exocytosis as a basic molecular mechanism of intracellular detoxification. Charnolophagy occurs during acute phase of drug addiction as an efficient molecular mechanism of intracellular detoxification. However chronic drug addiction destabilizes CS. The CS buds off to synthesize CS bodies. CS bodies subsequently coalesce with the plasma membrane to form apoptotic bodies, which enhance membrane permeabilization. Chronic drug addiction (nicotine) induces CS destabilization (represented by permeabilization, sequestration, and fragmentation) and release of toxic substances to cause neurodegenerative apoptosis as illustrated in Figure 7.

Figure 7. Three major types of addiction.

Acute vs Chronic Nicotine during Intrauterine Life

Intrauterine exposure to nicotine can have acute as well as chronic deleterious effects. Acute exposure of nicotine to the developing fetus can induce mitochondrial oxidative stress to cause free radical overproduction. Free radicals are generated as a byproduct of mitochondrial oxidative phosphorylation during ATP synthesis. The energy (ATP) requirements are significantly increased in the neural progenitor cells, derived from induced pluripotent cells during nicotine exposure. Free radicals-induced lipid peroxidation causes degeneration of the mitochondrial membranes. The degenerated mitochondrial membranes condense to form electron-dense penta or hepta-lamellar structures. These quasi-crystalline intra-cellular inclusions are named as Charnoly bodies (CB). CB is very efficiently phagocytosed by energy-driven lysosome-dependent charnolophagy. The lysosome containing phagocytosed CB is named as charnolophagosome (CPS). CPS is transformed to charnolosome (Cs) when the CB is completely hydrolyzed by the lysosomal enzymes. During acute phase the CS is expcytosed by an energy (ATP)-dependent process as an efficient basic molecular mechanism of intracellular detoxification. The CS is structurally and functionally highly labile intracellular organelle and is easily destabilized by free radical attack. Free radical attack causes lipid peroxidation of CS membranes to trigger structural and functional breakdown of polyunsaturated fatty acids (linoeic acid, Linolenic acid, and Arachidonic acid). At certain very weak points, the CS membrane exhibits protuberances in the form of CS bodies.

The CS bodies can coalesce with the plasma membranes to induce the formation of apoptotic bodies which can cause membrane perforations. Thus free radicals induced permeabilization, sequestration, and degradation of CS releases highly toxic substances, such as cytochrome-C, 8-OH-2dG, 2, 3-dihydroxy nonenal, iron, acetaldehyde, hydrogen peroxide, and ammonia to cause degenerative apoptosis as illustrated in Figure 8.

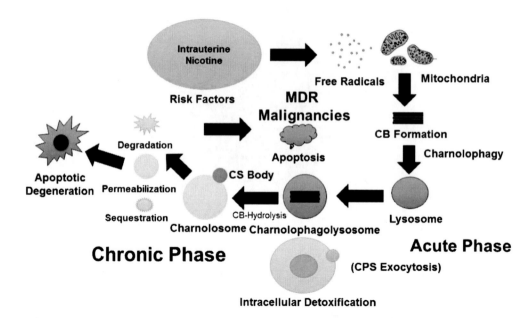

Figure 8. Acute vs Chronic Nicotine during Intrauterine Life.

Inhibition of AgNOR by Nicotine-Induced CS Body Prevents Protein Synthesis to Cause Apoptosis

The inhibition of argyrophilic nucleolar organizer (AgNOR) by nicotine induces CS body formation which prevents protein synthesis to cause degenerative apoptosis. Ribosomes are involved in the protein synthesis for cell growth and proliferation in mDR malignancies even in the presence of anticancer drugs. In addition to BCl_2, HSP, SOD, and catalase, CSscs releases MTs in the nucleus. MTs in the nucleus release Zinc to induce transcriptional activation of genes involved in DNA cell cycle, growth, proliferation, migration, and development in MDR malignancies. MTs are induced in severe malnutrition and in response to environmental toxins (nicotine, ethanol. Cd, Pb, Hg, As, Cr), microbial (bacteria, virus, and fungus) infections, and in numerous physico-chemical injuries as a defensive mechanism. Nuclear translocation of MTs through CS bodies renders MDR malignancies refractory to conventional therapeutic interventions, because MTs-induced release of Zinc is involved in transcriptional regulation of genes involved in cell growth, proliferation, migration, and development of malignant tumors even in the presence of anticancer drugs. In addition, MTs serve as potent free radical scavengers to prevent AgNOR down-regulation in MDR malignancies. Hence, conventional protein synthesis inhibitors are unable to inhibit protein synthesis due to MTs-mediated attenuation of AgNOR down-regulation and CS stabilization as presented in Figure 9.

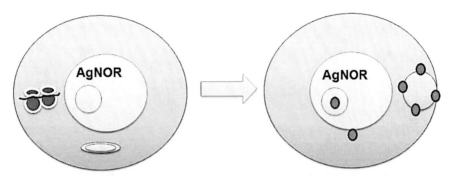

AgNOR in the Nucleolus is involved in the regulation of ribosomes synthesis. Ribosomes are involved in protein synthesis for cell growth and proliferation in MDR malignancies even in the presence of anticancer drugs. In addition to BCl2, HSPs, SOD and catalase, CSscs releases MTs in the nucleus. MTs release Zn^{2+}, to induce transcriptional activation of genes involved in growth, proliferation, and development in MDR malignancies. MTs are induced in malnutrition, and in response to environmental toxins (Nicotine, Ethanol), microbial infections, and in any physicochemical cell injury as a defensive mechanism Nuclear translocation of MTs through CS bodies renders MDR malignancies refractory to conventional treatment, because MTs-induced release of Zinc is involved in the transcriptional regulation of genes involved in growth, proliferation, migration, and tumor development even in the presence of anticancer drugs.

Figure 9. Inhibition of AgNOR by Nicotine-Induced CS Body Prevents Protein Synthesis to Cause Apoptosis.

Nicotine and Ethanol-Induced Charnolosome (CS) Destabilization

Abuse of nicotine and ethanol in combination induce charnolosome (CS) destabilization triggering inhibition of Purkinje cell AgNOR to cause SIDS. A pictorial diagram illustrating nicotine and ethanol-Induced CS destabilization causing inhibition of Purkinje cell AgNOR in SIDS. In general malnutrition, environmental neurotoxins (nicotine, ethanol) and microbial infections induce oxidative and nitrative stress to cause free radical production, involved in mitochondrial degeneration and CB formation, which is immediately phagocytosed by lysosomes to form charnolophagosome (CPS). The CPS is transformed to charnolosome (CS), when the entire phagocytosed CB is completely hydrolyzed by the lysosomal enzymes. CS are highly labile single layered intracellular organelles and can be easily destabilized to form CS bodies. The endonucleosis of CS bodies causes the release of toxic substances including cytochrome C, iron, and acetaldehyde, and ammonia, hydrogen peroxide to inhibit AgNOR, which is involved in the synthesis of ribosomes depending on the zinc-mediated transcriptional activation of nuclear genes involved in DNA cell cycle, growth, proliferation, migration and development. Thus, blockade of AgNOR-induced ribosomal production inhibits protein synthesis involved in cell survival, and leads to apoptotic degeneration as presented in Figure 10.

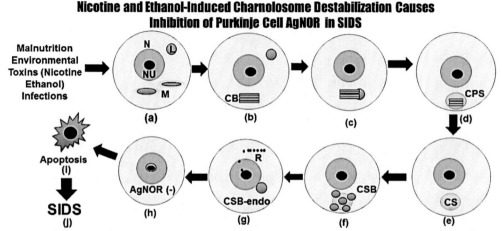

Figure 10. Nicotine and ethanol-induced charnolosome (CS) destabilization.

Molecular Mechanism of Nicotine -Induced MDR Malignancies (Involvement of CSscs Bodies)

Nicotine induces MDR malignancies by destabilizing stem cell specific CS formation. The stem cell specific CS is highly rich in MTs, which provide invasive characteristics to this highly unstable subcellular organelle. Endocytosis of CSscs is involved in malignant transformation of non-proliferating cell. The Nicotine-induced CSscs body is highly rich in antioxidant proteins such as BCl_2, MTs, HSPs, SOD, and Catalase, which protect argyrophilic nucleolar organizer (AgNOR) from free radical attack and from various protein synthesis inhibitors used in cancer chemotherapy, in addition to antibacterial, antifungal, and antiviral therapy. The therapeutic effect of various protein synthesis inhibitors used for the treatment of cancer, bacterial infections, fungal infections, and viral infections is nullified by Nicotine abuse because Nicotine inhibits AgNOR to prevent ribosomes production required for the protein synthesis. The cancer stem cell-specific CSscs are rich in metallothioneins (MTs), which store, donate, sequester, and buffer Zinc ions for the transcriptional activation of genes involved in induction of AgNOR to synthesize ribosomes. The ribosomes are involved in proteins synthesis for growth, proliferation, and development of MDR malignancies as presented in Figure 11.

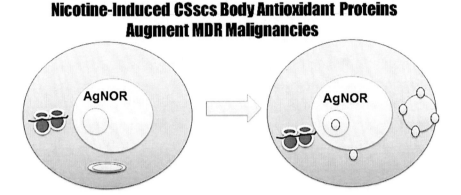

AgNOR in the nucleolus sustains protein synthesis by synthesizing the , required cell growth, development, and proliferation in MDR malignancies even in the presence of anticancer drugs. CSscs releases MTs in the nucleus, which release Zn^{2+}, involved in the transcriptional activation of genes involved in growth, proliferation, and development, which happens MDR malignancies. MTs are induced in malnutrition, and in response to environmental toxins and any physicochemical cell injury.

Figure 11. Molecular mechanism of nicotine-induced MDR malignancies. (Involvement of CSscs Bodies).

Environmental Pollution and Metal Ion Speciation of Metallothioneins

Although, MTs are primarily Zinc-binding proteins and under normal physiological conditions store, buffer, donate, and release Zinc. Zinc is translocated from the mitochondria to the nucleus, where it is involved in the transcriptional regulation of genes involved in DNA cell cycle, cell growth, proliferation, migration, differentiation, and development particularly in highly proliferating and metabolically-active cells. Environmental pollution of heavy metals such as Cd, Hg, Lead, Cr, As, Fe can also bind with this metal binding protein which render MTs either non-functional in several cardiovascular and neurodegenerative diseases (where cellular differentiation is very crucial), or aggressive, as noticed during malignant transformations. Thus MTs may become highly-induced to cause MDR malignancies. Hence, metal ion speciation of MTs is extremely important to determine the exact pathophysiological significance of these anti-apoptotic, anti-inflammatory, and free radical scavenging antioxidant proteins. Naturally, impaired metal ion speciation of MTs would be unable to prevent CB formation, CPS induction and CS destabilization and disintegration. Metal ion speciation of MTs can be precisely estimated employing metalomics analyses by inductively-coupled plasma mass spectrometry (ICP-MS) which is a matrix-independent procedure and can estimate as many at 32 metal ions from MTs within 20 minutes. Argon plasma torch burns at 5000-8000^{0}C, which can very efficiently induce pyration, atomization, and ionization within seconds and analyze the nature and quantity of metal ions in MTs.

Metallothioneins Stabilize Charnolosome to Prevent Apoptosis and Render Immortalization to Cancer Stem Cells in MDR Malignancies. (Charnolosome-Metallothioneins (CS-MTs) interaction)

There are primarily four major types of charnolosomes (CS) depending on the level of MTs in these structurally and functionally labile intracellular organelles. These charnolosomes (CS) include (a) MTs-Deficient CS; (b) MTs-Inadequate CS; (c) MTs-Normal CS; and (d) MTs-Over-expressing CS. MTs are low molecular weight, cysteine-rich, metal (Zn^{2+})-binding proteins, which can serve as antioxidants, antiapoptotic and anti-inflammatory factors. MTs inhibit CB formation, enhance charnolophagy, and stabilize charnolosomes (CS) by serving as potent free radical scavengers. The translocation of MTs in the nucleus, triggers genes involved in cell proliferation, cell migration, cell differentiation by donating zinc ions resulting in hyper-proliferation of cells. The structural and functional integrity of charnolosomes (CS) depends on the levels of MTs in these intracellular organelles. MTs deficient charnolosomes (CS) are most unstable and vulnerable to free radical-induced permeabilization, sequestration, and disintegration. Free radicals induce lipid peroxidation by causing structural and functional breakdown of polyunsaturated fatty acids (Linoic acid, Linolinic acid, and Arachidonic acid) resulting in the formation and rupture of charnolosome (CS) bodies to enhance permeabilization of charnolosome (CS) membrane to release highly toxic substances such as cytochrome-C, acetate, ammonia, hydrogen peroxide, iron, bax and bak to cause further apoptotic neurodegeneration. The free radicals are partially scavenged around the charnolosomes (CS) having inadequate MTs, whereas, MTs over-expressing charnolosomes (CS) remain structurally and functionally stable because these can readily scavenge free radicals. Thus, CS-MTs interaction renders the cancer cells either susceptible or resistant to anticancer therapy.

- **MTs Deficient CS**: These CSs can be readily disintegrated by free radical overload due to MTs deficiency.

- **MTs-Inadequate CS**: These CSs are also susceptible to free radicals synthesized as a byproduct of mitochondrial oxidative phosphorylation.
- **MTs-Normal CS**: The cells possessing CS with normal levels of MTs are relatively more stable because these organelles can scavenge free radicals to a certain extent.
- **CS Possessing High Levels of MTs**: The cell possessing CS with high levels of MTs are highly resistant to free radical attack and provide MDR malignancies and majority of adverse effects during anticancer therapy.

Thus, MTs-Over-expressing CS render structural and functional stability to CS to trigger MDR malignancies as illustrated in Figure 12.

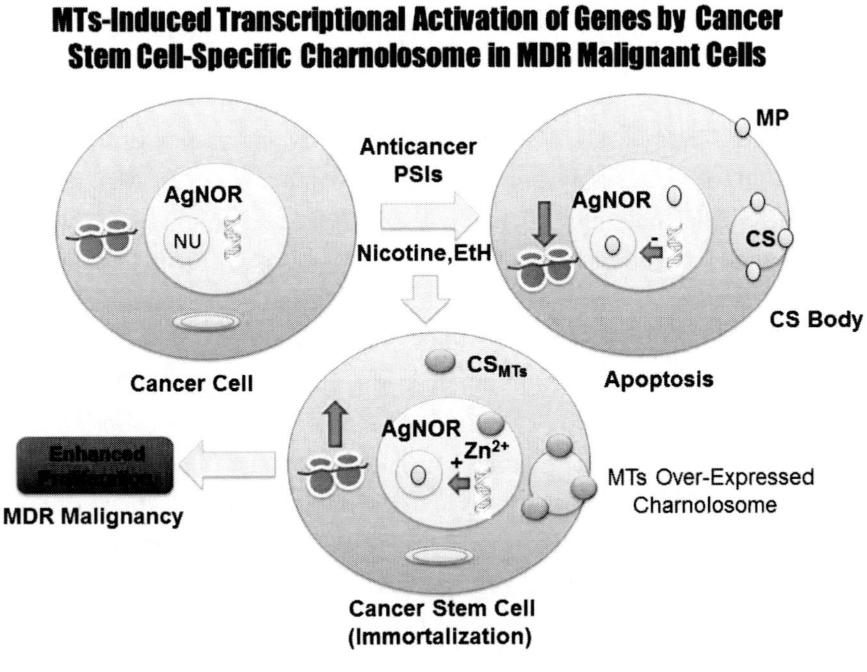

Figure 12. Metallothioneins-induced transcriptional activation of genes.

Nicotine-Induced CSscs Body Antioxidant Proteins Augment MDR Malignancies

Nicotine induces CSscs body Antioxidant Proteins Augment MDR Malignancies. AgNOR in the nucleolus maintains and sustains protein synthesis by synthesizing the ribosomes, required for the cell growth, development, proliferation and development in MDR malignancies even in the presence of various protein synthesis inhibitors which serve as anticancer agents. Because CSscs release antioxidant proteins such as MTs,

HSPs, BCl2, SOD, and Catalase to protect the AgNOR. As a consequence it goes on producing ribosomes involved in protein synthesis during MDR malignancy. The translocation and/or release of MTs from the CSscs in the nucleus donates Zinc, which causes the transcriptional activation of genes involved in the induction of DNA cell cycle, cell proliferation, migration, development, and invasion in MDR malignancies. MTs particularly are induced in severe malnutrition, environmental toxicity of nicotine, ethanol, during microbial infection, and numerous physico-chemical injuries to the most vulnerable cell as a basic molecular mechanism of cellular repair and growth. Uncontrolled induction of MTs in response to nicotine or ethanol-induced cell injury is involved in malignant transformation. Thus, MDR malignancies develop as a consequence of uncontrolled synthesis and induction of CSscs Body.

Pre-Term Neonatal Urinary Renal Developmental and Acute Kidney Injury Metabolomic Profiling

Acute kidney injury (AKI) staging has been developed in the adult and pediatric populations, but these do not yet exist for the neonatal population. Mercier et al., (2017) recently utilized metabolomics to uncover biomarkers of normal and AKI-associated renal dysfunction in preterm infants. The study comprised 20 preterm infants with an AKI diagnosis who were matched by gestational age and gender to 20 infants without an AKI diagnosis. Urine samples from pre-term newborn infants collected on day 2 of life were analyzed using broad-spectrum nuclear magnetic resonance (NMR) metabolomics. Multivariate analysis were used to identify metabolite profiles that differentiated AKI and no AKI, and to identify a metabolomics profile correlating with gestational age in infants with and without AKI. There was a clear distinction between the AKI and no-AKI profiles. Two previously identified biomarkers of AKI, hippurate and homovanillate, differentiated AKI from no-AKI profiles. Pathway analysis revealed similarities to cholinergic neurons, prenatal nicotine exposure on pancreatic β cells, and Amitraz-induced inhibition of Insulin secretion. Additionally, a pH difference was noted. Both pH and the metabolites were associated with AKI; however, only the metabotype was a significant predictor of AKI. Pathways for the no-AKI group that correlated with gestational age included aminoacyl-t-RNA biosynthesis, whereas pathways in the AKI group yielded potential metabolite changes in pyruvate metabolism, indicating that metabolomics can differentiate the urinary profiles of neonates with and without an AKI diagnosis and metabolic developmental profiles correlated with gestational age. These investigators recommended further studies in larger cohorts to validate these findings.

Gambling and Its Association with Drug Severity and Emotion-Related Impulsivity

Neural biomarkers for the active detrimental effects of cocaine dependence (CD) are lacking. Direct comparisons of brain connectivity in cocaine-targeted networks between CD and behavioral addictions (i.e., pathological gambling, PG) may be informative. Therefore, Contreras-Rodríguez et al., (2016) contrasted the resting-state functional connectivity networks of 20 individuals with CD, 19 individuals with PG and 21 healthy individuals (controls). Study groups were assessed to rule out psychiatric co-morbidities (except alcohol abuse and nicotine dependence) and current substance use or gambling (except PG). Thee investigators first examined global connectivity differences in the corticolimbic reward network and then utilized seed-based analyses to characterize the connectivity of regions displaying between-group differences. They examined the relationships between seed-based connectivity and trait impulsivity and cocaine severity. CD compared with PG displayed increased global functional connectivity in a large-scale ventral corticostriatal network involving the orbitofrontal cortex, caudate, thalamus and amygdala. Seed-based analyses showed that CD compared with PG exhibited enhanced connectivity between the orbitofrontal and subgenual cingulate cortices and between caudate and lateral prefrontal cortex, which are involved in representing the value of decision-making feedback. CD and PG compared with controls showed overlapping connectivity changes between the orbitofrontal and dorsomedial prefrontal cortices and between amygdala and insula, which are involved in stimulus-outcome learning. Orbitofrontal-subgenual cingulate cortical connectivity correlated with impulsivity and caudate/amygdala connectivity correlated with cocaine severity, suggesting that CD is linked to enhanced connectivity in a large-scale ventral corticostriatal-amygdala network that is relevant to decision making and likely to reflect an active cocaine detrimental effect.

Apoptosis of Testis in Rats after Cigarette Smoke Inhalation

Recently, He et al., (2016) studied the effects of differences in smoke concentration and exposure duration in Sprague Dawley rats to determine variation in type and severity of the testis apoptosis. The daily dosages were 10, 20 and 30 non-filter cigarettes for a period of 2, 4, 6, 8 and 12 weeks. Mainstream smoke exposure suppressed body weight gain in all regimens. A dose-related increase in plasma nicotine concentration was observed in smoke-exposed groups for 4, 6, 8 and 12 week regimens. Histopathological examination of the exposed groups showed disturbances in the stages of spermatogenesis, tubules atrophying and these appeared to be dose-related. Cytoplasmic caspase-3 immunostaining was detected both in Sertoli cells and germ cells in smoke-exposure groups. An increase in TUNEL-positive testicular cells was observed after 6 weeks of cigarette exposure, indicating that depending on the duration and concentration, cigarette exposure can induce apoptosis in the rat testes.

Metabolic Activation of Biomarkers of Tobacco-Specific Carcinogenic Nitrosamines

Lung cancer is the leading cause of death in the world, and cigarette smoking is the primary cause. Oral cavity cancer is another debilitating and often fatal cancer closely linked to tobacco product use. While great strides have been made in decreasing tobacco use in the US and some other countries, there are still an estimated 1 billion men and 250 million women in the world who are cigarette smokers and there are hundreds of millions of smokeless tobacco users, all at risk for cancer. Worldwide, lung cancer kills about three people per minute. In a recent review, Hecht et al., (2016) highlighted that this account focuses on metabolites and biomarkers of two powerful tobacco-specific nitrosamine carcinogens, 4-(methylnitrosamino)-1-(3-pyridyl)-1-butanone (NNK) and N'-nitrosonor nicotine (NNN), considered to be among the main causes of lung cancer and oral cavity cancer in people who use tobacco products. Three properties of NNK and NNN are critical for successful biomarker studies: (i) they are present in all tobacco products, (ii) they are tobacco-specific and are not found in any other product, (iii) and they are strong carcinogens. NNK and NNN are converted in humans to urinary metabolites that can be quantified by mass spectrometry as biomarkers of exposure to these carcinogens. They are also metabolized to diazonium ions and related electrophiles that react with DNA to form addition products that can be detected and quantified by mass spectrometry. These urinary metabolites and DNA addition products can serve as biomarkers of exposure and metabolic activation, respectively. The biomarkers of exposure, in particular the urinary NNK metabolites 4-(methylnitrosamino)-1-(3-pyridyl)-1-butanol (NNAL) and its glucuronides, have been extensively applied to document tobacco-specific lung carcinogen uptake in smokers and nonsmokers exposed to second-hand tobacco smoke. Highly sensitive mass spectrometric procedures have been developed for the quantitative analysis of these NNK metabolites as well as metabolites of NNN in human urine, blood, and toenails. Urinary and serum NNAL have been related to lung cancer risk, and urinary NNN has been related to esophageal cancer risk in prospective epidemiology studies. These are consistent with carcinogenicity studies of NNK, NNAL, and NNN in rats, which show that NNK and NNAL induce mainly lung tumors, while NNN causes tumors of the esophagus and oral cavity. Biomarkers of metabolic activation of NNK and NNN applied in human studies include the metabolism of deuterium labeled substrates to distinguish NNK and NNN metabolism from that of nicotine and the determination of DNA and hemoglobin adducts in tissues, blood, and oral cells from people exposed to tobacco products. As these are continually improved in parallel with the ever increasing sensitivity and selectivity of mass spectrometers, development of a comprehensive biomarker panel for identifying tobacco users at high risk for cancer appears to be a realistic goal. Targeting high risk individuals for smoking cessation and cancer surveillance with LC-MS can potentially decrease the risk of developing fatal cancers.

Circulating Monoamine Precursors and Smoking in Patients with Schizophrenia

Smoking is highly prevalent in patients with schizophrenia and exerts a negative impact on cardiovascular mortality in these patients. Smoking has complex interactions with monoamine metabolism through the ability of cigarette smoke to suppress Type 1 T helper cell (Th1) type immunity, the immunophenotype that is implicated in phenylalanine hydroxylase (PAH) dysfunction and tryptophan (Trp) breakdown to kynurenine (Kyn) via indoleamine 2, 3-dioxygenase. Nicotine also induces tyrosine hydroxylase (TH) gene expression, leading to increased synthesis of catecholamines. Furthermore, there is evidence for PAH dysfunction in schizophrenia. Mathai et al., (2016) recently compared the plasma levels of selected monoamine precursors and their metabolites in smokers vs. non-smokers in a large sample of patients with schizophrenia. They estimated plasma phenylalanine (Phe), tyrosine (Tyr), Trp, and Kyn levels using HPLC and calculated Phe:Tyr and Kyn:Trp ratios in 920 patients with schizophrenia. Analysis of variance and linear regression analyses were used to compare these endpoints between three groups of patients with schizophrenia: (1) current smokers, (2) past smokers, and (3) non-smokers. There were significant differences among the three groups with regards to Tyr levels [$F_{(2,789)} = 3.77$, $p = 0.02$], with current smokers having lower Tyr levels when compared with non-smokers ($p = 0.02$). Kyn levels and Kyn: Trp ratio were different among the three groups [$F_{(2,738)} = 3.17$, $p = 0.04$, $F_{(2,738)} = 3.61$, $p = 0.03$] with current smokers having lower Kyn levels ($p = 0.04$) and higher Kyn: Trp ratio ($p = 0.02$) when compared with past smokers. These findings required replication with protocols that include healthy controls to further elucidate the neurobiological underpinnings of altered Tyr and Kyn levels in smokers. Based on these findings, these investigators suggested potential molecular links between schizophrenia and smoking that may represent biomarkers and treatment targets for reducing an important modifiable cause of general morbidity and mortality in patients with schizophrenia.

Salivary Stress Biomarkers of Recent Nicotine Abuse and Dependence

Although stress plays a critical role in vulnerability to nicotine use and dependence, the stress response factors that contribute to smoking behaviors remain poorly elucidated. To minimize the confounding effects of chronic nicotine use, assessing individuals with relatively short smoking histories is critical for characterizing the neurobiological substrates associated with nicotine dependence early in the course of illness. Morris et al., (2016) recently conducted a pilot study to examine the sympathetic nervous system (α-amylase) and hypothalamic-pituitary-adrenal axis (Cortisol, Dehydroepiandrosterone) responses to the Trier Social Stress Test (TSST) in young adult smokers. Associations among indices of recent smoking (salivary cotinine, carbon monoxide in the breath [CO]), behavioral measures of nicotine dependence and withdrawal, and salivary biomarkers in response to the TSST were investigated. Smokers (N = 64; 28 males, 36 females) provided saliva samples at 30 min intervals for 2 hrs. prior to the TSST and every 10 min for 1 hr. following the TSST. α-Amylase responses to the TSST were positively associated with salivary cotinine levels but negatively associated with CO levels. Individuals with a lower level of nicotine dependence had increased Cortisol responses to the stressor, whereas those with a higher level of nicotine dependence did not show any Cortisol changes in response to the stressor, indicating that different mechanisms may be involved at different levels of nicotine dependence severity. Recent nicotine use and lower dependence severity was associated with increased activation of the stress response systems. In contrast, more severe levels of dependence downregulated stress response systems.

Personalized (Precision) Medicine in Smoking Cessation Treatments

Cigarette smoking is highly addictive and modern genetic research has identified robust genetic influences on nicotine dependence. An important step in translating these genetic findings to clinical practice is identifying the genetic variants as biomarkers. Hence, Chen et al., (2016) recently reviewed various factors affecting smoking cessation in order to enhance current smoking cessation treatments. These researchers reviewed the significant genetic variants that predict nicotine dependence, smoking cessation, and response to cessation pharmacotherapy. These data suggested that genetic risks can predict smoking cessation outcomes and moderate the effect of pharmacological treatments. Some pharmacogenetic findings have been replicated in meta-analyses or in multiple smoking cessation trials. The variation in efficacy between smokers with different genetic biomarkers supports the notion that personalized smoking cessation intervention based upon genotype could maximize the efficiency of such treatment while minimizing side effects, thus influencing the number needed to treat (NNT) and the number needed to harm. As personalized (precision) medicine is revolutionizing healthcare, smoking cessation may be one of the first areas where genetic variants may identify individuals at increased risk. Current evidence strongly suggests that genetic variants predict cessation failure and that cessation pharmacotherapy effectiveness is modulated by biomarkers such as nicotinic cholinergic receptor α5 subunit (CHRNA5) genotypes or nicotine metabolism ratio (NMR). These findings strengthen the development and rigorous testing of personalized treatments that target patients with different biological risk profiles. Hence, further research in this direction will go a long way in the safe and effective clinical management of individuals trapped in nicotnism associated with smoking conventional cigarettes and/or emerging e-cigarettes.

References

Chabenne, A., Moon C, Ojo C, Khogali A, Nepal B, and Sharma, S., 2014. Biomarkers in Fetal Alcohol Syndrome (Recent Update) *Biomarkers and Genomic Medicine* 6, 12-22.

Chen, L. S., Horton, A., Bierut, L. 2016. Pathways to precision medicine in smoking cessation treatments. *Neurosci Lett.* 2016 May 18.

Contreras-Rodríguez, O., Albein-Urios, N., Vilar-López, R., Perales J. C., Martínez-Gonzalez, J. M., Fernández-Serrano, M. J., Lozano-Rojas, O., Clark, L., Verdejo-García, A. 2016. Increased corticolimbic connectivity in cocaine dependence versus pathological gambling is associated with drug severity and emotion-related impulsivity. *Addict Biol.* 21(3), 709-718.

He, L., Gong, H., Zhang, J., Zhong, C., Huang, Y., Zhang, C., Aqeel Ashraf, M. 2016. Interaction of exposure concentration and duration in determining the apoptosis of testis in rats after cigarette smoke inhalation. *Saudi J Biol Sci.* 23(4), 531-541.

Hecht, S. S., Stepanov, I., Carmella, S. G., 2016. Exposure and Metabolic Activation Biomarkers of Carcinogenic Tobacco-Specific Nitrosamines. *Acc Chem Res.* 49(1), 106-114.

Jacob, N., Golmard, J.L., Berlin, I., 2017. Fetal exposure to tobacco: Nicotine and cotinine concentration in amniotic fluid and maternal saliva. *J Matern Fetal Neonatal Med.* 30(2), 233-239.

Jagtap, A., Gawande, S., Sharma, S., 2015. Biomarkers in Vascular Dementia. (A Recent Update). *Biomarkers and Genomic Medicine.* 7, 43-56.

Kim, N. H., Kim, H. C., Lee, J. Y., Lee, J. M., Suh, I., 2016. Active and Passive Smoking and Serum Total Bilirubin in a Rural Korean Population. *Nicotine Tob Res.* 18(5), 572-579.

Lavezzi, A. M., Alfonsi, G., Pusiol, T., Matturri, L., 2016. Decreased argyrophilic nucleolar organiser region (AgNOR) expression in Purkinje cells: first signal of neuronal damage in sudden fetal and infant death. *J Clin Pathol.* 69(1), 58-63.

Lindsay, R. P., Tsoh, J. Y., Sung, H. Y., Max, W., 2016. Secondhand smoke exposure and serum cotinine levels among current smokers in the USA. *Tob Control.* 25(2), 224-231.

Mathai, A. J., Kanwar, J., Okusaga, O., Fuchs, D., Lowry, C. A., Peng, X., Giegling, I., Hartmann, A. M., Konte, B., Friedl, M., Gragnoli, C., Reeves, G. M., Groer, M. W., Rosenthal, R. N., Rujescu, D., Postolache, T. T., 2016. Blood Levels of Monoamine Precursors and Smoking in Patients with Schizophrenia. *Front Public Health.* 4, 182.

Mercier, K., McRitchie, S., Pathmasiri, W., Novokhatny, A., Koralkar, R., Askenazi, D., Brophy, P. D., Sumner, S., 2017. Preterm neonatal urinary renal developmental and acute kidney injury metabolomic profiling: an exploratory study. *Pediatr Nephrol.* 32(1), 151-161.

Morris, M. C., Mielock, A. S., Rao, U., 2016. Salivary stress biomarkers of recent nicotine use and dependence. *Am J Drug Alcohol Abuse.* 42(6), 640-648.

Nascimento, S. N., Göethel, G., Baierle, M., Barth, A., Brucker, N., Charão, M. F., Moro, A. M., Gauer, B., Sauer, E., Durgante, J., et al., 2017. Environmental exposure and effects on health of children from a tobacco-producing region. *Environ Sci Pollut Res Int.* 24(3), 2851-2865.

Sharma, S., 2017a. *Zika Virus Disease (Prevention and Cure).* Nova Science Publishers, New York, U.S.A.

Sharma, S., 2017b *Fetal Alcohol Spectrum Disorders (Concepts, Mechanism, and Cure).* Nova Science Publishers, New York, U.S.A.

Sharma, S., 2017c *Charnolosome-Metallothioneins Interaction in Health and Disease.* Nova Scicnes Publishers. U.S.A. (in Process)

Sharma, S., 2017d *The Charnoly Body (A Novel Biomarker of Mitochondrial Bioenergetics in Health and disease).* CRC Press Boca Raton, FL. U.SA. (In process).

Sharma, S., 2017e. Multimodality Translational Neuroimaging. *Current Drug Targets.* 18, (in press).

Sharma, S., 2017f. *Nicotinism and emerging Electrornic Cigarettes.* Nova Science Publishers, New York, U.S.A. Vol. 2.

Sharma, S., Lippincott, W., 2017. Emerging Biomarkers in Alzheimer's Disease (Recent Update). *Current Alzheimer Research.* 14 (in press).

Sharma, S., 2016a. *Personalized Medicine (Beyond PET Biomarkers).* Nova Science Publishers. New York. U.S.A.

Sharma, S., 2016b. *Charnoly body as a novel biomarker of Zika virus induced microcephaly.* Conference: Drug Discovery & Therapy World Congress-2016

(Track: CNS Drug Discovery & Therapy), At John B. Hynes Veterans Memorial Convention Center, Boston, USA. Aug 22-25.

Sharma, S., 2016. *Progress in PET Radiopharmaceuticals (Quality Control & Theranostics)*. Nova Science Publishers. New York. U.S.A.

Sharma, S., 2016c. PET Radiopharmaceuticals for Personalized Medicine. *Curr Drug Targets.* 17, 1894-1907.

Sharma, S., Choga, J., Gupta, V. et al., 2016d. Charnoly body as Novel Biomarker of Nutritional Stress in Alzheimer's Disease. *Functional Foods in Health and Disease.* 6(6), 344-377.

Sharma, S., Gawande, S., Jagtap, A., Abeulela, R., Salman, Z., 2015. Fetal Alcohol Syndrome; Prevention, Diagnosis, & Treatment. In *Alcohol Abuse: Prevalence, Risk Factors.* Nova Science Publishers, New York, U.S.A.

Sharma, S., 2015a. *Monoamine Oxidase Inhibitors: Clinical Pharmacology, Benefits, & Adverse Effects.* Nova Science Publishers, New York. U.S.A.

Sharma, S., 2015b. *Alleviating Stress of the Soldier & Civilian.* Nova Science Publishers, New York. U.S.A.

Sharma, S., 2014. *Beyond Diet and Depression (Volume-1)* Book. Nova Sciences Publishers, New York, U.S.A.

Sharma, S., 2014. *Beyond Diet and Depression (Volume-2)* Book. Nova Science Publishers, New York, U.S.A.

Sharma, S., 2014. Nanotheranostics in Evidence Based Personalized Medicine. *Current Drug Targets.* 15: 915-930.

Sharma, S., Ebadi, M., 2014. Significance of Metallothioneins in Aging Brain. *Neurochemistry International.* 65, 40-48.

Sharma, S., Ebadi, M., 2014 Charnoly body as a Universal Biomarker of Cell Injury. *Biomarkers and Genomic Medicine* 6, (No 4), 89-98.

Sharma, S., 2014. Molecular Pharmacology of Environmental Neurotoxins. In *Kainic Acid: Neurotoxic Properties, Biological Sources, and Clinical Applications.* Nova Science Publishers. New York. P1-47.

Sharma, S., Nepal, B., Moon, C. S., Chabenne, A., Khogali, A., Ojo, C., Hong, E., Goudet, R., Sayed-Ahmad, A., Jacob, A., Murtaba, M., Firlit, M., 2014. Psychology of Craving. *Open Jr of Medical Psychology.* 3, 120-125.

Sharma, S., Rais, A., Sandhu, R., Nel, W., Ebadi, M. M., 2013. Clinical significance of metallothioneins in cell therapy and nanomedicine. *International Journal of Nanomedicine.* 8, 1477–1488.

Sharma, S., Moon, C. S., Khogali, A., Haidous, A., Chabenne, A., Ojo, C., Jelebinkov, M., Kurdi, Y., Ebadi, M., 2013. Biomarkers of Parkinson's Disease (Recent Update). *Neurochemistry International.* 63, 201-229.

Sharma, S. K., Selvamurthy, W. and Dakshinamurti, K., 1993. Effect of environmental neurotoxins in the developing brain. *Biometeorology.* 2, 447-455.

Sharma, S. K., 1988. Nutrition and Brain Development. Published in the *Proceedings of the First World Congress of Clinical Nutrition. New Delhi*, (India) p 5-8.

Sharma, S. K., Nayar, U., Maheshwari, M. C. and Singh, B., 1987. Effect of undernutrition on developing rat cerebellum: Some Electrophysiological and Neuromorphological Correlates. *J. Neurol. Sciences.* 78, 261-272.

Sharma, S. K., Nayar, U., Maheshwari, M. C, and Gopinath, G., 1986. Ultrastructural studies of P-cell morphology in developing normal and undernourished rat cerebellar cortex. Electrophysiological Correlates. *Neurology. India.* 34, 323-327.

Section 2:
Clinical Management of Nicotinism

Chapter 8

Harmful and Beneficial Effects of Tobacco and Clinical Management of Nicotinism

Abstract

This chapter highlights recent update on the deleterious effects of nicotinism and its clinical management. The chapter also highlights some of the therapeutic benefits of tobacco smoking. However, the list of health risks seems endless. Despite serious health risks, global population smokes tobacco in the entire world. Particularly, young adolescents are highly vulnerable to tobacco addiction and its deleterious consequences in their later life, associated with early morbidity and mortality. It has been shown that IL-6 and IL-10 levels in the cord blood of newborns with a history of crack/cocaine exposure in utero are significantly increased, indicating induction of a proinflammatory response to these drugs of abuse, whereas Agmatine protected rat liver from nicotine induced hepatic damage. The plasma suPAR level was lowered by smoking cessation. An experimental study indicated that antimicrobial photodynamic therapy minimizes the deleterious effect of nicotine in female rats suffering from induced periodontitis. Recently, reduced nicotine content cigarettes have been introduced in the market as alternative nicotine products and snus vs medicinal nicotine among smokers interested in product switching, and tobacco heating system (THS), as a modified tobacco risk product have been evaluated. A significant non-compliance was noticed among switchers to reduced nicotine content cigarettes. A comparative health-related analysis of conventional cigarettes vs THS has provided evidence of their relative safety. Although, not exactly identical, similar biomarkers of exposure were identified in smokers switching to a carbon-heated tobacco product. Moreover, caffeine in coffee, tea, chocolate, and energy-drink flavored e-liquids also significantly influenced health risks of e-cigarettes. In a recent study, a metabolomic profiling of Menthol smokers was carried out, which is used as a flavor enhancer in the e-cigarettes. Particularly, reno-protective effects of Curcumin against diabetes and nicotine have been reported and biomarker feedback intervention to motivate smoking cessation during pregnancy have been tried with limited success. The beneficial effects of the compounds of smilax China have been reported on the nicotine-induced endothelial dysfunction. In addition, Nicotine replacement therapy has been advocated to reduce harm from continued tobacco use and RCT has been employed for the evaluation of e-cigarettes. The effect of reduced nicotine content cigarettes on smoking behavior has been explored. Biomarkers of second-hand tobacco smoke exposure among nonsmokers have also been evaluated. Notably, nicotine and 6-hydroxy-l-nicotine improved behavioral deficits in an animal model of AD. It has been demonstrated that CB2 receptors mediate nicotine-induced anti-inflammation in N9 microglial cells exposed to β-amyloid, implicated in the etiopathogenesis of AD. In an experimental model of AD, the therapeutic benefits of nicotine versus 6-hydroxy-l-nicotine were evaluated against Chlorisondamine-induced memory impairment and oxidative stress in the rat hippocampus. It has been shown that the biomarkers of depression are significantly elevated in MS patients, whereas nicotine in tobacco smoke may alleviate some of the symptoms of depression in these patients. Hence, nicotinic acetylcholine receptors have been evaluated in an experimental model of MS. To evaluate nicotine intake from e-cigarettes, tobacco consumption and toxicant exposure of e-cigarettes was determined. Recently, analytical methods have been developed for the measurement of parent drug and metabolites in the oral fluid and plasma samples of cigarette smokers. In addition, assessment of tobacco-specific nitrosamines (TSNAs) have been estimated in the oral fluid as biomarkers of cancer risk among conventional and e-cigarette smokers. Behavioral and physiological responses to nicotine patch among nonsmokers were determined. Recently, reduced nicotine products have been evaluated from their safety profile. Nicotine had a moderating effect and impact on cannabis use. Serious health related consequences were noticed due to incomplete smoke-free legislation in the Republic of Korea. Supervised, vigorous intensity exercise intervention have been introduced for depressed female smokers. In addition to alternative nicotine delivery systems (ANDS) and the effectiveness of CO-Oximetry and anti-smoking brief advice have been tried in a cohort of kidney transplant patients who smoke. The biomarkers of exposure and effect in smokers and moist snuff consumers has been established. Human pharmacology for addiction medicine has been established. It has been discovered that mood, stress and longevity converge on ANK3 gene. Light and intermittent smoking has also been evaluated. The spectrum of nicotine has been characterized in variable nicotine research cigarettes. Racial differences have been noticed in nicotine metabolism, and nicotine intake from cigarette smoking. The puff characteristics, nicotine dependence, and nicotine metabolism were interlinked among tobacco smokers. A weight gain was observed among smokers consuming low nicotine content cigarettes. A recent study evaluated the prevalence and impact of long-term use of nicotine replacement therapy in UK stop-smoking services. The melancholia was associated with serum cytokine receptor levels among tobacco smokers. Hence, staging of illness was evaluated in depressive and manic phases, and severity of depression in bipolar disorder and the adverse effects of smoking on health outcomes in bipolar disorder were determined. It has been established that a single controlled exposure to secondhand smoke may not influence thrombogenesis or trigger platelet activation. Particularly, Benzene has been identified as one of the toxic chemical in tobacco smoke. An association of exposure to Benzene and smoking with oxidative damage to nucleic acids has been established. Microarray analyses determined the protective effects of elafin against cigarette smoking adult asthma patients. Supervised, vigorous intensity exercise intervention has been recommended for depressed female smokers. In addition, estimates of tobacco use has been made by wastewater analysis of anabasine and anatabine to assess the environmental exposure of nicotine to general public. An agreement between wastewater-based epidemiology and survey data on Alcohol and nicotine was noticed in circumscribed community. Substance use disorders have been determined in individuals with mild to borderline intellectual disability and tobacco alkaloids nornicotine, anatabine, and anabasine have been estimated in smokers' urine. A genome-wide meta-analysis of cotinine levels in cigarette smokers has been performed. Care-giver health literacy and preschool children's secondhand smoke exposure has been established. Furthermore, self-report and biological measures of cigarette use in nondaily smokers has been evaluated. Tobacco-specific N-nitrosamines and polycyclic aromatic hydrocarbons (PAH) in cigarettes have been estimated to determine their carcinogenic potential. It has been demonstrated that white matter integrity is impaired in young smokers. Genetic determinants of CYP2A6 activity and biomarkers of tobacco smoke exposure have been determined in relation to risk of lung cancer. A randomized controlled trial of reduced nicotine cigarettes was performed in smokers with mood and/or anxiety disorders and various biomarkers of tobacco exposure were established. Regional homogeneity changes were identified in nicotine addicts by performing resting-state fMRI. Recently, cDNA-AFLP biotechnology was applied for novel biomarker discovery in a non-model species *Grandidierella japonica*. The deleterious effects of fetal exposure to tobacco have also been demonstrated. Furthermore, psychometric properties of the Fagerström test for nicotine dependence in Mexican smokers, and the determinants of light and intermittent smoking in the US population have been established to accomplish the personalized theranostics of nicotinism.

Keywords: antimicrobial photodynamic therapy, endothelial dysfunction, bipolar disorders, nicotinism, resting state fMRI, cDNA-AFLP biotechnology, genetic feterminants of CYP2A6 activity, e-cigarettes, tobacco-specific nitrosamines (TSNAs)

Introduction

It has been reported that within 10 seconds after a cigarette smoker inhales, nicotine is absorbed through the skin and the mucosal linings in the nose, mouth and lungs, and enters through the bloodstream to the brain. Nicotine stimulates adrenal glands to synthesize epinephrine, a hormone and neurotransmitter as adrenaline, which causes tachycardia and increase in BP by inducing vasoconstriction. It also stimulates the production of DA, a neurotransmitter that controls the brain's pleasure center. Inhaling nicotine confers the most immediate effects, and that's not a coincidence; it's because lungs are lined with millions of alveoli, which provide an enormous surface area, >40 times the surface area of the skin, making it the most efficient way to get nicotine into circulation. Nicotine only stays in the human body for a few hrs; it has a half-life of about a hr. or two, meaning that 6 hrs. after smoking a cigarette, only about 0.031 mg of the 1 mg of nicotine inhaled remains. Nicotine is also able to absorb through GIT system and skin. This is how smokeless tobacco products such as chewing tobacco, skin patches and gum deliver their nicotine in this system. It's because nicotine can help people feel calmer, causing temporary feelings of relaxation as well as reducing stress, anxiety and even pain. In spite of relaxation, nicotine actually increases physical stress; its effects are considered a paradox. It boosts the CNS, but depending on the dosage some smokers find nicotine also acts as a sedative. Some studies, though, suggest it may just be the ritual of smoking that induces a calming effect, because nicotine is actually considered a stimulant, not a depressant. When nicotine is first inhaled, it causes body to release epinephrine, which is the "fight or flight" hormone. Epinephrine activates the sympathetic nervous system, making breathing become rapid and shallow, the heart rate increase, and blood pressure rise to cause alertness. Nicotine can also lead to Insulin sensitivity and Insulin resistance, as well as an increased risk of developing metabolic syndrome, type 2 diabetes and cardiovascular disease. It affects thyroid hormones, pituitary hormones, sex hormones and adrenal hormones. Insulin resistance in cigarette smokers may be partly because nicotine stimulates the body to produce high levels of adrenal androgens i.e., nicotine influences the body's glucose metabolism, leading to hyperglycemia associated with insulin resistance. Insulin resistance not only increases the risk of developing type 2 diabetes but also cardiovascular disease.

Tobacco plant belong to the same family as some of our favorite edibles including: potatoes, tomatoes, eggplant and hot peppers. Although, nicotine is addictive, as addictive as cocaine or heroin, it is difficult to quit even if body absorbs only a tenth of the amount of nicotine in every cigarette smoke -- just 1 mg out of the 10 an average cigarette contains is sufficient to get trapped in the vicious circle of nicotinism. Most smokers report they want to quit the habit, but without cessation help, >85% of those who try to quit, start smoking again in about a week (NIDA). Trying to quit nicotine habit may cause physical reactions such as strong cravings for the substance, an increased appetite, insomnia, sleep disturbances, gastrointestinal problems and mood-related complaints including anxiety, anger and frustration, depression, irritability and restlessness [Mayo Clinic].

Many health risks have been associated with tobacco consumption. Although, nicotine has been used as a commercial insecticide and fumigant in the recent past, the news doesn't get better. According to CDC report, each year, 440,000 cigarette smokers die, and for every one death caused by a smoking-related disease there are 20 more people living with at least one serious smoking-related illness. Tobacco use of any type is accompanied with numerous health risks. Out of as many as 7000 chemical identified from the tobacco smoke, at least 250 chemicals are known to be toxic or to cause cancer. A smoking habit of just one to four cigarettes a day is enough to increase the chance of developing cardiovascular disease. Pneumonia, emphysema and respiratory infections, cataracts and ocular problems, and certain cancers including cancers of the mouth, pharynx, larynx, esophagus, lungs, stomach, pancreas, cervix, kidney, ureter and bladder as well as some leukemias are all recognized risks of a nicotine addiction. The risk of dying from cancer (lung or another type) doubles if someone is a smoker, and as many as 9 out of 10 people diagnosed with lung cancer can directly blame their tobacco habits [MedicineNet, Mayo Clinic]. Smokers are also more likely to suffer from periodontal disease, diabetes (or insulin resistance), infertility and pregnancy complications, and deleterious changes in their physical appearance (including early aging and yellow-stained, sallow skin). On an average, nonsmokers live about a decade longer than smokers [CDC].

Although smoking tobacco is linked with certain diseases and chronic conditions that will lead to an early mortality, nicotine is also lethal if ingested in high doses. An oral dose (consumed rather than inhaled) of 50 to 60 mg is sufficient to cause fatality in a 160-pound person [NIOSH]. For example, manufacturers recommend that no one should chew >24 pieces of nicotine gum in single day, because if we ingest more nicotine then there is a risk an overdose. Nicotine is a stimulant and when someone exposed to too much, it causes excitation of the cholinergic neurons by binding with the cholinergic receptors to cause excitation. The same cholinergic receptors are involved in the poisoning of organophosphate insecticides such as DDT and nerve agents such as sarin gas. When exposed to toxic levels of organophosphate, ACh builds up at synapses and impairs nerve impulses. Ach induces electrical stimulation normally associate with vagus nerve, and the excess Ach overstimulates the neurons. Because nicotine is also similar to ACh, it binds to nicotinic cholinergic receptors and, in excess, produces overstimulation -- the more nicotine available in body to bind to the nicotinic cholinergic receptors, the greater will be its severity of poisoning.

In this chapter, a recent update on the harmful and therapeutic effects of Nicotine are described briefly. The chapter is also devoted to describe various clinical and psychological interventions to safely and successfully manage nicotinism and its deleterious health-related consequences.

IL-6 and IL-10 in the Cord Blood of Newborns with a History of Crack/Cocaine Exposure in Utero

It is well established that prenatal cocaine exposure (PCE) is associated with neurobehavioral problems during childhood and adolescence. Early activation of the inflammatory response may contribute to such changes. Hence, Mardini et al., (2016) conducted a study to compare inflammatory markers (IL-6 and IL-10) both in umbilical cord blood and in maternal peripheral blood at delivery between newborns with history of crack/cocaine exposure in utero and non-exposed newborns. In this cross-sectional study, 57 newborns with a history of crack/cocaine exposure in utero (EN) and 99 non-exposed newborns (NEN) were compared for IL-6 and IL-10 levels. Sociodemographic and perinatal data, maternal psychopathology, consumption of nicotine and other substances were systematically collected in cases and controls. After adjusting for potential confounders, mean IL-6 was significantly higher in EN than in NEN (10,208.54, 95% confidence interval [95%CI] 1,328.54-19,088.55 vs. 2,323.03, 95%CI 1,484.64-3,161.21; $p = 0.007$; generalized linear model [GLM]). Mean IL-10 was also significantly higher in EN than in NEN (432.22, 95%CI 51.44-812.88 vs. 75.52, 95%CI 5.64-145.39, $p = 0.014$;

GLM). Adjusted postpartum measures of IL-6 were significantly higher in mothers with a history of crack/cocaine use (25,160.05, 95%CI 10,958.15-39,361.99 vs. 8,902.14, 95%CI 5,774.97-12,029.32; p = 0.007; GLM), with no significant differences for IL-10. There was no correlation between maternal and neonatal cytokine levels, indicating that IL-6 and IL-10 might be early biomarkers of PCE in newborns. These findings could help to elucidate neurobiological pathways underlying neurodevelopmental changes and broaden the possibilities for early intervention.

Agmatine Protects Rat Liver from Nicotine -Induced Hepatic Damage

Tobacco smoking with its various forms is a global problem with proven hazardous effects to human health. El-Sherbeeny et al., (2016) recently planned a study to define the role of Agmatine (AGM) on hepatic oxidative stress and damage induced by nicotine in rats. Thirty-two rats divided into four groups were employed: control group, nicotine-only group, AGM group, and AGM-nicotine group. Measurements of serum hepatic biochemical markers, lipid profile, and vascular cell adhesion molecule-1 were done. In addition, malondialdehyde (MDA), superoxide dismutase (SOD), glutathione (GSH) activity, and nitrate/nitrite (NOx) levels were estimated in the liver homogenates. Immunohistochemistry for Bax and transforming growth factor beta (TGF-β1) and histopathology of the liver were also included. This study demonstrated that nicotine administration exhibits marked liver deterioration, an increase in liver enzymes, changes in lipid profile, and an elevation in MDA with a decline in levels of SOD, GSH, and NOx (nitrate/nitrite). Also, levels of proapoptotic bax and profibrotic TGF-β1 showed marked elevation in the liver. AGM treatment to rats in nicotine-only group ameliorated all the aforementioned deleterious changes, indicating that AGM could successfully avert nicotine-evoked hepatic oxidative stress and tissue injury, apoptosis, and fibrosis.

Plasma suPAR is Lowered by Smoking Cessation

It is well-established that soluble urokinase plasminogen activator receptor (suPAR) is a stable inflammatory biomarker. In patients, suPAR is a marker of disease presence, severity, and prognosis. In the general population, suPAR is predictive of disease development, such as diabetes and cardiovascular disease and, in smokers, predictive of long-term lung cancer development. Whether smoking cessation impacts the suPAR level remains unknown. In a recent study, Eugen-Olsen et al., (2016) randomized 48 smokers into three groups of 16: (i) continued to smoke 20 cigarettes per day, (ii) refrained from smoking and used transdermal nicotine patches and (iii) refrained from smoking and used placebo patches. Nonsmokers were included for comparison. SuPAR and C-reactive protein (CRP) levels were measured by ELISA. At baseline, the suPAR level was significantly higher in the 48 smokers (median 3·2 ng mL, IQR (2·5-3·9)) than in 46 never smokers (1·9 ng/mL (1·7-2·2)). In smokers randomized to smoking cessation, suPAR levels after 4 weeks of stopping were decreased and no longer significantly different from the never smokers values. SuPAR decreased in both those who received a placebo as well as nicotine patch. Interestingly, those with the highest suPAR level at time of smoking were also those with the highest level of suPAR after smoking cessation. In contrast, smoking or smoking cessation had no influence on CRP levels, suggesting that the suPAR level may aid to personalize the risk of smoking by identifying those smokers with the highest risk of developing disease and who may have the most benefit of smoking cessation.

Antimicrobial Photodynamic Therapy Minimizes the Deleterious Effect of Nicotine in Female Rats with Induced Periodontitis

In a study, Gualberto et al (2016) compared the use of antimicrobial photodynamic therapy (aPDT) as an adjunct to scaling and root planning (SRP) in the treatment of experimentally-induced periodontitis in female rats that were systemically treated with or without nicotine. Female rats (n = 180) were divided into two groups: vehicle administration (Veh) and nicotine administration (Nic). Mini-pumps containing either vehicle or nicotine were implanted in the rats 30 days before the induction of experimental periodontitis (EP). EP was induced by placing a cotton ligature around the left mandibular first molar. After 7 days, the ligature was removed, and the rats were randomly divided into three treatment subgroups: SRP (only SRP), DL (SRP plus diode laser), and aPDT (SRP plus aPDT). The aPDT consisted of phenothiazine photosensitizer deposition followed by diode laser irradiation. Ten rats from each subgroup were euthanized at 7, 15, and 30 days after treatment. Alveolar bone loss (ABL) in the furcation region was evaluated using histological, histometric, and immunohistochemical analyses. The rats that were treated with nicotine showed more ABL compared to those treated with vehicle. In both the Veh and Nic groups, SRP plus aPDT treatment resulted in reduced ABL, smaller numbers of both TRAP- and RANKL-positive cells, and higher numbers of PCNA-positive cells compared to SRP treatment alone, indicating that APDT was an effective adjunctive therapy for the treatment of periodontitis in female rats regardless of whether they received nicotine.

Reduced Nicotine Content Cigarettes and Alternative Nicotine Products

To compare the use of alternative nicotine products, smoking behavior and tobacco biomarker exposure in smokers unwilling to quit who were assigned randomly to normal nicotine content (NNC) cigarettes or very low nicotine content (VLNC) cigarette, Hatsukami et al., (2017) randomized, parallel-arm 8-week study with assignment to VLNC (VLNC 1, n = 53) or NNC (NNC, n = 27) with access to non-cigarette combusted and non-combusted tobacco/nicotine products or to VLNC with access to only non-combusted products (VLNC2, n = 56) in clinics in Minnesota, U.S.A. Smokers uninterested in quitting smoking with a mean [± standard deviation (SD)] age of 44(± 14) years and smoking 16 (± seven) cigarettes/day; 51% female, 72% white. During the experimental period, the measures taken included: rate of alternative products used, amount of and abstinence from combusted tobacco used and tobacco exposure biomarkers. There were higher rates of non-combusted alternative tobacco/nicotine product use in both VLNC conditions versus the NNC condition and in VLNC1 versus VLNC2 condition, accompanied by reduced biomarkers of exposure primarily in VLNC2 condition compared to NNC condition. Fewer combusted products were smoked at almost all visits (Ps ≤ 0.02) and there were higher rates of abstinence for both VLNC conditions compared with the NNC condition. The offer of, and instructions to use, reduced nicotine content cigarettes during an 8-week period led to greater use of alternative tobacco/nicotine products compared with continued use of normal nicotine cigarettes and also reductions in smoking rates.

Snus vs Medicinal Nicotine among Smokers Interested in Product Switching

An essential component of evaluating potential modified risk tobacco products is to determine how consumers use the product and resulting effects on biomarkers of toxicant exposure. In a recent study, Hatsukami et al., (2016) recruited cigarette smokers (n = 391) in Minnesota and Oregon to either snus or 4 mg nicotine gum for 12 weeks. Participants were instructed to completely switch from cigarettes to these products. Urine samples were collected to analyze carcinogenic tobacco-specific nitrosamine metabolites (4-(methylnitrosamino)-1-(3-pyridyl)-1-butanol and N'-nitrosonor nicotine and their glucuronides) and nicotine metabolites (total cotinine and nicotine equivalents) levels. Of the 391 participants randomized, 52.9% were male, the means age was 43.9 ± 12.5 years, baseline number of cigarettes/day was 18.0 ± 6.5 and Fagerström Test for nicotine Dependence score was 5.1 ± 2.0. The mean ± SD number of snus pouches used/week at week 6 prior to tapering was 39.1 ± 24.0 and nicotine gum pieces used was 37.6 ± 26.3. Dual use of cigarettes and these products were observed in 52.9% and 58.2% of those assigned to snus and nicotine gum, respectively, at week 12. The end of treatment biochemically verified (carbon monoxide, CO < 6 ppm) 7-day avoidance of cigarettes was 21.9% in the snus group and 24.6% in the nicotine gum group. Toxicant exposure in the nicotine gum group was significantly less when compared to snus. Snus performed similarly to nicotine gum in cigarette smokers who were interested in completely switching to these products, but was associated with less satisfaction and greater toxicant exposure than nicotine gum.

THS a Modified Risk Tobacco Product

The Tobacco Heating System (THS) 2.2, a candidate Modified Risk Tobacco Product (MRTP), is designed to heat tobacco without burning it. Tobacco is heated in order to reduce the formation of harmful and potentially harmful constituents (HPHC), and reduce the consequent exposure, compared with combustible cigarettes (CC). In a 5-day exposure, controlled, parallel-group, open-label clinical study, Haziza et al., (2016) randomized 160 smoking, healthy subjects to three groups and asked to: (1) switch from CCs to THS 2.2 (THS group; 80 participants); (2) continue to use their own non-menthol CC brand (CC group; 41 participants); or (3) to refrain from smoking (smoking abstinence (SA) group; 39 participants). Biomarkers of exposure, except those associated with nicotine exposure, were significantly reduced in the THS group compared with the CC group, and approached the levels observed in the SA group. Increased product consumption and total puff volume were reported in the THS group. However, exposure to nicotine was similar to CC at the end of the confinement period. Reduction in urge-to-smoke was comparable between the THS and CC groups and THS 2.2 product was well tolerated.

Non-Compliance in Switchers to Reduced Nicotine Content Cigarettes

Clinical trials on the impact and safety of reduced nicotine content cigarettes (RNCs) are ongoing, and an important logical concern is participant compliance with smoking only RNCs. Recently, Nardone et al., (2016) conducted a study to measure non-compliance biochemically with urine cotinine (COT) and total nicotine equivalents (TNEs), compare with self-reported non-compliance and identify associated covariates to perform a secondary analysis of a double-blind, parallel, randomized clinical trial. Volunteer sample of 242 participants (55% Caucasian), average age of 41.2 years, smoking at least five cigarettes per day (CPD). Smoking very low nicotine cigarettes (VLNCs; 0.4 mg nicotine/g tobacco) for 6 weeks. The primary outcome was biochemically verified non-compliance, measured as thresholds of COT/CPD and TNE/CPD ratios, considering changes in nicotine content from conventional levels to VLNCs, and as an absolute threshold of week 6 TNEs. Self-reported non-compliance was measured via daily phone calls. Key predictors included age, sex, race, Menthol preference, nicotine metabolite ratio, time to first cigarette dependence, CPD, TNEs, tar level and cigarette evaluation. Estimates of non-compliance with smoking the VLNCs exclusively include: the biochemical ratios (both 78%), the week 6 TNE threshold (76%) and self-report (39%). Of the key covariates, age, dependence and cigarette evaluations of satisfaction were significant; for age, younger participants more likely to be non-compliant. Dependence was associated with self-reported non-compliance. Cigarette evaluations of satisfaction were associated with non-compliance. Among smokers volunteering to smoke only very low nicotine cigarettes for 6 weeks, non-compliance was common and biochemical assessments detected more cases of non-compliance than self-report. Despite high levels of non-compliance, smokers reduced their intake of nicotine by an average of 60%.

Conventional Cigarettes vs Tobacco Heating System

It has been recognized that smoking conventional cigarettes (CCs) exposes smokers to harmful and potentially harmful constituents (HPHCs). The Tobacco Heating System 2.2 (THS 2.2), a candidate modified risk tobacco product, was developed to reduce or eliminate the formation of HPHCs, while preserving as much as possible the taste, sensory experience, nicotine delivery profile and ritual characteristics of CC. Recently, Haziza et al., (2016) measured levels of biomarkers of exposure to selected harmful and potentially harmful smoke constituents found in cigarette smoke, in addition to nicotine in 160 smokers randomized for 5 days to continuing smoking conventional cigarettes (41 participants), switching to Tobacco Heating System 2.2 (THS 2.2) (80 participants), or abstaining from smoking (39 participants). The descriptive statistics of the levels of each biomarker of exposure expressed as concentrations adjusted to creatinine; at baseline, and at the end of the study, and their relative change from baseline were analyzed. Reductions in the levels of biomarkers of exposure when expressed as quantity excreted, were also reported. These investigators also provided detailed descriptions of bioanalytical assays. These data were related to the article entitled "Evaluation of the Tobacco Heating System 2.2. Part 8: 5-Day randomized reduced exposure clinical study in Poland" In a further study, Haziza et al., (2016) conducted randomized, controlled, open-label study in confinement for 5 day exposure to demonstrate the reduction in exposure to selected HPHCs, to assess nicotine uptake and subjective effects, in participants switching to THS 2.2 (n = 80) compared to participants continuing smoking CCs (n = 40) and abstaining from smoking (n = 40). The subjects were randomized according to sex and daily CC consumption. The levels of biomarkers of exposure to HPHCs were significantly reduced in participants switching to THS 2.2, compared to CC use. Particularly, the magnitude of exposure reduction observed was close to that which was seen in participants who abstained from smoking for 5 days, while nicotine uptake was maintained. Reduction in urge-to-smoke was comparable between THS and CC groups, however THS 2.2 was slightly less satisfactory than CCs. The new, alternative tobacco product THS 2.2 was well tolerated.

Biomarkers of Exposure in Smokers Switching to a Carbon-Heated Tobacco Product

The primary aim of tobacco harm reduction is to provide reduced risk alternatives to smokers who would otherwise continue smoking combustible cigarettes (CCs). Hence, Ludicke et al., (2016) performed a randomized, open-label, three-arm, parallel-group, single-center, short-term confinement study to investigate the effects of exposure to selected harmful and potentially harmful constituents (HPHCs) of cigarette smoke in adult smokers who switched to a carbon-heated tobacco product (CHTP) compared with adult smokers who continued to smoke CCs and those who abstained from smoking for 5 days. Biomarkers of exposure to HPHCs, including nicotine and urinary excretion of mutagenic, were measured in 24-hrs. urine and blood samples in 112 male and female Caucasian smokers switching from CCs to the CHTP ad libitum use. Puffing topography was assessed during product use. Switching to the CHTP or smoking abstinence (SA) resulted in marked decreases from baseline to Day 5 in all biomarkers of exposure measured, including carboxyhemoglobin (43% and 55% decrease in the CHTP and SA groups, respectively). The urinary excretion of mutagenic was also markedly decreased on Day 5 compared with baseline (89% and 87% decrease in the CHTP and SA groups, respectively). No changes in biomarkers of exposure to HPHCs or urinary mutagenic were observed between baseline and Day 5 in the CC group. This study provided clear evidence supporting a reduction in the level of exposure to HPHCs of tobacco smoke in smokers who switched to CHTP under controlled conditions, similar to that observed in SA. The reductions observed in biomarkers of exposure to HPHCs of tobacco smoke in this short-term study could potentially reduce the incidence of cancer, cardiovascular and respiratory diseases in those smokers who switch to a heated tobacco product.

Influence of Caffeine in Coffee, Tea, Chocolate, and Energy-Drink Flavored E-Liquids

Most e-cigarettes contain a solution of propylene glycol/glycerin and nicotine, as well as flavors. E-cigarettes and their associated e-liquids are available in numerous flavor varieties. A subset of the flavor varieties include coffee, tea, chocolate, and energy drink, which, in beverage form, are commonly recognized sources of caffeine. Recently, some manufacturers have begun marketing e-liquid products as energy enhancers that contain caffeine as an additive. Lisko et al., (2016) recently developed a gas chromatography-mass spectrometry (GC-MS) for the quantitation of caffeine in e-liquids to assess caffeine concentrations in 44 flavored e-liquids from cartridges, disposables, and refill solutions. Products chosen were flavors associated with caffeine (i.e., coffee, tea, chocolate, and energy drink), marketed as energy boosters, or labeled as caffeine-containing by the manufacturer. Caffeine was detected in 42% of coffee-flavored products, 66% of tea-flavored products, and 50% of chocolate-flavored e-liquids (limit of detection [LOD] - 0.04 µg/g). Detectable caffeine concentrations ranged from 3.3 µg/g to 703 µg/g. Energy drink-flavored products did not contain detectable concentrations of caffeine. Eleven of 12 products marketed as energy enhancers contained caffeine, though in widely varying concentrations (31.7 µg/g to 9290 µg/g). E-liquid flavors commonly associated with caffeine content like coffee, tea, chocolate, and energy drink often contained caffeine, but at concentrations significantly lower than their dietary counterparts. Estimated daily exposures from all e-cigarettes products containing caffeine were much less than ingestion of traditional caffeinated beverages like coffee. This study presented an optimized and validated for the measurement of caffeine in e-liquids. The developed procedure was applicable to all e-liquid matrices and could potentially be used to ensure regulatory compliance for those geographic regions that forbid caffeine in e-cigarettes products. Caffeine concentrations and estimated total caffeine exposure from e-cigarettes products was significantly lower than oral intake from beverages. However, because very little is known about the effects of caffeine inhalation, e-cigarettes users should proceed with caution when using caffeine containing e-cigarettes products. Further research is necessary to determine associated effects from inhaling caffeine.

Metabolomic Profiling of Menthol Smokers

The use of Menthol in cigarettes and marketing is under consideration for regulation by the FDA. However, the effects of Menthol on smoking behavior and carcinogen exposure have been inconclusive. Hsu et al., (2017) recently reported metabolomic profiling for cigarette smokers, and a Menthol-glucuronide (MG) as the most significant metabolite directly related to smoking. These investigators studied MG in relation to smoking behavior and metabolomic profiles in a cross-sectional study of 105 smokers who smoked two cigarettes in the laboratory one hr. apart. Blood nicotine, MG, and exhaled carbon monoxide (CO) boosts were determined (the difference before and after smoking). Spearman correlation, χ^2, and ANCOVA adjusted for gender, race, and cotinine levels for menthol smokers assessed the relationship of MG boost, smoking behavior, and metabolic profiles. Multivariate metabolite characterization using supervised partial least squares-discriminant analysis (PLS-DA) was carried out for the classification of metabolomics profiles. MG boost was positively correlated with CO boost, nicotine boost, average puff volume, puff duration, and total smoke exposure.

Classification using PLS-DA, MG was the top metabolite discriminating metabolome of Menthol versus non-Menthol smokers. Among Menthol smokers, 42 metabolites were significantly correlated with MG boost, which linked to cellular functions, such as of cell death, survival, and movement, suggesting that plasma MG boost is a new smoking behavior biomarker that may provide novel information over self-reported use of Menthol cigarettes by integrating different smoking measures for understanding smoking behavior and harm of Menthol cigarettes. These studies provided further insight into the biological effect of Menthol smoking.

Reno-Protective Effects of Curcumin against Diabetes and Nicotine

It is known that the progression of diabetic nephropathy (DN) is accelerated by smoking. Recently, Ibrahim et al., (2016) investigated the ability of Curcumin to protect the kidneys against damage from oxidative stress induced by diabetes mellitus (DM) and nicotine (NC). A total of 24 male Wistar rats were divided into four groups of six rats each. DM was induced by a single i.p. injection of Streptozotocin 60 mg/kg body weight. DM rats were treated with or without NC in the absence or presence of curcumin for 8 weeks. As compared with the controls, DM rats exhibited reduced serum levels of high density lipoprotein, SOD and glutathione peroxidase, and decreased renal mRNA expression levels of synaptopodin, connexin 43 and erythropoietin (EPO), which were further suppressed by NC and restored to normal levels by Curcumin treatment. Additionally, DM rats exhibited increases in their lipid profiles (cholesterol, triacylglycerol and phospholipids), oxidative markers (malondialdehyde, γ-glutamyltranspeptidase and nitric oxide), and kidney function markers (urea and creatinine) and the mRNA expression levels of vimentin, desmin, SREBP-1, iNOS and TGF-β1. These effects were further enhanced by NC, but counteracted by Curcumin treatment. Kidneys from DM rats displayed glomerular hypertrophy, sclerosis and tubulo-interstitial changes represented by tubular lipid deposition, interstitial mononuclear cell infiltration and fibroplasia. Pancreatic islets exhibited cellular vacuolation, morphological irregularity and damaged or reduced in size β-cells. These renal and pancreatic changes became more severe following NC treatment and were ameliorated by Curcumin. Therefore, NC-induced DM progression may predominantly operate by increasing oxidative stress, reducing the levels of antioxidants, suppressing EPO levels, and causing perturbations to gap junction and podocyte structure. Based on above findings, these investigators suggested that Curcumin may ameliorate the damaging effects of DM and NC on the kidney through normalization of the mRNA expression levels of several genes involved in the progression of DM.

Biomarker Feedback Intervention to Motivate Smoking Cessation during Pregnancy

The prevalence of smoking during pregnancy for Alaska Native (AN) women is more than triple that of non-Native Alaska women. In a qualitative study, Koller et al., (2016) solicited input from AN women and others to determine how best to present findings from an earlier study demonstrating a strong correlation between biomarkers for maternal smoking (cotinine) and neonatal exposure to a tobacco-specific carcinogen 4-(methylnitrosamino)-1-(3-pyridyl)-1-butanol (NNAL) to motivate cessation. These investigators developed a brochure incorporating generalized biomarker information. Using in-depth individual interviews with pregnant and postpartum a women and partners/family members, they explored applicability and acceptability of the information. Postpartum women, who had participated in the earlier correlation study, additionally received their individual biomarker. They assessed whether being presented general or individual biomarker information would motivate cessation using content analysis. They conducted 39 interviews: 16 pregnant women, 12 postpartum women, and 11 partners/family members. Overall, participants agreed the biomarker information was new, but understandable as presented. Postpartum women shared that learning their personal inspired them to want to quit or cut back smoking while pregnant women indicated the generalized correlation information was less helpful in motivating cessation. These data was interpreted to suggest that generalized information about fetal exposure to carcinogens may be more effective in motivating pregnant women to quit smoking when combined with individual cotinine testing. Using feedback from this study, they refined and evaluated an intervention incorporating generalized correlation information from Phase I and cotinine testing to determine its effectiveness in motivating smoking cessation among pregnant AN women.

Effects of Compounds of Smilax China on Nicotine-Induced Endothelial Dysfunction

This study investigated the effects of compounds isolated from 70% ethanol (EtOH) extraction of smilax China L. (SCE), a plant belonging to the family solenaceae on nicotine-induced endothelial dysfunction (ED) in human umbilical vein endothelial cells. In a recent study, Lincha et al., (2016) isolated 10 compounds from ethyl acetate (EtOAc) fraction of 70% EtOH extract of SCE and investigated their inhibitory effect on nicotine-induced ED in endothelial cells. kaempferol, kaempferol 7-O-α-L-rhamnopyranoside, puerarin and ferulic acid showed inhibition of nicotine-induced vascular cell adhesion molecule (VCAM-1) expression while kaempferol, kaempferin, and caffeic acid attenuated intercellular adhesion molecule (ICAM-1) expression. Lepidoside, caffeic acid and methylsuccinic acid caused the highest up-regulated expression of endothelial nitric oxide synthase at the protein level with caffeic acid and ferulic acid showing strong inhibitory effects on iNOS expression. In addition, ferulic acid and Kaempferol showed inhibition against IL-8 and IL-1β expression while ferulic acid and caffeic acid showed comparatively higher inhibition of ED associated TNF-α expression. These findings demonstrated the potential of the aforementioned compounds to reverse the toxic effects of nicotine on the endothelium.

Reducing Harm from Continued Tobacco Use

Although smoking cessation is currently the only guaranteed way to reduce the harm caused by tobacco smoking, a reasonable secondary tobacco control approach may be to try and reduce the harmful effects of continued tobacco use amongst smokers unable or unwilling to quit. Possible approaches to reduce the exposure to toxins from smoking include reducing the amount of tobacco used, and using less toxic products, such as pharmaceutical, nicotine and potential reduced-exposure tobacco products (PREPs), as an alternative to cigarettes. Hence, Lindson-Hawley et al., (2016) performed a study to assess the effects of interventions intended to reduce the harm to health of continued tobacco use. They considered the following specific questions: do interventions intended to reduce harm have an effect on long-term health status?; do they lead to a reduction in the number of cigarettes smoked?; do they have an effect on smoking abstinence?; do they have an effect on biomarkers of tobacco exposure?; and do they have an effect on biomarkers of damage caused by tobacco? They searched the Cochrane Tobacco Addiction Group Trials Register (CRS) on the 21st October 2015, using free-text and MeSH terms for harm reduction, smoking reduction and cigarette reduction. Randomized or quasi-randomized controlled trials of interventions to reduce the amount smoked, or to reduce harm from smoking by means other than cessation. They included studies carried out in smokers with no immediate desire to quit all tobacco use. Primary outcomes were change in cigarette consumption, smoking cessation and any markers of damage or benefit to health, measured six months from the start of the intervention. They assessed study eligibility for inclusion using standard Cochrane. They pooled trials with similar interventions and outcomes (>50% reduction in cigarettes a day (CPD) and long-term smoking abstinence), using fixed-effect models. Where it was not possible to Meta-analyze data, they summarized findings narratively. Twenty-four trials evaluated interventions to help those who smoke to cut down the amount smoked or to replace their regular cigarettes with PREPs, compared to placebo, brief intervention, or a comparison intervention. None of these trials directly tested whether harm reduction strategies reduced the harms to health caused by smoking. Most trials (14/24) tested nicotine replacement therapy (NRT) as an intervention to assist reduction. In a pooled analysis of eight trials, NRT significantly increased the likelihood of reducing CPD by at least 50% for people using nicotine gum or inhaler or a choice of product compared to placebo (risk ratio (RR) 1.75, 95% confidence interval (CI) 1.44 to 2.13; 3081 participants). Where average changes from baseline were compared for different measures, carbon monoxide (CO) and cotinine generally showed smaller reductions than CPD. Use of NRT versus placebo also increased the likelihood of ultimately quitting smoking (RR 1.87, 95% CI 1.43 to 2.44; 8 trials, 3081 participants; quality of the evidence: low). Two trials comparing NRT and behavioral support to brief advice found a significant effect on reduction, but no significant effect on cessation. They found one trial investigating each of the following harm reduction intervention aids: Bupropion, Varenicline, e-cigarettes, snus, plus another of nicotine patches to facilitate temporary abstinence. The evidence for all five intervention types was therefore imprecise, and it remained uncertain whether or not these aids increase the likelihood of smoking reduction or cessation. Two trials investigating two different types of behavioral advice and instructions on reducing CPD also provided imprecise evidence. Therefore, the evidence base for this comparison was insufficient to support the use of these types of behavioral advice to reduce smoking. Four studies of PREPs (cigarettes with reduced levels of tar, carbon and nicotine, and in one case delivered using an electronically-heated cigarette smoking system) showed some reduction in exposure to some toxicants, but it remained uncertain whether this would substantially alter the risk of harm. They judged the included studies to be generally at a low or unclear risk of bias; however, there were some ratings of high risk, due to a lack of blinding and the potential for detection bias. Using the GRADE system, they rated the overall quality of the evidence for cessation outcomes as 'low' or 'very low', due to imprecision and indirectness. A 'low' grade meant that further research was very likely to have an important impact on our confidence in the estimate of effect and may likely to change the estimate. A 'very low' grade meant that they were very uncertain about the estimate. These data were interpreted to suggest that people who do not wish to quit can be helped to cut down the number of cigarettes they smoke and to quit smoking in the long term, using NRT, despite original intentions not to do so. However, they rated the evidence contributing to the cessation outcome for NRT as 'low' by GRADE standards. There was a lack of evidence to support the use of other harm reduction aids to reduce the harm caused by continued tobacco smoking. This could simply be due to the lack of high-quality studies, meaning that these investigators might have missed a worthwhile effect, or due to a lack of effect on reduction or quit rates. It was therefore important that more high-quality RCTs are conducted, and that these also measure the long-term health effects of treatments.

RCT for Electronic Cigarette Evaluation

Recently, Lopez et al., (2016) conducted a systematic evaluation of a novel tobacco product, e-cigarettes (ECIGs) using a two-site, four-arm, 6-month, parallel-group randomized controlled trial (RCT) with a follow-up to 9 months. Virginia Commonwealth University was the primary site and Penn State University was the secondary site. This RCT design was important because it was informed by analytical work, clinical laboratory, and qualitative/quantitative findings regarding the specific ECIG products used. Participants (N = 520) were randomized across sites and were healthy smokers of >9 cigarettes for at least one year, who have not had a quit attempt in the prior month, were not planning to quit in the next 6 months, and were interested in reducing cigarette intake. Participants were randomized into one of four 24-week conditions: a cigarette substitute that does not produce an inhalable aerosol; or one of three ECIG conditions that differ by nicotine concentration 0, 8, or 36 mg/ml. Blocked randomization were accomplished with a 1:1:1:1 ratio of condition assignments at each site. Specific aims were to: characterize ECIG influence on toxicants, biomarkers, health indicators, and disease risk; determine tobacco abstinence symptom and adverse event profile associated with real-world ECIG use; and examine the influence of ECIG use on conventional tobacco product use. Liquid nicotine concentration-related differences on these study outcomes were predicted. Participants and research staff in contact with participants were blinded to the nicotine concentration in the ECIG conditions. This study informed knowledge concerning ECIG use as well as demonstrated a model that may be applied to other tobacco products. These investigators suggested that the model of using prior empirical testing of ECIG devices should be considered in other RCT evaluations.

Effect of Reduced Nicotine Content Cigarettes on Smoking Behavior, Biomarkers of Exposure, and Subject Rating

The U.S. FDA has the authority to reduce cigarette nicotine content if found to benefit public health. Reduced nicotine content (RNC) cigarette use does not appear to increase harm exposure, but studies have not rigorously assessed smoking behavior or used a comprehensive panel of biomarkers. This study examined the effects of decreasing RNC cigarettes on smoking behaviors, biomarkers of exposure, and subjective ratings. Mercincavage et al., (2016) recently performed a study on 158 daily, non-treatment-seeking smokers in a 35-day randomized, unblinded, parallel investigation. After a 5-day baseline period, participants were randomly assigned to an experimental group (n = 80) that smoked progressively decreasing RNC cigarettes during three 10-day periods, or control group (n = 78) that smoked their own brand throughout the study. Daily cigarette consumption significantly increased for the intermediate RNCs but approached baseline rate for the lowest RNC; in contrast, puffing behavior significantly decreased at intermediate levels and increased for the lowest RNC. Cotinine and NNAL significantly decreased by RNC period, whereas CO boost initially increased. 1-HOP did not change by period. Smoking behaviors changed by RNC period via CPD and puffing behavior. Generally, biomarkers of exposure decreased with nicotine content, suggesting that RNC use does not ubiquitously reduce smoking behaviors or biomarkers, yet the lowest RNC level tested may reduce harm exposure, emphasizing the importance of using multiple behavioral and biologic measures to address the impact of RNC cigarette smoking.

Biomarkers of Secondhand Tobacco Smoke Exposure among Nonsmokers

It has been recognized that secondhand tobacco smoke (SHS) exposure causes several adverse physical health outcomes. Conceptual differences in survey measures of 'psychosocial' (SHS exposure from smokers in an individual's life) and 'physical' (environments where an individual is exposed to SHS) SHS exposure exist. Few studies have examined the association between psychosocial and physical SHS exposures measures in comparison to biomarkers of SHS exposure. Okoli (2016) recently examined the secondary analysis of cross-sectional data among a convenience sample of 20 adults. The data included survey items on SHS exposure and hair nicotine and saliva cotinine levels. Spearman analysis was used to assess correlations among variables. Medium and strong correlations were found among SHS exposure measures with the exception of saliva cotinine levels. Strong correlations were found among and between psychosocial and physical SHS exposure measures. Hair nicotine levels had medium strength associations with only perceived frequency of SHS exposure. As psychosocial measures of exposure were associated with biomarkers, such measures (particularly perceived frequency of SHS exposure) should be added to surveys in addition to physical SHS exposure measures to enhance accuracy of SHS measurement. Based on their findings, this investigator recommended that future explorations with robust sample sizes should further examine the strength of relationship between psychosocial and physical SHS exposure measures.

Tobacco Consumption and Toxicant Exposure of Cigarette Smokers Using E-Cigarettes

There is considerable debate about the benefits and risks of e-cigarettes (ECs). To better understand the risk-benefit ratio of ECs, more information is needed about net nicotine consumption and toxicant exposure of cigarette smokers switching to ECs. Pulvers et al., (2016) recently enrolled 40 cigarette smokers (>1 year of smoking) interested in switching to ECs but not necessarily quitting smoking in a four-week observational study and provided an e-Go C non-variable battery and refillable atomizers and choice of 8 flavors in 12 mg or 24 mg nicotine dosage. Measurement of urinary cotinine (metabolite of nicotine), 4-(Methylnitrosamino)-1-(3-Pyridyl)-1-Butanol (NNAL; a pulmonary carcinogen), and eight volatile organic compounds (VOCs) that are toxic tobacco smoke constituents was conducted at baseline and Week-4. All participants with follow-up data (92.5%) reported using the study EC. Of the 40 smokers, 16 reported no cigarettes at Week-2 (40%) and 6 continued to report no cigarettes at Week-4 (15%). Change in nicotine intake over the 4-weeks was not significant ($p = 0.90$). Carbon monoxide ($p < 0.001$), NNAL ($p < 0.01$) and metabolites of Benzene ($p < 0.01$) and Acrylonitrile ($p=0.001$) were significantly decreased in the study sample. Smokers switching exclusively to ECs for at least half of the study period demonstrated significant reductions in HEMA ($p >= 0.03$) and AAMA ($p < 0.01$). Smokers using ECs over 4-weeks maintained cotinine levels and experienced significant reductions in carbon monoxide, NNAL, and two out of eight measured VOC metabolites. Those who switched exclusively to ECs for at least half of the study period significantly reduced two additional VOCs. This study extended current literature by measuring change in smoking dependence and disease-associated biomarkers, NNAL and a panel of eight common volatile organic compounds (VOCs) that were toxic tobacco smoke constituents in smokers who switch to E-cigarettes. The findings supported the idea of harm reduction, however some levels of toxicant exposure are still of clinical concern, particularly for dual users. Extrapolation of these must be careful to separate the different toxic exposure for exclusive switchers versus dual cigarette+EC users, and not to equate harm reduction with the idea that using ECs is harmless.

Nicotine Intake from E-Cigarettes: Measurement of Parent Drug and Metabolites in Oral Fluid and Plasma

E-cigarettes known as electronic nicotine devices recently gained popularity among smokers. Despite many studies investigating their safety and toxicity, few examined the delivery of e-cigarettes-derived nicotine and its metabolites in alternative biological fluids. Therefore, Papaseit et al., (2017) performed a randomized, crossover, and controlled clinical trial in nine healthy smokers. Nicotine (NIC), cotinine (COT), and trans-3'-hydroxycotinine (3-HCOT) were measured in plasma and oral fluid by liquid chromatography-tandem mass spectrometry (LC-MS) after consumption of two consecutive e-cigarettes administrations or two consecutive tobacco cigarettes. NIC and its metabolites were detected both in oral fluid and plasma following both administration conditions. Concentrations in oral fluid resulted various orders of magnitude higher than those observed in plasma. Oral fluid concentration of tobacco cigarette and e-cigarettes-derived NIC peaked at 15 min after each administration and ranged between 1.0 and 1396 μg/L and from 0.3 to 860 μg/L; those of COT between 52.8 and 110 μg/L and from 33.8 to 94.7 μg/L; and those of 3-HCOT between 12.4 and 23.5 μg/L and from 8.5 to 24.4 μg/L. The oral fluid to plasma concentration ratio of both e-cigarettes-and tobacco cigarette-derived NIC peaked at 15 min after both administrations and correlated with oral fluid NIC concentration. These supported the measurement of NIC and metabolites in oral fluid in the assessment of intake after e-cigarettes use and appeared to be a suitable alternative to plasma when monitoring nicotine delivery from e-cigarettes for clinical and toxicological studies.

Assessment of Tobacco-Specific Nitrosamines (TSNAs) in Oral Fluid as Biomarkers of Cancer Risk

Smoke-free laws are expected to reduce smoking habits and exposure to secondhand smoke. Pérez-Ortuño et al., (2016) recently measured tobacco specific carcinogens (TSNAs) in oral fluid to assess the most suitable biomarker of cancer risk associated with tobacco smoke. TSNAs, N'-nitrosonor nicotine (NNN), 4-(methylnitrosamino)-1-(3-pyridyl)-1-butanone (NNK) and 4-(methylnitrosamino)-1-(3-ppyridyl)-1-butanol (NNAL), as well as nicotine and cotinine were measured in oral fluid samples from 166 smokers and 532 non-smokers of the adult population of Barcelona, Spain. A simple procedure with an alkaline single liquid-liquid extraction with Dichloromethane/ Isopropanol was used and lower limits of quantification for cotinine, NNN, NNK and NNAL were set at 0.10ng/mL, 1.0, 2.0 and 0.50pg/mL respectively. The NNN/cotinine ratio was also calculated. NNN was the most abundant TSNA present in oral fluid with a significant difference between smokers and non-smokers (mean concentrations of 118 pg/ml and 5.3 pg/mL, respectively, $p < 0.001$). NNK and NNAL were detectable in fewer samples. NNN and cotinine concentrations had a moderate correlation within both groups (Spearman's rank correlation coefficient of 0.312, $p < 0.001$ in smokers and 0.279, $p = 0.022$ in non-smokers). NNN/cotinine ratio was significantly higher ($p < 0.001$) in non-smokers than in smokers, in line with equivalent findings for the NNAL/cotinine ratio in urine. TSNAs were detectable in oral fluid of smokers and non-smokers. NNN was the most abundant, in line with its association with esophageal and oral cavity cancers. The NNN/cotinine ratio confirmed the relative NNN increase in secondhand smoke. These findings provided a new oral fluid biomarker of cancer risk associated with exposure to tobacco smoke

Therapeutically-Beneficial Effects of Nicotine

6-Hydroxy-l-Nicotine Improves Behavioral Deficits in AD Model

6-hydroxy-l-nicotine (6HLN), a nicotine derivative from nicotine degradation by Arthrobacter nicotinovorans pAO1 strain was found to improve behavioral deficits and to reverse oxidative stress in the rat hippocampus. Recently, Hritcu et al., (2017) prepared animal model of AD by injecting CHL (chlorisondamine) (10 mg/kg, i.p.) in rats. The nicotine (0.3 mg/kg) and 6HLN (0.3 mg/kg) were administered alone or in combination in the CHL-treated rats. Memory-related behaviors were evaluated using Y-maze and radial arm-maze tests. The antioxidant enzymes activity and the levels of the biomarkers of oxidative stress were measured in the hippocampus. Statistical analyses were performed using two-way ANOVA and Tukey's post hoc test. F values for which $p < 0.05$ were regarded as statistically significant. CHL caused memory deficits and oxidative stress. Both nicotine and 6HLN administration attenuated the cognitive deficits and recovered the antioxidant capacity in the rat hippocampus of the CHL rat model of AD, suggesting that 6HLN versus nicotine confers anti-amnesic properties in the CHL-induced a rat model of memory impairment via reversing cholinergic function and decreasing brain oxidative stress, suggesting the use of this compound as an alternative agent in AD treatment.

CB2 Receptor Mediates Nicotine-Induced Anti-Inflammation in N9 Microglial Cells Exposed to β Amyloid

Reducing β amyloid-(Aβ)-induced microglial activation is considered to be effective in treating AD. Nicotine attenuates Aβ-induced microglial activation; the mechanism, however, is still elusive. Microglia could be activated into classic activated state (M1 state) or alternative activated state (M2 state); the former is cytotoxic and the latter is neurotrophic. In a study, Jia et al., (2016) hypothesized that nicotine attenuates Aβ-induced microglial activation by shifting microglial M1 to M2 state, and cannabinoid CB2 receptor and protein kinase C mediate this process. These investigators used Aβ1-42 to activate N9 microglial cells and observed nicotine-induced effects on microglial M1 and M2 biomarkers by using western blot, immunocytochemistry, and enzyme-linked immunosorbent assay (ELISA). Nicotine reduced the levels of M1 state markers, including iNOS expression and TNF-α and IL-6 releases; meanwhile, it increased the levels of M2 state markers, including arginase-1 (Arg-1) expression and BDNF release, in the Aβ-stimulated microglia. Co-administration of cannabinoid CB2 receptor antagonist or PKC inhibitor partially abolished the nicotine-induced effects, indicating that cannabinoid CB2 receptor mediates nicotine-induced anti-inflammation in microglia exposed to Aβ via PKC.

Biomarkers of Depression in Multiple Sclerosis

There is evidence that activated immune-inflammatory and oxidative and nitrosative stress (IO&NS) pathways play a role in the pathophysiology of MS and depression. Kallaur et al., (2016) examined serum levels of interleukin (IL)-1β, IL-4, IL-6, and IL-10; peroxides (LOOH); nitric oxide metabolites (NOx); albumin; ferritin; C-reactive protein (CRP); and TNF-β NcoI polymorphism (rs909253) and gadolinium-enhanced MRI in MS patients with (n = 42) and without (n = 108) depression and normal controls (n = 249). Depression was scored using the depressive subscale of the Hospital Anxiety and Depression Scale (HADS). The extent of neurological disability was measured using the Expanded Disability Status Scale (EDSS) at the same time of the afore-mentioned measurements and 5 years earlier. Disease progression was assessed as actual EDSS-EDSS 5 years earlier. Three variables discriminated MS patients with depression from those without depression, i.e., increased IL-6 and lower IL-4 and albumin. Binary logistic regression showed that MS with depression (versus no depression) was characterized by more GIT symptoms and disease progression, higher serum IL-6, and lower albumin levels. In subjects with MS, the HADS score was predicted by three EDSS symptoms, i.e., pyramidal, GIT, and visual symptoms. Fifty-eight percent of the variance in the HADS score was predicted by GIT symptoms, visual symptoms, the TNFB1/B2 genotype, and contrast enhancement (both inversely associated). There were no significant associations between depression in MS and type of MS, duration of illness, age, sex, nicotine dependence, and BMI. MS with depression was associated with signs of peripheral inflammation, more disability, disease progression, GIT, and visual symptoms, but less contrast enhancement as compared to MS without depression, indicating that depression is part of the neurological symptoms of MS and that its expression is primed by peripheral inflammation while acute neuroinflammation and the TNFB1/B2 genotype may be protective.

Nicotinic Acetylcholine Receptors in an Experimental Model of Multiple Sclerosis

It has been recognized that myeloid cells, including proinflammatory monocytes and neutrophils, have important roles in the pathology of multiple sclerosis and its animal model, experimental autoimmune encephalomyelitis (EAE). These cells infiltrate the CNS in the early stages of disease development and contribute to the inflammatory response that is associated with symptom severity. It is thus crucial to identify and understand new mechanisms that can regulate the CNS infiltration of proinflammatory myeloid cells. Nicotinic acetylcholine receptors (nAChRs) have been studied for their immune-regulatory properties. In a study, Jiang et al., (2016) assessed the ability of nicotine, a nAChR ligand, to modulate proinflammatory myeloid cell numbers within the bone marrow, spleen, blood, and CNS of EAE mice. They found that nicotine inhibits the infiltration of proinflammatory monocytes and neutrophils into the CNS at time points where these cells are known to play critical roles in disease pathology. In contrast, nicotine does not affect the expansion of other monocytes. These investigators also demonstrated that nicotine exerts these effects by acting on α7 and α9 nAChR subtypes. Finally, mRNA transcript levels for CCL2 and CXCL2, chemokines involved in the chemotaxis of proinflammatory monocytes and neutrophils, respectively, are reduced in the brain of nicotine-treated EAE mice before the massive infiltration of these cells. These data provided evidence that nAChRs can regulate proinflammatory cell infiltration into the CNS, which could be of significant value for the treatment of neuroinflammatory disorders such as MS.

Clinical and Other Management of Nicotinism

Consequences of Incomplete Smoke-Free Legislation in the Republic of Korea

In some countries with high smoking prevalence, smoke-free legislation has only been implemented in specific public places, as opposed to a comprehensive ban on smoking in all public places. Park et al., (2016) recently conducted a study to provide valid data on secondhand smoke (SHS) exposure that reflect the consequences of incomplete smoke-free legislation, and provide a rationale for expanding this legislation. Indoor and outdoor environmental exposure (fine particulate matter [PM2.5], air nicotine, and dust 4-(methylnitrosamino)-1-(3-pyridyl)-1-butanone [NNK]) was monitored in 35 public places where smoking is prohibited by law in Goyang, Republic of Korea. Biomarkers of SHS exposure (urinary cotinine, hair nicotine, and urinary 4-(methylnitrosamino)-1-(3-pyridyl)-1-butanol) were measured in 37 non-smoking employees. Geometric means and standard deviations were used in comparison of each measure. Considerable exposure of SHS was detected at all indoor monitoring sites (PM2.5, 95.5 µg/m (3) in private educational institutions; air nicotine, 0.77 µg/m (3) in large buildings; and dust NNK, 160.3 pg/mg in large buildings); environmental measures were higher in private or closed locations, such as restrooms. Outdoor measures of SHS exposure were lowest in nurseries and highest in government buildings. Biochemical measures revealed a pattern of SHS exposure by monitoring site, and were highest in private educational institutions. The evidence of SHS exposure in legislative smoke-free places in Korea suggested that incomplete smoke free legislation and lack of enforcement of it might not protect people from exposure to smoke. Therefore, active steps should be taken toward a comprehensive ban on smoking in all public places and its enforcement.

Supervised, Vigorous Intensity Exercise Intervention for Depressed Female Smokers

Few studies have evaluated exercise interventions for smokers with depression or other psychiatric comorbidities. This pilot study evaluated the potential role of supervised vigorous exercise as a smoking cessation intervention for depressed females. Recently, Patten et al., (2016) enrolled 30 adult women with moderate-severe depressive symptoms and randomly assigned to 12 weeks of thrice weekly, in person sessions of vigorous intensity supervised exercise at a YMCA setting (EX; n = 15) or health education (HE; n = 15). All participants received behavioral smoking cessation counseling and nicotine patch therapy. Assessments were done in person at baseline, at the end of 12 weeks of treatment, and at 6 months post-target quit date. Primary end points were exercise adherence (proportion of 36 sessions attended) and biochemically confirmed 7-day point prevalence abstinence at Week 12. Biomarkers of inflammation were explored for differences between treatment groups and between women who smoked and those abstinent at Week 12. Treatment adherence was high for both groups (72% for EX and 66% for HE; p = .55). The Week 12 smoking abstinence rate was higher for EX than HE (11/15 [73%] vs. 5/15 [33%]; p = .028), but no significant differences emerged at 6-month follow-up. Interleukin-6 levels increased more for those smoking than women abstinent at Week 12 (p = .040). Based on these findings, these investigators recommended that vigorous intensity supervised exercise enhances short-term smoking cessation among depressed female smokers. Innovative and cost-effective strategies to bolster long-term exercise adherence and smoking cessation need evaluation in this population. Inflammatory biomarkers could be examined in future research as mediators of treatment efficacy. This preliminary study found that vigorous intensity supervised exercise is feasible and enhances short-term smoking cessation among depressed female smokers. This research addressed an important gap in the field. Despite decades of research examining exercise interventions for smoking cessation, few studies were done among depressed smokers or those with comorbid psychiatric disorders. A novel finding was increases in levels of a pro-inflammatory biomarker observed among women who smoked at the end of the intervention compared to those who did not.

Alternative Nicotine Delivery Systems (ANDS)

Alternative nicotine delivery systems (ANDS) such as e-cigarettes are battery-powered devices that aerosolize nicotine and other substances to simulate smoking without using tobacco. Little is known about the ANDS initiation process among adult smokers. Hence, Pearson et al., (2016) conducted a study with a primary objective to examine: (1) how ANDS use affects cigarette use; (2) how the immediate environmental and psychosocial contexts of cigarette and ANDS use vary within-and between-participants in general and by Menthol preference and race; and, (3) participants' 'lived experience' of the subjective perceptions, meaning, influences and utility of cigarette and ANDS use. These investigators highlighted that this study's mixed, 6-week longitudinal design will produce a detailed description of the ANDS initiation process among adult smokers (N=100). Qualitative and quantitative data collection will include 3 weeks of: (1) ecological momentary assessment of patterns of cigarette/ANDS use, satisfaction, mood and craving; (2) geospatial assessment of participants' environment, including indoor and outdoor cigarette/ANDS norms and rules; (3) in-depth interviews about the meaning and utility of cigarette smoking and ANDS use; and, (4) saliva cotinine and exhaled carbon monoxide (CO) biomarkers. A diverse sample will be recruited with an equal number of Menthol and non-Menthol cigarette smokers. As the primary independent variable, the investigators will investigate how ANDS use affects cigarette consumption. They will also examine how smoking-related and ANDS-related rules and norms surrounding product use influence cigarette and ANDS product use, and how the subjective effects of ANDS use affect ANDS perceptions, beliefs and use.

Effectiveness of CO-Oximetry and Anti-Smoking Brief Advice in a Cohort of Kidney Transplant Patients Who Smoke

The cardiovascular risk in renal transplant patients is increased in patients who continue to smoke after transplantation. Pita-Fernández et al., (2016) recently conducted a study to measure the effectiveness of exhaled carbon monoxide (CO) measurement plus brief advisory sessions, in comparison to brief advice, to reduce smoking exposure and smoking behavior in kidney transplant recipients who smoke. The effectiveness was measured by: (1) abandonment of smoking, (2) increase in motivation to stop smoking, and (3) reduction in the number of cigarettes smoked per day. This was a randomized, controlled, open clinical trial with blinded evaluation. Renal transplant patients who smoked in the precontemplation, contemplation or preparation stages according to the Prochaska and DiClemente's Stages of Change model, and who gave their consent to participate were included in this study. The smokers attempting to stop smoking, patients with terminal illness or mental disability that prevented them from participating were excluded from this study. The patients were randomized to the control group (brief advisory session) or the intervention group (brief advisory session plus measuring exhaled CO). The sample target size was n = 112, with 56 patients in each group. Allowing for up to 10% loss to follow-up, this would provide 80% power to detect a 13% difference in attempting to give up smoking outcomes at a two-tailed significance level of 5%. Sociodemographic characteristics, cardiovascular risk factors, treatment, rejection episodes, infections, self-reported smoking habit, drug use, level of dependence (the Fagerström test), stage of change (Prochaska and DiClemente's Stages of Change model), and motivation to giving up smoking (the Richmond test) were estimated. The effectiveness was evaluated every 3, 6, 9 and 12 months as: pattern of tobacco use (self-reported tobacco use), smoking cessation rates, carbon monoxide (CO) levels in exhaled air measured by CO-oximetry, urinary cotinine tests, nicotine dependence (Fagerström test), motivational stages of change (Prochaska and DiClemente's stages) and motivation to stop smoking (the Richmond test). Descriptive statistics and linear/logistic multiple regression models were performed. Clinical relevance was measured as relative risk reduction, absolute risk reduction and the number needed to treat. Informed consent of the patients and Ethical Review Board was obtained. Based on these findings, it was inferred that tobacco is a modifiable risk factor that increase the risk of morbidity and mortality in kidney transplant recipients. If effectiveness of CO-oximetry is confirmed to reduce tobacco exposure, necessary intervention can be easy to use, low cost and with great success about cardiovascular risk prevention in these patients.

Biomarkers of Exposure and Effect in Smokers and Moist Snuff Consumers

Cigarette smoking is a major risk factor for several chronic diseases. Epidemiological data indicate the use of smokeless tobacco (ST) is associated with significantly lower risk for smoking-related diseases compared to cigarettes. Several biomarkers of exposure (BioExp) and effect (BioEff) associated with smoking and use of moist snuff (ST) were evaluated. Recently, Prasad et al., (2016) performed a single site, cross-sectional clinical study by enrolling three groups of generally healthy male smokers (SMK), moist snuff consumers (MSC), and non-tobacco consumers (NTC). These investigators evaluated several BioExp and BioEff. Blood and urinary BioExp, including total nicotine equivalents and tobacco-specific nitrosamines, were higher in MSC compared to SMK. Biomarkers of combustion-related toxicants and cadmium were elevated in SMK. Elevated levels of some BioEff associated with oxidative stress (urinary isoprostanes and leukotriene E4), inflammation (white blood cell count), platelet activation (thromboxane metabolites), and lipid metabolism (apolipoprotein B100 and oxidized low-density lipoprotein) were observed in SMK relative to NTC and MSC. The non-smoking groups (MSC and NTC) showed similar levels of combustion-related BioExp and BioEff. Higher levels of exposure to nicotine and some N'-nitrosamines may be observed in MSC, and

SMK are exposed to higher levels of combustion-related toxicants. Changes in BioEff consistent with some aspects of inflammation, oxidative stress, and altered lipid metabolism were detected in SMK compared to the non-smoking groups. These biomarker data further improved our understanding of pathophysiological changes and the risk continuum associated with various tobacco products, and could be useful components of future assessments of tobacco products.

Evaluation of a Reduced Nicotine Product Standard: Moderating Effects and Impact on Cannabis Use

The Family Smoking Prevention and Tobacco Control Act authorized the FDA to reduce the nicotine content in cigarettes. Hence, research is needed to guide proposed regulations, including evaluation of consequences to public health. Recently, Pacek et al., (2016) conducted a study to evaluate how a reduced nicotine product standard might be moderated by and impact cannabis use. Secondary analysis of a controlled clinical trial examining the effects of nicotine content in cigarettes in adult daily smokers. Linear regression assessed whether baseline cannabis use moderated behavioral, subjective, or physiological effects of smoking very low nicotine content (VLNC) versus normal nicotine content (NNC) cigarettes. Repeated measures analysis of associations between nicotine condition and prevalence and frequency of cannabis use was completed using generalized estimating equations (GEE). Cannabis use did not moderate most of the following effects of VLNC cigarettes: Among cannabis users and non-users, smokers randomized to VLNC cigarettes reported lower nicotine dependence, cigarettes per day, biomarkers of nicotine exposure, and craving compared to smokers randomized to NNC cigarettes. Non-cannabis using smokers randomized to VLNC cigarettes also reported lower smoking dependence motives and had lower tobacco-specific nitrosamine exposure and total puff volume versus smokers randomized to NNC cigarettes. For cannabis users, smokers randomized to VLNC cigarettes reported decreased positive affect. VLNC cigarette use did not impact the prevalence or frequency of cannabis use. These findings provided evidence that nicotine reduction in cigarettes could have beneficial effects on cigarette smoking regardless of cannabis use and that transitioning to VLNC cigarettes is unlikely to alter current rates of cannabis use.

Behavioral and Physiological Responses to Nicotine Patch Administration among Nonsmokers

Despite the large amount that is known about the physical health effects of second-hand tobacco smoke (SHS) exposure, little is known about the behavioral health effects. Nicotine, the principle psychoactive substance in SHS, elicits subjective mood and physiological responses in nonsmokers. However, no studies have examined the subjective mood or physiological responses to nicotine in nonsmokers while accounting for prior chronic or acute SHS exposure. Okoli et al., (2016) administered a 7-mg nicotine patch to 17 adult nonsmokers for 2 hrs. Main outcome measures obtained at ½ hr., 1 hr., and 2 hrs. were subjective behavioral drug effects (based on eleven 10-cm Visual Analog Scales [VASs]) and the physiological measures of heart rate, blood pressure, and serum nicotine levels. Analysis of outcome data was based on participants' chronic (using hair nicotine) or acute (using saliva cotinine) SHS exposure. Greater chronic SHS exposure was negatively associated with pleasurable responses to nicotine administration ("drug feels good" score at 2-hr time point, Spearman's $\rho = -.65$, $p < .004$), whereas greater acute SHS exposure was associated with positive responses ("like feeling of drug" score at 2-hr time point, Spearman's $\rho = .63$, $p < .01$). There were no associations between chronic or acute exposure and physiological changes in response to nicotine administration. The findings of this study may be useful in providing preliminary empirical data for future explorations of the mechanism whereby SHS exposure can influence behavioral outcomes in nonsmokers. Such studies can inform future interventions to reduce the physical and behavioral health risks associated with SHS exposure.

Human Pharmacology for Addiction Medicine

Substance use disorders (SUD) are complex and often chronic diseases with negative health outcomes and social consequences. Pharmacological treatment options for SUD can be separated in medications for (i) intoxication, (ii) withdrawal, and (iii) reduction of use together with relapse prevention. Quednow and, Herdener (2016) focused on approved or clinically established pharmacological strategies suited to manage symptoms of withdrawal, and to reduce substance use or to promote abstinence. Hereby SUD involving alcohol, nicotine, stimulants, and opioids were primarily discussed as these substances are considered most harmful for both the individual and the society. Moreover, the pharmacotherapy of SUD related to the use of cannabis, Benzodiazepines, and Gamma-hydroxybutyrate was also briefly reviewed. Since most approved pharmacological treatment options showed only moderate effect sizes especially in the long term, the development of new treatment strategies including new drugs, new combinations of available compounds, and biomarkers for response prediction is still warranted.

Mood, Stress and Longevity: Convergence on ANK3

Antidepressants have been shown to improve longevity in C. elegans. It is plausible that orthologs of genes involved in mood regulation and stress response are involved in such an effect. Recently, Rangaraju et al., (2016) sought to understand the underlying biology. First, these investigators analyzed the transcriptome from worms treated with the antidepressant Mianserin, previously identified in a large-scale unbiased drug screen as promoting increased lifespan in worms. They identified the most robust treatment-related changes in gene expression, and identified the corresponding human orthologs. These analyses uncovered a series of genes and biological pathways that may be at the interface between antidepressant effects and longevity, notably pathways involved in drug metabolism/degradation (nicotine and Melatonin). Second, they examined which of these genes overlap with genes which may be involved in depressive symptoms in an aging non-psychiatric human population (n = 3577), discovered using a genome-wide association study (GWAS) approach in a design with extremes of distribution of phenotype. Third, they used a convergent functional genomics (CFG) approach to prioritize these genes for relevance to mood disorders and stress. The top gene identified was ANK3. To validate these findings, they conducted genetic and gene-expression studies, in C. elegans and in humans. They studied C. elegans inactivating mutants for ANK3/unc-44, and showed that they survive longer than wild-type, particularly in older worms, independently of mianserin treatment. They also showed that some ANK3/unc-44 expression was necessary for the effects of Mianserin on prolonging lifespan and survival in the face of oxidative stress, particularly in younger worms. Wild-type ANK3/unc-44 increased in expression with age in C. elegans, and was maintained at lower youthful levels by Mianserin treatment. These lower levels might be optimal in terms of longevity, offering a favorable balance between sufficient oxidative stress resistance in younger worms and survival effects in older worms. Thus, ANK3/unc-44 might represent an example of antagonistic pleiotropy, in which low-expression level in young animals were beneficial, but the age-associated increase became detrimental. Inactivating mutations in ANK3/unc-44 reversed this effect and caused detrimental effects in young animals (sensitivity to oxidative stress) and beneficial effect in old animals (increased survival). In humans, these investigators studied if the most significant single nucleotide polymorphism (SNP) for depressive symptoms in ANK3 from our GWAS had a relationship to lifespan, and showed a trend towards longer lifespan in individuals with the risk allele for depressive symptoms in men (odds ratio (OR) 1.41, $P = 0.031$) but not in women (OR 1.08, $P = 0.33$). They also examined whether ANK3, by itself or in a panel with other top CFG-prioritized genes, acted as a blood gene-expression biomarker for biological age, in two independent cohorts, one of live psychiatric patients (n = 737), and one of suicide completers from the coroner's office (n = 45). They showed significantly lower levels of ANK3 expression in chronologically younger individuals than in middle age individuals, with a diminution of that effect in suicide completers, who presumably had been exposed to more severe and acute negative mood and stress. Of note, ANK3 was previously reported to be overexpressed in fibroblasts from patients with Hutchinson-Gilford progeria syndrome, a form of accelerated aging. Taken together, these studies uncovered ANK3 and other genes as biological links between mood, stress and longevity/aging that might serve as biomarkers as well as targets for preventive or therapeutic interventions. Drug repurposing bioinformatics analyses identified the relatively innocuous omega-3 fatty acid DHA (docosahexaenoic acid), Piracetam, Quercetin, Vitamin D and Resveratrol as potential longevity promoting compounds, along with a series of existing drugs, such as estrogen-like compounds, antidiabetics and Sirolimus/Rapamycin. Intriguingly, some of the top candidate genes for mood and stress-modulated longevity were changed in expression in opposite direction in previous studies in the Alzheimer disease (AD). Additionally, a whole series of others were changed in expression in opposite direction in previous studies on suicide, suggesting the possibility of a "life switch" actively controlled by mood and stress.

Light and Intermittent Smoking in the United States

Light and/or intermittent smokers have been the fastest growing segment of cigarette smokers in the U.S over the past two decades. Defining their behavioral characteristics is a critical public health priority. Hence, Reyes-Guzman et al., (2017) performed a study on 78,229 U.S. adults from three pooled contemporary population-based surveys: the 2012 NHIS, 2012 NSDUH, and 2011-2012 NHANES. They classified current smokers into four categories (light and intermittent [LITS], light-daily, heavier-intermittent, and heavier-daily) and assessed smoking behaviors, illicit drug use, and mental health indicators using weighted analyses. Analyses associated smoking categories with nicotine dependence, age of smoking initiation, race/ethnicity, and other demographic and behavioral factors. Compared with heavier-daily smokers, smokers who were LITS were most likely to have mild or no nicotine dependence (weighted odds ratio [OR], 16.92; 95% confidence interval [CI], 13.10-21.85), to start smoking cigarettes regularly after age 21 (OR, 3.42; 95% CI, 2.84-4.12), and to be Hispanic (OR, 5.38; 95% CI, 4.38-6.61). Additional significance was found for other categories of smokers. Based on pooled data from three large national surveys, light and/or intermittent smokers differed in smoking, drug use, and mental health behaviors from heavier-daily, former, and never smokers. Significance differences by level of smoking frequency and intensity were observed for nicotine dependence, age of smoking initiation, and race/ethnicity. Based on this study, these investigators indicated that afore-mentioned parameters may help focus preventive measures and developing policies for the growing number of light and/or intermittent smokers because smoking patterns vary by behavioral and socioeconomic factors.

Characterization of Spectrum Variable Nicotine Research Cigarettes

To provide researchers an extensive characterization of the SPECTRUM variable nicotine research cigarettes, Richter et al., (2016) compiled data on cigarette physical properties, nicotine content, harmful and potentially harmful constituents in the tobacco filler. Data on physical properties, concentrations of Menthol, nicotine and minor alkaloids, tobacco-specific nitrosamines, polycyclic aromatic hydrocarbons, Ammonia, and toxic metals in the filler tobacco for all available varieties of Spectrum research cigarettes were provided. The similarity in the chemistry and physical properties of SPECTRUM cigarettes to commercial cigarettes rendered them acceptable for use in behavioral studies. Baseline information on harmful and potentially harmful constituents in research tobacco products, particularly constituent levels such as minor alkaloids that fall outside typical ranges reported for commercial, provided researchers with the opportunity to monitor smoking behavior and to identify biomarkers that will inform efforts to understand the role of nicotine in creating and sustaining addiction. Well characterized research cigarettes suitable for human consumption were an important tool in clinical studies for investigating the physiological impacts of cigarettes delivering various levels of nicotine, the impact of reduced nicotine cigarettes on nicotine addiction, and the relationship between nicotine dose and smoking behavior.

Racial Differences, Nicotine Metabolism, and Nicotine Intake from Cigarette Smoking

Rate of nicotine metabolism has been identified as an important factor influencing nicotine intake and can be estimated using the nicotine metabolite ratio (NMR), a validated biomarker of CYP2A6 enzyme activity. Individuals who metabolize nicotine faster (higher NMR) may alter their smoking behavior to titrate their nicotine intake in order to maintain similar levels of nicotine in the body compared to slower nicotine metabolizers. There are known racial differences in the rate of nicotine metabolism with African Americans on average having a slower rate of nicotine metabolism compared to Whites. Ross et al., (2016) recently conducted a study to determine if there are racial differences in the relationship between rate of nicotine metabolism and measures of nicotine intake assessed using multiple biomarkers of nicotine and tobacco smoke exposure. Using secondary analyses of the screening data collected in a recently completed clinical trial, treatment-seeking African American and White daily smokers (10 or more cigarettes per day) were grouped into NMR quartiles so that the races could be compared at the same NMR, even though the distribution of NMR within race differed. The rate of nicotine metabolism was important factor influencing nicotine intake in White smokers. Specifically, Whites were more likely to titrate their nicotine intake based on the rate at which they metabolize nicotine. However, this relationship was not found in African Americans. Overall, there was a greater step-down, linear type relationship between NMR groups and cotinine or cotinine/cigarette in African Americans, suggesting that differences in blood cotinine levels between the African

American NMR groups were primarily due to differences in CYP2A6 enzyme activity without titration of nicotine intake among faster nicotine metabolizers.

Puff Characteristics, Nicotine Dependence, and Nicotine Metabolism

It has been identified that African American (AA) smokers experience greater tobacco-related disease burden than Whites, despite smoking fewer cigarettes per day (CPD). Understanding factors that influence daily nicotine intake in AA smokers is an important step toward decreasing tobacco-related health disparities. One factor of interest is smoking topography, or the study of puffing behavior. To create a model using puff characteristics, nicotine dependence, and nicotine metabolism to predict daily nicotine exposure, and to compare puff characteristics and nicotine intake from two cigarettes smoked at different times to ensure the reliability of the puff characteristics, Ross et al., (2016) conducted a study on 60 AA smokers who smoked their preferred brand of cigarette at two-time points through a topography device. These investigators measured plasma nicotine, expired CO, and changes in subjective before and after each cigarette. Total nicotine equivalents (TNE) was measured from 24-hrs. urine collected during ad libitum smoking. Daily nicotine exposure, total puff volume, CPD, sex, and Menthol status were significant predictors. Total puff volume was significantly greater and inter-puff intervals were significantly shorter after ad lib smoking compared with the first cigarette of the day, but puffing behaviors for both cigarettes were highly correlated within-subjects. This was the first study to show that puff characteristics of individual cigarettes are predictive of daily nicotine intake. These findings enhance our understanding of the relationship between smoking behavior and nicotine intake in AA smokers.

Weight Gain in Smokers Consuming Low Nicotine Content Cigarettes

The Food and Drug Administration (FDA) can reduce the nicotine content in cigarettes to very low levels. This potential regulatory action is hypothesized to improve public health by reducing smoking, but may have unintended consequences related to weight gain. Hence, Rupprecht et al., (2016) evaluated weight gain from a double-blind, parallel, randomized clinical trial of 839 participants assigned to smoke 1 of 6 investigational cigarettes with nicotine content ranging from 0.4 to 15.8 mg/g or their own usual brand for 6 weeks. Additional analyses evaluated weight gain in the lowest nicotine content cigarette groups (0.4 and 0.4 mg/g, high tar) to examine the effect of study product in compliant participants as assessed by urinary biomarkers. Differences in outcomes due to gender were also explored. There were no significant differences in weight gain compared to the reduced nicotine conditions with the 15.8 mg/g control group across all treatment groups and weeks. However, weight gain at week 6 was negatively correlated with nicotine exposure in the 2 lowest nicotine content cigarette conditions. Within the 2 lowest nicotine content cigarette conditions, male and female smokers biochemically verified to be compliant on study product gained significantly more weight than non-compliant smokers and control groups. The effect of random assignment to investigational cigarettes with reduced nicotine on weight gain was likely obscured by non-compliance with study product. Men and women who were compliant in the lowest nicotine content cigarette conditions gained 1.2 kg over 6 weeks, indicating that weight gain is a likely consequence of reduced exposure to nicotine.

Prevalence and Impact of Long-Term Use of Nicotine Replacement Therapy in UK Stop-Smoking Services

Nicotine replacement therapy (NRT) was licensed for harm reduction in the United Kingdom in 2005, and guidance to UK Stop-Smoking Services (SSS) to include long-term partial or complete substitution of cigarettes with NRT was issued in 2013. Yet, NRT prevalence data and data on changes in biomarkers associated with long-term NRT use among SSS clients are scarce. Recently, Shahab et al., (2016) followed up SSS clients abstinent 4 weeks post quit date at 12 months. At baseline standard sociodemographic, smoking and SSS use characteristics were collected and of those eligible, 60.6% (1047/1728) provided data on smoking status and NRT use at follow-up. A subsample also provided saliva samples at baseline and of those eligible, 36.2% (258/712) provided follow-up samples. Saliva was analyzed for cotinine (a metabolite of nicotine) and α-amylase (a stress biomarker). Among those who had used NRT during their initial quit attempt were still using NRT at 1 year, significantly more ex-smokers than relapsed smokers. In adjusted analysis, NRT use interacted with smoking status to determine change in cotinine, but not α-amylase, levels: cotinine levels remained unchanged in relapsed smokers and ex-smokers with long-term NRT use but decreased in ex-smokers without long-term NRT use. Long-term NRT use is uncommon in SSS clients, particularly among relapsed smokers. Its use was associated with continued high intake of nicotine among ex-smokers but did not increase nicotine intake in smokers. It did not appear to affect stress response. Little is known about the long-term effects of NRT. Given an increasing shift towards harm reduction in tobacco control, reducing the harm from combustible products by partial or complete substitution with noncombustible products, more data on long-term use are needed. This study demonstrated that in the context of SSS, clients rarely use products for up to a year and that NRT use does not affect users' stress response. Hence, ex-smokers using NRT long-term can completely replace nicotine from cigarettes with nicotine from NRT; long-term NRT use by continuing smokers did not increase nicotine intake. Hence, long-term NRT appears to be a safe and effective way to reduce exposure to combustible nicotine.

Associations of Serum Cytokine Receptor Levels with Melancholia, Staging of Illness, Depressive and Manic Phases, and Severity of Depression in Bipolar Disorder

To examine cytokine receptor biomarkers in bipolar disorder (BD), Siwek et al., (2016) recruited 133 well-phenotyped BD patients and 50 normal controls and measured serum levels of soluble interleukin 1 receptor antagonist (sIL-1RA), soluble interleukin-2 receptor (sIL-2R), sIL-6R, and TNF receptor 60 and 80 kDa (sTNFR60/80). sIL-1RA and sTNFR80 were significantly higher in BD than in controls and sTNFR80 and higher in melancholic than in non-melancholic patients and controls. Kapczinski's stages 3 + 4 were characterized by lowered sIL-2R and increased sTNFR80 levels. Acute phase depression was characterized by increased sTNFR80 levels as compared with controls, manic, and euthymic patients. Both sTNFR60 and sTNFR80 levels were significantly and positively related with severity of depression but not mania. Logistic regression analysis showed that the significant predictors for BD are increased sIL-1RA levels, nicotine dependence and a family history of depression and alcoholism. The risk factors for stages 3 + 4 were lowered sIL-2R levels and nicotine dependence. Melancholia was predicted by higher sTNFR80 levels and female sex. Severity of depression was predicted by female sex, nicotine dependence, and increased sTNFR60 and sTNFR80 levels. Cell-mediated immunity was activated during a current episode of depression but not (hypo) mania or the euthymic state. There were no associations between the biomarkers and age at onset, duration of illness, severity of mania, bipolar (BP) 2 or BP1 subtypes, rapid cycling, atypical depression, psychotic or suicidal symptoms, and a family history of psychiatric disease. These findings revealed that increased sIL-1RA may be a trait marker of BD, increased sTNFR80 a state marker of the depressive phase, especially melancholia, while lower sIL-2R but higher sTNFR80 may be considered as staging biomarkers.

The Adverse Effects of Smoking on Health Outcomes in Bipolar Disorder

In a recent narrative review, Slyepchenko et al., (2016) provided evidence and putative mechanisms of comorbid effects of BD, cigarette use, and nicotine dependence, and discussed the clinical significance of these interactions. These investigators highlighted that several biological systems are implicated in the progression of bipolar disorder including but not limited to cytokine levels, oxidative stress markers, monoamine levels, tryptophan catabolite and glutamate-mediated excitotoxicity, microglial activation as well as structural and functional changes. The high rate of smoking behavior in individuals with bipolar disorder provides the impetus for exploring shared and discrete pathogenetic mechanisms. Based on the literature evidence, these researchers highlighted that in addition to contributing to increased mortality, smoking activates several neurobiological effector systems implicated in the progression of bipolar disorder.

A Single Controlled Exposure to Secondhand Smoke May Not Alter Thrombogenesis or Trigger Platelet Activation

It is known that chronic secondhand smoke (SHS) exposure increases cardiovascular events, particularly acute thrombotic events. There is limited human data on acute SHS exposure. Therefore, Srikanth et al., (2016) conducted a study to determine whether a single controlled exposure of humans to SHS increased thrombogenesis. After 6-8 hours fast, subjects (n = 50) were exposed to constant dose SHS (particulate level of 500 μg/m (3)) for 120 minutes in a temperature-regulated and ventilated, simulated bar environment. Blood was drawn before and immediately after SHS exposure for thromboelastography (TEG) and flow cytometry. Maximum clot strength (MA) was measured using TEG and platelet leukocyte aggregates (LPA) were measured as an index of platelet activation. Anti-CD 14 antibodies were used as leukocyte markers and anti-CD 41 antibodies as platelet markers for cytometry. There was no effect of acute exposure to SHS on platelet activation or thrombogenesis. Also, intra group (smokers [n = 19] and nonsmokers [n = 31]) comparisons of LPA and TEG parameters did not show changes with SHS exposure. While there are abundant data showing enhanced thrombogenesis and platelet activation following repeated exposure to SHS, this study suggested that a single exposure does not appear to significantly alter thrombin kinetics nor in platelet activation, suggesting that the effects of SHS on thrombogenesis might be nonlinear.

Association of Exposure to Benzene and Smoking with Oxidative Damage to Nucleic Acids

Tranfo et al., (2016) recently conducted a study to validate liquid chromatography-tandem mass spectrometry (HPLC-MS/MS t-muconic acid) isotopic dilution for the determination of Benzene and nicotine metabolites in urine. These investigators calculated limit of detection 0.026 μg/L for S-phenylmercapturic acid (SPMA), 0.55 μg/L for t, (t, t-MA), and 12.41 μg/L for the cotinine, and the relative uncertainty. The study involved 446 healthy volunteer residents since at least 10 years in an area of central Italy.

SPMA was strongly correlated with cotinine, its concentration in smokers (93) being about ten times than in non/ex-smokers (197/156), while the t, t-MA of smokers was about twice the non/ex-smokers value. A cutoff value for the definition of smoker was set at 100 μg/g. Oxidative stress was studied in smokers and non- and ex-smokers by means of the determination of the biomarkers 8-oxo-7,8-dihydro-2'-deoxyguanosine (8-oxodGuo), 8-oxo-7,8-Dihydroguanosine (8-oxoGuo), and 8-oxo-7,8-dihydroguanine (8-oxoGua): no significant differences were found between smokers and non/ex-smokers, but when subjects were classified according to the cotinine cutoff value, a correlation in smokers' urinary 8-oxodGuo was found with SPMA and cotinine. These findings were confirmed by chemometric analysis that also identified the experimental variables contributing the discrimination as cotinine and t, t-MA.

Protective Effects of Elafin against Adult Asthma (Microarray Analyses)

It has been established that elafin inhibits serine proteases, such as human neutrophil elastase and proteinase 3, to prevent excessive damage during inflammation. However, the relationship between elafin and asthma is still unclear. Hence, Tsai et al., (2016) utilized microarray technology to evaluate smoking- and asthma-related biomarkers in a discovery-driven manner. They identified candidate genes, e.g., proteinase inhibitor 3 (PI3), related to asthma and smoking from gene expression microarray data sets and evaluated their potential as biomarkers for asthma. They used human genome microarray data sets from smoking-and asthma-related gene expression data sets and performed real-time quantitative polymerase chain reaction to measure and validate differences in gene expression. They also recruited adult patients with asthma and age- and sex-matched control patients who were administered a structured questionnaire and evaluated for lung function and plasma elafin levels, which are encoded by the PI3 gene. Six significantly altered candidate genes, PI3, protein kinase C iota, phosphoserine phosphatase, IQ motif-containing GTPase activating protein 1, interleukin 13 receptor α 1, signal transducing adaptor molecule SH3 domain, and ITAM motif 2, were identified from comparisons across the four asthma-and four smoking-related data sets included in this study. An in vitro study of human airway epithelial cells (A549) and a human monocytic cell line (THP-1) demonstrated that PI3 messenger RNA levels were significantly altered by nicotine exposure. Elafin concentration was significantly higher in control patients than in patients with asthma. The plasma elafin concentration in the highest quartile (≥12.69 ng/mL) was inversely associated with asthma compared with the lowest quartile (<5.82 ng/mL) after adjusting for age, sex, smoking status, waist-to-hip ratio, percentage predicted forced expiratory volume in 1 second, cockroaches in the home, incense burning, and family history, suggesting that high elafin levels identified in smoking- and asthma-related microarray data sets and an epidemiologic study significantly reduced the risk of asthma. These investigators recommended further studies of elafin as a potential therapy for asthma.

Supervised, Vigorous Intensity Exercise Intervention for Depressed Female Smokers

Few studies have evaluated exercise interventions for smokers with depression or other psychiatric comorbidities. A pilot study evaluated the potential role of supervised vigorous exercise as a smoking cessation intervention for depressed females. In this study, Patten et al., (2017) enrolled 30 adult women with moderate-severe depressive symptoms and randomly assigned to 12 weeks of thrice weekly, in person sessions of vigorous intensity supervised exercise at a YMCA setting (EX; n = 15) or health education (HE; n = 15). All participants received behavioral smoking cessation counseling and nicotine patch therapy. Assessments were done in person at baseline, at the end of 12 weeks of treatment, and at 6 months post-target quit date. Primary end points were exercise adherence (proportion of 36 sessions attended) and biochemically confirmed 7-day point prevalence abstinence at Week 12. Biomarkers of inflammation were explored for differences between treatment groups and between women who smoked and those abstinent at Week 12. Treatment adherence was high for both groups (72% for EX and 66% for HE; p = .55). The Week 12 smoking abstinence rate was higher for EX than HE (11/15 [73%] vs. 5/15 [33%]; p = .028), but no significant differences emerged at 6-month follow-up. Interleukin-6 levels increased more for those smoking than women abstinent at Week 12. Vigorous intensity supervised exercise was feasible and enhanced short-term smoking cessation among depressed female smokers. Innovative and cost-effective strategies to bolster long-term exercise adherence and smoking cessation need evaluation in this population. Hence, inflammatory biomarkers could be examined in future research as mediators of treatment efficacy. This preliminary study found that vigorous intensity supervised exercise is feasible and enhances short-term smoking cessation among depressed female smokers. This research addressed an important gap in the field. Despite decades of research examining exercise interventions for smoking cessation, few studies have been done among depressed smokers or those with comorbid psychiatric disorders. A novel finding of this study was increases in levels of a pro-inflammatory biomarker observed among women who smoked at the end of the intervention compared to those who did not.

Estimates of Tobacco Use by Wastewater Analysis of Anabasine and Anatabine

Wastewater analysis and the chemical analysis of municipal sewage, is becoming the technique of choice to monitor changes in community consumption of a range of compounds over time. Currently wastewater analyses which estimate tobacco consumption focus on the major alkaloid nicotine and its urinary metabolite, cotinine. Nicotine is also present in replacement therapies such as nicotine gum and patches, this analysis is unspecific and hence does not truly reflect the harmful consumption of tobacco. Therefore, Tscharke et al., (2016) assessed two alkaloids - anabasine and anatabine - which are specific to dried tobacco, as biomarkers for tobacco consumption in wastewater, together with nicotine and cotinine. Consequently, solid phase extraction (SPE) and liquid chromatography-mass spectrometry (LC-MS) for the detection of anabasine, anatabine, nicotine, and cotinine in municipal wastewater were validated. All compounds were detected in wastewater extracts and found to have satisfactory recovery, accuracy, precision, and stability in wastewater. Daily flow volume and catchment population of the wastewater facility were used to estimate normalized consumption figures of mg/day/1000 people for composite samples collected over one week. Anabasine and anatabine were found to be suitable wastewater biomarkers of tobacco and can be used to assess tobacco consumption of communities via wastewater analysis. Application of this methodology can be used to collect temporal consumption data which could be used to determine the efficacy of tobacco reduction strategies.

Agreement between Wastewater-Based Epidemiology and Survey Data on Alcohol and Nicotine Use in a Community

Alcohol and nicotine are the two most commonly used substances world-wide and associated with increased burden of disease. Since surveys on substance use may be difficult due to response biases, van Wel ET a (2016) developed wastewater-based epidemiology (WBE) as a more efficient measure of nicotine and alcohol abuse. This study compared estimates of nicotine and alcohol use from a wastewater sampling campaign in a medium-sized Belgian city with a concurrently executed population survey. 29,083 letters about participation in an online survey study on weekly alcohol and tobacco use were sent to the inhabitants of Lier, Belgium. Wastewater samples were collected from the associated treatment plant in four bi-weekly periods. Samples were analyzed using liquid chromatography coupled to tandem mass spectrometry (LC-MS/MS). Ethylsulfate was used as alcohol biomarker and cotinine and trans-3'-hydroxycotinine as nicotine biomarker. 263 (1%) surveys were filled out on average per week. According to survey data, alcohol and nicotine were used less than in the rest of Belgium and this was matched by the wastewater data. Nicotine use, but not alcohol use, showed a significant variation over the sampling periods. Both nicotine and alcohol showed increase use during the weekend while only alcohol showed a different use pattern throughout the week. No correlation between WBE and survey data could be demonstrated, due to small sample sizes. However, this study provided evidence that weekly trends in alcohol and nicotine use can be quickly detected from wastewater analysis and the occurrence of major events such as festivals can be identified.

Substance Use in Individuals with Mild to Borderline Intellectual Disability

It is known that individuals with mild or borderline intellectual disability (MBID) are at risk of substance use (SU). At present, it remains uncertain which strategy is the best for assessing SU in individuals with MBID. Therefore, VanDerNagel et al., (2016) conducted a study to compare three strategies, namely self-report, collateral-report, and biomarker analysis. In a sample of 112 participants with MBID from six Dutch facilities providing care to individuals with intellectual disabilities, willingness to participate, SU rates, and agreement between the three strategies were explored. The Substance use and misuse in Intellectual Disability - Questionnaire (SumID-Q; self-report) assesses lifetime use, use in the previous month, and recent use of tobacco, alcohol, cannabis, and stimulants. The Substance use and misuse in Intellectual Disability - Collateral-report questionnaire (SumID-CR; collateral-report) assesses staff members' report of participants' SU over the same reference periods as the SumID-Q. Biomarkers for SU, such as cotinine (metabolite of nicotine), ethanol, Tetrahydrocannabinol (THC), and its metabolite THCCOOH, benzoylecgonine (metabolite of cocaine), and amphetamines were assessed in urine, hair, and sweat patches. Willingness to provide biomarker samples was significantly lower compared to willingness to complete the SumID-Q. Most participants reported smoking, drinking alcohol, and using cannabis at least once in their lives, and about a fifth had ever used stimulants. Collateral reported lifetime use was significantly lower. However, self-reported past month and recent SU rates did not differ significantly from the rates from collateral-reports or biomarkers with the exception of lower alcohol use rates found in biomarker analysis. The agreement between self-report and biomarker analysis was substantial (kappas 0.60-0.89), except for alcohol use (kappa 0.06). Disagreement between SumID-Q and biomarkers concerned mainly over-reporting of the SumID-Q. The agreement between SumID-CR and biomarker analysis was moderate to substantial (kappas 0.48 - 0.88), again with the exception of alcohol (kappa 0.02). In this study, the three strategies that were used to assess SU in individuals with MBID differed significantly in participation rates, but not in SU rates. Several explanations for the better-than-expected performance of self- and collateral-reports were presented. Based on these findings, these investigators concluded that for individuals with MBID, self-report combined with collateral report can be used to assess current SU, and this combination may contribute to collaborative, early intervention efforts to reduce SU and its related harms in this vulnerable group.

Tobacco Alkaloids NorNicotine, Anatabine, and Anabasine in Smokers' Urine

It is now well established that nicotine is the most abundant alkaloid in tobacco accounting for 95% of the alkaloid content. There are also several minor tobacco alkaloids; among these are nor nicotine, anatabine, and anabasine. Von Weymarn et al., (2016) recently developed and applied a 96 well plate-based capillary LC-tandem mass spectrometry for the analysis of nor nicotine, anatabine, and anabasine in urine. This was validated with regard to accuracy and precision. Anabasine was quantifiable to low levels with a limit of quantitation (LOQ) of 0.2 ng/mL even when nicotine, which was isobaric, was present at concentrations >2500-fold higher than anabasine. This attribute was important since anatabine and anabasine in urine have been proposed as biomarkers of tobacco use for individuals using nicotine replacement therapies. These investigators analyzed the three minor tobacco alkaloids in urine from 827 smokers with a wide range of tobacco exposures. Nor nicotine (LOQ 0.6 ng/mL) was detected in all samples, and anatabine (LOQ, 0.15 ng/mL) and anabasine were detected in 97.7% of the samples. The median urinary concentrations of nor nicotine, anatabine, and anabasine were 98.9, 4.02, and 5.53 ng/mL. Total nicotine equivalents (TNE) were well correlated with Anatabine ($r(2) = 0.714$) and anabasine ($r(2) = 0.760$). TNE was most highly correlated with nor nicotine, which is also a metabolite of nicotine. Urine samples from a subset of subjects ($n = 110$) were analyzed for the presence of glucuronide conjugates by quantifying any increase in anatabine and anabasine concentrations after β-glucuronidase treatment. The median ratio of the glucuronidated to free anatabine was 0.74 (range, 0.1 to 10.9), and the median ratio of glucuronidated to free anabasine was 0.3 (range, 0.1 to 2.9). This was the largest population of smokers for whom the urinary concentrations of these three tobacco alkaloids had been reported.

Genome-Wide Meta-Analysis of Cotinine Levels in Cigarette Smokers

Genome-wide association studies (GWAS) of complex behavioral phenotypes such as cigarette smoking typically employ self-report phenotypes. However, precise biomarker phenotypes may afford greater statistical power and identify novel variants. Ware et al., (2016) recently reported the GWAS meta-analysis of levels of cotinine, the primary metabolite of nicotine, in 4,548 daily smokers of European ancestry. They identified a locus close to UGT2B10 at 4q13.2 (minimum $p = 5.89 \times 10^{-10}$ for rs114612145), which was consequently replicated. This variant is in high linkage disequilibrium with a known functional variant in the UGT2B10 gene which is associated with reduced nicotine and cotinine glucuronidation activity, but is not associated with nicotine intake. Additionally, these investigators observed association between multiple variants within the 15q25.1 region and cotinine levels, all located within the CHRNA5/A3/B4 gene cluster or adjacent genes, consistent with previous much larger GWAS using self-report measures of smoking quantity. These investigators illustrated the increase in power afforded by using precise biomarker measures in GWAS and highlighted that biomarkers do not always mark the phenotype of interest. Hence, the use of metabolite data as a proxy for environmental exposures should be carefully considered in the context of individual differences in metabolic pathways.

Caregiver Health Literacy and Preschool Children's Secondhand Smoke Exposure

Recently, Welkom et al., (2016) conducted a study to examine the associations between caregiver health literacy (HL) and smoking-related outcome expectancies, implementation of home/car smoking bans (H/CSBs), and child secondhand smoke exposure (SHSe). Caregivers of Head Start children residing with a smoker(s) completed measures assessing HL, outcome expectancies, and H/CSB implementation. Biomarkers of child SHSe included home air nicotine monitors and child salivary cotinine. Caregivers with lower HL had higher levels of home air nicotine and child salivary cotinine in the full sample and among smokers. After controlling for child age and number of smokers in the home, lower HL was associated with higher endorsement of negative smoking expectancies in the full sample and in smokers. HL was not associated with H/CSB implementation across groups. Caregiver HL was associated with child SHSe and was important in shaping smoking-related beliefs. HL was not directly related to adoption of SHSe-reduction behaviors such as H/CSBs.

Self-Report and Biological Measures of Cigarette Use in Nondaily Smokers

Although, a large subset of individuals who smoke cigarettes do not smoke regularly, the assessments used to collect data on cigarette consumption in nondaily smokers have not been rigorously evaluated. Therefore, Wray et al., (2016) conducted a study to examine several self-report and biomarker approaches to the assessment of cigarette use in a sample of nondaily smokers (n = 176). Participants were randomly assigned to a daily monitoring condition (n = 89), requiring a daily report of the number of cigarettes smoked in the previous 24 hrs. or a no monitoring condition (n = 87). Number of cigarettes smoked over the first 28 days of the study was assessed using 2 quantity frequency measures, a graduated frequency measure, and a timeline follow back (TLFB) interview at the Session 5 study visit. Hair nicotine (NIC), hair cotinine (COT), and expired-air carbon monoxide (CO) were collected from each participant. Total cigarettes reported via daily report were strongly correlated with all Session 5 measures of total cigarettes, but were most strongly associated with TLFB total cigarettes. Collapsed CO across 5 sessions was the biomarker most strongly correlated with daily report total cigarettes. These data supported the use of daily report and TLFB of assessing cigarette use in nondaily smokers. The data also supported the use of CO and hair biomarkers as most appropriate biomarkers of nicotine exposure in nondaily smokers.

Tobacco-Specific N-Nitrosamines and Polycyclic Aromatic Hydrocarbons in Cigarettes

Recent studies on tobacco smoke carcinogen and toxicant biomarkers and cancer risk among male smokers in the Shanghai Cohort Study demonstrated that exposure to tobacco-specific nitrosamines (TSNA) and polycyclic aromatic hydrocarbons (PAH) is associated with the risk of cancer. These findings supported the hypothesis that the smokers' cancer risk is a function of the dose of selected tobacco carcinogens and highlighted the importance of understanding the factors that affect the intake of these carcinogens by smokers. Given that tobacco constituent exposures are driven by the levels of these constituents in cigarette smoke, Yershova et al., (2016) measured mainstream smoke TSNA and PAH levels in 43 Chinese cigarette brands that participants of the Shanghai Cohort Study reported to smoke. In all brands analyzed, mainstream smoke levels of NNN and NNK, the two carcinogenic TSNA, were relatively low, averaging ($\pm$SD) 16.8($\pm$25.1) and 14.2($\pm$9.5) ng/cigarette, respectively. The levels of PAH were comparable to those found in U.S. cigarettes, averaging 15($\pm$9) ng/cigarette for benzo[a]pyrene, 119($\pm$66) ng/cigarette for phenanthrene and 37($\pm$19) ng/cigarette for pyrene. These findings indicated that the generally low levels of NNN and NNK are most likely responsible for relatively low levels of corresponding biomarkers in the urine of the Shanghai Cohort Study participants as compared to those found in the U.S. smokers, supporting the role of the levels of these constituents in cigarette smoke in smokers' exposures. These findings also suggested that, in addition to smoking, other sources contribute to Chinese smokers' exposure to PAH.

White Matter Integrity in Young Smokers

Previous diffusion tensor imaging (DTI) studies revealed contradictory effects of smoking on fractional anisotropy (FA). Multiple DTI-derived indices may help to deduce the pathophysiological type of white matter (WM) changes and provide more specific biomarkers of WM neuropathology in the whole brain of young smokers. Yu et al., (2016) recently performed a study on 23 young smokers and 22 age-, education- and gender-matched healthy non-smoking controls. Tract-based spatial statistics was employed to investigate the WM microstructure in young smokers by integrating multiple indices, including FA, mean diffusivity (MD), radial diffusivity (RD) and axial diffusivity (AD). Compared with healthy non-smoking controls, young smokers showed significantly increased FA with increased AD and decreased RD in several brain regions, while no difference in MD was observed. Specifically, the overlapped WM regions with increased FA, increased AD and decreased RD were found in the right posterior limb of the internal capsule, the right external capsule and the right superior corona radiata. Additionally, average FA and RD values in the WM regions mentioned earlier were significantly correlated with pack-years and Fagerström Test for Nicotine Dependence, while no correlation in AD was found. The WM tracts with increased FA may be more associated with RD, rather than AD in young smokers, suggesting that WM properties of several fibers in young smokers may serve as biomarker of cumulative effect and severity of nicotine dependence.

Genetic Determinants of CYP2A6 Activity and Biomarkers of Tobacco Smoke Exposure in Relation to Risk of Lung Cancer

Cytochrome P450 2A6 (CYP2A6) catalyzes nicotine metabolism and contributes to the metabolism of the tobacco-specific lung carcinogen, NNK. Genetic variation in CYP2A6 may affect smoking behavior and contribute to lung cancer risk. Yuan et al., (2016) recently performed a nested case-control study of 325 lung cancer cases and 356 controls within a prospective cohort of 18,244 Chinese men in Shanghai, China. Quantified were 4 allelic variants of CYP2A6 [*1(+51A), *4, *7, and *9] and urinary total nicotine, total cotinine, total trans-3'-Hydroxycotinine (3HC) and total NNAL (an NNK metabolite). Calculated values were total nicotine equivalents (TNE), the sum of total nicotine, total cotinine and total 3HC and the total 3HC: total cotinine ratio as a measure of CYP2A6 activity. The nicotine metabolizer status (normal, intermediate, slow and poor) was determined by CYP2A6 genotypes. The smoking-adjusted odds ratios (95% confidence intervals) of lung cancer for the highest vs lowest quartile of total nicotine, total cotinine, total 3HC, TNE and total NNAL were 3.03 (1.80-5.10), 4.70 (2.61-8.46), 4.26 (2.37-7.68), 4.71 (2.61-8.52), and 3.15 (1.86-5.33) (all Ptrend < 0.001), respectively. Among controls CYP2A6 poor metabolizers had a 78% lower total 3HC: total cotinine ratio and 72% higher total nicotine (Ptrend ≤ 0.002). Poor metabolizers had an odds ratio of 0.64 (95% confidence interval = 0.43-0.97) for lung cancer, which was statistically nonsignificant (odds ratio = 0.74, 95% confidence interval = 0.48-1.15) after adjustment for urinary TNE and smoking intensity and duration. The lower lung cancer risk observed in CYP2A6 poor metabolizers was partially explained by the influence of CYP2A6 genetic polymorphisms on nicotine uptake and metabolism.

Randomized Controlled Trial of Reduced Nicotine Cigarettes in Smokers with Mood and/or Anxiety Disorders

The Food and Drug Administration (FDA) can set standards for cigarettes that could include reducing their nicotine content to improve public health without causing unintended serious consequences for sub-populations. Allen et al., (2017) recently performed a study to evaluate the effect of progressive nicotine reduction in cigarettes on smoking behavior, toxicant exposure, and psychiatric symptoms in smokers with comorbid mood and/or anxiety disorders using a two-site, two-arm, double-blind, parallel group, randomized controlled trial (RCT) in four phases over 34 weeks. Adult smokers (N = 200) of 5 or more cigarettes per day were randomized across two sites (Penn State and Massachusetts General). Participants must have not had a quit attempt in the prior month, nor be planning to quit in the next 6 months, meet criteria for a current or lifetime unipolar mood and/or anxiety disorder based on the structured Mini-International Neuropsychiatric Interview, and must not have an unstable medical or psychiatric condition. After a week of smoking their own cigarettes, participants received two weeks of Spectrum research cigarettes with usual nicotine content (11.6 mg). After this baseline period, participants were randomly assigned to continue smoking Spectrum research cigarettes that contain either (a) Usual nicotine Content (11.6 mg); or (b) Reduced nicotine Content: the nicotine content per cigarette was progressively reduced from ~11.6 mg to 0.2 mg in five steps over 18 weeks. At the end of the randomization phase, participants were offered the choice to either (a) quit smoking with assistance, (b) continue smoking free research cigarettes, or (c) return to purchasing their own cigarettes, for the final 12 weeks of the study. The primary outcome measure was blood cotinine; key secondary outcomes were: exhaled carbon monoxide, urinary total NNAL- 4-(methylnitrosamino)-1-(3-Pyridyl)-1-butanol and 1-hydroxypyrene, oxidative stress biomarkers including 8-Isoprostanes, measures of psychiatric symptoms (e.g., depression, anxiety), smoking behavior and dependence (e.g., cigarette consumption, quit attempts), and health effects (e.g., blood pressure, respiratory symptoms). The results from this study were used to inform FDA on the potential effects of regulating the nicotine content of cigarettes and help determine whether smokers with mood and/or anxiety disorders can safely transition to significantly reduced nicotine content cigarettes.

Regional Homogeneity Changes in Nicotine Addicts by Resting-State fMRI

To reveal the brain functional changes of nicotine addicts compared with those of non-smokers and explore the biomarker for nicotine dependence evaluation, Chen and Mo (2017) recruited a total of 14 smokers and 11 non-smoking controls. Resting-state fMRI and regional homogeneity (ReHo) were applied in the neural activity analysis.

Two-sample t-test was performed to examine the voxel-wise difference between the smokers and the controls. Correlation analysis between the ReHo values and the Fagerström Test for Nicotine Dependence (FTND) scores were performed to explore the biomarkers for the clinical characteristics of smokers. The ReHo values from the right superior frontal gyrus of the Brodmann's area (BA) 9 to the right middle frontal gyrus and the ReHo value from the left and right precuneus (BA 23) to the left and right middle cingulum gyrus were lower in the smokers than in the non-smokers. The ReHo value in the precuneus (BA 23) was positively correlated with the FTND score of smokers. Hence, ReHo values in the right superior frontal gyrus and left precuneus can be used to separate the smokers from the non-smokers. In particular, the left precuneus is a potential neuroimaging biomarker for nicotine addicts.

Application of cDNA-AFLP to Biomarker Exploration in a Non-Model Species *Grandidierella japonica*

Biomarkers of exposure can be used to identify specific contaminants that are adversely affecting aquatic organisms. However, it remains costly to investigate multiple novel biomarkers of exposure in a non-model species, despite the development of next-generation sequencing technology. In a recent study, Hiki et al., (2017) focused on the use of cDNA-amplified fragment length polymorphism (AFLP) as a cost-effective biomarker discovery tool to test whether it could identify biomarkers of exposure in the non-model amphipod species *Grandidierella japonica*. Loci were identified that were differentially expressed in amphipods exposed to reference chemicals (Cu, Zn, and nicotine) and to an environmental sample (road dust) at sublethal concentrations. Eight loci responded consistently to nicotine at different concentrations, but not to Cu or Zn. Some of the loci also responded to an environmental road dust sample containing nicotine. These findings suggested that loci identified using cDNA-AFLP could be used as biomarkers of nicotine exposure in environmental samples with complex matrices. Further studies with other organisms and toxicants are needed, but these investigators highlighted that the use of cDNA-AFLP to identify biomarkers for eco-toxicological studies of non-model species is at least feasible.

Fetal Exposure to Tobacco

It is well established that fetal exposure to tobacco constituents is a risk factor for negative birth outcomes. Recently, Jocob et al., (2017) determined the relationships between nicotine and cotinine concentrations in amniotic fluid and maternal saliva. As part of a therapeutic trial, 42 pregnant smokers agreed to sample amniotic fluid (8 samples from amniocentesis, 34 at birth). Their smoking characteristics were collected along with the newborns' birth outcomes. The median concentrations [IQR] in amniotic fluid and saliva were 11 [7-31] and 38 [7-174] μg/L for nicotine and 72 [22-123] μg/L and 55 [17-109] μg/L for cotinine, respectively. Multivariate models showed that saliva cotinine concentration predicted amniotic fluid nicotine and cotinine concentrations. Amniotic fluid nicotine or cotinine concentration was not associated with birth weight. In multivariate analysis, the time elapsed since the last cigarette was the only variable associated with increased birth weight. Maternal saliva sampling for the determination of cotinine concentration is of interest to monitor fetal exposure to nicotine of any origin. Nevertheless, the time elapsed since the last cigarette was a better predictor of birth weight than the biomarkers' concentrations in amniotic fluid or maternal saliva.

Psychometric Properties of the Fagerström Test for Nicotine Dependence in Mexican Smokers

The Fagerström Test for Nicotine Dependence (FTND) is a widely used six-item questionnaire, often used as a measure of physical dependence on nicotine, although evidence of its validity in Spanish-language studies is scarce. Hence, Moreno-Coutiño et al., (2017) conducted a study to assess the psychometric properties of FTND in Spanish speakers. These investigators recruited 136 regular adult smokers to answer the FTND. They assessed the internal consistency of the FTND with a Cronbach's alpha and convergent and divergent validity with the Pearson product-moment coefficient between variables of external criteria, both measure and nonmeasure related; the FTND items, and the total score. They performed a binary logistic regression model to determine predictive validity of the questionnaire, using the FTND total scores as an independent variable and cessation as the outcome and performed a confirmatory factor analysis to assess the robustness of a single-factor model. The internal consistency had a lower coefficient than current standards. The FTND was unable to predict cessation at any assessed time point. The FTND total score showed significant correlation with exhaled carbon monoxide, urinary cotinine, and self-report of cigarettes smoked per day. However, Items 5 (smoke in the first hours) and 6 (smoke if ill) failed to obtain a significant correlation with biological biomarkers. Although the FTND showed an adequate construct validity, these data suggested that its convergent and predictive validity was limited. Therefore, it might not be suitable for the Mexican population. These investigators suggested more studies in other populations to establish the generalizability of these findings.

References

Allen, S. I., Foulds, J., Pachas, G. N., Veldheer, S., Cather, C., Azzouz, N., Hrabovsky, S., Hameed, A., Yingst, J., Hammett, E., Modesto, J., Krebs, N. M., Zhu, J., Liao, J., Muscat, J. E., Richie, J., Evins, A. E. 2017. A two-site, two-arm, 34-week, double-blind, parallel-group, randomized controlled trial of reduced nicotine cigarettes in smokers with mood and/or anxiety disorders: trial design and protocol. *BMC Public Health.* 17(1), 100.

Chen, H., Mo, S., 2017. Regional Homogeneity Changes in nicotine Addicts by Resting-State fMRI. *PLoS One.* 12(1), e0170143.

Durazzo T. C., Mattsson N., Weiner M. W., Korecka M., Trojanowski J. Q., et al., (2014) History of cigarette smoking in cognitively-normal elders is associated with elevated cerebrospinal fluid biomarkers of oxidative stress. *Drug Alcohol Depend* 142, 262-268.

Fagan, P., Pokhrel, P., Herzog, T. A., Pagano, I. S., Franke, A. A., Clanton, M. S., Alexander, L. A., Trinidad, D. R., Sakuma, K. L., Johnson, C. A., Moolchan, E. T., 2016. Nicotine Metabolism in Young Adult Daily Menthol and Nonmenthol Smokers. *Nicotine Tob Res.* 18(4), 437-446.

Goniewicz, M. L., Gawron, M., Smith, D. M., Peng, M., Jacob, P. 3rd., Benowitz, N. L. 2017. Exposure to nicotine and Selected Toxicants in Cigarette Smokers Who Switched to E-Cigarettes: A Longitudinal Within-Subjects Observational Study. *Nicotine Tob Res.* 19(2), 160-167.

Gualberto, E. C. Jr., Theodoro, L. H., Longo, M., Novaes, V. C., Nagata, M. J., Ervolino, E., Garcia, V. G. 2016. Antimicrobial photodynamic therapy minimizes the deleterious effect of nicotine in female rats with induced periodontitis. *Lasers Med Sci.* 31(1), 83-94.

Harats D, Ben-Naim M, Dabach Y, Hollander G, Stein O, et al., (1989) Cigarette smoking renders LDL susceptible to peroxidative modification and enhanced metabolism by macrophages. *Atherosclerosis* 79, 245-252.

Hatsukami, D. K., Luo, X., Dick, L., Kangkum, M., Allen, S. S., Murphy, S. E., Hecht, S. S., Shields, P. G., al'Absi, M. 2017. Reduced nicotine content cigarettes and use of alternative nicotine products: exploratory trial. *Addiction.* 112(1), 156-167.

Hatsukami, D. K., Severson, H., Anderson, A., Vogel, R. I., Jensen, J., Broadbent, B., Murphy, S. E., Carmella, S., Hecht, S. S. 2016. Randomized clinical trial of snus versus medicinal Nicotine among smokers interested in product switching. *Tob Control.* 25(3), 267-274.

Haziza, C., de La Bourdonnaye, G., Merlet, S., Benzimra, M., Ancerewicz, J., Donelli, A., Baker, G., Picavet, P., Lüdicke, F., 2016. Assessment of the reduction in levels of exposure to harmful and potentially harmful constituents in Japanese subjects using a novel tobacco heating system compared with conventional cigarettes and smoking abstinence: A randomized controlled study in confinement. *Regul Toxicol Pharmacol.* 81, 489-499.

Haziza, C., de La Bourdonnaye, G., Skiada, D., Ancerewicz, J., Baker, G., Picavet, P., Lüdicke, F., 2016. Evaluation of the Tobacco Heating System 2.2. Part 8: 5-Day randomized reduced exposure clinical study in Poland. *Regul Toxicol Pharmacol.* 81 Suppl 2, S139-S150.

Haziza, C., de La Bourdonnaye, G., Skiada, D., Ancerewicz, J., Baker, G., Picavet, P., Lüdicke, F., 2016. Biomarker of exposure level data set in smokers switching from conventional cigarettes to Tobacco Heating System 2.2, continuing smoking or abstaining from smoking for 5 days. *Data Brief.* 10, 283-293.

He, L., Gong, H., Zhang, J., Zhong, C., Huang, Y., Zhang, C., Aqeel Ashraf, M. 2016. Interaction of exposure concentration and duration in determining the apoptosis of testis in rats after cigarette smoke inhalation. *Saudi J Biol Sci.* 23(4), 531-541.

Hecht, S. S., Stepanov, I., Carmella, S. G., 2016. Exposure and Metabolic Activation Biomarkers of Carcinogenic Tobacco-Specific Nitrosamines. *Acc Chem Res.* 49(1), 106-114.

Hiki, K., Nakajima, F., Tobino, T., 2017. Application of cDNA-AFLP to biomarker exploration in a non-model species *Grandidierella japonica*. *Ecotoxicol Environ Saf.* 140, 206-213.

Hritcu, L., Ionita, R., Motei, D. E., Babii, C., Stefan, M., Mihasan, M., 2017. Nicotine versus 6-hydroxy-l-nicotine against chlorisondamine induced memory impairment and oxidative stress in the rat hippocampus. *Biomed Pharmacother.* 86, 102-108.

Hritcu, L., Ionita, R., Motei, D. E., Babii, C., Stefan, M., Mihasan, M., 2017. Nicotine versus 6-hydroxy-l-nicotine against chlorisondamine induced memory impairment and oxidative stress in the rat hippocampus. *Biomed Pharmacother.* 86, 102-108.

Hsu, P. C., Lan, R. S., Brasky, T. M., Marian, C., Cheema, A. K., Ressom, H. W., Loffredo, C. A., Pickworth , W. B., Shields, P G., 2017. Menthol Smokers: Metabolomic Profiling and Smoking Behavior. *Cancer Epidemiol Biomarkers Prev.* 26(1), 51-60.

Hsu, P. C., Lan, R. S., Brasky, T. M., Marian, C., Cheema, A. K., Ressom, H. W., Loffredo, C. A., Pickworth, W. B., Shields, P. G., 2017. Menthol Smokers: Metabolomic Profiling and Smoking Behavior. *Cancer Epidemiol Biomarkers Prev.* 26(1), 51-60.

Ibrahim, Z. S, Alkafafy, M. E., Ahmed, M. M., Soliman, M. M., 2016. Renoprotective effect of curcumin against the combined oxidative stress of diabetes and nicotine in rats. *Mol Med Rep.* 13(4), 3017-3026.

Jacob, N., Golmard, J. L., Berlin, I., 2017. Fetal exposure to tobacco: Nicotine and cotinine concentration in amniotic fluid and maternal saliva. *J Matern Fetal Neonatal Med.* 30(2), 233-239.

Jacob, N., Golmard, J. L., Berlin, I., 2017. Fetal exposure to tobacco: Nicotine and cotinine concentration in amniotic fluid and maternal saliva. *J. Matern Fetal Neonatal. Med.* 30(2), 233-239.

Jansen, E. H., Beekhof, P., and Ruskovska, T. 2014. The Effect of Smoking on Biomarkers of (Anti) oxidant Status. *J. Mol Biomark. Diagn.* 5, 6.

Jia, J., Peng, J., Li, Z., Wu, Y., Wu, Q., Tu, W., Wu, M., 2016. Cannabinoid CB2 Receptor Mediates Nicotine -Induced Anti-Inflammation in N9 Microglial Cells Exposed to β Amyloid via Protein Kinase C. *Mediators Inflamm.* 2016, 4854378.

Jiang, W., St-Pierre, S., Roy, P., Morley, B. J., Hao, J., Simard, A. R., 2016. Infiltration of CCR2+Ly6C high Proinflammatory Monocytes and Neutrophils into the Central Nervous System Is Modulated by Nicotinic Acetylcholine Receptors in a Model of Multiple Sclerosis. *J Immunol.* 196(5), 2095-2108.

Kallaur, A. P., Lopes, J., Oliveira, S. R., Simão, A. N., Reiche, E. M., de Almeida, E. R., Morimoto, H. K., de Pereira, W. L., Alfieri, D. F, Borelli, S. D., Kaimen-Maciel, D. R., Maes, M., 2016. Immune-Inflammatory and Oxidative and Nitrosative Stress Biomarkers of Depression Symptoms in Subjects with Multiple Sclerosis: Increased Peripheral Inflammation but Less Acute Neuroinflammation. *Mol Neurobiol.* 53(8), 5191-5202.

Kaluarachchi, M. R., Boulangé, C. L., Garcia-Perez, I., Lindon, J. C., Minet, E. F., 2016. Multiplatform serum metabolic phenotyping combined with pathway mapping to identify biochemical differences in smokers. *Bioanalysis.* 8(19), 2023-2043.

Kim, N. H., Kim, H. C., Lee, J. Y., Lee, J. M., Suh, I., 2016. Active and Passive Smoking and Serum Total Bilirubin in a Rural Korean Population. *Nicotine Tob Res.* 18(5), 572-579.

Koller, K. R., Flanagan, C. A., Day, G. E., Thomas, T. K., Smith, C. A., Wolfe, A. W., Meade, C., Hughes, C. A., Hiratsuka, V. Y., Murphy, N. J., Patten, C. A., 2016. Developing a Biomarker Feedback Intervention to Motivate Smoking Cessation During Pregnancy: Phase II MAW Study. *Nicotine Tob Res.* Dec 21. pii: ntw330.

Lavezzi, A. M., Alfonsi, G., Pusiol, T., Matturri, L., 2016. Decreased argyrophilic nucleolar organiser region (AgNOR) expression in Purkinje cells: first signal of neuronal damage in sudden fetal and infant death. *J Clin Pathol.* 69(1), 58-63.

Lincha, V. R., Zhao, B. T., Woo, M. H., Yang, I. J., Shin, H. M., 2016. Effects of Constituent Compounds of Smilax China on Nicotine -Induced Endothelial Dysfunction in Human Umbilical Vein Endothelial Cells. *Biol Pharm Bull.* 39(6), 984-992.

Lindsay, R. P., Tsoh, J. Y., Sung, H. Y., Max, W., 2016. Secondhand smoke exposure and serum cotinine levels among current smokers in the USA. *Tob Control.* 25(2), 224-231.

Lindson-Hawley, N., Hartmann-Boyce, J., Fanshawe, T. R., Begh, R., Farley, A., Lancaster, T., 2016. Interventions to reduce harm from continued tobacco use. *Cochrane Database Syst Rev.* 10, CD005231.

Lisko, J. G., Lee, G. E., Kimbrell, J .B., Rybak, M. E., Valentin-Blasini, L., Watson, C. H., 2016. Caffeine Concentrations in Coffee, Tea, Chocolate, and Energy Drink Flavored E-liquids. *Nicotine & Tob Res.* 2016.

Liu, K. H., Hwang, S. J., 2016. Effect of smoking cessation for 1 year on periodontal biomarkers in gingival crevicular fluid. *J Periodontal Res.* 51(3), 366-375.

Lopez, A. A., Cobb, C. O., Yingst, J. M., Veldheer, S., Hrabovsky, S., Yen, M. S., Foulds, J., Eissenberg, T., 2016. A transdisciplinary model to inform randomized clinical trial for electronic cigarette evaluation. *BMC Public Health.* 16, 217.

Lüdicke, F., Baker, G., Magnette, J., Picavet, P., Weitkunat, R., 2017. Reduced Exposure to Harmful and Potentially Harmful Smoke Constituents With the Tobacco Heating System 2.1. *Nicotine Tob Res.* 19(2), 168-175.

Lüdicke, F., Haziza, C., Weitkunat, R., Magnette, J., 2016. Evaluation of Biomarkers of Exposure in Smokers Switching to a Carbon-Heated Tobacco Product: A Controlled, Randomized, Open-Label 5-Day Exposure Study. *Nicotine & Tob Res.* 18(7), 1606-1613.

Lüdicke, F., Picavet, P., Baker, G., Haziza, C., Poux, V., Lama, N., Weitkunat, R., 2017. Effects of Switching to the Tobacco Heating System 2.2 Menthol, Smoking Abstinence, or Continued Cigarette Smoking on Biomarkers of Exposure: A Randomized, Controlled, Open-Label, Multicenter Study in Sequential Confinement and Ambulatory Settings (Part 1). *Nicotine Tob Res.* Feb 8.

Mardini, V., Rohde, L. A., Ceresér, K. M., Gubert Cde, M., da Silva, E. G., Xavier, F., Parcianello, R., Röhsig, L. M., Pechansky, F., Pianca, T. G., Szobot, C. M. 2016. IL-6 and IL-10 levels in the umbilical cord blood of newborns with a history of crack/cocaine exposure in utero: a comparative study. *Trends Psychiatry Psychother.* 38(1), 40-49.

Mathai, A. J., Kanwar, J., Okusaga, O., Fuchs, D., Lowry, C. A., Peng, X., Giegling, I., Hartmann, A. M., Konte, B., Friedl, M., Gragnoli, C., Reeves, G. M., Groer, M. W., Rosenthal, R. N., Rujescu, D., Postolache, T. T., 2016. Blood Levels of Monoamine Precursors and Smoking in Patients with Schizophrenia. *Front Public Health.* 4, 182.

Mayne ST (2003) Antioxidant nutrients and chronic disease: use of biomarkers of exposure and oxidative stress status in epidemiologic research. *J. Nutr.* 133 Suppl 3, 933S-940S.

Mercier, K., McRitchie, S., Pathmasiri, W., Novokhatny, A., Koralkar, R., Askenazi, D., Brophy, P. D., Sumner, S., 2017. Preterm neonatal urinary renal developmental and acute kidney injury metabolomic profiling: an exploratory study. *Pediatr Nephrol.* 32(1), 151-161.

Mercincavage, M., Souprountchouk, V., Tang, K. Z., Dumont, R. L., Wileyto, E. P., Carmella, S. G., Hecht, S. S., Strasser, A. A., 2016. A Randomized Controlled Trial of Progressively Reduced Nicotine Content Cigarettes on Smoking Behaviors, Biomarkers of Exposure, and Subjective Ratings. *Cancer Epidemiol Biomarkers Prev.* 25(7), 1125-1133.

Mezzetti A., Lapenna D., Pierdomenico S. D., Calafiore A. M., Costantini F., et al., (1995) Vitamins E, C and lipid peroxidation in plasma and arterial tissue of smokers and non-smokers. *Atherosclerosis* 112, 91-99.

Mikheev, V. B., Brinkman, M. C., Granville, C. A., Gordon, S. M., Clark, P. I., 2016. Real-Time Measurement of Electronic Cigarette Aerosol Size Distribution and Metals Content Analysis. *Nicotine Tob Res.* 18(9), 1895-1902.

Mohod, K., Ninghot, A., Ansari, A. K., Garg, N., 2014. Circulating lipid peroxide and antioxidant status in cigarette smokers: an oxidative damage phenomena. *Int J Health Sci Res* 4, 59-65.

Moreno-Coutiño, A., Villalobos-Gallegos, L., 2017. Psychometric Properties of the Fagerström Test for Nicotine Dependence in a Sample of Mexican Smokers. *J Addict Nurs.* 28(1), 27-33.

Morris, M. C., Mielock, A. S., Rao, U., 2016. Salivary stress biomarkers of recent nicotine use and dependence. *Am J Drug Alcohol Abuse.* 42(6), 640-648.

Murphy, S. E., Sipe, C. J., Choi, K., Raddatz, L. M., Koopmeiners, J. S., Donny, E. C., Hatsukami, D. K., 2017. Low cotinine glucuronidation in higher serum and saliva cotinine in African American compared to White smokers. *Cancer Epidemiol Biomarkers Prev.* Mar 6.

Murphy, S. E., 2017. Nicotine Metabolism and Smoking: Ethnic Differences in the Role of P450 2A6. *Chem Res Toxicol.* 30(1), 410-419.

Nardone, N., Donny, E. C., Hatsukami, D. K., Koopmeiners, J. S., Murphy, S. E., Strasser, A. A., Tidey, J. W., Vandrey, R., Benowitz, N. L., 2016. Estimations and predictors of non-compliance in switchers to reduced Nicotine content cigarettes. *Addiction.* 111(12), 2208-2216.

Nascimento, S. N., Göethel, G., Baierle, M., Barth, A., Brucker, N., Charão, M. F., Moro, A. M., Gauer, B., Sauer, E., Durgante, J., Arbo, M. D., Thiesen, F. V., Pierre, T. D., Gioda, A., Moresco, R., Garcia, S. C., 2017. Environmental exposure and effects on health of children from a tobacco-producing region. *Environ Sci Pollut Res Int.* 24(3), 2851-2865.

Ochoa, V., George, A. A., Nishi, R., Whiteaker, P., 2016. The prototoxin LYPD6B modulates heteromeric α3β4-containing nicotinic acetylcholine receptors, but not α7 homomers. *FASEB J.* 30(3),1109-1119.

O'Connell, G., Graff, D. W., D'Ruiz, C. D., 2016. Reductions in biomarkers of exposure (BoE) to harmful or potentially harmful constituents (HPHCs) following partial or complete substitution of cigarettes with E-cigarettes in adult smokers. *Toxicol Mech.* 26(6), 443-454.

Okoli, C., 2016. A Comparison of Survey Measures and Biomarkers of Secondhand Tobacco Smoke Exposure among Nonsmokers. *Public Health Nurs.* 33(1), 82-89.

Okoli, C., Kodet, J., Robertson, H. 2016. Behavioral and Physiological Responses to Nicotine Patch Administration among Nonsmokers Based on Acute and Chronic Secondhand Tobacco Smoke Exposure. *Biol Res Nurs.* 18(1), 60-67.

Pacek, L. R., Vandrey, R., Dermody, S. S., Denlinger-Apte, R. L., Lemieux, A., Tidey, J. W., McClernon, F. J., Bangdiwala, A. S., Drobes, D. J., al'Absi, M., Strasser, A. A., Koopmeiners, J. S., Hatsukami, D. K., Donny, E. C., 2016., Evaluation of a reduced nicotine product standard: Moderating effects of and impact on cannabis use. *Drug Alcohol Depend.* 167, 228-232.

Papaseit, E., Farré, M., Graziano, S., Pacifici, R., Pérez-Mañá, C., García-Algar, O., Pichini, S., 2017. Monitoring nicotine intake from e-cigarettes: measurement of parent drug and metabolites in oral fluid and plasma. *Clin Chem Lab Med.* 55(3), 415-423.

Park, E. Y., Yun, E. H., Lim, M. K., Lee, D. H., Yang, W., Jeong, B. Y., Hwang, S. H., 2016. Consequences of Incomplete Smoke-Free Legislation in the Republic of Korea: from Environmental and Biochemical Monitoring: Community Based Study. *Cancer Res Treat.* 48(1), 376-383.

Patten, C. A., Bronars, C. A., Vickers Douglas, K. S., Ussher, M. H., Levine, J. A., Tye, S. J., Hughes, C. A., Brockman, T. A., Decker, P. A., DeJesus, R. S., Williams, M. D., Olson, T. P., Clark, M. M., Dieterich, A. M., 2017. Supervised, Vigorous Intensity Exercise Intervention for Depressed Female Smokers: A Pilot Study. *Nicotine Tob Res.* 19(1), 77-86.

Patten, C. A., Bronars, C. A., Vickers Douglas, K. S., Ussher, M. H., Levine, J. A., Tye, S.J., Hughes, C. A., Brockman, T. A., Decker, P. A., DeJesus, R. S., Williams, M. D., Olson, T. P., Clark, M. M., Dieterich, A. M., 2017. Supervised, Vigorous Intensity Exercise Intervention for Depressed Female Smokers: A Pilot Study. *Nicotine Tob Res.* Jan;19(1), 77-86.

Pearson, J. L., Smiley, S. L., Rubin, L. F., Anesetti-Rothermel, A., Elmasry, H., Davis, M., DeAtley, T., Harvey, E., Kirchner, T., Abrams, D. B. 2016., The Moment Study: protocol for a mixed observational cohort study of the Alternative Nicotine Delivery Systems (ANDS) initiation process among adult cigarette smokers. *BMJ Open.* 6(4), e011717.

Pérez-Ortuño, R., Martínez-Sánchez, J. M., Fu, M., Ballbè, M., Quirós, N., Fernández, E., Pascual, J. A., 2016. Assessment of tobacco specific nitrosamines (TSNAs) in oral fluid as biomarkers of cancer risk: A population-based study. *Environ Res.* 151, 635-641.

Peterson, L. A., Hecht, S. S., 2017. Tobacco, e-cigarettes, and child health. *Curr Opin Pediatr.* 29(2), 225-230.

Pita-Fernández, S., Seijo-Bestilleiro, R., Pértega-Díaz, S., Alonso-Hernández, Á., Fernández-Rivera, C., Cao-López, M., Seoane-Pillado, T., López-Calviño, B., González-Martín, C., Valdés-Cañedo, F., 2016. A randomized clinical trial to determine the effectiveness of CO-oximetry and anti-smoking brief advice in a cohort of kidney transplant patients who smoke: study protocol for a randomized controlled trial. *Trials.* 17, 174.

Prasad, G. L., Jones, B. A., Chen, P., Gregg, E. O., 2016. A cross-sectional study of biomarkers of exposure and effect in smokers and moist snuff consumers. *Clin Chem Lab Med.* 54(4), 633-642.

Pulvers, K., Emami, A. S., Nollen, N. L., Romero, D. R., Strong, D. R., Benowitz, N. L., Ahluwalia, J. S., 2016. Tobacco Consumption and Toxicant Exposure of Cigarette Smokers Using E-Cigarettes. *Nicotine Tob Res.* Dec 21.

Quednow, B. B., Herdener, M., 2016. Human pharmacology for addiction medicine: From evidence to clinical recommendations. *Prog. Brain Res.* 224, 227-250.

Rangaraju, S., Levey, D. F., Nho, K., Jain, N., Andrews, K. D., Le-Niculescu, H., Salomon, D. R., Saykin, A. J., Petrascheck, M., Niculescu, A. B., 2016. Mood, stress and longevity: convergence on ANK3. *Mol Psychiatry.* 21(8), 1037-1049.

Reyes-Guzman, C. M., Pfeiffer, R. M., Lubin, J., Freedman, N. D., Cleary, S. D., Levine, P. H., Caporaso, N. E. 2017. Determinants of Light and Intermittent Smoking in the United States: from Three Pooled National Health Surveys. *Cancer Epidemiol Biomarkers Prev.* 26(2), 228-239.

Richter, P., Steven, P. R., Bravo, R., Lisko, J. G., Damian, M., Gonzalez-Jimenez, N., Gray, N., Keong, L. M., Kimbrell, J. B., Kuklenyik, P., Lawler, T. S., Lee, G. E., Mendez, M., Perez, J., Smith, S., Tran, H., Tyx, R., Watson, C. H., 2016. Characterization of SPECTRUM Variable Nicotine Research Cigarettes. *Tob Regul Sci.* 2(2), 94-105.

Ross, K. C., Dempsey, D. A., St Helen, G., Delucchi, K., Benowitz, N. L., 2016. The Influence of Puff Characteristics, Nicotine Dependence, and Rate of Nicotine Metabolism on Daily Nicotine Exposure in African American Smokers. *Cancer Epidemiol Biomarkers Prev.* 25(6), 936-943.

Ross, K. C., Gubner, N. R., Tyndale, R. F., Hawk, L. W. Jr., Lerman, C., George, T. P., Cinciripini, P., Schnoll, R. A., Benowitz, N. L., 2016. Racial differences in the relationship between rate of Nicotine metabolism and Nicotine intake from cigarette smoking. *Pharmacol. Biochem. Behav.* 148, 1-7.

Rupprecht, L. E., Koopmeiners, J. S., Dermody, S. S., Oliver, J. A., al'Absi, M., Benowitz, N. L., Denlinger-Apte, R., Drobes, D. J., Hatsukami, D., McClernon, F. J., Pacek, L. R., Smith, T. T., Sved, A. F., Tidey, J., Vandrey, R., Donny, E. C., 2016.

Reducing Nicotine exposure in weight gain in smokers randomised to very low Nicotine content cigarettes. *Tob Control.* Nov 17.

Shahab, L., Dobbie, F., Hiscock, R., McNeill, A., Bauld, L., 2016. Prevalence and Impact of Long-term Use of Nicotine Replacement Therapy in UK Stop-Smoking Services: Findings From the ELONS Study. *Nicotine Tob. Res.* 2016 Sep 24.

Shahab, L., Goniewicz, M. L., Blount, B. C., Brown, J., McNeill, A., Alwis, K. U., Feng, J., Wang, L., West, R., 2017. Nicotine, Carcinogen, and Toxin Exposure in Long-Term E-Cigarettes and Nicotine replacement therapy Users: A Cross-sectional Study. *Ann Intern Med.* Feb. 7.

Siwek, M., Sowa-Kućma, M., Styczeń, K., Misztak, P., Nowak, R. J., Szewczyk, B., Dudek, D., Rybakowski, J. K., Nowak, G., Maes, M., 2016. Associations of Serum Cytokine Receptor Levels with Melancholia, Staging of Illness, Depressive and Manic Phases, and Severity of Depression in Bipolar Disorder. *Mol Neurobiol.* Sep 23.

Slyepchenko, A., Brunoni, A. R., McIntyre, R. S., Quevedo, J., Carvalho, A. F., 2016. The Adverse Effects of Smoking on Health Outcomes in Bipolar Disorder: A Review and Synthesis of Biological Mechanisms. *Curr Mol Med.* 16(2), 187-205.

Srikanth, S., Sy, F., Kotak, K., Kiel, R. G., Bajwa, M., Tandon, A., Loures-Vale, A. A., Aftab, W., Tringali, S., Ambrose, J. A. 2016. A Single Controlled Exposure to Secondhand Smoke May Not Alter Thrombogenesis or Trigger Platelet Activation. *Nicotine & Tob Res.* 18(5), 580-584.

Thompson RL, Margetts BM, Wood DA, Jackson AA (1992) Cigarette smoking and food and nutrient intakes in relation to coronary heart disease. *Nutr Res Rev* 5, 131-152.

Tranfo, G., Pigini, D., Paci, E., Marini, F., Bonanni, R. C., 2016. Association of exposure to benzene and smoking with oxidative damage to nucleic acids by means of biological monitoring of general population volunteers. *Environ Sci Pollut Res Int.* Mar 14.

Tsai, Y. S., Tseng, Y. T., Chen, P. S., Lin, M. C., Wu, C. C., Huang, M. S., Wang, C. C., Chen, K. S., Lin, Y. C., Wang, T. N. 2016. Protective effects of elafin against adult asthma. *Allergy Asthma Proc.* 37(2), 15-24.

Tscharke, B. J., White, J. M., Gerber, J. P. 2016. Estimates of tobacco use by wastewater analysis of anabasine and anatabine. *Drug Test Anal.* 8(7), 702-707.

van Wel, J. H., Gracia-Lor, E., van Nuijs, A. L., Kinyua, J., Salvatore, S., Castiglioni, S., Bramness, J. G., Covaci, A., Van Hal, G., 2016. Investigation of agreement between wastewater-based epidemiology and survey data on alcohol and nicotine use in a community. *Drug Alcohol Depend.* 162, 170-175.

VanDerNagel, J. E., Kiewik, M., van Dijk, M., Didden, R., Korzilius, H. P., van der Palen, J., Buitelaar, J. K., Uges, D. R., Koster, R. A., de Jong, C. A., 2016. Substance use in individuals with mild to borderline intellectual disability: A comparison between self-report, collateral-report and biomarker analysis. *Res. Dev. Disabil.* 2016 Apr 25.

von Weymarn, L. B., Thomson, N. M., Donny, E. C., Hatsukami, D. K., Murphy, S. E., 2016. Quantitation of the Minor Tobacco Alkaloids Nornicotine, Anatabine, and Anabasine in Smokers' Urine by High Throughput Liquid Chromatography-Mass Spectrometry. *Chem Res Toxicol.* 29(3), 390-397.

Ware, J. J., Chen, X., Vink, J., Loukola, A., Minica, C., Pool, R., Milaneschi, Y., Mangino, M., Menni, C., Chen, J., Peterson, R. E., Auro, K., Lyytikäinen, L. P., Wedenoja, J., Stiby, A. I., et al., 2016. Genome-Wide Meta-Analysis of Cotinine Levels in Cigarette Smokers Identifies Locus at 4q13.2. *Sci Rep.* 6, 20092.

Welkom, J. S., Riekert, K. A., Rand, C. S., Eakin, M. N., 2016. Associations Between Caregiver Health Literacy and Preschool Children's Secondhand Smoke Exposure. *J. Pediatr. Psychol.* 41(4), 462-472.

Wray, J. M., Gass, J. C., Miller, E. I., Wilkins, D. G., Rollins, D. E., Tiffany, S. T., 2016. A comparative evaluation of self-report and biological measures of cigarette use in nondaily smokers. *Psychol. Assess.* 28(9), 1043-1050.

Xu, H., Wang, F., Kranzler, H. R., Gelernter, J., Zhang, H., 2017. Alcohol and nicotine codependence-associated DNA methylation changes in promoter regions of addiction-related genes. *Sci Rep.* 7, 41816.

Yershova, K., Yuan, J. M., Wang, R., Valentin, L., Watson, C., Gao, Y. T., Hecht, S. S., Stepanov, I., 2016. Tobacco-specific N-nitrosamines and polycyclic aromatic hydrocarbons in cigarettes smoked by the participants of the Shanghai Cohort Study. *Int J Cancer.* 139(6), 1261-1269.

Yu D., Yuan, K., Zhang, B., Liu, J., Dong, M., Jin, C., Luo, L., Zhai, J., Zhao, L., Zhao, Y., Gu, Y., Xue, T., Liu, X., Lu, X., Qin, W., Tian, J., 2016. White matter integrity in young smokers: a tract-based spatial statistics study. *Addict Biol.* 21(3), 679-687.

Yuan, J. M., Nelson, H. H., Butler, L. M., Carmella, S. G., Wang, R., Kuriger-Laber, J. K., Adams-Hauch, J., Hecht, S. S., Gao, Y. T., Murphy, S. E., 2016. Genetic determinants of cytochrome P450 2A6 activity and biomarkers of tobacco smoke exposure in relation to risk of lung cancer development in the Shanghai cohort study. *Int J Cancer.* 138(9), 2161-2171.

Zainol Abidin, N., Zainal Abidin, E., Zulkifli, A., Karuppiah, K., Syed Ismail, S. N., Amer Nordin, A. S., 2017. E-cigarettes and indoor air quality: a review of studies using human volunteers. *Rev Environ Health.* Jan 20.

Chapter 9

Recent Update on Nicotine Research

Abstract

This chapter highlights recent update on nicotine research. Recent studies established the deleterious effects of cigarette smoke constituents on myeloid cell lineage. Cigarette smoke condensate and nicotine impaired growth and development of periodontal tissue to cause early tooth decay. Epigenetic studies of nicotinism have established the exact etiopathogenesis of oral lesions. Recently, topping responsive proteins in tobacco roots have been identified and smoking behavior among alcohol and other substance use disorders has been investigated. Some economic perspective on smoking behavior in mental illness have been established. Nicotine influenced working versus reference memory in a dual component odor span task. Recent studies also established that prenatal tobacco exposure shortens the telomere length in children, implicated in early morbidity and reduced life span. A study was performed to establish the influence of telephone-based care on tobacco cessation medications. It is known that self-administered nicotine suppresses body weight gain independent of food intake. Tobacco smoking significantly reduces hunger to ultimately cause loss of weight, whereas those who attempt to quit smoking, develop depression, anxiety, and increased food intake and eventually increase their body weight. A recent epidemiological survey reported relatively lower prevalence of female smoking in developing countries as compared to industrially-developed countries like Europe, Australia, and U.S.A. and Canada. Tobacco significantly influenced aging-related alterations in eNOS and nNOS responsiveness and smooth muscle reactivity to cause early cardiovascular morbidity. A recent study reported increased incidence of suicidality among tobacco smokers in the U.S.A. The risk of suicidality was particularly enhanced among those who were on smoking cessation regimens. Some newly developed devices have been introduced with a primary objective of reducing the risks of tobacco smoking. These are classified as nicotine replacement devices. However, nicotine remains the primary ingredient in varying doses and formulations in these devices. For example, nicotine metered dose inhaler vs nicotine patch have been evaluated for smoking cessation and the predictors of the onset of cigarette smoking have been explored. It is now well established that A7β2 nicotinic acetylcholine receptor, with which nicotine binds, is heterogeneously distributed in the CNS. Linkage and association analyses on susceptibility genes for smoking and other addictions have been performed and the basic molecular mechanisms and treatments to avoid heavy drinking and cigarette smoking have been explored. For example, nicotine receptor partial agonists such as Bupropion have been tried for smoking cessation, in addition to Varenicline. It has been identified that substances of abuse by mother during pregnancy increases the chances of consumption of drug of abuse in the offsprings. Recently, highly sensitive procedures have been developed to detect cotinine level to establish the severity of nicotinism. Smoking influenced the production of ovarian hormones and menstrual cycle in women because nicotine in the tobacco smoke inhibits the enzyme aromatase involved in the conversion of testosterone to estrogen. Furthermore, nicotine binds with the α7β2 nicotinic acetylcholine receptors on the mitochondria in the spermatocytes to cause reduced mobility and/or infertility due to CB formation, impaired charnolophagy, and CS destabilization. Various drug interactions have been noticed with tobacco smoking. Particularly, physiologically and pharmacologically-intricate interactions between nicotine, Alcohol, and Cannabinoids are the most significant. These interactions are currently being investigated to develop safe, effective, and successful personalized theranostics of nicotinism with currently limited success.

Keywords: myeloid cell lineage, nicotine self-administration, body weight reduction, eNOS and nNOS, cardiovascular disease, meter dose inhaler, nicotine, patch, tobacco cessation, α7β2 nicotinic acetylcholine receptor, Bupropion, Varenicline, suicidality, cotinine, ovarian hormones, aromatase, menstrual cycle, spermatocyte motility, male infertility, nicotine, alcohol, and cannabinoids interactions, smoking cessation

Introduction

It is now well-established that serious mental illness (SMI) is associated with high rates of cigarette smoking. The identification of factors that contribute to persistent smoking in people with SMI may lead to the development of tobacco control policies and treatment approaches that help these smokers quit smoking.

Recently, Tidey (2016) examined factors underlying smoking persistence in people with SMI from the perspective of behavioral economics, a discipline that applies economic principles to understand drug abuse and dependence. Studies were conducted in the Northeastern US within the past 30 years that compared the reinforcing effects of nicotine and the costs of smoking in smokers with and without schizophrenia and depression, and interventions to reduce the reinforcing efficacy of nicotine and increase the costs of smoking in people with SMI.

This chapter describes the deleterious effect of tobacco smoking on myeloid cell lineage, Nicotine self-administration and body weight reduction; the functional significance of eNOS and nNOS in cardiovascular diseases and nicotinism; Nicotine replacement therapy employing meter dose inhaler and nicotine patch and other tobacco cessation products. The chapter also describes the role of nicotine on α7β2 nicotinic acetylcholine receptor in causing spermatocyte immobility and infertility in men and inhibition of the enzyme aromatase (involved in the conversion of testosterone to estrogen) causing menstrual irregularities and diversified charnolopathies in women. Partial Nicotine AChR agonist, Bupropion and a full agonist Varenicline are described as smoking cessation drugs with a potential risk of suicidality. A highly sensitive method to detect cotinine is described to determine the severity of nicotinism. In addition, nicotine, alcohol, and cannabinoids interactions are described to determine the basic molecular mechanism of nicotinism and to develop safe and effective personalized smoking cessation products in near future.

Effect of Cigarette Smoke Constituents on Myeloid Cell Lineage

Although cigarette smoking is prevalent amongst HIV-infected patients, the effects of cigarette smoke constituents in cells of myeloid lineage remain poorly understood. Recently, Rao et al., (2016) demonstrated that nicotine induces oxidative stress through cytochrome P450 (CYP) 2A6-mediated pathway in U937 monocytic cells. These investigators evaluated the effect of cigarette smoke condensate (CSC), which contains majority of tobacco constituents, on oxidative stress, cytotoxicity, expression of CYP1A1, and/or HIV-1 replication in HIV-infected (U1) and uninfected U937 cells. The effects of CSC on induction of CYP1 enzymes in HIV-infected primary macrophages were also analyzed. The CSC-mediated increase in production of ROS in U937 cells was dose-and time-dependent. CSC induced cytotoxicity in U937 cells through the apoptotic pathway via activation of caspase-3. Pretreatment with Vitamin C attenuated the CSC-mediated production of ROS and induction of caspase-3 activity. In U1 cells, acute treatment of CSC increased ROS production at 6H (>2-fold) and both ROS (>2 fold) and HIV-1 replication (>3-fold) after chronic treatment. The CSC mediated effects were associated with robust induction in the expression of CYP1A1 mRNA upon acute CSC treatment of U937 and U1 cells (>20-fold), and upon chronic CSC treatment to U1 cells (>30-fold). The CYP1A1 induction in U937 cells was mediated through the aromatic hydrocarbon receptor pathway. Lastly, CSC, which is known to increase viral replication in primary macrophages, induced CYP1 enzymes in HIV-infected primary macrophages. Although mRNA levels of both CYP1A1 and CYP1B1 were elevated following CSC treatment, only CYP1B1 protein levels were increased in HIV-infected primary macrophages, suggesting association between oxidative stress, CYP1 expression, and viral replication in CSC-treated cells of myeloid lineage. These investigators suggested further studies to examine the precise role of CYP1B1 in smoking-mediated enhanced HIV replication.

Effect of Cigarette Smoke Condensate and Nicotine on Periodontal Tissue

Although cigarette smoking is a major lifestyle-related risk factor for periodontal diseases, the exact pathophysiological role of cigarette smoking in periodontal disease remains unknown. Kubota et al., (2016) recently reported that the systemic administration of cigarette smoke condensate or nicotine, which is the major ingredient of cigarette smoke, enhanced alveolar bone loss. The number of osteoclasts in periodontal tissues increased and the expression of receptor activator of nuclear factor κB ligand was upregulated at the ligated side in mice with periodontitis. Nicotine also attenuated alveolar bone repair after ligature removal, suggesting the destruction of periodontal tissue by smoking and the unfavorable clinical course of periodontal disease in patients with a cigarette smoking habit. This study demonstrated that periodontal disease models are useful for elucidating the pathogenesis of cigarette smoking-related periodontal diseases.

Topping Responsive Proteins in Tobacco Roots

It is well-known that the process of topping elicits many responses in the tobacco plant, including an increase in nicotine biosynthesis, and the secondary growth of roots. Recently, Li et al., (2016) identified some topping responsive miRNAs and genes in their previous study, but the exact mechanism of the tobacco response to topping remains unknown. In the present study, these investigators screened topping responsive proteins isolated from tobacco roots using two-dimensional electrophoresis. Of the proteins identified, Calreticulin, Auxin-responsive protein, and Indole acetic acid (IAA9) were involved in the secondary growth of roots; leucine-rich repeat disease resistance, heat shock protein 70, and farnesyl pyrophosphate synthase 1 were involved in the wounding stress response; and F-box protein in promoting the ability of nicotine synthesis after topping. In addition, these investigators identified 5 tobacco bHLH proteins (NtbHLH, NtMYC1a, NtMYC1b, NtMYC2a, and NtMYC2b) related to nicotine biosynthesis. NtMYC2 was the main positive transcription factor, with NtbHLH protein being a negative regulator in the Jasmonic acid (JA)-mediated activation of nicotine biosynthesis after topping. Tobacco topping activated several biological processes involving the IAA and JA signaling pathways. These investigators suggested that proteins involved in these processes will improve our understanding of cigarette nicotine content to benefit public health.

Reduced Nicotine Content Cigarette Biomarkers and General Beliefs

Recently, Mercincavage et al., (2017) reported that smokers may misconstrue RNC cigarettes as less harmful than regular cigarettes. These beliefs, in conjunction with favorable subjective ratings, may increase product use. It has been realized that reduced nicotine content (RNC) cigarette use did not apply comprehensive panel of biomarkers. In a recent study, these investigators examined the effects of using RNC cigarettes on smoking behaviors, biomarkers of exposure, and subjective ratings. In a randomized, unblinded, parallel study, these investigators included a sum of 158 daily, non-treatment-seeking smokers in a 35-day clinical trial. After a 5-day baseline period, participants were randomly assigned to an experimental group (n = 80) that smoked progressively decreasing RNC cigarettes during three 10-day periods, or control group (n =78) that smoked their own brand throughout the study. Daily cigarette consumption significantly increased for the intermediate RNCs (P's < 0.001) but approached baseline rate for the lowest RNC (P = 0.686); in contrast, puffing behavior significantly decreased at intermediate levels and increased for the lowest RNC (P's < 0.001). Cotinine and NNAL significantly decreased by RNC period (P's {less than or equal to} 0.001-0.02), while CO boost initially increased (P's = 0.001-0.005). 1-HOP did not change by period (P = 0.109). Smoking behaviors changed by RNC period via CPD and puffing behavior. Biomarkers of exposure decreased with nicotine content, suggesting that RNC use does not reduce smoking behaviors or biomarkers, yet the lowest RNC level may reduce harm exposure, emphasizing the importance of behavioral and biological measures to address this study.

Smoking Behavior among Alcohol & Other Substance Use Disorders

Persons with alcohol use disorders (AUDs) and substance use disorders (SUDs) appear to be severely affected by cigarette smoking. To address the consequences of smoking in this population, an understanding of the current state of knowledge is needed. Epidemiologic research provides the opportunity to obtain detailed information on smoking behaviors in large community samples. Recently, Weinberger et al., (2016) synthesized the epidemiologic evidence on smoking among persons with AUDs/SUDs and suggested directions for future research. Literature searches of Medline and PubMed were used to identify articles and additional articles were collected from publication reference lists. To be included in the review, papers had to be published in English, analyze epidemiologic data, and examine an aspect of smoking behavior in persons with AUDs/SUDs. Twenty-nine studies met inclusion criteria. Epidemiologic evidence suggested greater lifetime and current smoking, nicotine dependence, and non-cigarette tobacco use; lower quitting; and differences in quit attempts and withdrawal symptoms for persons with AUDs/SUDs compared to other subjects. Most studies examined nationally representative data and were conducted on persons in the US and Australia. Few publications examined outcomes by demographics (e.g., gender, age) but these studies suggested that specific patterns differ by demographic subgroups. Based on this study, these investigators suggested that more research is needed on persons with AUDs/SUDs to develop the most effective public health and clinical interventions to reduce smoking behaviors, improve cessation outcomes, and reduce the harmful consequences of smoking for those with AUDs/SUDs.

Epigenetics to Determine Etiopathogenesis of Oral Lesions

A controversy has existed over the etiopathogenesis and management of oral lesions, especially oral malignancies. The knowledge of genetic basis is proving to be inadequate in the light of emerging new mechanisms termed epigenetic phenomena. In a recent study, Singh et al., (2016) presented a review article aimed to understand the role of epigenetic mechanisms in oral lesions. Epigenetics is the study of acquired changes in chromatin structure that arise independently of a change in the underlying DNA nucleotide sequence. Key components involved in epigenetic regulation are DNA methylation, histone modifications and modifications in micro ribonucleic acids (miRNA). Epigenetics is a reversible system that can be affected by various environmental factors such as diet, drugs, mental stress, physical activity and addictive substances such as tobacco, nicotine and alcohol. Epigenetics may also play a pivotal role in explaining the etiopathogenesis of developmental anomalies, genetic defects, cancer as well as substance addiction (tobacco, cigarette and alcohol). Epigenetic modifications may contribute to aberrant epigenetic mechanisms seen in oral precancers and cancers. Epigenetic variations detected in oral dysplastic cells can act as a molecular fingerprint for malignancies. These investigators searched literature and a structured scientific review and meta-analysis of publications from the year 2000-2015 and found that epigenetic biomarkers can prove to be novel for early diagnosis, prognosis and treatment of oral cancers as well as other diseases.

Working vs Reference Memory in a Dual Component Odor Span Task

Developed as a tool to assess working memory capacity in rodents, the odor span task (OST) has significant potential to advance drug discovery in animal models of psychiatric disorders. Prior investigations indicate OST performance is impaired by systemic administration of N-methyl-d-aspartate receptor (NMDA-r) antagonists and is sensitive to cholinergic manipulations. MacQueen et al., (2016) recently determined whether an impairment in OST performance can be produced by systemic administration of the competitive NMDA-r antagonist 3-(2-Carboxypiperazin-4-yl) Propyl-1-Phosphonic acid (CPP; 3, 10, 17 mg/kg i.p.) in a dual-component variant of the OST, and whether this impairment is ameliorated by nicotine (0.75 mg/kg i.p.). Male Sprague-Dawley rats were trained to asymptotic level of performance on a 24-trial two-comparison incrementing nonmatching to sample OST. In addition, rats were administered a two-comparison olfactory reference memory (RM) task, which was integrated into the OST. The RM task provided an assessment of the effects of drug administration on global behavioral measures, long-term memory and motivation. Several measures of working memory (span, longest run, and accuracy) were impaired by CPP without adversely affecting RM. Analysis of drug effects across trial blocks demonstrated a significant impairment of performance even at low memory loads, suggesting a CPP-induced deficit of olfactory short-term memory that was not load-dependent. Although nicotine did not ameliorate CPP-induced impairments in span or accuracy, it did block the impairment in longest run produced by the 10 mg/kg dose of CPP, indicating that performance in 24 odor two-comparison OST is capacity-dependent and that CPP impaired OST working, but not reference memory.

Prenatal Tobacco Exposure Shortens Telomere Length in Children

Preliminary evidence suggests a possible association between prenatal tobacco exposure and telomere length in children. Recently, Ip et al., (2016) conducted a study to investigate whether maternal smoking during pregnancy was associated with telomere shortening in their children, and whether prenatal and childhood exposure to environmental tobacco had any impact on this association. This was a population-representative study on the association between prenatal tobacco exposure and telomere length in children. 98 Hong Kong Chinese children aged under 15 years with prenatal tobacco exposure and 98 age-and gender-matched controls were recruited from a population health study with stratified random sampling. Telomere length in children with prenatal tobacco exposure was significantly shorter than in those with no exposure (mean T/S ratio = 24.9 [SD = 8.58] in exposed vs. 28.97 [14.15] in control groups; p = 0.02). A negative dose-response relationship was observed between the T/S ratio and tobacco exposure duration: the longer the duration of maternal smoking in pregnancy, the shorter the child's telomere length. The association between the child's telomere length and prenatal tobacco exposure remained significant after considering the influence of family socioeconomic status and exposure to environmental tobacco smoke during pregnancy and childhood. This study demonstrated that prenatal tobacco exposure was associated with telomere shortening in children. Based on afore-mentioned findings, these investigators recommended that as this may impose significant health impacts through fetal genetic programming, efforts should be made to reduce fetal tobacco exposure by educating pregnant women to not smoke and motivating smokers to quit in early pregnancy. As reflected by telomere shortening, prenatal tobacco exposure in children can cause premature aging and increased health risks, which is absolutely-preventable. Not smoking during pregnancy or quitting smoking is critical to improving the health outcome of future generations as prenatal tobacco exposure may affect children's biological programming.

The Influence of Telephone-Based Care on Cessation Medications

Post-Hospital Discharge Smokers benefit from ongoing cessation support upon leaving the hospital and returning to their home environment. Hence, Tague et al., (2016) examined the impact of telephone-delivered care coordination on utilization of and adherence to cessation pharmacotherapy after hospital discharge. Inpatient smokers (n = 606) were randomized to receive counseling with care coordination (CCC) or counseling alone (C) for smoking cessation. Both groups received written and telephone-based cessation counseling during hospitalization and post-discharge. CCC recipients received help in selecting, obtaining, and refilling affordable pharmacotherapy prescriptions during and after hospitalization. Study outcomes included self-reported utilization, duration of use, and type of medication during the 3 months post-discharge. Of the 487 (80%) of participants completing 3 month follow-up, 211 (43.3%) reported using cessation pharmacotherapy post-discharge; this did not differ by study arm (CCC: 44.7%, C: 42.0%, p = 0.55). Use of pharmacotherapy post-discharge was associated with smoking at least 20 cigarettes per day at baseline (OR 1.48; 95%CI: 1.00-2.19) and receipt of pharmacotherapy during hospitalization (OR 4.00; 95% CI: 2.39-6.89). Smokers with Medicaid (OR 2.29; 95% CI: 1.32 - 4.02) or other insurance (OR 1.69; 95% CI: 1.01 - 2.86) were more likely to use pharmacotherapy post-discharge than those with no healthcare coverage. Less than one in four (23.8% of CCC; 22.2% of C) continued pharmacotherapy beyond 4 weeks. These investigators discovered that supplemental care coordination did not improve use of post-discharge pharmacotherapy beyond that of inpatient treatment and behavioral counseling. Insurance coverage and use of medications during the hospitalization were associated with higher use of evidence-based treatment post-discharge. Many hospitalized smokers did not receive the benefits of cessation pharmacotherapy post-discharge and telephone quit-line programs often failed to help smokers procure pharmacotherapy. Based on these findings, they suggested that effective strategies are needed to improve utilization and adherence to evidence-based cessation therapies when smokers leave the hospital. They also noticed that use of post-discharge pharmacotherapy was strongly associated with receipt of pharmacotherapy during the hospitalization and with the availability of insurance to cover the costs of treatment. However, additional efforts to coordinate pharmacotherapy services did not improve either utilization or adherence to therapy.

Self-Administered Nicotine Suppresses Body Weight Gain Independent of Food Intake

The action of nicotine to suppress body weight is often cited as a factor impacting smoking initiation and the failure to quit. Despite the weight-suppressant effects of nicotine, smokers and nonsmokers report equal daily caloric intake. The weight-suppressive effects of nicotine in animal models of smoking are poorly understood. Furthermore, the FDA has authority to implement a policy markedly reducing nicotine levels in cigarettes; such a reduction could reduce smoking behavior, but have detrimental effects on body weight. Recently, Rupprecht et al., (2016) examined the effects of self-administered nicotine on body weight and food intake in rats. In Experiment 1, rats with ad libitum access to chow responded for i.v infusions of nicotine (60 µg/kg/infusion) or saline in daily 1-hr sessions; body weight and 24-hour food intake were measured. Experiment 2 tested the effects of s.c injections of nicotine on food intake. In Experiment 3, rats were food restricted and self-administered nicotine across a range of doses (3.75-60 µg/kg/infusion) while body weight was measured. In Experiment 4, rats self-administered 60 µg/kg/infusion nicotine before reduction to one of several doses (1.875-15 µg/kg/infusion) for 50 days. Self-administered nicotine suppressed weight gain independent of food intake. In food restricted rats, self-administered nicotine suppressed body weight gain. In rats self-administering 60 µg/kg/infusion nicotine, dose reduction increased body weight. Self-administered nicotine, even at low doses, suppressed body independent of food intake; this may have important role for nicotine reduction policy. This study demonstrated that self-administered nicotine suppresses body weight independent of food intake in rats and established that self-administered nicotine suppresses body weight even at very low doses and that reduction of nicotine dose in weight gain. These findings have important role for nicotine reduction policy.

Lower Prevalence of Female Smoking in Developing Countries

Generally, female smoking prevalence is lower in developing countries (3.1%) than developed countries (17.2%), whereas male smoking is similar (32% vs. 30.1%). Low female smoking has been linked to high gender inequality. Alternatively, to protect their offspring from teratogenic substances, pregnant and lactating women appear to have evolved aversions to toxic plant substances like nicotine, which are reinforced by cultural proscriptions. Higher total fertility rates (TFR) in developing countries could therefore explain their lower prevalence of female smoking. To compare the associations of TFR, gender inequality, and older postmenopausal age on national prevalence rates of female and male smoking, Hagen et al., (2016) analyzed data from a previous study of smoking prevalence vs. gender inequality in 74 countries with a regression model that also included TFR. These investigators replicated this analysis with three additional measures of gender equality and 2012 smoking data from 173 countries. A one standard deviation increase in TFR predicted a decrease in female smoking prevalence by factors of 0.58 - 0.77, adjusting for covariates. TFR had a smaller and unexpected negative association with male smoking prevalence. Increased gender equality was associated with increased female smoking prevalence, and, with decreased male smoking prevalence. TFR was also a positive predictor of an increase in smoking prevalence among postmenopausal women. High TFR and gender inequality both predicted reduced prevalence of female smoking across nations. In countries with high TFR, adaptations and cultural norms that protect fetuses from plant toxins might suppress smoking among frequently pregnant and lactating women.

Aging-Related Alterations in eNOS and nNOS Responsiveness and Smooth Muscle Reactivity

It is known that aging causes major alterations of all components of the neurovascular unit and compromises brain blood supply. Recently, Lubomirov et al., (2016) tested how aging affects vascular reactivity in basilar arteries from young (<10 weeks; y-BA), old (>22 months; o-BA) and old (>22 months) heterozygous MYPT1-T-696A/+ knock-in mice. In isometrically mounted o-BA, media thickness was increased by ~10% while the passive length tension relations were not altered. Endothelial denudation or pan-NOS inhibition (100 μmol/L L-NAME) increased the basal tone by 11% in y-BA and 23% in o-BA, while inhibition of nNOS (1 μmol/L L-NPA) induced ~10% increase in both ages. eNOS expression was ~2-fold higher in o-BA. In o-BA, U46619-induced force was augmented (pEC_{50} ~6.9 vs. pEC_{50} ~6.5) while responsiveness to DEA-NONOate, electrical field stimulation or nicotine was decreased. Basal phosphorylation of MLC_{20}-S19 and MYPT1-T-853 was higher in o-BA and was reversed by Apocynin. Furthermore, permeabilized o-BA showed enhanced Ca^{2+}-sensitivity. Old T-696A/+ BA displayed a reduced phosphorylation of MYPT1-T696 and MLC_{20}, a lower basal tone in response to L-NAME and a reduced eNOS expression, suggesting that the vascular hypercontractility found in o-BA is mediated by inhibition of MLCP and is partially compensated by an upregulation of endothelial NO release.

Tobacco Use and Suicidality in USA

To examine how 12-month prevalence of suicidality vary by tobacco use, Han et al., (2016) applied regression models to data from 325,800 adults who participated in the 2008-2014 National Survey on Drug Use and Health. Descriptive analyses and multivariable multinomial logistic were applied. Among adults aged 18 or older in the U.S. during 2008-2014, 27.4% (annual average, Standard Error (SE) = 0.14%) were never tobacco users, 38.8% (SE = 0.17%) were former tobacco users, 5.9% (SE = 0.07%) were past-year users of other types of tobacco (non-cigarette), 20.2% (SE = 0.13%) were past-year cigarette-only users, and 7.7% (SE = 0.07%) were past-year users of cigarettes plus other types of tobacco; 2.6% (SE = 0.04%) had suicidal ideation only, 0.7% (SE = 0.02%) had suicidal ideation and suicide plan only, and 0.5% (SE = 0.02%) attempted suicide. After controlling for covariates, compared with never tobacco users, past-year users of cigarettes plus other types of tobacco were at elevated risk of all examined suicidality outcomes (adjusted relative risks (ARRs) = 1.2-1.7), and past-year cigarette-only users were at higher risk of suicide attempt (ARR = 1.4). Early age of first tobacco use was associated with higher risk of suicidal ideation and suicide plan among former tobacco users, past-year tobacco users, and past-year cigarette users (ARRs = 1.2-1.6). Among past-year tobacco users, frequencies of cigarette and cigar use were associated with suicide attempt (ARRs = 1.4-1.7). Nicotine dependence was associated with suicide attempt among past-year cigarette users (ARR = 1.2), suggesting that tobacco use is associated with 12-month suicidality among adults and patients who use tobacco should be assessed further for mental health status and suicide risk. This study revealed that tobacco use is independently associated with the 12-month suicidality outcomes among adults and identified how the prevalence of 12-month suicidality outcomes vary by tobacco use status and use characteristics among adults. These researchers suggested that these findings are clinically significant and future research should assess the effectiveness of tobacco use questions as simple screeners for more extensive assessment of mental health status and suicide risk.

Smoking Cessation Treatments and Suicidality Risk

Risk of suicidality during smoking cessation treatment is an important, but often overlooked, aspect of nicotine addiction research and treatment. Recently, Penberthy et al., (2016) explored the relationship between smoking cessation interventions and suicidality and common treatments, their associated risks, and effectiveness in promoting smoking reduction and abstinence. Although active smokers have been reported to have twofold to threefold increased risk of suicidality when compared to nonsmokers, research regarding the safest way to stop smoking does not always provide clear guidelines for practitioners wishing to advise their patients regarding smoking cessation strategies. These investigators reviewed pharmacological and cognitive behavioral therapy (CBT) options for people seeking to quit smoking, focusing on the relationship between the ability of these therapies to reduce smoking behavior and promote abstinence and suicidality risks as assessed by reported suicidality on validated measures, reports of suicidal ideation, behaviors, actual attempts, or completed suicides. Pharmacotherapies such as Varenicline, Bupropion, and nicotine replacement therapy, and CBTs, including contextual CBT interventions, have been found to help reduce smoking rates and promote and maintain abstinence. Suicidality risks, while present when trying to quit smoking, do not appear to demonstrate a consistent or significant rise associated with use of a particular smoking cessation pharmacotherapy, or CBT/contextual CBT intervention.

Nicotine Metered Dose Inhaler and Nicotine Patch for Smoking Cessation

To replicate the rewarding effects of smoking, nicotine replacement therapies must deliver nicotine via the pulmonary route. Caldwell et al., (2016) measured the efficacy of a simple pressurized metered dose inhaler containing nicotine combined with a nicotine patch for smoking cessation. Double-blind randomized placebo-controlled, parallel group trial was conducted at the University of Otago, Wellington, New Zealand. Five-hundred two adults ($\geq$18 years) who smoked at least nine cigarettes per day, with a Fagerström Test for Nicotine Dependence $\geq$3 who wanted to quit, were randomized (1:1). These investigators studied the effect of active nicotine pressurized metered dose inhaler (pMDI) plus active nicotine patch, versus placebo pMDI plus active nicotine patch. Subjects were instructed to use the aerosols for 6 months when they felt an urge to smoke and the patches daily for 5 months, reduce their smoking and quit by the end of the fourth week. Subjects were followed for 7 months. The primary outcome was prolonged 6 months not smoked on 7 consecutive days, analyzed by intention-to-treat. 78/246 (31.71%) in the active group versus 46/256 (17.97%) in the control group were abstinent. Adverse events were reported by 245/246 (99.6%) and 247/256 (96.5%) subjects in the active and control groups, respectively. Mild coughing which decreased with regular use was common with the nicotine aerosols. Inhaled nicotine from a metered dose inhaler combined with a nicotine patch substantially improved abstinence for 6 months amongst adult nicotine dependent smokers wanting to quit. In 2012, these investigators published a systematic review of the use nicotine by inhalation. At that time these investigators were unable to find any studies that had measured the effects of nicotine delivery by pMDI on smoking cessation, and they were not aware of any since 2012. This was the first study to evaluate nicotine by pMDI in smoking cessation. This clinical trial demonstrated that a simple nonproprietary nicotine inhaler, using relatively inexpensive standard technology, increases smoking cessation rates over nicotine patch therapy, and could enhance nicotine replacement in smoking cessation treatment.

Predictors of the Onset of Cigarette Smoking

In general, the onset of cigarette smoking typically occurs during childhood or early adolescence. Nicotine dependence symptoms can manifest soon after onset, contributing to sustained, long-term smoking. Previous reviews have not clarified the determinants of onset. In 2015, a systematic review of the literature in PubMed and EMBASE was undertaken to identify peer-reviewed prospective longitudinal studies published between January 1984 and August 2015 that investigated predictors of cigarette smoking onset among youth aged <18 years who had never smoked. Wellman et al., (2016) recently identified 98 conceptually different potential predictors in 53 studies. An increased risk of smoking onset was consistently (i.e., in four or more studies) associated with increased age/grade, lower SES, poor academic performance, sensation seeking or rebelliousness, intention to smoke in the future, receptivity to tobacco promotion efforts, susceptibility to smoking, family members' smoking, having friends who smoke, and exposure to films, whereas higher self-esteem and high parental monitoring/supervision of the child appeared to protect against smoking onset psychological weaknesses were identified in numerous studies, including failure to account for attrition or for clustering in samples, and misidentification of potential confounders, which may have led to biased estimates of associations. These investigators recommended that predictors of smoking onset for which there is robust evidence should be considered in the design of interventions to prevent first puff to optimize their effectiveness and future research should seek to define onset as the transition from never use to first use (e.g., first few puffs).

Heteromeric α7β2 Nicotinic Acetylcholine Receptors in the Brain

It is well-established that the α7 nicotinic acetylcholine receptor (α7 nAChR) is highly expressed in the brain, where it maintains various neuronal functions including learning, intelligence, memory, and behavior. In addition, the protein expression levels of α7 nAChRs are altered in various brain disorders. The classic rule governing α7 nAChR assembly in the mammalian brain was that it was assembled from five α7 subunits to form a homomeric receptor pentamer. However, emerging evidence demonstrates the presence of heteromeric α7 nAChRs in heterologously expressed systems and naturally in brain neurons, where α7 subunits are co-assembled with β2 subunits to form a novel type of α7β2 nAChR. Interestingly, the α7β2 nAChR exhibits distinctive function and pharmacology from traditional homomeric α7 nAChRs. Recently, Wu et al., (2016) reviewed recent advances in probing the distribution, function, pharmacology, pathophysiology, and stoichiometry of the heteromeric α7β2 nAChR, which provide new insights into the understanding of a novel target of cholinergic signaling.

Mechanisms and Development of Treatments for Heavy Drinking Cigarette Smokers

It is well established that there is a strong association between cigarette smoking and alcohol use at the epidemiological, behavioral, and molecular levels, and this co-use creates impediments to smoking cessation among smokers who are also heavy drinkers. Compared with individuals who only smoke, those who both drink and smoke heavily experience more severe health consequences and have greater difficulty in quitting smoking. During smoking abstinence, greater alcohol use is associated with decreased odds of smoking cessation, and smokers are more likely to experience a smoking lapse during drinking episodes. As heavy drinking smokers are less responsive to the currently available pharmacological treatments, this subgroup of high-risk substance users possesses a unique clinical profile and treatment needs. Thus, treatment development for heavy drinking smokers represents a significant and understudied research area within the field of smoking cessation. Recently, Roche et al., (2016) briefly described findings from epidemiological, behavioral, and molecular studies illustrating alcohol and tobacco co-use and identified how the behavioral and neurobiological mechanisms underlying the interaction of alcohol and nicotine may inform the development of targeted treatments for this specific population of smokers.

Nicotine Receptor Partial Agonists for Smoking Cessation

Nicotine receptor partial agonists may help people to stop smoking by a combination of maintaining moderate levels of DA to counteract withdrawal symptoms (acting as an agonist) and reducing smoking satisfaction (acting as an antagonist). To review the efficacy of nicotine receptor partial agonists, including Varenicline and Cytisine, for smoking cessation, Cahill et al., (2016) searched the Cochrane Tobacco Addiction Group's specialized register for trials, using the terms ('Cytisine' or 'Tabex' or 'Dianicline' or 'Varenicline' or 'nicotine receptor partial agonist') in the title or abstract, or as keywords. The register was compiled from searches of MEDLINE, EMBASE, and PsycINFO using MeSH terms and free text to identify controlled trials of interventions for smoking cessation and prevention. These investigators contacted authors of trial reports for additional information where necessary. The latest update of the specialized register was in May 2015, although they included a few key trials published after this date. They also searched online clinical trials registers and included randomized controlled trials which compared the treatment drug with placebo, and also included comparisons with Bupropion and nicotine patches where available, and excluded trials which did not report a minimum follow-up period of 6 months from start of treatment. They extracted data on the type of participants, the dose and duration of treatment, the outcome measures, the randomization procedure, concealment of allocation, and completeness of follow-up. The main outcome measured was abstinence from smoking at longest follow-up. They used the most rigorous definition of abstinence, and preferred biochemically validated rates where they were reported. These investigators also pooled risk ratios (RRs), using the Mantel-Haenszel fixed-effect model. Two trials of Cytisine (937 people) found that more participants taking Cytisine stopped smoking compared with placebo at longest follow-up, with a pooled risk ratio (RR) of 3.98 (95% confidence interval (CI) 2.01 to 7.87; low-quality evidence). One recent trial comparing cytisine with NRT in 1310 people found a benefit for cytisine at six months (RR 1.43, 95% CI 1.13 to 1.80). One trial of Dianicline (602 people) failed to find evidence that it was effective (RR 1.20, 95% CI 0.82 to 1.75). This drug is no longer in development. They identified 39 trials that tested Varenicline, 27 of which contributed to the primary analysis (Varenicline versus placebo). Five of these trials also included a Bupropion treatment arm. Eight trials compared Varenicline, with nicotine replacement therapy (NRT). Nine studies tested variations in Varenicline, dosage, and 13 tested usage in disease-specific subgroups of patients. The included studies covered 25,290 participants, 11,801 of whom used Varenicline. The pooled RR for continuous or sustained abstinence at six months or longer for Varenicline at standard dosage versus placebo was 2.24 (95% CI 2.06 to 2.43; 27 trials, 12,625 people; high-quality evidence). Varenicline at lower or variable doses was also shown to be effective, with an RR of 2.08 (95% CI 1.56 to 2.78; 4 trials, 1266 people). The pooled RR for Varenicline versus Bupropion at six months was 1.39 (95% CI 1.25 to 1.54; 5 trials, 5877 people; high-quality evidence). The RR for Varenicline versus NRT for abstinence at 24 weeks was 1.25 (95% CI 1.14 to 1.37; 8 trials, 6264 people; moderate-quality evidence). Four trials which tested the use of Varenicline beyond the 12-week standard regimen found the drug to be well-tolerated during long-term use. The number needed to treat with Varenicline for an additional beneficial outcome, based on the weighted mean control rate, is 11 (95% CI 9 to 13). The most commonly reported adverse effect of Varenicline was nausea, which was mostly at mild to moderate levels and usually subsided over time. The analysis of reported serious adverse events occurring during or after active treatment suggested that there may be a 25% increase in the chance of SAEs among people using Varenicline (RR 1.25; 95% CI 1.04 to 1.49; 29 trials, 15,370 people; high-quality evidence). These events included comorbidities such as infections, cancers and injuries, and were considered unrelated to the treatments. There was also evidence of higher losses to follow-up in the control groups compared with the intervention groups, leading to a likely under-ascertainment of the true rate of SAEs among the controls. Early concerns about a possible association between Varenicline and depressed mood, agitation, and suicidal behavior or ideation led to the addition of a boxed warning to the labelling in 2008. However, subsequent observational cohort studies and meta-analyses have not confirmed these fears, and the findings of the EAGLES trial did not support a causal link between Varenicline and neuropsychiatric disorders, including suicidal ideation and suicidal behavior. The evidence was inconclusive, however, in people with past or current psychiatric disorders concerns were raised that Varenicline may slightly increase cardiovascular events in people already at increased risk of those illnesses. Current evidence neither supported nor refuted such an association, but the findings of the CATS trial are still awaited, which should establish whether this is a valid concern. Based on these observations, these investigators concluded that Cytisine increases the chances of quitting, although absolute quit rates were modest in two recent trials. Varenicline at standard dose increased the chances of successful long-term smoking cessation between two- and three-fold compared with pharmacologically unassisted quit attempts. Lower dose regimens also conferred benefits for cessation, while reducing the incidence of adverse events. More participants quit successfully with Varenicline than with Bupropion or with NRT. Limited evidence suggested that Varenicline may have a role to play in relapse prevention. The most frequently recorded adverse effect of Varenicline was nausea, but mostly at mild to moderate levels and tending to subside over time. Early reports of possible links to suicidal ideation and behavior was not been confirmed by current research. These authors recommended that future trials of Cytisine may test extended regimens and intensive behavioral support.

Substances of Abuse during Pregnancy Increases Consumption in Offspring

Correlative human observational studies on substances of abuse have been highly dependent on the use of rodent models to determine the neuronal and molecular mechanisms that control behavioral outcomes. This is particularly true for gestational exposure to non-illicit substances of abuse, such as excessive dietary fat, ethanol, and nicotine, commonly consumed in our society. Exposure to these substances during the prenatal period has been shown in offspring to increase their intake of these substances, induce other behavioral changes, and affect neurochemical systems in several brain areas that are known to control behavior. More importantly, emerging studies are linking the function of the immune system to these neurochemicals and ingestion of these abused substances. Recently, Poon et al., (2016) summarized the prenatal rodent models used to study developmental changes in offspring caused by prenatal exposure to dietary fat, ethanol, or nicotine. These investigators discussed various techniques used for the administration of these substances into rodents and summarized the published outcomes induced by prenatal exposure to these substances. In addition, this review covered some of the recent evidence for the role of immune factors in causing these behavioral and neuronal changes.

Detection of Cotinine Level in Tobacco Users

It is now realized that the greatest disease-producing product known to man is tobacco. It is a cause of many oral diseases and adverse oral conditions. Recently, Raja et al., (2016) reported that in India, tobacco is available in smokeless and smoking form. Tobacco contains nicotine which metabolizes to form a toxic alkaloid i.e., cotinine, which stimulates autonomic ganglia and CNS. Cotinine is the best indicator of tobacco smoke exposure. Various methods are used to measure cotinine level in blood, saliva and urine such as HPLC, colorimetric assay, gas chromatography, NicAlert saliva test, etc. Thus such wide range of tests for cotinine detection in tobacco users requires a detailed knowledge regarding their utility. These investigators reviewed various comparative methods for cotinine detection to make scientifically informative decision.

Ovarian Hormones, Menstrual Cycle Phase, and Smoking

Cigarette smoking continues to be the leading cause of preventable morbidity and mortality. Similar to other addictive substances, the prevalence of cigarette smoking is greater among men than women, yet women are less successful at quitting smoking. Preclinical and clinical research suggests that ovarian hormones (i.e., Estradiol and Progesterone), which fluctuate over the course of the menstrual cycle, may contribute to these sex differences. Specifically, research suggests that Progesterone may protect against cigarette smoking and nicotine addiction; whereas Estradiol may underlie enhanced vulnerability. Recently, Wetherill et al., (2016) discussed emerging research on ovarian hormone and menstrual cycle phase effects on smoking-related responses and behavior in women, including studies examining neural responses to smoking cues, hormonal influences on medication-assisted smoking cessation, and acute smoking abstinence. These authors highlighted innovative studies with up-to-date research methodology and provided suggestions for future research that allowed evidence-based knowledge for translation to the clinic to guide novel, hormonally-informed personalized treatment strategies. Thus, rigorous scientific study holds the potential to reduce relapse rates, thus improving the health and saving the lives of many women who do not respond to current treatments.

Nicotinic Acetylcholine Receptors and Cancer

Recently, Dang et al., (2016) reported that nicotine, the primary addictive constituent of cigarettes, is believed to contribute to cancer promotion and progression through the activation of nicotinic acetylcholine receptors (nAChRs), which are membrane ligand-gated cation channels. nAChRs activation can be triggered by the neurotransmitter Ach, or certain other biological compounds, such as nicotine. In recent years, genome-wide association studies (GWAS) have indicated that allelic variation in the α5-α3-β4 nAChR cluster on chromosome 15q24-15q25.1 is associated with increased lung cancer risk. The role of nAChRs in other types of cancer has also been reported. This review highlighted the role of nAChRs in various types of human cancer.

Drug Interactions with Tobacco, Cannabinoids and Smoking Cessation Products

Recently, Anderson and Chan (2016) reported that tobacco smoke contains large number of compounds in the form of metals, volatile gases and insoluble particles, as well as nicotine, a highly addictive alkaloid. Marijuana is the most widely used illicit drug of abuse in the world, with a significant increase in the USA due to the increasing number of states that allow medical and recreational use. Of the over 70 phytocannabinoids in marijuana, Δ^9-Tetrahydrocannabinol (Δ^9THC), cannabidiol (CBD) and cannibinol are the three main constituents. Both marijuana and tobacco smoking induce cytochrome P450 (CYP) 1A2 through activation of the aromatic hydrocarbon receptor, and the induction effect between the two products is additive. Smoking cessation is associated with rapid downregulation of CYP1A enzymes. On the basis of estimated half-life of CYP1A2, dose reduction of CYP1A drugs may be necessary as early as the first few days after smoking cessation to prevent toxicity, especially for drugs with a narrow therapeutic index. Nicotine is a substrate of CYP2A6, which is induced by Estrogen, resulting in lower concentrations of nicotine in females than in males, especially in females taking oral contraceptives. The significant effects of CYP3A4 inducers and inhibitors on the PKs of Δ^9THC/CBD oromucosal spray suggest that CYP3A4 is the primary enzyme responsible for the metabolism of Δ^9THC and CBD. Limited data also suggest that CBD may significantly inhibit CYP2C19. With the increasing use of marijuana and cannabis products, clinical studies are needed to determine the effects of other drugs on PKs and pharmacodynamics to successfully accomplish personalized treatment of multiple drug addiction such as tobacco, alcohol, and marijuana co-abuse.

References

Anderson, G. D., Chan, L. N., 2016. Pharmacokinetic Drug Interactions with Tobacco, Cannabinoids and Smoking Cessation Products. *Clin Pharmacokinet.* Apr 22.

Cahill, K., Lindson-Hawley, N., Thomas, K. H., Fanshawe, T. R., Lancaster, T., 2016. Nicotine receptor partial agonists for smoking cessation. *Cochrane Database Syst Rev.* May 9.

Caldwell, B. O., Crane, J., 2016. Combination Nicotine Metered Dose Inhaler and Nicotine Patch for Smoking Cessation: A Randomized Controlled Trial. *Nicotine Tob Res.* May 16.

Dang, N., Meng, X., Song, H., 2016. Nicotinic acetylcholine receptors and cancer. *Biomed Rep.* 4(5), 515-518.

Hagen, E. H., Garfield, M., Sullivan, R. J., 2016. The low prevalence of female smoking in the developing world: gender inequality or maternal adaptations for fetal protection? *Evol Med Public Health.* May 18.

Han, B., Compton, W. M., Blanco, C., 2016. Tobacco Use and 12-Month Suicidality among Adults in the United States. *Nicotine Tob Res.* May 17.

Ip, P., Chung, B. H., Ho, F. K., Chan, G. C., Deng, W., Wong, W. H., Lee, S. L., Chan, P. Y., Ying, D., Wong, W. L., Tung, K. T., Lau, Y. L., 2016. Prenatal tobacco exposure shortens telomere length in children. *Nicotine & Tob Res.* May 18.

Kubota, M., Yanagita, M., Mori, K., Hasegawa, S., Yamashita, M., Yamada, S., Kitamura, M., Murakami, S., 2016. The Effects of Cigarette Smoke Condensate and Nicotine on Periodontal Tissue in a Periodontitis Model Mouse. *PLoS One.* 11(5), e0155594.

Li, F., Zhang, H., Wang, S., Xiao, W., Ding, C., Liu, W., Guo, H., 2016. Identification of Topping Responsive Proteins in Tobacco Roots. *Front Plant Sci.* 7, 582.

Lubomirov, L. T, Papadopoulos, S., Pütz, S., Welter, J., Klöckener, T., Weckmüller, K., Ardestani, M. A., Filipova, D., Metzler, D., Metzner, H., Staszewski, J., Zittrich, S., Gagov, H., Schroeter, M. M., Pfitzer, G., 2016. Aging-related alterations in eNOS and nNOS responsiveness and smooth muscle reactivity of murine basilar arteries are modulated by apocynin and phosphorylation of myosin phosphatase targeting subunit-1. *J Cereb Blood Flow Metab.* May 18.

MacQueen, D. A., Dalrymple, S. R., Drobes, D. J., Diamond, D. M., 2016. Influence of pharmacological manipulations of NMDA and cholinergic receptors on working versus reference memory in a dual component odor span task. *Learn Mem.* 23(6), 270-277.

Mercincavage, M., Saddleson, M. L., Gup, E., Halstead, A., Mays, D., Strasser, A. A., 2017. Reduced nicotine content cigarette advertising: How false beliefs and subjective ratings affect smoking behavior. *Drug Alcohol Depend.* 173, 99-106.

Poon, K, Leibowitz, S. F., 2016. Consumption of Substances of Abuse during Pregnancy Increases Consumption in Offspring: Possible Underlying Mechanisms. *Front Nutr.* 3, 11.

Raja, M., Garg, A., Yadav, P., Jha, K., Handa, S., 2016. Diagnostic for Detection of cotinine Level in Tobacco Users: A Review. *J Clin Diagn Res.* 10(3), ZE04-6.

Roche, D. J., Ray, L. A., Yardley, M. M., King, A. C., 2016. Current insights into the mechanisms and development of treatments for heavy drinking cigarette smokers. *Curr Addict Rep.* 3(1), 125-137.

Rupprecht, L. E., Smith, T. T., Donny, E. C., Sved, A. F., 2016. Self-Administered Nicotine Suppresses Body Weight Gain Independent of Food Intake in Male Rats. *Nicotine Tob Res.* May 18.

Singh, N. N., Peer, A., Nair, S., Chaturvedi, R. K., 2016. Epigenetics: A possible answer to the undeciphered etiopathogenesis and behavior of oral lesions. *J Oral Maxillofac Pathol.* 20(1), 122-128.

Tague, C., Richter, K. P., Cox, L. S., Keighley, J., Hutcheson, T., Fitzgerald, S. A., Ellerbeck, E. F., 2016. Impact of Telephone-Based Care Coordination on Use of Cessation Medications Post-Hospital Discharge: A Randomized Controlled Trial. *Nicotine Tob Res.* May 18.

Tidey, J. W., 2016. A behavioral economic perspective on smoking persistence in serious mental illness. *Prev Med.* May 16.

Weinberger, A. H., Funk, A. P., Goodwin, R. D., 2016. A review of epidemiologic research on smoking behavior among persons with alcohol and illicit substance use disorders. *Prev Med.* May 16.

Wellman, R. J., Dugas, E. N., Dutczak, H., O'Loughlin, E. K., Datta, G. D., Lauzon, B., O'Loughlin, J., 2016. Predictors of the Onset of Cigarette Smoking: A Systematic Review of Longitudinal Population-Based Studies in Youth. *Am J Prev Med.* May 11.

Wetherill, R. R., Franklin, T. R., Allen, S. S., 2016. Ovarian hormones, menstrual cycle phase, and smoking: a review with recommendations for future studies. *Curr Addict Rep.* 3(1), 1-8.

Wu, J., Liu, Q., Tang, P., Mikkelsen, J. D., Shen, J., Whiteaker, P., Yakel, J. L., 2016. Heteromeric α7β2 Nicotinic Acetylcholine Receptors in the Brain. *Trends Pharmacol Sci.* May 11.

Yang, J., Li, M. D., 2016. Converging findings from linkage and association analyses on susceptibility genes for smoking and other addictions. *Mol Psychiatry.* May 10.

Conclusion and Recommendations

It is now well established that nicotinism is a globally-preventable healthcare challenge and is the most significant cause of loss of national and international economy and productivity. It poses a significant challenge to general health and well-being of an individual. Several preventive as well as therapeutic measures have been already implemented to minimize the risks of numerous diseases associated with tobacco smoking. However, a considerable amount of work is needed to minimize this devastating preventable addiction from the entire world. A recent trend of reduction in smoking among adolescent population in several countries including U.S.A, Canada, and Australia, seems quite encouraging. However, smoking in several other countries such as Serbia, Slovania, Russia, China, and India, remains a significant challenge. The public awareness and proper education particularly to the adolescent population will go a long way in the early prevention and successful personalized theranostics of nicotinims in the entire world.

Nicotine in tobacco plant is a very potent drug, which is highly addictive when regularly consumed, and its abuse should be avoided. Given the serious health risks associated with cigarette smoking (particularly in young adolescents), primarily by the addictive properties of nicotine, the best recommendation is to avoid smoking from the very beginning. We may call it as "nip the evil in the bud"; or "prevention is better than cure." Unfortunately, despite the obvious health hazards and cost to society, thousands of young adolescents start smoking each year and become permanently addicted to nicotine in their entire life. It is important to mention here, that all nicotine-containing products should be handled with care and kept out of the reach of children. Secondhand smoke should be avoided, particularly for infants and children, and laws limiting exposure to secondhand smoke should be encouraged. Furthermore, laws restricting or defining smoking areas that reduce exposure to secondhand smoke and tobacco prevention programs and research should be encouraged.

Now we know that the effects of dose, age, race, and gender may be related to the prevalence of nicotinism. Hence, the number of cigarettes smoked per day and the duration of smoking are positively related to the percentage with diagnosis of nicotine dependence. Prevalence of nicotine dependence among adolescent smokers may be higher than that among adult smokers, particularly for those who smoke fewer cigarettes per day. Indeed! The prevalence of nicotine dependence, as defined by DSM criteria, was higher among Whites than among Blacks but was lower in Whites when time to the first cigarette of the day was the criterion of dependence. However, it remains uncertain whether the prevalence of nicotine dependence differs by gender, suggesting the need for further studies to explore underlying reasons for the inconsistent findings across subgroups of smokers.

A significant association also exists between psychiatric disorders and smoking, but the nature of this association also remains uncertain. Depending on the disorder, the relationship may be causal; for example, smoking may increase the risks of panic disorder and major depressive disorder (MDDs) and may lead to self-medication with tobacco use. On the other hand, this association may result from common underlying factors that involve psychological or physiological processes, such as intolerance to states of negative affect or neurotransmitter dysfunction, which may lead to nicotine dependence, substance abuse, and depression.

To date, understanding the causal relationships has relied primarily on cross-sectional data. Prospective studies are limited and have examined only a few psychiatric disorders, but this type of study is highly crucial to lend concrete evidence for any bidirectional causality or for common underlying causes of cigarette smoking and nicotine dependence with specific psychiatric disorders. A better understanding of these relationships will result in a deeper understanding of the pathophysiology of nicotine addiction. Moreover, the studies of adults are limited in that the focus has been primarily on internalizing rather than externalizing disorders. In adolescent studies, externalizing disorders may play greater role than do internalizing disorders in the development of nicotine addiction. Hence, studies encompassing a broader range of diagnoses are needed.

The ventral tegmental area (VTA) of the brain and the DAergic neurotransmission are primarily involved in the positive reinforcement of nicotine addiction. Nicotine-induced DA release occurs by stimulating nAChRs, primarily $\alpha4\beta2$ and $\alpha7$ homomeric nAChRs in the VTA. Nicotine stimulates nAChRs on glutamatergic terminals that release glutamate (excitatory neurotransmitter), which also increases DA release in the nucleus accumbens and the frontal cortex. Nicotine also stimulates nAChRs on GABA-releasing terminals. Thus, levels of GABA, an inhibitory neurotransmitter, are also increased by nicotine. However, the interaction between the quick desensitization of nAChRs on the GABA neuron and the higher doses of nicotine required to desensitize nAChRs on the glutamate neuron results in a greater increase in DA levels. Although, a critical role may also be played by nicotine-induced increases in NE-ergic neurotransmission, its precise role in nicotine dependence has not been investigated as extensively as that of the DAergic, glutamatergic, and GABAergic systems. Similarly, the role of endocannabinoids, serotonin, and endogenous opiates in nicotine addiction remains uncertain. Recent advances have been made in this direction as described in this book.

A comprehensive study is needed to understand the basic molecular mechanism of nicotine-induced withdrawal symptoms. The neurophysiology associated with withdrawal symptoms may be based on the symptoms experienced (e.g., somatic versus affective) by a nicotine addict. Recent studies suggest that nAChRs is involved in both the somatic and affective components of nicotine withdrawal. Animal studies suggest that β4 plays an important role in the somatic symptoms, whereas β2 plays an important role in the affective symptoms of withdrawal. The neuronal subunit α7 may be involved only in some of the somatic (e.g., hyperalgesia) symptoms of withdrawal. Although, the role of α4 remains uncertain, it may influence both affective and somatic withdrawal effects. In addition, decreased mesolimbic DAergic neurotransmission mediates various aspects of the withdrawal syndrome. NE-ergic and 5-HTergic systems may also play a pivotal role in withdrawal. Decreased glutamatergic neurotransmission mediates the withdrawal symptoms, however, GABAergic neurotransmission does not change with withdrawal.

Although some studies suggest that a dysregulation in the hypothalamic-pituitary axis occurs subsequent to nicotine withdrawal, which is associated with relapse to smoking, a further study is warranted to delineate the involvement of specific neurotransmitters and neuroreceptors relevant to the numerous aspects of nicotinism and other form of addictions.

Finally, understanding the pathophysiology of depression and schizophrenia, other psychiatric illnesses, and substance abuse disorders (SUDs), (particularly nicotinism) as well as the effects of medications used to treat these disorders in smokers, may enhance basic understanding of the pathophysiology of nicotine addiction. Because of the overlap between prevalence of nicotine dependence and comorbid psychiatric disorders, the similar monoamines affected by these disorders, and the use of similar treatment medications, it is possible that common substrates mediate nicotine dependence and depression or schizophrenia, as well as other psychiatric disorders and may provide further insight into safe and effective personalized theranostics.

A brief overview of "Personalized Theranostics of Nicotinism" is described in this book with a primary objective to emphasize the importance of emerging omics technology, molecular imaging, and viccinomics, because conventional treatment with Nicotine replacement therapy (NRT), nicotine patch, cognitive behavioral therapy (CBT), telemedicine, and pharmacological agents such as Varenicline, Cysitine, and Bupropion remain inefective in certain patients possessing unique pharmacogenomic, pharmacokinetic, and pharmacodynamic profile. Particularly, this book highlights the clinical significance of Charnoly body (CB) and mitochondrial bioenergetics-based charnolopharmacotherapeutics in nicotinism for the regulation of CHRNA-1-5 genes, involved in the transcriptional activation of nitotinic acetyl choline receptor (nAChR) subgroups in lung epithelial cells and in other vulnerable organs such as CNS, heart, vessels, liver, kidneys, ovaries, and testis. Chronic exposure of nicotine in these sensitive organs can compromise the mitochondrial bioenergetics to induce diversified charnolopathies including embryopathies (such as abortion, still birth, sudden infant death syndrome, microcephaly, craniofacial abnormalities, growth retardation, ADHD, autism, and craniofacial abnormalities) in the developing infants, and asthma, COPD, and cancer in adults as the author has described in his books "Zika Virus Disease: Prevention and Cure," and "Fetal Alcohol Spectrum Disorders: Concepts, Mechanisms, and Cure" by Nova Science Publishers, New York, U.S.A.

The most unique feature of this book is that it confers basic molecular biology and pharmacogenomics of Nicotinism and the emerging role of e-cigarettes as a wishful alternative to reduce tobacco craving and related second-hand smoking-related health risks. The book highlights specifically mitochondrial bioenergetics-based charnolopharmacotherapeutics for the clinical management of Nicotinims with minimum withdrawal symptoms and reduce early morbidity and mortality due to asthma, emphysema, cancer, heart attack, diabetes, obesity, infertility, MDDs, and schizophrenia by inhibiting Charnoly body (CB) formation, augmenting charnolophagy, and by augmenting charnolosome stabilization and its exocytosis in the most vulnerable cells as a basic molecular mechanism of intracellular detoxification to remain healthy for a better quality of life.

In view of the above, novel disease-specific-CB antagonists, charnolophagy agonists, charnolosome stabilizers, and CS exocytosis enhancers may be developed as promising charnolopharmacotherapeutics for the prevention and treatment of chronic neurodegenerative diseases and cardiovascular disease and vice versa for the clinical management of malignancies associated with nicotinism, Alcoholism, and other drugs of abuse, as described and illustrated with pictorial diagrams for easy comprehension of young adolescent population.

Emerging biotechnologies (such as flow cytometry with sorting, LC-MS, capillary electrophoresis, and multimodality molecular imaging with PET, CT, SPECT, MRI/MRS) to understand the basic molecular pathogenesis and pharmacogenomics of nicotinism and the emerging role of e-cigarettes have been discussed in detail in this book. It is envisaged that the readers (particularly high school and college going students) will enjoy learning the most recent and novel approaches those are being implemented in this clinically-significant discipline by carefully going through and following these brand-new volumes on "Nicotinism and the Emerging Role of E-Cigarettes" by Nova Science Publishers, New York, U.S.A. for their better future and quality of life.

Appendix

Tobacco Harm Reduction

Tobacco harm reduction describes actions taken to lower the health risks associated with using tobacco or nicotine. A very important part of tobacco harm reduction is simply educating people about the risks of different sources of nicotine. Smokers can quit nicotine entirely, that is, quit smoking and not use any other type of nicotine. They can also get nicotine from a much less harmful source. Neither one will immediately eliminate all of the health risks caused by their previous smoking, but both come very close. Quitting entirely is probably the slightly healthier option for most people. This is because nicotine itself may slightly increase your risk of heart attack and stroke, though not nearly as much as smoking does. But switching to a highly-reduced-risk nicotine product is almost as good as quitting entirely. Because the longer you smoke the worse it is for you, switching now may be better than quitting later. You are probably aware of the many programs, drugs, and therapies available to help smokers quit using nicotine entirely. And we very much hope that if you are a smoker and elect to quit entirely, that you are successful. But since you are reading this, it is likely that you or someone you know has tried to quit and failed, or wants to continue using nicotine but wants to reduce the risk. The most popular highly-reduced-risk nicotine product is smokeless tobacco (ST), specifically modern Western moist snuff (the Swedish word for which is snus) and chewing tobacco. A newer and rapidly growing alternative product is the electronic cigarette. Another product category is pharmaceutical nicotine (such as nicotine gum, lozenges, patches, and inhalers). Someone who uses any of these products rather than smoking reduces the risks by around 99%.

But it shouldn't be. Most all of public health, and a large part of medical care, is devoted to harm reduction. The term "harm reduction" is most often used in controversial contexts, like encouraging condom use and other safe sex practices, or providing heroin users with clean needles or Methadone. Calling it "harm reduction" reminds us that though people would be at less risk of disease if they just avoided sex or gave up narcotics entirely, we cannot really expect that to happen.

In general, harm reduction is also our policy in matters of health. Even though driving is dangerous, we don't suggest that people give it up. We do not even ask them to limit it to "necessary" trips. Instead, we have rules of the road that make it safer, encourage (or mandate) seatbelt use, and build cars with safety features. Similarly, we do not tell people they have to give up playing hockey, bicycling, or other sports, even though there is some risk, but we do try to encourage the use of protective equipment.

When physicians or public health practitioners try to get you to change your cholesterol, eat less meat, or exercise more, the target is to improve your health but seldom do they insist that you have only one choice: Do the best possible thing or forget it. Taking most health advice will reduce your health risks but not get them to the lowest possible level.

When it comes to diet, exercise, sex, transportation, sports, and even heroin use, public health experts generally agree that scolding people to do the healthiest thing possible is just not practical or reasonable (indeed, it would be downright cruel in most cases). Instead we realize that people will decide that the benefits of certain behaviors are worth some risks, so we try to help them reduce their risks. Of all the things people do, nicotine use is about the only one where health officials do not promote harm reduction, and think they have a right to just demand you do what they want; and will even lie to you to keep you from learning about reduced harm alternatives. If you find yourself dealing with someone who seems to be insisting that comparative risk does not matter - that a lot better is not good enough and therefore not worth pursuing - think about this. Eating more fruits and vegetables reduces the risk of stomach and colon cancers and is beneficial in many other ways. Yet this too is not without its own dangers. There are a fair number of cases of foodborne disease that are traced to plant foods, some of which are fatal. People die from allergic reactions to fruits. Fruits and vegetables contain pesticides (some natural, some not) and other organic chemicals, heavy metals (calcium, lead), and even radioactive isotopes that probably sometimes cause cancers and other diseases.

Though you are much better off (or safer) eating more fruits and vegetables rather than less, it is not perfect. But, it is still very good. Over the last few decades, men in Sweden have smoked less and used more "snus" (the Swedish word for moist snuff) instead.

This was not caused by any public health campaign or government meddling. It was a normal social process of people changing their tastes. But the result was a huge public health triumph. Swedish men have a very low rate of lung cancer and other smoking related diseases, as we would expect from a population that quit smoking. The scientific evidence shows that the widespread use of ST is not causing any substantial disease risk.

(Swedish women, unfortunately, continue to smoke at the higher rates typical of other countries, and their rates of smoking-related diseases remain high.

Could the Swedish experience be repeated elsewhere? It might be happening in Norway right now, where ST is also culturally popular. But to duplicate it in other cultures will require some effort on the part of health promoters to educate people and persuade them of the advantages of harm reduction. That is what we are attempting to do. The rapidly growing popularity of e-cigarettes, a much safer nicotine source that is not even available in many brick and mortar stores, indicates that people are looking for alternatives.

References

Rodu, B., Cole, P., 2004. The Burden of Mortality from Smoking: Comparing Sweden with Other Countries in the European Union. *European Journal of Epidemiology* 19: 129-131.

FDA has established a list of harmful and potentially harmful constituents (HPHCs) in tobacco products and tobacco smoke (the established HPHC list) as required by the Federal Food, Drug, and Cosmetic Act (the FD&C Act).

Contact FDA
1-877-287-1373
(9am EST-4pm EST)
Tobacco
For General Inquiries:
AskCTP@fda.hhs.gov
Center for Tobacco Products
Food and Drug Administration
10903 New Hampshire Avenue
Document Control Center
Building 71, Room G335
Silver Spring, MD 20993-002

Important Sites to Help Quit Smoking

Quit line: 1-800-TRY-TO-STOP (English)
1-800-DEJALO (Espanol)

1-800-TDD-1477 Deaf/Hearing Impaired)
National Cancer Institute Cancer Information line: 1-800-4-CANCER

I. Groups:
There are many support groups to help people quit smoking. They teach people to make the changes needed to stop smoking.

Cambridge Hospital
Department of Behavioral Medicine
Cambridge, MA
(617)498-1520

Harvard Pilgrim Health Plan
Freedom From Smoking Program
Various sites/cities
(617)731-8223

Mount Auburn Hospital
Cambridge, MA
(617)499-4214

Mass. Alliance of Portuguese Speakers
Somerville, MA
(617)628-6065

II. Self-Help:
The following organizations offer quitting kits and free brochures with guidelines and tips on quitting: American Cancer Society (Fresh Start Program): 1-800-952-7664 X4664

American Lung Association: (617) 272-2866; National Cancer Institute: 1-800-4-CANCER; Cambridge Tobacco Education Program: (617)349-6353; Mass. Tobacco Education Clearinghouse: (617)482-9485; Tobacco Education Clearinghouse of California: 1-800-258-9090

III. Web Resources:
American Cancer Society
http://www.cancer.org

American Lung Association
http://www.lungusa.org
National Cancer Institute
http://cancernet.nci.nih.gov

Try-To-Stop TOBACCO Resource Center of Massachusetts
(for Massachusetts residents only)
http://www.trytostop.org

External Links

North American Agencies

- Health Canada - Tobacco (CDC). Online: < http://www.hc-sc.gc.ca/hl-vs/tobac-tabac/index-eng.php > Heath Canada information on the health effects of tobacco products.
- US Centers for Disease Control and Prevention (CDC). Online: <http://www.cdc.gov/tobacco/> US CDC site has multiple listings on health, tobacco, and Nicotine.
- US National Institute on Drug Abuse (NIDA). Online: <http://www.drugabuse.gov/drugpages/Nicotine.html>. US NIDA site has general information on Nicotine.
- US Medline plus - Smoking Tobacco. Online: <http://www.nlm.nih.gov/medlineplus/smoking.html>. Site has many good reference on smoking tobacco.

European, Asian, and International Agencies

- England - Department of Health - Public Health and Tobacco. Online: http://www.dh.gov.uk/en/Publichealth/Healthimprovement/Tobacco/index.htm
- Society for Research on Nicotine and Tobacco. Online: <http://www.srnt.org/> "An international society with a mission to stimulate the generation of new knowledge concerning nicotine in all its manifestations – from molecular to societal."
- World Health Organization (WHO). Online: <http://www.who.int/health_topics/tobacco/en/> Covers tobacco and international efforts to track and reduce use of tobacco.
- National Tobacco Information Online System (NATIONS). Online: <http://apps.nccd.cdc.gov/nations/>

"The National Tobacco Information Online System (NATIONS) is an electronically integrated information system containing country-specific information on a wide variety of tobacco control issues."

- Pan American Tobacco Information Online System (PATIOS). Online: <http://www.paho.org/tobacco/PatiosHome.asp>
PATIOS is a web-based information system containing country-specific data on a wide variety of tobacco control topics.

Non-Government Organizations

- Neuroscience For Kids - Nicotine. Online: http://faculty.washington.edu/chudler/nic.html. Addresses the health effects of tobacco and Nicotine.
- Society for Neuroscience (SfN). Online: < http://www.sfn.org/index.cfm?pagename=brainBriefings_Nicotine and the Brain> this article, part of the SfN series on Brain Briefing, covers nicotine and the brain.
- Tobacco and Nicotine - The Vaults of Erowid. Online: <http://www.erowid.org/plants/tobacco/tobacco.shtml> (accessed: 27 August 2008). Site has information on tobacco and nicotine.

Glossary

- *Addiction.* Other words like "compulsion" or "obsession" or "craving" also have slightly different meanings, and on several occasions addiction is confused with them. Addiction may be defined as consuming a lot of something, even though it may have harmful consequences for health. But this definition is weak. Addiction has to do with wanting more of something the more you consume, rather than becoming satisfied and bored by it, as we might with most things. We should distinguish between addiction and compulsion or merely liking something a lot. It is possible to be addicted to exercise, work, listening to music, or other things that we would not tell people to quit, just because they are addicted. Some people cannot or will not quit smoking (or using nicotine).
- *Apoptotic Body.* A blebbing on the surface of the plasma membrane following a tertiary or quaternary free radical attack. The fusion of CS body with the plasma membrane releases highly toxic metabolites of the mitochondrial metabolism as described above to cause phosphatidyl serine externalization and eventually release of intracellular constituents in the microenvironment to induce apoptosis resulting in chronic MDR diseases as described systematically in this book.
- *Cardiovascular Disease.* Diseases of the heart and circulatory system, including heart attacks and stroke.
- *Chain Smoking.* A practice of smoking several cigarettes in succession, using the ember of a finished cigarette to light the next. This term refers to a person who smokes relatively constantly, not necessarily chaining each cigarette.
- *Charnolocidal.* An agent which eliminates Charnoly body (CB) in a physicochemically-injured cell.
- *Charnologenetics.* Genetic changes involved in Charnoly body (CB) formation.
- *Charnolomimetic.* An agent which augments Charnoly body (CB) formation.

- *Charnolophagosome.* A highly unstable and functionally labile intracellular organelle which is formed following charnolophagy. It is electron-dense and almost 2.5 times larger than the size of a lysosome. A lysosome containing phagocytosed Charnoly Body (CB).
- *Charnolophagy.* Energy (ATP)-dependent phagocytosis of Charnoly body (CB).
- *Charnolopharmaceuticals.* Charnoly Body (CB)-targeted pharmaceutical agents for the safe and effective clinical management of chronic multi-drug resistant (MDR) diseases such as malignancies.
- *Charnolopharmacogenomics.* Genomic changes associated with induction and inhibition of Charnoly body (CB).
- *Charnolopharmacology.* Charnoly Body (CB)-targeted mitochondrial bioenergetics-based therapeutic drugs with their precise pharmacokinetics (PKs), pharmacodynamics (PDs), beneficial effects, and adverse effects.
- *Charnolopharmacotherapeutics.* Charnoly Body (CB)-targeted therapeutic drugs designed based on the compromised mitochondrial bioenergetics involving Charnoly body (CB), charnolophagy, charnolophagosome/charnolosome and their exocytosis and endocytosis as a basic molecular mechanisms of intracellular detoxification for a normal cellular function.
- *Charnoloscopy.* A microscopic (usually confocal, atomic force, and TEM) evaluation of Charnoly Body (CB), charnolophagy, charnolophagosome, charnolosome and its exocytosis/endocytosis as a basic molecular mechanism of intracellular detoxification.
- *Charnolosome Body.* A blebbing on the surface of a charnolosome following a secondary or tertiary free radical attack due to lipid peroxidation. The charnolosome body pinches off from the charnolosome and fuses with the plasma and nuclear membrane to synthesize apoptotic body.
- *Charnolosome.* A charnolosome is formed when the phagocytosed CB in the charnolophagosome is completely hydrolyzed by the lysosomal enzymes. It is a single layered highly unstable and functionally labile intracellular organelle containing toxic metabolites of mitochondrial metabolism.
- *Charnolostatic.* An agent which inhibits Charnoly body (CB) formation.
- *Charnoly Body Epigenetics.* Methylation of mitochondrial DNA at N-4 position of cytosine.
- *Charnoly Body.* A pleomorphic, multi-lamellar, electron-dense, quasi-crystalline, intracellular inclusion body which is generated in the most vulnerable cell (such as neural progenitor cells, derived from induced pluripotent cells) due to malnutrition, toxins, and microbial (bacteria, viral, and fungal) infection-induced free radical overproduction as a byproduct of mitochondrial oxidative phosphorylation in the electron transport chain. Free radicals cause degeneration of mitochondrial

membranes and CB formation as an initial attempt to contain highly toxic metabolites of the mitochondria such as 2,3-dihydroxy nonenal, 8-OH 2dG, cytochrome-C, acetaldehyde, hydrogen peroxide, ammonia, GAPDH, lactate, monoamine oxidases, TSPO (18 kDa protein), which serves as a cholesterol transport channel (for the synthesis of intra-mitochondrial steroid hormones to stabilize the mitochondrial and other intracellular membranes), and a canonical TRPC (a calcium transport channel) protein. These proteins are delocalized during CB formation.

- *E-Cigarettes.* Consumption of steamed smoke by heating the nicotine solution electronically rather than conventional incineration of tobacco to consume tobacco smoke.
- *Free Radicals.* Free radicals are highly unstable, reactive chemical species (including OH, NO, CO) which are formed in the mitochondria as a byproduct to oxidative phosphorylation in the electron transport chain. They cause lipid peroxidation of cellular membranes by inducing structural and functional breakdown of polyunsaturated fatty acids (including: linoic acid, linolenic acid, and arachidonic acid).
- *Free Radical Attack:*

  o *Primary Free Radical Attack.* Is attenuated by endogenously synthesized antioxidants such as glutathione, metallothioneins, heat chock proteins, heat shock factor-α, theiredoxin, superoxide dismutase (SOD), and catalase.
  o *Secondary Free Radical Attack.* Requires endogenously-synthesized antioxidants as well as naturally-produced antioxidants such Resveratrol, Lycopene, sirtuins, rutins, catchsin, polyphenols, and flavonoids to maintain intracellular detoxification and sustain intra-mitochondrial homeostasis.
  o *Tertiary Free Radical Attack.* Requires endogenously-synthesized antioxidants, naturally synthesized antioxidants as describe above, and pharmacological antioxidants such as all B-Vitamins, Vitamin-A, D, E, Probucol, statins, and several other drugs in the pharmaceutical industry.
  o *Quaternary Free Radical Attack.* Difficult to attenuate and can't be prevented by all the above three sources of antioxidants. In general, quaternary free radical attack is associated with degenerative and pro-inflammatory apoptosis to cause chronic MDR diseases.

- *Inveterate Smokers.* Smokers who either cannot quit, or who don't want to quit.
- *Nicotine Replacement Therapy (NRT).* This term is generally used to describe pharmaceutical nicotine products. Even though the term is popular, we avoid it because it is confusing. The term comes from the use of nicotine patches, gum, and other products for helping smokers quit using nicotine entirely. Because we are interested in exploring the use of long-term substitutes for smoking for those who

cannot quit using nicotine, we find the term distracting. The word "therapy" suggests physicians and medicine and other unpleasantness, and is not a good way to describe something people might want to use. It implies that nicotine users have a disease that needs to be treated. We try to focus on low risk alternatives that smokers might voluntarily switch to, rather than treating smokers. Replacement therapy usually refers to medical interventions. The products are manufactured primarily by pharmaceutical companies, involving marketing, profits, research funding, regulation, and other political and economic issues. Hence, more accurate and descriptive term, could be "pharmaceutical nicotine products."

- *Nicotonism:* Nicotine addiction associated with physical tolerance and dependence.
- *Pharmaceutical Nicotine Products.* A variety of medical devices that provide nicotine, such as nicotine patches and gum, which are available without a prescription in many places, as well as inhalers, nasal sprays, topical gels, and lozenges. These products, designed primarily to help wean smokers off of nicotine entirely, are usually called NRT, though the term is misleading. Sometimes these are described as reduced-harm substitute for smoking.
- *Quit or Die.* Harm reduction advocates characterize the anti-tobacco-harm-reduction position this way. The usual messages to smokers are that smoking kills, and the only way to avoid this risk is to quit using nicotine entirely - there are no other choices, including: switching products, cutting back, or anything else. This simplification seems a bit harsh. Often anti-tobacco and anti-harm-reduction advocates come close to saying exactly this.
- *Snus.* It is a Swedish word for moist snuff, a product that is popular there than anywhere else in this world. Because the term "smokeless tobacco" is awkward and the word "snuff" is not very appealing (and makes it sound like you inhale the product), some companies call their moist snuff products "snus." Some North American anti-smokeless-tobacco advocates have suggested that the Swedish product is different from the U.S. products. It remains unknown that whether the health risks are different.
- *Stages of Free Radical Attack.* There are primarily 4 different stages of free radical attacks:

    - *Primary free radical attack,*
    - *Secondary free radical attack,*
    - *Tertiary free radial attack*, and
    - *Quaternary free radical attack.*

- *Vaping.* Heating the nicotine solution electronically rather than conventional burning (incineration) of tobacco in conventional cigarettes.

About the Author

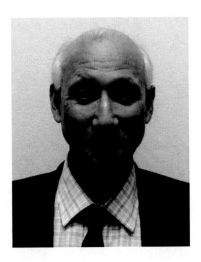

Sushil Sharma, PhD, DMRIT
Academic Dean of the American International School of Medicine,
Georgetown, Guyana (South America)
US Corporate Headquarters
Georgia, USA
Email: Sharmabharmar@gmail.com

Sushil Sharma is Academic Dean of the American International School of Medicine, Georgetown, Guyana (South America). He was serving as Professor of Pharmacology & Course Director at the Saint James School of Medicine, St Vincent & Grenadines, West Indies. Before joining this school, he served as a Professor of Pharmacology & Course Director at the Saint James School of Medicine, Bonaire, Dutch Caribbean, Netherland Antilles for four years. He served as a Scientist at the University of Texas Health

Sciences Center, Department of Neurology, at Houston, TX as a Research Scientist, and as an Associate Professor and Director at the Cyclotron and PET-RPs laboratory of the Weil Cornell University affiliated Methodist Hospital, Houston. He also served as an Associated Professor and Director at the University of North Dakota, Center of Excellence in Neuroscience, Grand Forks in the Cyclotron and Positron Imaging Research Laboratory for 5 years and as an Assistant Professor in the Department of Pharmacology, Physiology, and Therapeutics, Grand Forks, ND for 4 years. He was invited to deliver a lecture on "DAergic Neurotransmission in Drug Addiction" in the Office of National Drug Control Policy (ONDCP), Executive Office of the President, and Washington DC on April 29, 2004. He received several advanced trainings on the synthesis and quality control of PET-RPs from Siemens Medical Solutions, Cardinal Health, EBCO, Agilent Technologies, and General Electrics, USA. He served as a Research scientist at the Saint Boniface Hospital Research Center, Department of Cardiovascular Pharmacology in Winnipeg, Canada and worked on the therapeutic potential of 5-HT2A receptor antagonist (Sarpogrelate) and angiotensin-2 receptor antagonist, Losartan on hypertension, atherosclerosis, vascular neointimal hyperplasia, and cardiovascular remodeling for 2.5 years. Dr. Sharma was selected as a Scientist-E (Deputy Director) in the Defense Institute of Physiology and Allied Sciences, New Delhi in 1997.

Dr. Sharma served as a Senior Scientist in the Clinical Research Institute of Montreal in the Peptide Pharmacology laboratory and in the McGill University on pain mechanisms and analgesia for 2 years. As a Research Officer in the University of Montreal, Andre Viallet Clinical Research Center, Hospital St Luc in Montreal for one year, he studied the deleterious effects of Vitamin-D Deficiency and Hypocalcemia in experimental animals. He served 6 years as a Research Associate in the Department of Biochemistry and Molecular Biology on the Neuropharmacology of Vitamin B_6 and published several research papers on the influence of Vitamin B_6 deficiency and excess on the developing adult rat brain and in human cultured cell lines. He was awarded Manitoba Health Research Council Post-Doctoral Fellowship for 2 years. The primary goal of this study was to determine the precise role of Vitamin B_6 (Pyridoxine) as a coenzyme in GABA-ergic, DAergic, and serotonergic neurotransmission and seizure susceptibility in the developing and adult brain. This research was extended to examine the deleterious effects of environmental neurotoxins including: picrotoxin, and pentylene tetrazole on pyridoxine-deficient adult rats. Dr. Sharma discovered that Kainic Acid, and Domoic Acid induce excito-neurotoxicity and selective neurodegeneration in the hippocampal CA-3 and dentate gyrus regions and loss of memory, as observed in AD patients. Brain regional GABA as well as serotonin were significantly reduced in pyridoxine-deficient rats as observed in patients suffering from depression and seizures. Domoic acid-induced seizure discharge activity and thresholds were significantly reduced in pyridoxine-deficient rats and they exhibited seizure discharge activity of prolonged duration and delayed spontaneous or drug-induced neuronal recovery; as confirmed by computerized EEG analysis. He discovered that a specific 5-HT_{1A} agonist, 8-OH-DPAT suppresses, whereas the antagonist, spiroxatrine augments domoic acid-induced seizures in adult rats. Dr. Sharma was awarded Royal Society Fellowship in the University of Sheffield U.K in 1988.

As a Scientific Officer at the All India Institute of Medical Sciences (A.I.I.M.S), New Delhi, he conducted his doctoral research on the neuropharmacology of the antiepileptic drugs in the developing normal and undernourished rats under the worthy guidance of late Emeritus Professor, Dr. Baldev Singh (Father Neuron). He served at the A.I.I.M.S, New Delhi for 10 Years where he discovered that protein undernourished developing postnatal rats are highly susceptible to Kainate neurotoxicity, and exhibit electro cortical inhibition of prolonged duration, in response to relatively reduced doses of KA as compared to their normal litter mates. He was selected at the Bio-medical group of the Bhabha Atomic Research Center (BARC), Bombay to receive training on the synthesis of clinical radiopharmaceuticals (RPs) for personalized treatment of cancer, cardiovascular diseases, and neurodegenerative diseases. He received postgraduate diploma in Medical Radiopharmaceutical Technology (D.M.R.I.T) from the Bombay University and later on served as a research fellow in the Medical Radiopharmaceutical laboratory at the Postgraduate Institute of Medical Education and Research, Chandigarh (India).

Dr. Sharma has throughout first class academic career in his master and undergraduate studies in Biophysics from the Panjab University Basic Medical School, Chandigarh. He was invited to serve as a scientific consultant, chairperson, and speaker in numerous international congresses. He is the recipient of five Gold Medals. He was awarded E. Merck (German) Gold Medal for the best doctoral research, and a Gold Medal for his significant contributions in cardiovascular research on the basic molecular mechanism of vascular neointimal hyperplasia and the therapeutic potential of a specific 5-HT_{2A} receptor antagonist, sarpogrelate in the World Heart Congress, Winnipeg, Canada in July 2001. He organized 5 international conferences and has more than 262 publications including 120 research abstracts, published in the international journals of high impact factor.

Dr. Sharma invented an electro-micro-injector for which he was invited in the Invention and Innovation session of the 3rd world congress of Nuclear Medicine and Biology in Paris, France in Sep 1982. As a doctoral student, he discovered Charnoly Body (CB) in the developing undernourished Purkinje neurons for which he was invited as a Chairperson in the 13th World Congress of Neurology, Hamburg, Germany in Sep 1985, and as a Guest Speaker in the International Conference of Biometeorology in Calgary, Canada in Sep 1993. Recently he was invited in the first and IInd International Translational Conferences on Nanomedicine in Boston, to deliver a lecture on CB as a Sensitive Biomarker in Nanomedicine, and was awarded the Certificate of Honor for his excellent research in drug addiction, and other progressive neurological and neurodegenerative disorders in July 2015 in the 4th International Conference on Drug Addiction & Therapy, in Orlando, Florida, U.S.A. Dr. Sharma was also invited as an international scientific consultant, chairperson, and invited speaker to deliver lectures in the area of his expertise in several biomedical institutes in India, China, Canada, and U.S.A.

Dr. Sharma conducted studies on the mitochondrial genome knock out (RhO_{mgko}) human DAergic neurons as an experimental model of aging to authenticate that the mitochondrial bioenergetics is severely compromised in progressive neurodegenerative disorders and aging. Hence agents including monoamine oxidase inhibitors (MAOIs), that inhibit CB formation and antioxidants derived from the natural sources, may provide better therapeutic strategies for the clinical management of ZIKV disease, depression, Parkinson's disease, epilepsy, Alzheimer's disease, and other diseases. Recently, he reported that cysteine-rich, Zn^{2+}-binding proteins metallothioneins (MTs) prevent CB formation, enhance chranolophagy, and eliminate structurally-labile charnolosome by energy-driven exocytosis as a basic molecular mechanism of intracellular detoxification and sanitation; by serving as free potent radical scavengers. MTs are induced in severe nutritional stress, infections (i.e., ZIKV), and following exposure to toxic environmental neurotoxins including; nanoparticles. CB formation occurs in the developing undernourished rats or in response to neurotoxins such as: kainic acid, domoic acid, and acromelic acid in the sea foods, and in wild mushrooms, respectively. Although MTs have been implicated in PD, AD, and depression; their exact pathophysiological significance in the etiopathogenesis of these progressive neurodegenerative disorders is yet to be established. Whether depression augments brain regional CB formation to compromise the mitochondrial bioenergetics and MTs inhibit CB formation in depression, remains unknown. He proposed that hippocampal neurodegeneration due to MTs down-regulation and free radicals-mediated CB formation triggers depression and progressive neurodegenerative disorders, such as PD, AD, and drug addiction. Recently, Dr. Sharma proposed three types of nanoparticles including (a) Protective, (b) Neutral, and (c) Toxic. Protective nanoparticles inhibit CB formation and augment charnolophagy; neutral nanoparticles do not exert any influence on the cell; whereas toxic nanoparticles induce CB formation, inhibit charnolophagy, and destabilize charnolosome to trigger progressive apoptotic degeneration. Hence, CB can be utilized as novel disease-specific biomarker in nanomedicine.

Dr. Sharma serves as an expert reviewer, editor, and consultant for several international journals of high impact factor. He also serves as an expert reviewer for the evaluation of research grants including Michael Smith Foundation in Vancouver (Canada), New Zeeland Neurological Society, and The University of Leuven, Belgium. He has guided several MD and Ph. D students. He developed several genetically-engineered mouse models of drug addiction, drug rehabilitation and genetic resistance including: α-Syn metallothionein triple knockout (α-Syn-MT_{tko}) mice, metallothioneins over-expressing weaver mutant mice (wv/wv-MTs) mice and a sensitive method of Coenzyme Q_{10} estimation from rare biological samples. He discovered α-Syn Index (SI) which can be utilized as an early and sensitive biomarker of progressive neurodegenerative α-synucleinopathies and proposed the role of CB in various neurodegenerative disorders including PD, AD, drug addiction, depression, cardiovascular diseases, cancer, fetal alcohol spectrum disorder (FASD), and in ZIKV disease. His recent research articles on "Effect of Tryptophan-Rich Diet on Depression" and "Biomarkers in Parkinson's disease," were published in the journal "Neurochemistry International," "Biomarkers in Alzheimer's Disease" (Recent Update) was published in the journal "Current Alzheimer Research," and PET Radiopharmaceuticals in Personalized Medicine" in "Current Drug Targets."

Dr. Sharma studied the effect of environmental neurotoxins including Kainic Acid and Domoic Acid, which induce dementia as a consequence of selective loss of hippocampal CA-3 and dentate gyrus neurons. He proposed that the neuroprotective drugs could be targeted to specifically inhibit CB formation in the CNS, as their accumulation at the junction of the axon hillock may block axoplasmic flow of various enzymes, neurotransmitters, ions, and mitochondria at the synaptic terminals to hinder normal neurotransmission, as observed in PD, AD, HD, ALS, MS, diabetic neuropathy, and several other neurodegenerative disorders including treatment resistant depression and ZIKV disease, which may result in early morbidity and mortality. Hence, drugs may be developed to induce cancer stem cell specific CB formation in order to treat multidrug-resistant malignancies, and prevent CB formation in NPCs in microbial (ZIKV) infections. Nonspecific CB formation causes GIT symptoms, myelosuppression, and alopecia in multi-drug-resistant malignancies. Hence drugs may be targeted to specifically induce cancer stem cell-specific CB formation to prevent undesirable adverse effects and accomplish maximum therapeutic benefits. Based on the specific brain regional localization of MAO-A and MAO-B on the mitochondrial membranes, Dr. Sharma proposed MA0-A and MAO-B specific CB formation in progressive neurobehavioral and neurodegenerative disorders. Hence, novel drugs may be developed to specifically target either MAO-A and/or MAO-B–specific CB formation, for the effective treatment of PD, AD, drug addiction, ADHD, schizophrenia, multiple drug-resistant depression, and ZIKV embryopathies.

Dr. Sharma has several publications on the neuroprotective role of coenzyme Q_{10}, Zinc, and MTs in cultured human DAergic (SK-N-SH) neurons *in vitro* and genetically modified α-Syn and MTs mouse models of neurodegeneration such as PD, AD, and drug addiction *in vivo*. Recently, therapeutic potential of Serotonin, Coenzyme Q_{10}, Zn^{2+}, and Vitamin B_6 has gained popularity as antidepressant agents. These neuroprotective agents can be derived from several dietary sources as discussed in one of his book entitled "Beyond Diet & Depression by Nova Science Polishers, New York, U.S.A. The diet rich in these important nutraceuticals may have great promise as compared to conventionally-prescribed antidepressants with serious adverse effects including anorexia, weight loss, and osteoporosis in young adolescent women, who are at increased risk of developing depression as compared to men. Effective treatment of PD, AD, drug addiction, and major depression requiring specific MAOIs such as Selegiline, Rasagiline, Moclobemide, Safinamide, Lazabemide, and multifunctional Ladostigil, has been described in greater detail in his recently published book entitled "Monoamine Oxidase Inhibitors: Clinical Pharmacology, Therapeutic Application, & Adverse Effects by Nova Science Publishers, New York, U.S.A. His researches on mitochondrial genome knock out (RhO_{mgko}) human DAergic neurons and on homozygous weaver (wv/wv) mutant mice demonstrated that MTs and CoQ_{10} are clinically important for drug addicts as well as in aging subjects, who suffer frequently from major depression and suicidal ideation. Dr. Sharma reported that MAOIs, including Selegiline and Rasagiline augment MTs to prevent CB formation, implicated in progressive neurological and neurodegenerative disorders; such as PD, AD, drug addiction, and depression.

Dr. Sharma was invited in several international conferences, symposia, and workshops across the globe as a scientific consultant, chairperson, and an invited speaker. Recently, he published series of articles on fetal alcohol syndrome (FAS) and presented his original research findings at the Harvard Medical School, Boston and in the 4th International Conference of Drug Addiction and Therapy in Orlando, Florida, Aug 2-5, 2015, where he was invited to deliver a keynote lecture on "Charnoly Body as a Novel Biomarker in Drug Addiction." This lecture can be retrieved from Google.com. In addition, author's three intimately related invited lectures can be retrieved from Google website. In addition to his 8 books, the author has written 3 chapters on the Biomarkers of Fetal Alcohol Syndrome published by Nova Science Publishers and Elsevier Science Publishers. He has also published the following chapter in his recent book "Personalized Medicine (Beyond PET Biomarkers) Nova Science Publishers. New York. U.S.A. "Biomarkers in Personalized Theranostics of Fetal Alcohol Syndrome. Chapter-8, pp. 183-215. In his earlier research, he studied the deleterious effect of intrauterine exposure of "Kainic acid and Domoic acid on the developing hippocampal CA-3 and dentate gyrus regions of the mouse progeny and discovered that these glutamate analogs can induce apoptosis by CB formation as noticed in chronic Alcoholism and Alzheimer's disease (AD) patients (Dakshinamurti et al 1993; Sharma and Dakshinamurti 1992).

Recently Dr. Sharma introduced following books entitled "Beyond Diet and Depression" (2014) (Volume-1 and Volume-2) and "Alleviating Stress of the Soldier and Civilian" (2015), and Therapeutic Potential of Monoamine Oxidase Inhibitors," Personalized Medicine (Beyond PET Biomarkers, Progress in PET Radiopharmaceuticals (Quality Control & Theranostics)", Zika Virus Disease (Prevention and Cure)" released by Nova Science Publishers, New York. He was invited to present a lecture on "Charnoly Body as a Novel Biomarker of ZIKV-Induced Microcephaly" in the Drug Discovery & Therapy World Congress, in Boston in Aug 21-25, 2016 and to deliver a lecture on

"Charnoly Body as a Novel Biomarker of Nutritional Stress in Alzheimer's Disease" in Sep 22-23, 2016 at the Harvard Medical School, Boston, Massachusetts, U.S.A. The information provided in his books provides updated knowledge and wisdom regarding mitochondrial bioenergetics, CB formation, charnolophagy, and charnolosome exocytosis as a basic molecular, mechanism of intracellular detoxification, charnolosome stabilization, and CB sequestration inhibitors; as novel biomarkers for the diagnosis as well as novel targets for drug therapy and vaccine development for a better quality of life to enjoy healthy aging.

In this book Dr. Sharma has described the neuroprotective role of antioxidants such as MTs and glutathione (G-SH) as potent free radical scavengers to prevent/inhibit organ and disease-specific CB formation, augment charnolophagy to restore intracellular detoxification, inhibit CB sequestration and stabilize charnolosome by regulating Zinc-mediated transcriptional activation of metallothioneins (MTs) and other genes involved in growth, proliferation, differentiation, and development to eventually overcome "tobacco smoking-induced charnolopathies" at an earlier stage in the most vulnerable spermatocytes, oocytes, neural progenitor cells, cardiac progenitor cells (derived from induced pluripotent cells), osteoblasts, and other cells for therapeutic and prophylactic interventions against nicotinism and other related diseases.

Index

α

α2-adrenoceptor agonist, 17
α3-containing nAChRs, 6
α4β2 and α7 homomeric nAChRs, 226
α5-α3-β4 nAChR cluster, 222
α7 homomeric nAChRs, 17
α7 nAChR antagonist, 18
α7-containing nicotinic acetylcholine receptors (nAChRs), 3, 4, 5, 6, 7, 8, 10, 13, 16, 17, 19, 23, 67, 68, 70, 74, 99, 100, 107, 108, 113, 171, 217, 222, 226, 227
α7-nAChR subunit inhibitor, 113
α7nicotnic receptors (α7 nAChRs), 6, 8, 13, 18, 217
α7β2 nicotinic acetylcholine receptor, 206
α-amino-3-hydroxy-5-methyl-4-isoxazole proprionic/kainate receptors, 18
α-amylase, 142, 181
α-BT, 113
α-syn index (SI), xxxix, 242
α-syn metallothionein triple knockout (α-Syn-MT$_{tko}$) mice, 242
α-synuclein, 243

β

β-amyloid, 150

γ

γ-glutamyltranspeptidase and nitric oxide, 161
γ-vinyl GABA (Vigabatrin), 10

Δ

Δ^9-Tetrahydrocannabinol (Δ^{9}THC), 222

#

2, 3-dihydroxy Nonenal, 237
2015 ecstasy and related drugs reporting system (EDRS), xxxvi, 75
2dG, 94, 132
2-electrode voltage-clamp, 99
2-methyl-6-(phenyl-ethynyl)pyridine (MPEP), 9, 38
3-dioxygenase, 141
4-(methylnitrosamino)-1-(3-pyridyl)-1-butanone [NNK], xxxviii, 102, 140, 168, 171, 190, 191
5 tobacco bHLH proteins (NtbHLH), 208
5-HT, xxi, 13, 17, 21, 24, 37, 39, 70, 240, 241
5HT$_{1A}$ receptor antagonists, 21
5-HT-ergic dorsal raphe neurons, 13
636 pilot DNA samples, 120
6-hydroxy-l-nicotine (6HLN), 150, 169, 196
7-ethyl-10-hydroxycamptothecin (SN-38), 112
8-hydroxy-2'-deoxy-guanosine (8-OH 2dG), 93, 94, 237
8-hydroxy-2-dipropylaminotetralin (8-OH-DPAT), 21, 240
8-isoprostanes, 192
8-oxo-7,8-dihydro-2'-deoxyguanosine (8-oxodGuo), 184
8-oxo-7,8-dihydroguanine (8-oxoGua), 184

A

aberrant epigenetic mechanisms, 210
abortion, ix, 228
abuse, v, xviii, xix, xx, xxix, xxxv, xxxvi, xxxvii, xxxviii, 6, 7, 11, 15, 16, 19, 26, 27, 33, 34, 35, 45, 47, 48, 49, 51, 52, 53, 54, 56, 57, 67, 68, 69, 72, 73, 74, 81, 82, 83, 85, 86, 89, 130, 133, 142, 144, 145, 149, 199, 206, 220, 222, 224, 225, 226, 227, 228, 233
acetaldehyde, 130, 132, 134, 237
acetate, 136, 162
acetylcholine, xxxviii, 3, 5, 7, 23, 24, 26, 31, 32, 33, 34, 35, 36, 38, 39, 40, 41, 42, 64, 67, 68, 69, 98, 99, 105, 107, 110, 116, 150, 170, 171, 197, 199, 205, 217, 222, 223
acetylcholine nicotinic receptors, 67, 68
acetylcholinesterase, 109, 110
acetylcholinesterase activities, 109
acromelic acid, 242
acrylonitrile, 167
acute kidney injury (AKI), 93, 94, 96, 105, 125, 126, 138, 144, 198
acute kidney injury (AKI) diagnosis, 97, 138
acute thrombotic events, 183
addiction, ix, xx, xxi, xxii, xxiii, xxvii, 3, 4, 19, 21, 25, 28, 34, 36, 46, 47, 61, 64, 67, 68, 69, 70, 73, 81, 85, 86, 90, 98, 101, 111, 117, 119, 120, 122, 130, 131, 149, 179, 201, 210, 225, 226, 235, 244
addiction-related genes, 98
AD-ND co-dependence, 98
adolescent population, xxxii, 67, 68, 69, 225, 228
Adrianycin, 112
affective and somatic withdrawal effects, 18, 227
affective disorder, xix
African American smokers, 93, 94, 95, 98, 104, 122
age, xviii, xix, xx, xxi, xxvii, 4, 21, 50, 51, 54, 58, 59, 69, 76, 78, 87, 91, 95, 97, 98, 115, 116, 119, 127, 138, 156, 157, 170, 177, 178, 182, 184, 189, 190, 210, 211, 215, 217, 226
agitation, 220
Agmatine, 124, 149, 154
AgNOR down-regulation, 133
alanine aminotransferase, 128
albumin, 170
alcohol, ix, xii, xx, xxi, xxiii, xxvii, xxix, xxxv, 11, 21, 23, 25, 26, 29, 33, 35, 45, 47, 49, 52, 53, 54, 57, 62, 65, 67, 68, 69, 70, 71, 81, 83, 89, 93, 94, 98, 101, 105, 119, 122, 139, 143, 144, 145, 150, 176, 186, 187, 195, 199, 200, 202, 203, 205, 206, 207, 209, 210, 218, 222, 223, 224, 244
alcohol abuse, 45, 47, 53, 54, 57, 139, 186
alcohol and nicotine codependence, 93, 94, 105, 203
alcohol use, xxiii, 89, 101, 119, 186, 187, 209, 218
Alcohol Use Disorder and Associated Disabilities Interview Schedule-DSM-IV Version (AUDADIS-IV), 54, 71
alcohol use disorders (AUDs) and substance use disorders (SUDs), 209
alcoholism, xxi, 23, 25, 27, 29, 46, 47, 57, 62, 182, 228
alkaline phosphatase (ALP), 107, 108, 112, 113, 118, 121, 122
alopecia, 116, 243
alsouric acid, 115
alternative nicotine delivery systems (ANDS), xxxv, 150, 173, 200
Alzheimer's disease (AD), xxxv, 54, 85, 86, 87, 98, 150, 169, 178, 191, 240, 242, 243, 244
AM404, 65, 67, 68, 69, 71
American Heart Association recommendations for CV health, 58
aminoacyl-t-RNA biosynthesis, 97, 138
Amitraz, 97, 138
ammonia, 130, 132, 134, 136, 179, 237
amniotic fluid, 126, 143, 193, 196, 197
amphetamine(s), xix, xxix, 16, 31, 34, 38, 39, 40, 187
amygdala and insula, 139
anabasine and anatabine, 55, 102, 104, 130, 150, 185, 186, 188, 202, 203
analysis, ix, xxxii, xxxv, xxxviii, xxxix, 13, 49, 54, 56, 80, 82, 84, 89, 97, 102, 105, 108, 113, 114, 118, 119, 121, 123, 127, 138, 140, 141, 149, 157, 160, 162, 163, 166, 175, 176, 181, 182, 185, 187, 188, 192, 194, 199, 203, 210, 211, 214, 219, 240
anandamide transport inhibitor, 65, 67, 68, 69, 71
anandamide transport inhibitor VDM11, 71
ancestry-specific genome-wide association scans (GWAS), xxxvi, 108, 119, 177, 188, 222
anger, xxiii, 152
anhedonia, 15, 36
ANK3 gene, 150
antagonist/inverse agonist Rimonabant, 72
anti-apoptotic, 136
antiapoptotic and anti-inflammatory factors, 136
anti-CD 14 antibodies, 183

anti-CD 41 antibodies, 183
anti-CD38-positive type 2 diabetes, 116
antidiabetics and Sirolimus/Rapamycin, 178
antigen-presenting cells (APCs), 111
anti-inflammatory, 136
antimicrobial photodynamic therapy (aPDT), 149, 151, 155, 195
antioxidant proteins, 134, 137
antioxidants, 136, 161, 237, 242, 245
antipsychotic drugs, 22
antiretroviral therapy (ART), 67, 68, 69, 79, 83
antisocial personality disorder, 71
anxiety, xi, xx, xxiv, xxvi, 17, 25, 45, 47, 53, 54, 62, 70, 79, 151, 192, 195, 205
aortic endothelial cells, 113, 121
Apocynin, 214, 223
APOE carrier(s), 85, 86
apolipoprotein B100 and oxidized low-density lipoprotein, 174
apoptosis, xi, 70, 96, 125, 130, 132, 133, 136, 139, 143, 154, 196, 235, 244
apoptosis in the rat testes, 140
apoptosis inducing factor, 130
apoptotic body(ies), 131, 132, 235, 236
apoptotic degeneration, 134, 242
apoptotic neurodegeneration, 136
arachidonic acid, 132, 136, 237
arginase-1 (Arg-1) expression, 169
argon plasma torch, 136
argyrophilic nucleolar organizer (AgNOR), xi, xxxii, 129, 132, 134
argyrophilic nucleolar organizer region (AgNOR), xi, xxxii, 125, 126, 129, 132, 133, 134, 137, 144, 197
aromatase, 206, 207
aromatic hydrocarbon receptor, 207, 222
aromatic hydrocarbon receptor pathway, 207
arsenic, xxi, 46
ART adherence, 79
as well as nicotine and cotinine, 168
association for the treatment of tobacco use and dependence (ATTUD), xxxv, 60, 62
asthma, ix, 45, 46, 47, 51, 66, 150, 184, 202, 228
atherosclerosis, 107, 108, 111, 113, 195, 199, 240
atherosclerotic lesions, 111, 121
atherosclerotic plaque, 111
atmospheric pressure solid analysis probe (ASAP), 93, 94, 102, 105, 123
atomization, 136

attention-deficit hyperactivity disorder (ADHD), ix, 53, 228, 243
attention-deficit-type problems, xxvi
auditory P50 gating, 23
auditory-verbal learning, 87
autism, ix, 228
Auxin-responsive protein, 208
axial diffusivity (AD), xxxv, 54, 85, 86, 87, 98, 150, 169, 178, 191, 240, 242, 243, 244
axonal pathfinding, 110
Aβ-induced microglial activation, 169

B

Baclofen, 10, 23, 27, 29, 35, 38, 41
Baclofen or CGP44532 [(3-Amino-2[S]-hydroxypropyl)-methylphosphinic Acid], 10
bad dreams, xxiv
bax and bak, 130, 136, 154
bax and transforming growth factor beta (TGF-β1), 154
BCl_2, 132, 134, 138
BDNF release, 169
behavioral therapy, 69
benzene, 150, 167, 183, 202
benzo[a]pyrene, 190
benzodiazepines, 176
benzoylecgonine, 187
Bergapten, 85, 90, 91
biological antioxidant potential (BAP), 115
biomarkers of exposure (BioExp), 104, 123, 128, 140, 149, 156, 157, 158, 159, 165, 174, 193, 198, 199, 201, 209
biomarkers of inflammation, 102, 172, 185
biomarkers of oxidative stress, 96, 115, 169, 195
biomarkers of tobacco smoke exposure, 99, 151, 203
bipolar disorder(s) (BD), xxix, 71, 74, 75, 150, 151, 182
bisexual populations, 88
body mass index (BMI), xxxv, 45, 47, 53, 57, 65, 99, 102, 119, 170
body weight gain, 139, 205, 213
body weight reduction, 206
brief Wisconsin inventory of dependence motives, 80
broad-spectrum nuclear magnetic resonance (NMR), xxxviii, 95, 97, 99, 119, 138, 143, 179
bronchitis, 45, 46

Bupropion, 13, 14, 16, 20, 22, 25, 26, 29, 33, 35, 37, 41, 74, 78, 164, 206, 207, 216, 219, 227
Bupropion sustained-release (SR), xxxix, 74, 88
Buspirone, 21, 32, 40, 42

C

cadmium, 46, 174
caffeic acid, 162
caffeine, xxiii, xxvi, 149, 159, 198
caffeine or Ritalin, xxvi
calmodulin-dependent protein kinases, 19
Calreticulin, 208
cancer, ix, xvii, xxiv, xxv, xxxvi, xxxvii, xxxviii, 46, 50, 59, 60, 63, 64, 65, 69, 70, 76, 97, 102, 105, 107, 108, 110, 114, 115, 122, 123, 134, 136, 140, 150, 152, 159, 168, 190, 191, 196, 199, 200, 201, 203, 210, 222, 223, 228, 232, 241, 243
cancer stem cell specific CB formation, 243
cancer stem cell-specific charnolosomes (CScsc), 107, 108, 115
cancer stem cell-specific charnolosomes (CScsc) destabilization, 107, 108
cancer stem cell-specific charnolosomes (CSscs), 116
cancers of the mouth, 152
cannabidiol (CBD) and cannibinol, 222
cannabinoid CB2 receptor, 169
cannabinoids, 72, 206, 207, 222, 223
cannabinoids (Δ (9)-tetrahydrocannabinol (THC) or anandamide) or cocaine, 72
cannabinoids interactions, 206, 207
cannabis, xxxv, 45, 47, 53, 54, 62, 65, 150, 175, 176, 187, 200, 222
cannabis abuse, 45, 47, 53, 54
canonical TRPC (a calcium transport channel) protein, 237
capillary electrophoresis, 228
carbohydrate intake, 77
carbon monoxide (CO), xxxvi, 46, 50, 78, 88, 99, 110, 128, 142, 150, 156, 160, 164, 166, 167, 173, 180, 189, 192, 194, 201, 209, 237
carbon monoxide (CO) reading, 50
carbon-heated tobacco, 149, 159
carcinogenic potential, 151
cardiac progenitor cells, xi, 130, 245
cardiovascular disease(s), xi, 74, 102, 114, 115, 128, 152, 154, 206, 228, 241, 243

cardiovascular health issues, 46, 47
caspase, 130, 207
catalase, xxxii, 132, 134, 138, 237
cataracts and ocular problems, 152
catchsin, 237
catecholamines, 31, 141
CB formation, xi, xxxi, xxxii, 93, 94, 96, 108, 116, 129, 133, 136, 206, 237, 242, 243, 244, 245
CB formation and CS sequestration, 129
CB sequestration, 245
CB sequestration inhibitors, 245
CBT interventions, 216
CBT/contextual CBT intervention, 216
CD38 autoimmunity, 107, 108, 109, 117, 122
CD38 knockout mice, 117
cDNA-AFLP biotechnology, 151
cDNA-amplified fragment length polymorphism (AFLP), 193
cell-mediated immunity, 182
cellular oxidative stress, 96
cervix, 152
cessation attempts, 85, 86, 88
cessation failure, 143
cessation pharmacotherapy, 142, 212
cessation pharmacotherapy effectiveness, 143
characteristics, xxxix, 51, 52, 58, 82, 83, 88, 119, 120, 126, 134, 150, 158, 178, 180, 181, 193, 194, 201, 215
charcoal, 46
charnolocidal, 235
charnologenetics, 235
charnolomimetic, 235
charnolophagosome (CPS), xxxvi, 129, 131, 133, 136, 236
charnolophagosome/charnolosome, 236
charnolophagy, xi, xxxi, xxxii, 93, 94, 96, 130, 131, 228, 236, 242, 245
charnolophagy agonists, 228
charnolopharmaceuticals, xxxix, 236
charnolopharmacogenomics, 236
charnolopharmacology, 236
charnolopharmacotherapeutics, ix, xxxii, 130, 228, 236
charnoloscopy, 236
charnolosome (CS), xi, xxxii, xxxvi, 4, 15, 93, 94, 96, 116, 129, 131, 132, 133, 134, 136, 137, 144, 206, 228, 235, 236, 242, 245
charnolosome (CS) Body (CS body), 129, 131, 132, 133, 134, 236

charnolosome (CS) destabilization, xi, 94, 133, 134
charnolosome (CS) exocytosis, 245
charnolosome (CS) stabilization, xxxii, 228, 245
charnolosome (CS) stabilizers, 228
charnolosome-metallothioneins (CS-MTs) interaction), 136
charnolostatic, 236
charnoly bodies (CBs), xi, xxxv, 94, 107, 129, 130, 131, 144, 145, 227, 228, 235, 236, 241, 244
charnoly bodies (CBs) epigenetics, 236
charnoly bodies (CBs) formation, xi, 107, 130, 228, 235, 236
charnoly body (CB) and mitochondrial bioenergetics-based charnolopharmacotherapeutics, 227
chemometric analysis, 184
chemotaxis of proinflammatory monocytes, 171
chewing tobacco, xxv, 151, 229
childhood abuse, 85, 86, 92
childhood parental loss, 54
childhood physical, v, 85, 86
chlorisondamine, 17, 150, 196
cholesterol, xxxvii, 161, 230, 237
cholesterol transport channel, 237
choline acetyltransferase, 42, 109, 110
cholinergic signaling, 98, 218
cholinergic synaptic impairment, 109
chranolophagy, 242
CHRNA4 and CHRNA5, 100
CHRNA5-A3-B4 gene cluster, 94, 189
CHRNA5-CHRNA3-CHRNB4 and CYP2A6-CYP2B6, 120
chromium (Cr), 128, 133, 135
chromosome 15q24-15q25.1, 222
chronic alcoholism, 244
chronic back pain, 46
chronic diseases, ix, 114, 128, 174, 176
chronic multidrug resistant malignancies, 46
chronic obstructive pulmonary diseases (COPD), ix, xvii, 45, 46, 47, 51, 64, 228
chronic pain, 45, 46, 47, 48
cigar smoking, xxv
cigarette exposure, 140
cigarette smoke condensate (CSC), 115, 205, 207, 208, 223
cigars, xxvii
circulating immunoglobulin, 93, 94
circulating monoamine precursors, 125, 126
Cisplatin, 112

Clonidine, 17, 30
Clozapine, 23, 30, 40
CNS infiltration of proinflammatory myeloid cells, 171
cocaine, xix, xxi, xxix, xxxv, 11, 16, 27, 28, 35, 36, 38, 39, 41, 45, 46, 47, 54, 55, 56, 65, 71, 123, 139, 143, 152, 153, 187
cocaine craving, 45, 47, 55
cocaine or heroin, 152
cochrane tobacco addiction group trials register (CRS), 163
Cochrane Tobacco Addiction Group's, 218
cockroaches in the home, 52, 184
Coenzyme Q_{10}, 242, 243
cognitive behavioral therapy(s) (CBT), xxxv, 54, 216, 227
cognitive decline, 45, 47, 64, 115
colorimetric assay, 221
competitive nAChR antagonist DHβE, 7
compromised mitochondrial bioenergetics, xi, 130, 236
conditioned place preference, 10, 11, 12
conduct disorder, xix
connexin 43 and erythropoietin (EPO), 161
convergent functional genomics (CFG), 177
CO-oximetry, 150, 173, 174, 201
coronary heart disease, 202
correlative and combinatorial bioinformatic, ix
cortical amyloid deposition, 86, 87
Cortisol, 23, 142
Cotinine (COT), 37, 60, 63, 93, 94, 95, 97, 99, 102, 103, 104, 105, 110, 122, 123, 125, 126, 127, 128, 142, 144, 151, 157, 160, 162, 164, 166, 167, 168, 173, 176, 179, 181, 183, 186, 187, 188, 189, 191, 192, 194, 197, 199, 203, 206, 207, 209, 221, 224
Cotinine glucuronidation, 105, 199
Coumarin, 85, 90
Coumarin derivatives, 85
Coumarin Umbelliferone, 85, 90
counseling with care coordination (CCC), 212
CPS induction and CS destabilization and disintegration., 136
crack/cocaine, 45, 47, 56, 64, 149, 153, 198
crack/cocaine-exposed newborn infants, 45, 47
craniofacial abnormalities, ix, 228
crash, xxi
craving, xxi, xxiv, xxvi, 4, 11, 19, 23, 25, 35, 36, 41, 49, 54, 63, 65, 67, 68, 69, 72, 73, 80, 101, 145, 173, 175, 228, 235

C-reactive protein (CRP), 102, 155, 170
CS bodies, 129, 131, 132, 133, 134
CS budding, 129
CS destabilization, 93, 94, 96, 131, 133, 206
CS exocytosis enhancers, 228
CS stabilization, 133
CS-induced AgNOR down-regulation, 130
cutting back, 238
cyanide (-CN), 46
cyclic adenosine monophosphate–response element binding protein (CREB), 19, 38
Cyclosporin A, 112
CYP1A1 mRNA, 207
CYP1B1, 207
CYP2A6, 40, 85, 90, 93, 94, 95, 97, 99, 100, 104, 111, 119, 121, 122, 123, 151, 179, 191, 222
CYP2A6 activity, 95, 99, 120, 151, 191
CYP2A6 alleles, 97
CYP2A6 and 5HTT and SNPs in the CHRNA5/A3/B4 gene cluster, 93, 94, 100
CYP2A6 and CYP2A7, 120
CYP2A6 diplotype predicted rate [CDPR], 95
CYP2A6 enzyme activity, 179
CYP2A6 genetic polymorphisms, 191
CYP2A6 genotype, 40, 95, 191
CYP2A6 inhibitors, 85, 90
cysitine, 227
cytisine, 219
cytochrome C, 134
cytochrome P450 (CYP) 1A2, 222
cytochrome P450 2A6 (CYP2A6), 40, 85, 90, 93, 94, 95, 97, 99, 100, 104, 111, 119, 121, 122, 123, 151, 179, 191, 203, 222
cytochrome P450-(2A6), 93, 94
cytochrome-C, 130, 132, 136, 237
cytokine levels, 56, 154, 182
cytoplasmic caspase-3 immunostaining, 139

D

DA receptor antagonists, 8
DA receptors D2 and D4 (DRD2 and DRD4) and DA transporter (DAT) genes, 100
DAergic, xix, xxi, xxii, xxiii, xxxvi, 6, 7, 8, 9, 13, 16, 22, 30, 65, 67, 68, 69, 73, 226, 227, 240, 243
DAergic neurotransmission, xix, 16, 226, 227
d-Ala^2,N-Me-Phe^4-Gly-ol-enkephalin, 11
DArgic neurons, 68

DEA-NONOate, 214
decision making, 139
decision making feedback, 139
decreased renal mRNA expression levels of synaptopodin, 161
dehydroepiandrosterone, 142
dendritic cell-mediated adaptive immunity, 107, 108, 121
dependence, xix, xx, xxiii, xxvii, xxviii, xxix, xxxv, xxxvi, xl, 4, 5, 6, 12, 14, 16, 19, 20, 21, 22, 23, 24, 25, 26, 29, 32, 33, 34, 36, 41, 57, 58, 60, 63, 70, 71, 78, 79, 80, 82, 83, 86, 88, 90, 92, 93, 94, 95, 98, 100, 101, 109, 117, 119, 120, 122, 123, 125, 139, 142, 143, 144, 151, 156, 158, 167, 174, 175, 178, 180, 182, 192, 194, 199, 201, 206, 226, 227, 238
depression, xi, xii, xix, xx, xxiv, xl, 5, 14, 20, 21, 22, 23, 24, 25, 27, 30, 34, 36, 38, 41, 53, 58, 65, 70, 89, 90, 145, 150, 152, 170, 172, 182, 185, 192, 197, 202, 205, 226, 227, 240, 242, 243, 244
depression and schizophrenia, 227
depressive disorders, 57
de-sensitization, xxii
desire, xxi, xxii, 163
desmin, 161
detoxification, 131, 228
deuterium labeled substrates, 140
diabetes, ix, 107, 116, 122, 149, 152, 154, 161, 196, 228
diabetes (or insulin resistance), 152
diabetes mellitus (DM), 53, 161
diabetic nephropathy (DN), 161
diabetic neuropathy, 243
Dianicline, 218
Diazonium ions, 140
dichlorodiphenyltrichloroethane (DDT), 153
diffusion tensor imaging (DTI), 190
digital image analysis (DIA), 114
diode laser irradiation, 155
discrimination, 80, 89, 184
disease-specific biomarker, 242
disease-specific CB formation, 245
disease-specific-CB antagonists, 228
disease-specific-spatiotemporal (DSST) charnolosomics, ix
disintegration, 129, 136
distal to CYP2A6, 120
disturbed family environment, 54
diversified charnolopathies, xi, 207, 228

diversified embryopathies, ix
DNA and hemoglobin adducts, 140
DNA cell cycle, 132, 134, 135, 138
DNA methylation, 93, 94, 98, 105, 203, 210
DNA nucleotide sequence, 210
domoic acid, 240, 242, 243, 244
doxorubicin, 115
doxorubicin and mitoxantrone, 115
drowsiness, xxiv
drug abuse disorder (DAD), xxxvi, 54
drug addiction, x, xxi, xxii, xxiii, 57, 108, 109, 130, 241, 242, 243
drug rehabilitation, 242
Dubin-Johnson syndrome, 111
DβH genes, 100

E

early aging, 152
early morbidity and reduced life span, 205
e-cigarettes, xxiii, xxiv, xxv, xxvi, xxvii, xxxi, xxxii, xxxvi, 63, 65, 67, 68, 69, 75, 80, 84, 123, 143, 149, 151, 159, 164, 165, 166, 167, 173, 195, 200, 201, 202, 228, 231, 237
e-cigarettes users, 80, 160
ecological momentary assessment (EMA) trial, 72
education, xiii, xvii, xviii, xxi, xxxviii, 54, 58, 64, 79, 89, 91, 92, 127, 172, 185, 190, 225, 232, 241
eight volatile organic compounds (VOCs), xxxviii, xl, 167
Elafin, 46, 47, 51, 66, 150, 184, 202
electron transport chain, 129, 236, 237
electronically-heated cigarette smoking system, 164
ellagic acid (EA), 98, 107, 108, 112, 117
embryopathies, 228
emotional impulsivity, 125, 126
emphysema, ix, 45, 46, 152, 228
emphysema and respiratory infections, 152
endocannabinoid(s), 3, 4, 11, 17, 227
endocytosis, 107, 109, 116, 134, 236
endocytosis of CSscs, 134
endogenous opiates in nicotine addiction, 227
endonucleosis of CS bodies, 134
endothelial cells, 107, 108, 113, 114, 122, 162, 197
endothelial denudation, 214
endothelial dysfunction, 113, 151
endothelial function, 107, 108, 128
endothelial NO release, 214

enhance charnolophagy, 136
enhanced HIV replication, 207
eNOS and nNOS, 205, 206, 214, 223
environmental tobacco smoke (ETS), xxxvi, 211
enzyme-linked immunosorbent assay (ELISA), 155, 169
epigenetic mechanisms, 210
epigenetics, 210, 224
epilepsy, xxxv, 27, 242
epinephrine, 13, 151
ER stress, 73
E-selectin, 107, 108, 113, 121
E-selectin gene, 113
esophagus, 140, 152
estradiol and progesterone, 221
estrogen levels, 119
estrogen-like compounds, 178
ethanol, xix, xxix, 16, 39, 40, 129, 133, 134, 138, 162, 187, 220
ethylsulfate, 186
event-related potentials (ERP), 73
evidence-based behavioral strategies, 60
evidence-based cessation therapies, 212
evidence-based smoking-cessation interventions, 60
evidence-based treatments, 60
exocytosis, 131, 228, 236, 242
expanded disability status scale (EDSS), 170
experimental autoimmune encephalomyelitis (EAE), 170

F

Fagerström, xxxvi, 60, 61, 69, 79, 151, 156, 174, 191, 193, 194, 199, 216
Fagerström test of nicotine dependence (FTND), xxxvi, 61, 191, 193, 194, 199, 216
family history, 52, 54, 182, 184
family history of SUDs, 54
Family Smoking Prevention and Tobacco Control Act, 175
farnesyl pyrophosphate synthase 1, 208
fatty acid amide hydrolase (FAAH) inhibitor URB597, 72
feeling tense, xxiv
female smoking prevalence, 213
ferric reducing ability of plasma (FRAP), 115
ferritin, 170
ferulic acid, 163

fetal alcohol spectrum disorder (FASD), xi, 7, 144, 228, 243
fibromyalgia, 45, 46
fibroplasia, 161
fibrosis, 154
flavonoids, 237
flow cytometry, 183, 228
flow cytometry with sorting, 228
Fluoxetine, 21, 31, 35, 39
Folic acid and Vitamin B_{12}, 96
food addiction, 130
Food and Drug Administration (FDA), 22, 104, 123, 160, 165, 175, 180, 192, 213, 231
food intake, 11, 77, 205, 213
fractional anisotropy (FA), 190
fragmentation, 131
free radical overproduction, 129, 131, 236
free radical scavengers, 133, 136, 245
free radical scavenging antioxidant proteins, 136
free radical-induced permeabilization, 136
frustrated, xxiv
frustration, 152
Fumitremorgin C, 116
functional MRI, 20, 70
furanocoumarins, 85, 90

G

GABA, 3, 7, 9, 10, 18, 27, 33, 34, 38, 226, 240
GABA metabolism, 10, 33
GABA transaminase, 10
GABAergic, 3, 4, 9, 11, 28, 57, 227
GABAergic neurons, 9
GABAergic systems, 227
GAD-negative/CD38-positive patients, 116
gadolinium-enhanced MRI, 170
gamma-glutamyl transferase, 128
gamma-hydroxybutyrate, 176
GAPDH, 237
gas chromatography, 160, 221
gas chromatography-mass spectrometry (GC-MS), 160
gastrointestinal problems and mood-related complaints including anxiety, 152
gay, xiii, xvi, 88
gender differences, 67, 68, 69, 80, 84, 118, 122
gender differences in smoking behavior, 80
gender inequality, 213, 223

gender predisposition, 85
gene expression profile, 74
generalized estimating equations (GEE), xxxvi, 102, 175
genes in the endogenous opioid pathway, 100
genetic predisposition, 45, 46
genetic resistance, 242
genetic variants as biomarkers, 142
genetically-engineered mouse models of drug addiction, 242
genome-wide analysis of candidate gene, 121
genome-wide association studies (GWAS), xxxvi, 70, 108, 109, 119, 177, 188, 222
genomics, ix, 104, 122
GIT disturbance, 116
GIT symptoms, 170, 243
gliogenesis, 110
glomerular hypertrophy, 161
glucose metabolism, 19, 41, 86, 87, 152
glucuronides, 140, 156
glutamate, 3, 7, 8, 9, 10, 18, 22, 26, 30, 31, 33, 34, 38, 39, 42, 107, 109, 117, 122, 226, 244
glutamatergic, 3, 4, 8, 10, 57, 117, 227
glutathione, xxxii, 154, 237, 245
glutathione (GSH) activity, 154
gout, 45, 46
Gramicidin, 112
Gramicidin D and Taxol, 112
Grandidierella japonica, 151, 193, 196
growth, ix, xxxii, xxxvi, 70, 95, 107, 108, 111, 132, 134, 135, 137, 205, 208, 228, 245
growth retardation, ix, 228
gums, xxv

H

hair nicotine, 166, 171, 176, 189
hair nicotine levels, 166
HapMap, 120
harm reduction, xxv, 118, 159, 163, 167, 181, 229, 230, 231, 238
harmful and potentially harmful constituents (HPHCs), xxxvii, 157, 158, 159, 178, 195, 199, 231
HbA1c, 96
headaches, xxiv
heart attack, ix, xxv, 228, 229, 235
heat chock proteins, 237

heat shock factor-α, 237
heat shock protein(s) (HSPs), xxxii, xxxvii, 70, 134, 138, 208
hedonic responses, 19
hematological alterations, 128
Hemicholinium-3, 110
hemoglobin, 128
hepatic cytochrome P-450 2A6 (CYP2A6), 90
heroin, xxi, 64, 67, 68, 69, 73, 229, 230
heteromeric α7β2 nicotinic acetylcholine receptors, 217, 224
high density lipoprotein, 161
high resolution mass spectrometry, 93, 94, 102
high-affinity choline transporter, 109, 110
high-performance liquid chromatography (HPLC), 141, 183, 221
hippocampal CB formation, xi
hippurate and homovanillate, 97, 138
histone modifications, 210
HIV-infected primary macrophages, 207
HIV-positive patients, 67, 68, 69, 79, 83
homomeric, 6, 8, 217
homozygous weaver (wv/wv) mutant mice, 244
hospital anxiety and depression scale (HADS), 170
human airway epithelial cells (A549), 52, 115, 184
human aortic endothelial cells (HAECs), 113
human DAergic neurons, 242, 244
human genetic variation, 120
human monocytic cell line (THP-1), 52, 184
human neutrophil elastase, 51, 184
human umbilical vein endothelial cells (HUVEC) in endothelial growth medium (EGM), 114
Hutchinson-Gilford progeria syndrome, 177
hydrogen peroxide, 130, 132, 134, 136, 237
hyperalgesia, 18, 227
hypothalamic-pituitary axis, 227
hypothalamic-pituitary-adrenal axis, 142

I

ICAM, 108, 114, 122, 162
IgA, 102
IgE, 102
IgG, 102
IgG subclasses, 102
IgM, 102
IL-1 receptor antagonist, 102
IL-10, 56, 153, 170
IL-4, 170
IL-6, 45, 47, 56, 64, 96, 102, 149, 153, 169, 170, 198
IL-8, 102, 163
illicit drug reporting system (IDRS), xxxvii, 75
immune-regulatory properties, 171
immunoregulation, 103
impaired charnolophagy, 206
impotencies, xi
in vivo microdialysis, 10, 12, 16, 29, 30, 34, 36, 37
incense burning, 52, 184
increased appetite, xxiv, 152
indole acetic acid (IAA9), 208
induced pluripotent cells, xi, 130, 131, 236, 245
inductively-coupled plasma mass spectrometry (ICP-MS), 136
infants and children, 225
infertility, ix, 126, 152, 206, 228
infertility and pregnancy complications, 152
inflammatory biomarkers and immunoglobulins, 103
inflammatory markers (IL-6 and IL-10), 45, 47, 56, 64, 149, 153, 198
inhalers, xxv, 229, 238
iNOS, 93, 94, 96, 122, 161, 163, 169
iNOS and TGF-β1, 161
insomnia, 152
insulin, 96, 97, 107, 108, 109, 116, 138, 152
insulin secretion, 97, 116, 138
insulin-resistant (type-2 diabetes), 107, 108, 109
intellectual disabilities, 187
intelligence, 217
interactive website, 78
intercellular adhesion molecule (ICAM-1), 162
interleukin (IL)-1α, 102
interleukin (IL)-1β, 170
interleukin 13 receptor α 1, 51, 184
Interleukin-1 beta (IL-1β) and Interleukin-6 (IL-6), 112, 118
intracellular adhesion molecule-1 (ICAM), 108, 114, 122, 162
intracellular detoxification, xxxi, xxxii, 129, 130, 132, 236, 237, 242, 245
intracellular protein synthesizing machinery, 130
intra-mitochondrial homeostasis, 237
intrauterine nicotine, 93, 94, 126
intronic, 120
ionization, xxxvi, 136
IQ motif-containing GTPase activating protein 1, 51, 184
iron, 130, 132, 134, 136

irritability and restlessness, 152
isotopic dilution, 183
ITAM motif 2, 51, 184

J

Jasmonic acid (JA)-, 208

K

Kaempferin, 162
Kaempferol, 162
Kainic Acid, 145, 240, 243, 244
kidney, xxiii, 74, 75, 96, 128, 138, 150, 152, 161, 173, 201
kidney dysfunction, 128
kidney transplant patients, 150, 201
kynurenine (Kyn) via indoleamine 2, 141

L

lactate, 237
Ladostigil, 244
larynx, 152
late positive potential (LPP), 48
Lazabemide, 244
LC-MS, xxxvii, 93, 94, 95, 103, 105, 123, 125, 141, 167, 186, 228
LC-tandem mass spectrometry, 188
learning, ix, x, xxiv, 4, 35, 38, 90, 91, 162, 217, 228, 230
Lepidoside, 162
lesbian, xiii, xvi, 88
leukemias, 152
leukocyte adhesion and expression of VCAM and ICAM, 107, 108
leukocyte adhesion assay (LAA), 114
leukocyte marker, 183
lifestyle factors, 102, 115, 128
ligand-gated cation channels, 222
ligand-gated ion channels, 5
linoeic acid, 132
linoic acid, 136, 237
linolenic acid, 132, 237
lipid peroxidation, 112, 118, 129, 131, 136, 199, 236, 237
lipidomics, ix

liquid chromatography coupled to tandem mass spectrometry (LC-MS/MS), 93, 94, 95, 103, 105, 123, 186
liquid chromatography-mass spectroscopy (LC-MS), xxxvii, 93, 94, 95, 103, 105, 123, 125, 141, 167, 186, 228
liquid chromatography-tandem mass spectrometry (HPLC-MS/MS), 167, 183
liquid chromatography-tandem mass spectrometry (LC-MS), 167, 183
L-NAME, 214
low nicotine content cigarettes, 150
low self-esteem, 54
low-dose computed tomography (LDCT), xxxvii, 50, 60
lozenges, 229, 238
lung cancer, 50, 60, 63, 65, 67, 68, 69, 97, 115, 140, 151, 152, 154, 191, 203, 222, 230
lung resistance related protein (LRP), xxxvii, 111
lung screen uptake trials (LSUT), xxxvii, 45, 46, 47, 50, 65
lungs, xi, xxiii, 151, 152
lycopene, 237

M

MA0-A, 243
magnetoencephalography, 70
major depressive disorders (MDDs), ix, xi, xxxvii, 226, 228
male infertility, 206
malignancies, xi, xxxii, 45, 46, 116, 132, 134, 135, 136, 137, 210, 228, 236, 243
malignant transformation, 134, 135, 138
malondialdehyde (MDA), 128, 154, 161
Mantel-Haenszel fixed-effect model, 219
MAOA, 20, 100
MAO-B specific CB formation, 243
marijuana, xii, 45, 46, 47, 53, 54, 62, 222
marijuana and tobacco smoking, 222
marijuana co-abuse, 222
maximum clot strength, 183
MDR malignancies, 107, 109, 132, 134, 135, 137
mean diffusivity (MD), xxix, 29, 31, 191, 231, 242
mechamylamine, xxviii, 13, 16, 17, 32, 37, 111, 116
melancholia, 150, 182, 202
melatonin, 177
membrane permeabiliza, 131

memory, xxii, xxiii, xxiv, 8, 24, 25, 30, 31, 34, 35, 85, 87, 90, 150, 169, 196, 205, 210, 217, 223, 240
menstrual cycle, 206, 221, 224
menstrual irregularities, 207
mental health screenings, 71
menthol, 93, 94, 99, 105, 111, 119, 149, 157, 160, 173, 179, 180, 195, 196, 198
menthol and non-menthol cigarette smokers, 173
menthol and nonmenthol smokers, 93, 94, 99
menthol cigarette, 99, 161
menthol exposure, 119
menthol preference, 157, 173
menthol smokers, 99, 149, 160
menthol versus non-menthol smokers, 161
menthol-glucuronide (MG), 160
meso-cortico-limbic brain system, 6
metabolism of nicotine, 90, 93, 94, 100, 122
metabolomics, ix, 96, 138, 160
metabotropic glutamate receptor type 5 (mGluR5), 9, 18, 38, 117
metal ion speciation of MTs, 135
metallomics, ix
metallothioneins (MTs), xxxii, 107, 108, 115, 116, 132, 134, 135, 136, 137, 144, 145, 237, 242, 243, 245
metallothioneins over-expressing weaver mutant mice (wv/wv-MTs), 242
metalomics, 94, 136
meter dose inhaler, 206
methadone, 73, 229
methadone maintenance treatment, 73
methamphetamine, xxxvii
methyllycaconitine, 8, 13, 18
methylsuccinic acid, 163
mGluR2/3 antagonist LY341495, 18
Mianserin, 177
micro ribonucleic acids (miRNA), 210
microalbuminuria (mALB) levels, 128
microarray analyses, 150
microarray technology, 51, 184
microcephaly, ix, xi, 144, 228, 244
microglial activation, 169, 183
migration and development, 134
mild or borderline intellectual disability (MBID), 187
mini-international neuropsychiatric interview, 192
minority stressors, 88
mitochondrial bioenergetics, xxxi, 228, 236, 242, 245

mitochondrial DNA, 93, 236
mitochondrial genome knock out (RhO$_{mgko}$) cells, 242, 244
mitochondrial membrane potential ($\Delta\Psi$), 96
mitochondrial oxidative phosphorylation, 131, 137, 236
mitochondrial oxidative stress, 107, 108, 131
mitogen-activated kinases ERK and p38 MAPK, 111
MLC$_{20}$-S19 and MYPT1-T-853, 214
Moclobemide, 244
modified risk tobacco product (MRTPs), 82, 156, 157
moist snuff consumers (MSC), 150, 174, 201
molecular biomarkers, 108
molecular fingerprint for malignancies, 210
molecular imaging, xxxii, 3, 4, 227
monoamine levels, 183
monoamine oxidase inhibitors (MAOIs),, 242
monoamine oxidases, 237
monocytes and dendritic cells (DCs), 111
mononuclear leukocyte (MNL), 114
mood management, 81
morphine, xxxvii
mortality due to asthma, ix, 228
motivation to stop smoking (the Richmond test), 174
motivational stages of change (Prochaska and DiClemente's stages), 174
MRI/MRS, 228
MTs, 107, 108, 115, 116, 132, 134, 135, 136, 137, 242, 243, 245
MTs-deficient CS, 136
MTs-inadequate CS, 136, 137
MTs-mediated attenuation of AgNOR down-regulation, 133
MTs-normal CS, 136, 137
MTs-over-expressing CS, 136, 137
multi-call phone counseling, 78
multi-call quit-line programs, 78
multidrug resistance protein (MRP or MRP1), 111
multidrug resistant (MDR), 45, 46, 107, 108, 111
multidrug resistant (MDR) diseases, 46
multidrug resistant (MDR) malignancies, 116, 243
multi-drug transporter ABCG, 115
multi-modal, 78
multimodality molecular imaging with PET, 228
multiple drug addiction, 222
multispecific organic anion transporter (cMOAT) gene, 111
multivariate analysis, 97, 126, 138, 194

myeloid cell lineage, 205, 206
myelosuppression, 116, 243

N

N-(4-Hydroxyphenyl)-Arachidonamide (AM404), 71
N-acetyl-β-D-glucosaminidase (NAG), 128
nAChR upregulation, 74
nAChRs on glutamatergic terminals, 8, 226
Naltrexone, 11, 27, 29, 34, 37, 39
nano-checkTM rapid nicotine test, 60
nanoparticles, 242
nasal spray(s), 238
national and international economy and productivity, 225
national epidemiologic survey on alcohol and related conditions (NESARC), 54, 71
nausea, xxiv, 74, 75, 219
N-diethylamide (LSD)-25, 70
NE-ergic and 5-HTergic systems, 227
NEergic pathways, 100
NEergic systems, 3, 4
negative reinforcement, 3, 4, 81
nephrotoxicities, xi
neural progenitor cells, xi, 130, 131, 236, 245
neurocognition, 86, 87, 91
neurodegenerative apoptosis, 131
neurodegenerative diseases, xi, 135, 228, 241
neurodegenerative disorders, 241, 242, 243, 244
neurogenesis, 110
neuroinflammatory disorders, 171
neurological and neuropsychiatric disorders, ix
neuronal maturation and plasticity, 110
neuronal nicotinic acetylcholine receptors (nAChRs), xxxviii, 6, 8, 13, 16, 17, 18, 23, 26, 28, 31, 70, 74, 100, 108, 171, 217, 228
neuropsychiatric disorders, 220
neuro-substrates of nicotine reinforcement, 3, 4
neutrophils, 171
next-generation sequencing, 193
NicAlert saliva test, 221
nicotine abuse, 45, 47, 53, 55, 73, 125, 135
nicotine addiction, xx, xxii, xxv, xxix, xxxii, 3, 4, 24, 28, 38, 47, 60, 70, 100, 107, 108, 117, 120, 152, 179, 215, 221, 226, 227, 238
nicotine administration, 5, 9, 11, 12, 13, 22, 23, 24, 28, 41, 77, 154, 155, 176

nicotine and cotinine, 95, 98, 119, 126, 143, 186, 188, 193, 196, 197
nicotine and cotinine glucuronidation, 98, 188
nicotine biosynthesis, 208
nicotine C-oxidation, 95
nicotine dependence (Fagerström test/FTND), xix, xx, xxviii, xxxvi, 3, 4, 5, 12, 14, 16, 18, 21, 22, 24, 25, 26, 29, 32, 35, 36, 37, 48, 50, 52, 54, 57, 60, 61, 65, 67, 68, 69, 70, 71, 72, 76, 79, 80, 83, 86, 90, 93, 94, 95, 99, 100, 117, 127, 139, 142, 150, 170, 174, 175, 178, 180, 182, 191, 192,194, 209, 215, 217, 226, 227
nicotine dependence syndrome scale (NDSS), 95
nicotine dependence with anxiety disorder, xix
nicotine exposure biomarkers, 94
nicotine gum, 85, 86, 90, 107, 109, 118, 122, 153, 156, 164, 186, 229
nicotine gum addiction, 85, 86, 90
nicotine gum and patches, 186
nicotine induced hepatic damage, 149
nicotine metabolism/metabolite ratio (NMR), xxxviii, 95, 97, 99, 119, 138, 143, 157, 179
nicotine metabolites (total cotinine and nicotine equivalents), 156
nicotine metabolizers, 179
nicotine metered dose inhaler vs nicotine patch, 216, 223
nicotine metered dose inhaler vs nicotine patch(es), 12, 65, 73, 78, 85, 86, 90, 92, 150, 154, 172, 175, 176, 185, 200, 205, 206, 216, 219, 223, 227, 237, 238
nicotine -N-glucuronide, 102
nicotine or ethanol-induced cell injury, 138
nicotine patch therapy, 172, 185, 217
nicotine pharmacokinetic, 95
nicotine receptor, 38, 61, 206, 218, 223
nicotine receptor agonist, 61
nicotine receptor partial agonist, 206, 218, 223
nicotine reinforcement, 3, 7, 8, 9
nicotine replacement devices, 205
nicotine replacement therapy (NRT), xxiv, xxv, xxxviii, 37, 46, 47, 60, 65, 69, 74, 78, 119, 150, 163, 181, 202, 206, 216, 219, 227, 237, 238
nicotine replacement therapy(ies) (NRT), xxiv, xxv, xxxviii, 37, 46, 47, 60, 65, 69, 74, 78, 119, 150, 163, 181, 188, 202, 206, 216, 219, 227, 237, 238
nicotine self-administration (NSA), 7, 8, 9, 10, 11, 13, 14, 27, 30, 31, 34, 36, 37, 38, 39, 40, 42, 46, 47, 55, 61, 62, 63, 64, 67, 68, 69, 77, 81, 83, 206

nicotine under concurrent fixed-ratio (FR) 1 schedules, 77
nicotine withdrawal, xix, xxiv, xxviii, 3, 4, 14, 15, 16, 17, 18, 20, 21, 22, 23, 24, 25, 29, 30, 32, 33, 34, 36, 37, 39, 40, 42, 77, 86, 92, 94, 227
nicotine-evoked hepatic oxidative stress and tissue injury, 154
nicotine-induced anti-inflammation, 150, 170
nicotine-induced endothelial dysfunction, 150, 162
nicotine-induced leukocyte adhesion, 114
nicotine-induced vascular cell adhesion molecule (VCAM-1), 162
nicotinic acetylcholine receptors (nAChRs), 3, 4, 5, 6, 7, 8, 10, 13, 16, 17, 19, 23, 67, 68, 70, 73, 99, 100, 107, 108, 113, 171, 217, 222, 226, 227
nicotinic acid adenine dinucleotide (NAADP+), 116
nicotinic and muscarinic receptors, 110
nicotinic cholinergic receptor α5 subunit (CHRNA5) genotypes, 143
nicotinic receptors, 23, 24, 27, 30, 31, 32, 34, 37, 39, 40, 42, 68, 74, 111
nicotinism, v, vii, ix, x, xi, xx, xxi, xxiv, xxxi, xxxii, 3, 4, 20, 45, 46, 47, 59, 67, 68, 85, 86, 90, 91, 92, 93, 94, 102, 104, 107, 108, 125, 126, 130, 144, 147, 149, 151, 152, 153, 171, 205, 206, 225, 226, 227, 228, 245
nightmares, xxiv
nitrate/nitrite (NOx), 154
nitric oxide metabolites (NOx), 170
NMDA-r antagonist 3-(2-Carboxypiperazin-4-yl) Propyl-1-Phosphonic acid, 211
N-methyl-d-aspartate receptor (NMDA-r), 23, 29, 40, 210
N-methyl-d-aspartate receptor (NMDA-r) antagonists, 210
NMR metabolomics, 97
N'-nitrosonor nicotine (NNN), xxxviii, 140, 168, 190
NNK 4-[methyl (nitroso) amino]-1-(3-pyridinyl)-1-butanone, 102
non-compliance, 149, 157, 181, 199
non-C-oxidation, 95
nonmenthol smokers, 99
non-proliferating cell, 109, 116, 134
non-tobacco consumers (NTC), 174
nor nicotine, 104, 130, 188
norepinephrine, 3, 13, 22, 29, 30, 35, 41
norproliferating cells, 107
nortriptyline, 17, 22
NtbHLH protein, 208

NtMYC1a, 208
NtMYC1b, 208
NtMYC2, 208
NtMYC2a, 208
NtMYC2b, 208
nuclear ATF6, 73
nuclear factor κB ligand, 208
nuclear magnetic resonance spectroscopy, 101
nuclear XBP1, 73
nucleolar organizer region (AgNOR), xi, xxxii, 125, 126, 129, 132, 133, 134, 137, 144, 197
nucleus accumbens (NA), xviii, xxvii, xxviii, 6, 7, 8, 9, 10, 11, 12, 13, 16, 17, 19, 24, 26, 27, 29, 32, 36, 37, 38, 39, 40, 42, 214, 226
nucleus accumbens shell, 10
nutrition, 58, 127, 146

O

obesity, ix, 57, 77, 116, 228
odor span task, 205, 210, 223
olfactory reference memory (RM) task, 211
omega-3 fatty acid DHA (docosahexaenoic acid), 178
omics technology, 227
opioid(s), 3, 4, 11, 17, 24, 27, 28, 34, 47, 57, 65, 176
oppositional defiant disorder, xix
oral health education (OHE), xxxviii, 46, 47, 59, 65
orbitofrontal and dorsomedial prefrontal cortices, 139
organizational justice questionnaire, 58
organophosphate insecticides, 153
osteocalcin (OCN), 107, 108, 112, 113, 118, 121, 122
osteoclasts, 208
ovarian hormones, 206, 221, 224
oxidative phosphorylation, 129, 237
oxidative stress biomarkers, 192
oxidative stress markers, 182

P

PA promotion, 58
pack-year history, 50, 60
PAH dysfunction in schizophrenia, 141
pain, v, xii, 45, 46, 47, 57, 65, 79, 151, 240
pancreas, 96, 152
pancreatic islets, 96, 116, 161

panic, xx, xxvi, 52, 226
panic disorder and major depressive disorder (MDDs), xi, xxxvii, 226, 228
panic/agoraphobia, 52
pan-NOS inhibition, 214
parental substance dependence, xix
past and present psychiatric disorders, 54
patch(es), 85, 86, 90, 154, 187, 206, 216, 229
pathological gambling, 123, 139, 143
pathway-based association analyses of addiction, 121
pedunculo-pontine tegmental nucleus, 8, 9, 10, 27, 34
percentage predicted forced expiratory volume in 1 second, 52, 184
periodontal disease, 152, 208
periodontal tissue(s), 205, 208
periodontitis, 149, 155, 195, 208
perionditis, 107, 108
permeabilization, 129, 131, 132, 136
peroxides (LOOH), 170
persistence of smoking, 3, 93, 94
persistent depression, 45, 47
personalized (precision) theranostics, 125, 126
personalized medicine, 125
personalized smoking cessation products, 207
personalized theranostic(s), ix, x, 107, 108, 109, 151, 206, 225, 227
personalized theranostics of nicotinism, ix, x, 107, 109, 125, 151, 206, 227
personalized treatment(s), 69, 143, 221, 222, 241
personalized treatment(s) strategies, 221
p-glycoprotein, 111
pharmaceutical nicotine, 229, 237
pharmacodynamic profile, 227
pharmacogenetic interventions, 119
pharmacogenomic(s), 93, 94, 228
pharmacogenomics of nicotinism, 93, 94, 228
pharmacokinetic(s), 93, 94, 95, 223, 227, 236
pharmacological, 3, 4, 23, 26, 28, 31, 32, 34, 43, 57, 74, 142, 176, 216, 218, 223, 227, 237
pharmacological chaperoning, 74
pharmacotherapies, 74, 119, 216
pharynx, 152
phenanthrene, 190
phencyclidine, 23, 41
phenothiazine, 155
phenylalanine hydroxylase (PAH) dysfunction, 141
phlegm, xxiv
phosphatidyl serine, 235

phosphatidyl serine externalization, 235
phosphorylated CREB, 19
phosphorylated eukaryotic initiation factor 2α, 73
phosphoserine phosphatase, 51, 184
physical activity (PA) program, 58
physical tolerance, 6, 46, 90, 238
phytocannabinoids, 222
PI3, 51, 111, 184
PI3 gene, 51, 184
PI3 kinase, 111
pipe smoking, xxv
piracetam, 178
plasminogen activator, 99
platelet activation, 150, 174, 183, 202
platelet markers, 183
platelets, 108
plus another of nicotine patches, 164
pneumonia, xvii, 152
polycyclic aromatic hydrocarbons (PAH), xxxviii, 141, 151, 179, 190, 203
polyphenols, 237
polysubstance abuse, 57
polyunsaturated fatty acids, 129, 132, 136, 237
population, xii, xiii, xiv, xv, xvi, xvii, xx, xxix, 21, 22, 34, 48, 54, 57, 58, 59, 72, 76, 88, 96, 107, 108, 115, 116, 119, 122, 127, 138, 143, 149, 154, 168, 172, 177, 178, 185, 186, 188, 194, 197, 200, 202, 209, 211, 218, 224, 225, 230
positive reinforcement, 3, 4, 81, 226
positive reinforcement of Nicotine addiction, 226
positive transcription factor, 208
post-discharge pharmacotherapy, 212
postmenopausal age, 214
posttraumatic stress disorder, 52
potential reduced-exposure tobacco products (PREPs), 163
PP2, 113
prenatal cocaine exposure (PCE), 56, 153
prenatal tobacco exposure, 205, 211, 223
pre-pulse inhibition of the startle response, 23
primary free radical attack, 238
prison inmates, 46, 47
proapoptotic bax and profibrotic TGF-β1, 154
Probucol, 237
progenitor cells proliferation and differentiation, 110
progressive neurodegenerative disorders, 242
pro-inflammatory apoptosis, 237
pro-inflammatory biomarker, 172, 185
pro-inflammatory cytokines, 45, 46, 47, 113, 118

proinflammatory monocytes and neutrophils, 170
proinflammatory response, 149
proliferation, 111, 132, 134, 135, 136, 137, 245
PROMIS nicotine dependence, 61
PROMIS smoking, 46, 47
promoter regions of addiction-related genes, 93, 94, 98, 105, 203
protein carbonyls (PCO), 128
protein kinase C iota, 51, 169, 184
proteinase 3, 51, 184
proteinase inhibitor 3 (PI3), 51, 111, 184
proteomics, ix
proximal, 119
proxy confirmation, 88
psilocybin, 70
psilocybin-assisted psychotherapy, 70
psychedelics serotonergic hallucinogens, 67, 68, 70
psychiatric comorbidities, 3, 4, 71, 172, 185
psychiatric comorbidities in nicotinism, 3, 4
psychiatric disorders, xx, xxvii, xxviii, 5, 21, 25, 45, 47, 54, 65, 67, 68, 69, 172, 185, 210, 220, 226, 227
psychiatric disorders and smoking, xx, 226
psychiatric vulnerability, 71
psychological, v, xii, xx, xxvi, xxvii, xxxix, 23, 26, 41, 46, 47, 57, 58, 78, 85, 86, 110, 153, 217, 226
psychological dependence, 46
puerarin and ferulic acid, 162
puff topography, 85, 86, 87
puff topography variables, 85, 86, 87, 92
puffing behavior, 88, 166, 180, 209
pulmonary carcinogen, 167
purkinje neurons, 125, 126, 241
pyration, 136
pyrene, 190
pyruvate metabolism, 97, 138

Q

quadrupole and time of flight (ASAP-MS-Q-TOF) detector, 93, 94
quaternary free radical attack, 235, 237, 238
Quercetin, 178
questionnaire of smoking urges (QSU), xxxix, 61
quit-line, 68, 77, 212
quit-line counseling, 68
quit-line services, 77
QuitPal, 76

R

radial diffusivity (RD), 191
rasagiline, 244
reactive oxygen metabolites (ROM), 115
reactive oxygen species (ROS), 96, 207
real-time quantitative polymerase chain reaction, 184
Reboxetine, 13, 36, 39
recent trauma, 54
receptor up-regulation, xxii
reduced nicotine content (RNC), 107, 108, 149, 156, 157, 165, 192, 195, 209, 223
reduced nicotine content (RNC) cigarette, 165, 209
reduced Nicotine content cigarettes (RNCs) biomarkers, 209
regular psychostimulant users (RPU), xxxix, 75
regulation of CHRNA-1-5 genes, 227
regulation of gene expression and cell survival, 110
reinforcing effect, 3, 5, 7, 8, 9, 10, 11, 12, 17, 18, 22, 27, 34, 36, 45, 47, 55, 56, 63, 72, 206
relapse, xxi, xxii, xxiii, xxiv, 3, 4, 15, 23, 45, 47, 49, 62, 63, 71, 76, 78, 82, 84, 93, 94, 101, 117, 119, 176, 220, 221, 227
relapse prevention, xxii, 176, 220
reno-protective effects of Curcumin, 161
resting-state fMRI, 151, 192, 195
restless, xxiv
resveratrol, 237
rheumatoid arthritis, 45, 46
Rimonabant, 12
risk for obesity, 77
risk of suicidality, 205, 207, 215
RNAi, 113
RNA-seq data, 120
rough endoplasmic reticulum, 130
Rush, xxi
rutins, 237

S

Safinamide, 244
saliva, xxiv, 88, 93, 94, 99, 102, 105, 123, 126, 142, 143, 166, 173, 176, 181, 193, 196, 197, 199, 221
salivary stress biomarkers, 125, 126, 144, 199
sanitation, xxxi, 242
sarin, 37, 153

schizophrenia, ix, xxvi, 20, 22, 23, 25, 26, 28, 29, 30, 31, 33, 36, 41, 125, 126, 141, 144, 198, 206, 227, 228, 243
schizophrenia and depression, 206
secondary free radical attack, 238
second-hand smoke (SHS), xiii, xxi, xxix, xxxix, 102, 125, 127, 150, 166, 168, 171, 175, 183, 189, 202, 203, 225
second-hand smoke exposure (SHSE), 127
second-hand smoking-related health risks, 228
Selegiline, 244
substance use and misuse in intellectual disability - questionnaire (SumID-Q, 187
sensory-gating deficits, 22
sequestration, 129, 131, 132, 136
serious mental illness (SMI), 67, 68, 76, 86, 206, 224
serious psychological distress (SPD), xxxix, 58, 63
serotonergic, 3, 4, 11, 39, 57, 69, 70, 240
serotonin, 3, 12, 21, 25, 31, 33, 39, 41, 70, 100, 227, 240, 243
serotonin biosynthesis, 100
serotonin transporter 5HTTLPR, 100
sertoli cells, 139
serum bilirubin, 125, 126, 127
serum bilirubin profiles, 128
severe sweating disorder, 90
sex, xvi, xxi, 34, 49, 50, 51, 89, 98, 119, 128, 130, 152, 157, 158, 170, 180, 182, 184, 221, 229, 230
sex addiction, 130
signal transducing adaptor molecule SH3 domain, 51, 184
sIL-6R, 182
single nucleotide polymorphism(s) (SNPs), xxxix, 70, 94, 98, 120, 177
sirtuins, 237
skin patches, xxv, 151
sleep disturbances, 152
smilax, 149, 162, 197
smokeless snuff, xxv
smokeless tobacco (ST), xxv, xxix, xxxix, 67, 68, 69, 82, 85, 86, 89, 104, 140, 151, 174, 198, 210, 229, 230, 231, 238
smokescreen, 108, 109, 119, 120, 122
smokescreen genotyping array, 120
smoking behaviors, 61, 78, 80, 88, 119, 142, 165, 178, 209
smoking cessation, xx, xxv, xxix, xxx, 10, 11, 13, 14, 16, 17, 22, 25, 27, 28, 30, 32, 33, 34, 37, 38, 40, 41, 46, 47, 49, 51, 58, 60, 61, 62, 66, 67, 68, 69, 74, 75, 76, 77, 78, 80, 82, 83, 88, 89, 90, 92, 100, 115, 119, 123, 124, 125, 141, 142, 143, 149, 154, 162, 163, 172, 174, 185, 197, 198, 205, 206, 207, 212, 215, 216, 218, 221, 222, 223
smoking cessation and relapse prevention, 58
smoking cessation pharmacotherapy, 216
smoking cessation regimens, 205
smoking cessation treatments, 123, 142, 143, 215
smoking status, 50, 52, 58, 76, 79, 85, 86, 87, 88, 119, 127, 181, 184
smoking topography, 110, 180
snus, xxvi, 82, 118, 122, 149, 156, 164, 195, 229, 230, 238
social deviance, 54
society for research on nicotine and tobacco (SRNT), xxxix, 41, 60, 63, 233
sociodemographic characteristics, 54, 174
SOD, xxxii, 112, 118, 132, 134, 138, 154, 161, 237
SOD and glutathione peroxidase, 161
sodium butyrate, 112
solid-phase extraction liquid chromatography with tandem mass spectrometry (LC-MS/MS), xxxvii, 93, 94, 95, 103, 105, 123, 125, 141, 167, 186, 228
soluble interleukin 1 receptor antagonist (sIL-1RA), 182
soluble interleukin-2 receptor (sIL-2R), 182
soluble urokinase plasminogen activator receptor (suPAR), 124, 149, 154
spermatocyte motility, 206
S-phenylmercapturic acid (SPMA), 183
spirometry test, 50
Src-kinase inhibitor, 113
SREBP-1, 161
stabilize charnolosomes (CS), xxxii, xxxvi, 4, 15, 93, 94, 96, 129, 131, 132, 133, 134, 136, 137, 206, 228, 235
statins, 237
still birth, ix, 228
stimulus-outcome learning, 139
stomach, 152, 230
stop-smoking services, 150, 181, 202
Streptozotocin, 161
stress, v, xi, xii, xvi, xviii, xxiii, xxvi, 23, 58, 73, 81, 91, 103, 114, 133, 142, 145, 150, 151, 154, 161, 169, 170, 174, 176, 181, 184, 196, 197, 198, 201, 207, 208, 210, 242, 244
stress management, 58
stress reduction, 81
stroke, xvii, 229, 235

substance abuse dependence, xix
substance use (SU), xviii, 33, 49, 53, 61, 139, 150, 176, 186, 187, 202, 205, 218, 224
substance use disorder(s) (SUDs), xviii, xxxix, 52, 53, 54, 150, 176, 205, 209, 224, 227
substance-related disorders, 117
sudden fetal and infant death, 129, 144, 197
sudden infant death syndrome (SIDS), ix, xxxix, 125, 126, 129, 133, 228
suicidal ideation and suicidal behavior, 220
suicidal ideation and suicidal behavior or ideation, 220
suicidality, 205, 206, 215, 223
suicidality risk, 215, 216
SuPAR and C-reactive protein (CRP), 155, 170
superoxide dismutase (SOD), xxxii, 112, 118, 132, 134, 138, 154, 161, 237
superoxide dismutase (SOD) and Thiobarbituric acid reactive substances (TBRAS), 112, 118
switching products, 238
synthetic cannabinoids, 75

T

Tabex, 218
tar, 22, 46, 157, 164, 180
target genotyping array, 108
targeted genotyping array biotechnology, 108, 109
Taxol, 112
T-cell proliferation, 111
T-cell proliferation and activation, 111
TEG and platelet leukocyte aggregates (LPA), 183
telemedicine, 227
telephone-based cessation counseling, 212
telomere length, 205, 211, 223
temporary abstinence, 164
teratogenic substances, 213
tertiary free radial attack, 238
testicular apoptosis, 125, 126
tetrahydrocannabinol (THC), 187
text messaging, 78
the nicotine metabolite ratio (NMR), xxxviii, 95, 97, 99, 119, 121, 138, 143, 179
The Patient Reported Outcomes Measurement Information System (PROMIS®) Smoking, xxxviii, 61
theiredoxin, 237
throat lozenges, xxv

thrombin kinetics, 183
thromboelastography (TEG), 183
thrombogenesis, 150, 183, 202
thromboxane metabolites, 174
time to first cigarette dependence, 157
TNF receptor 60 and 80 kDa (sTNFR60/80), 182
TNF-α, 93, 94, 96, 122, 163, 169
TNF-β NcoI polymorphism (rs909253), 170
tobacco cessation, 45, 48, 51, 60, 63, 65, 74, 205, 206
tobacco cessation products, 206
tobacco heating system (THS), xxxix, 149, 157, 158, 195, 196, 198
tobacco smoking behavior, 3
tobacco smoking-induced charnolopathies, 245
tobacco specific carcinogens (TSNAs), 150, 151, 168, 200
tobacco specific nitrosamines (TSNA) and polycyclic aromatic hydrocarbons (PAH), 110
tobacco use, xiii, xiv, xxi, xxv, xxviii, 5, 8, 63, 71, 73, 74, 75, 80, 89, 104, 110, 121, 140, 150, 152, 156, 163, 174, 186, 188, 198, 202, 209, 215, 221, 226
tobacco use disorder (TUDs), xxxix, 63, 74
tobacco-specific carcinogenic nitrosamines, 125, 126, 140
tobacco-specific lung carcinogen, 140, 191
tobacco-specific nitrosamine, 140, 150, 151, 156, 174, 175, 179, 190
tobacco-specific nitrosamines (TSNAs), 143, 150, 151, 168, 174, 179, 190, 196, 200
tobacco-specific N-nitrosamines, 151, 203
topical gels, 238
topping responsive miRNAs, 208
total antioxidant status (TAS), 115
total fertility rates (TFR), 213
total nicotine equivalent(s) (TNEs), 97, 118, 157, 174, 180, 188, 191
total oxidant status (TOS), 115
total thiol levels (TTL), 115
trans-3'-hydroxycotinine (3-HCOT), 167, 186
trans-3'-hydroxycotinine as nicotine biomarker, 186
trans-3-hydroxycotine to cotinine, 97
trans-3'-hydroxycotinine, 102, 119
trans-3'-hydroxycotinine/cotinine ratio, 119
transcriptional activation of genes, 132, 135, 137, 138
transgender-related minority stressors, 89
transmission electron microscopy (TEM), 236

triacylglycerol and phospholipids, 161
trier social stress test (TSST), 142
trigeminal neuralgia, 45, 46
trouble sleeping, xxiv
Trp ratios, 141
tryptophan catabolite and glutamate-mediated excitotoxicity, 183
tryptophan hydroxylase, 100
TSPO (18 kDa protein), 237
tumor necrosis factor alpha (TNFα), 102, 112, 118
TUNEL-positive testicular cells, 140
tunicamycin, 73
two-dimensional electrophoresis., 208
Type 1 T helper cell (Th1) type immunity, 141
tyrosine hydroxylase (TH) gene expression, 141
tyrosine hydroxylase (TH) immunoreactivity, xxviii, 73

U

UGT2B10 splice variant, 98
ultrahigh performance liquid chromatography with MS-triple quadrupole detector, 102
umbelliferone, 91
uncontrolled induction of MTs, 138
unfolded protein response (UPR), 67, 68, 69, 73
UPR suppression, 74
up-regulation of nAChR, xxii
ureter and bladder, 152
urinary 4-(methylnitrosamino)-1-(3-pyridyl)-1-butanol, 171
urinary cotinine, 167, 171, 174, 194
urinary cotinine tests, 174
urinary isoprostanes and leukotriene E4, 174
urinary NNK metabolites 4-(methylnitrosamino)-1-(3-pyridyl)-1-butanol (NNAL), 140
urokinase receptor, 99
US Preventive Services Task Force (USPSTF), xxxix, 60

V

vaping, xxiii, xxxii, 73, 238
Varenicline, 33, 46, 47, 61, 67, 68, 69, 74, 81, 119, 164, 206, 207, 216, 218, 227
Varenicline and Cytisine, 218
Varenicline and depressed mood, 220

vascular cell adhesion molecule-1 (VCAM), 108, 114, 122, 154, 162
vascular hypercontractility, 214
ventral corticostriatal-amygdala network, 139
ventral tegmental area (VTA), 6, 7, 8, 9, 10, 11, 12, 16, 17, 18, 20, 25, 26, 27, 29, 32, 34, 36, 37, 40, 42, 43, 226
verbal abuse, 85, 86
very low nicotine content (VLNC), xl, 109, 156, 175
vesicular acetylcholine transporter, 110
viccinomics, 227
vimentin, 161
vincristine, 112
visual analog scale (VAS), 79
vitamin A, 237
vitamin B, 237
vitamin B_{12}, 96
vitamin C, xxiii, 128
vitamin D, 240
vitamin D and Resveratrol, 178
volatile organic compounds (VOCs), xxxviii, xl, 167

W

waist-to-hip ratio, 52, 184
wastewater analysis, 150, 185, 187, 202
wastewater biomarkers of tobacco, 186
wastewater-based epidemiology (WBE), 150, 186, 202
WAY-100635, 21
weight control, 80, 81
weight gain, xxiv, 11, 77, 150, 180, 202, 213
weight management, 58
Western moist snuff, 229
white blood cell count, 174
Wisconsin inventory of smoking dependence motives (WISDM), xl, 61
withdrawal, xi, xviii, xxiii, xxiv, xxv, xxxvii, 3, 4, 5, 6, 12, 14, 15, 16, 17, 18, 19, 20, 21, 23, 24, 31, 36, 37, 38, 40, 41, 42, 43, 49, 67, 68, 69, 73, 77, 83, 85, 86, 93, 94, 101, 142, 176, 209, 218, 227, 228
withdrawal symptoms, xi, xix, xxiv, xxv, 5, 6, 14, 23, 37, 42, 85, 86, 93, 94, 101, 209, 218, 227, 228

X

xanthotoxin, 85, 90, 91

xenobiotics, 128

Y

Y-maze and radial arm-maze tests, 169
young adolescent smokers, 93, 94

Z

Zika virus disease, xi, 144, 228, 244
ZIKV disease, 242, 243
ZIKV embryopathies, 243